D1482804

# Management-Employee

## Relations in

## The Public Service

# "Management-Employee

# Relations in

# The Public Service"

By

FELIX A. NIGRO

PUBLIC PERSONNEL ASSOCIATION

1313 E. 60th Street • Chicago, Illinois 60637

TO EDNA

## Titles in the Series

# Policies and Practices in Public Personnel Administration

THIS VOLUME is the third of a group of books being published under the series title, *Policies and Practices in Public Personnel Administration*. This series title will be familiar to those readers who recall an earlier seven-volume set of the same title published during the era when the Public Personnel Association was known as the Civil Service Assembly of the United States and Canada.

As was true of the former series, the purpose of these new volumes is to give in-depth coverage of the major functional aspects of public personnel administration. The intent is to bring a broad perspective to the subject matter under treatment —one that gives insight into the purposes and policies of personnel administration as well as the techniques. This approach stems from the premise that effective personnel administration begins with well-conceived policies, and that achievement of desired objectives results from sound methodology intelligently adapted to its environment.

In reviving its earlier series title for this new major publishing effort, the Association does not wish to convey the impression that the new series will be essentially an updating and reissuance of the original books. The main thrust in this series will be to cover aspects of personnel administration that were not included in the earlier set. To the extent that overlap does occur between the old and the new, present-day trends will be noted.

Responsibility for the planning, editing, and production of the books in this new series is in the hands of J. J. Donovan, Associate Director of the Public Personnel Association. His background as a writer and editor in the public personnel field spans more than 25 years, including major staff work in producing the earlier seven-volume series.

In offering this new series, the Public Personnel Association hopes that it will prove useful to those who are concerned with personnel policy and operating management, as well as to those whose responsibilities require a mastery of special techniques. Each has an important contribution to make to a sound personnel program; all share in the opportunity to make personnel administration a dynamic force in modern public management.

Kenneth O. Warner
Executive Director
Public Personnel Association

# Table of Contents

# About the Author

A BOOK that sets out to deal in depth with management-employee relations in the public service in the midst of this unsettled era of change raises a formidable challenge to any author. The subject matter is broad and many-faceted; the tempo of new developments is ever-fresh; and emerging patterns are often the end-product not so much of applied theory as of controversy, compromise, and accommodation among conflicting forces. To view the scene with a knowing eye, to abstract the essential meaning of events, and to organize the bits and pieces into an understandable whole—these are tasks that call for more than passing skill.

Dr. Felix A. Nigro brings to this authorship task a background admirably suited to its demands. He has been intimately associated with the field of personnel and public management for many years, and in a variety of roles that have widened and sharpened his perspective. Since 1964 he has been Charles P. Messick Professor of Public Administration at the University of Delaware, and since 1967 he has been a member of the Personnel Board of New Castle County, Delaware. His earlier work experience in the public service was with several federal and international agencies, including the National Resources Planning Board, National Youth Administration, War Shipping Administration, National Housing Agency, Institute of Inter-American Affairs, Agency for International Development, the United Nations, and the United Nations Relief and Rehabilitation Administration. He has also served with various management firms as a consultant.

In more recent years Dr. Nigro has moved into the academic field, teaching political science and public administration at several colleges and universities. These include San Diego State College, Southern Illinois University, the University of Puerto Rico, Florida State University, and the University of Texas. He received his B.A., M.A., and Ph.D. degrees from the University of Wisconsin.

Dr. Nigro has contributed extensively to professional journals in the fields of public administration and personnel, and is the author of two earlier books: *Public Personnel Administration,* and *Modern Public Administration.* He is a frequent speaker before professional management groups and in governmental training programs.

In dealing with his present subject, Dr. Nigro brings to it a strong sense of its historical and evolutionary aspects in the public services of the United States, of Canada, and of other countries as well. His exposition of the "here and now" of management-employee relations in federal, state, provincial and local governments shows vividly the range and variety of policy and practice. His research and analysis have been undertaken, not with the object of buttressing any particular position, but rather to enlighten the reader and put at his command informational resources to help him resolve complex issues and find answers to a host of vexing questions.

As the author repeatedly shows, there is no one "magic formula" containing all the ingredients for a successful joint relationship between public management and organized employee groups. Only through patient mastery of the body of knowledge and experience gleaned from many sources can responsible parties on both sides create the means and methods to meet their own needs.

The editor and publisher join with the author in expressing appreciation to the many persons and organizations whose cooperation and assistance contributed substantially to the production of this book.

J. J. Donovan
Series Editor
"Policies and Practices in
Public Personnel Administration"

# Acknowledgments

M Y FIRST ACKNOWLEDGMENT must be to my wife who ever since this project began in December of 1964 has made herself indispensable by typing my notes and correspondence, mounting and filing numerous newspaper clippings, and typing the entire manuscript. At all times, I have had the help of the staff of the Public Personnel Association, as well as that of many PPA members with whom I have corresponded and consulted.

Following are those who reviewed the initial outline: Arvid Anderson, now Director of the Office of Collective Bargaining in New York City; Carl B. Barnes, Director of Personnel, U.S. Department of Agriculture; G. A. Blackburn, Director General of the Public Service Commission of Canada; Paul Camp, Deputy Personnel Officer, Public Health Service, U.S. Department of Health, Education, and Welfare; Merrill Collett, Executive Management Service, Inc., Arlington, Virginia; Franklin DeWald, Personnel Director, Department of Civil Service, State of Michigan; Bernard P. Donnelly, Standards and Surveys Division, California State Personnel Board; Dr. Robert C. Garnier, City Personnel Director, Milwaukee, Wisconsin; Elder Gunter, formerly City Manager, Pasadena, California; W. D. Heisel, City Personnel Officer, Cincinnati, Ohio; John R. James, Chief, Personnel Division, County of Los Angeles, California; Ralph Joy, Division of Urban Services, National Education Association; the late Louis J. Kroeger, Griffenhagen-Kroeger, Inc., San Francisco, California; Dr. Theodore Lang, Deputy Superintendent, Board of Education, New York, New York; Robert B. McKersie, Associate Professor of Industrial Relations, University of Chicago; Edward D. Meacham, Director of Personnel Services, New York State Department of Civil Service, Albany, New York; Dr. Hugh Morrison, Chairman, British Columbia Civil Service Commission; Muriel Morse, General Manager, City of Los Angeles, California; Harry P. Petrie, now retired and formerly Secretary and Chief Examiner, Los Angeles County Civil Service Commission; Thomas J. Plunkett of Plunkett and Associates, Municipal Affairs and Public Administration Consultants, Montreal, Cana-

1

da; Rollin B. Posey, Dean of Professional Studies, University of Wisconsin at Green Bay; Dr. Norman J. Powell, Professor of Political Science, City University of New York; Foster B. Roser, Personnel Director, City of Philadelphia, Pennsylvania; David Selden, Assistant to the President of the American Federation of Teachers; Robert H. Sharpe, formerly Assistant General Manager of the California State Employees' Association; Oscar S. Smith, Director, Division of Labor Relations, U.S. Atomic Energy Commission; O. Glenn Stahl, Director, Bureau of Policies and Standards, U.S. Civil Service Commission; Louis J. Van Mol, General Manager, Tennessee Valley Authority, Knoxville, Tennessee; Donald C. Wagner, Senior Research Investigator, Fels Institute of Local and State Government, University of Pennsylvania, Philadelphia, Pennsylvania; John A. Watts, Director of Civilian Personnel, Department of the Air Force; Douglas Weiford, formerly City Manager, Eau Claire, Wisconsin; Anthony C. Weinlein, Director, Department of Research and Education, Building Service Employees' International Union; Dr. Wesley A. Wildman, Research Associate, Industrial Relations Center, University of Chicago; Arnold S. Zander, now retired and formerly President of the American Federation of State, County, and Municipal Employees, AFL-CIO; and Frank P. Zeidler, labor relations consultant.

Those who read the manuscript are: G. A. Blackburn; Paul Camp; Melvin H. Cleveland, Director, State Civil Service Commission, State of Oregon; Professor Winston W. Crouch, Department of Political Science, University of California at Los Angeles; Thomas C. Enright, Executive Secretary, Oregon State Employees' Association; Professor Phillips L. Garman, Coordinator of Labor Programs, Institute of Labor and Industrial Relations, Division of University Extension, University of Illinois; Robert H. Hastings, Executive Assistant to the President, American Federation of State, County and Municipal Employees, AFL-CIO; L. David Korb, Assistant Director, Office of Labor-Management Relations, U.S. Civil Service Commission; R. O. MacFarlane, Director, School of Public Administration, Carleton University, Ottawa, Canada; John E. Massey, Director of Personnel, Tennessee Valley Authority; Dr. Chester A. Newland, Department of Political Science, University of Houston; Thomas J. Plunkett; Tom Page, Associate Professor, Institute of Government and Public Affairs, University of Illinois; Rollin B. Posey;

Foster B. Roser; Nelson Watkins, Executive Secretary, Ohio Civil Service Employees' Association, Inc.; Arnold S. Zander; and Frank P. Zeidler.

The author takes responsibility for all statements made and opinions expressed. I have profited from many valuable suggestions made by these reviewers, but do not in any sense speak for any or all of them. The more I plunged into my research, the more convinced I became of the importance of my assignment, and I am grateful to many colleagues, students, and others who have shared in my enthusiasm. Above all, it is hoped that this book will spur many individuals and groups to explore the problems in greater detail, as important developments continue to unfold in this, the decade of the public employee.

Felix A. Nigro

# Introduction

Our PURPOSE is to provide an up-to-date, book-length treatment of management-employee relations which will be of use not only to personnel specialists and personnel board and commission members but also to chief administrators, line department heads, supervisors at all levels, legislators, the officials and staffs of employee organizations, and students and others concerned with public personnel administration. Being "of use" means providing an adequate analysis of the basic issues and problems in developing effective management-employee relations. Illustrative materials will be drawn primarily from the United States and Canada, but it is hoped that the exposition of problems and issues will prove valuable to persons residing in other parts of the world.

### The Different Meanings of "Employee Relations"

Perhaps more than any other area of personnel administration, the phrase employee relations is subject to different interpretations as to exactly what it covers. While there is general agreement as to what is meant by recruitment, selection, and training, both the personnel literature and the usage of the practitioners show clearly that "employee relations" is defined in several different ways. Some definitions are very broad and encompass a wide scope of personnel activity; others are more narrow and include much less. The most common meanings seem to be as follows:

1. The management approach of taking into account employee reaction to present and proposed policies and the ways in which programs are administered.
2. Relationships between management and employee organizations.
3. Relationships between management and the individual employees, such as between supervisor and subordinate.
4. Relationships between the employees themselves.
5. Services and benefits provided by management to the

employees, such as health and welfare facilities, life insurance, pensions, sick and annual leave, and holidays.

### Employee Relations as an Approach

Let us discuss each of these meanings briefly and then explain what will be covered in this book. The first was stressed in the pioneering publication of the Civil Service Assembly of the United States and Canada, *Employee Relations in the Public Service*, where it was stated: [*69*, p. 4]

> The specialized field of employee relationships is more accurately characterized as an emphasis in personnel administration rather than as a series of related personnel activities. In this sense it can be distinguished, for example, from the fields of recruitment or service ratings. More than any other personnel function, perhaps, employee relationship policies are ways of doing the recognized tasks of personnel management, of providing for wider participation in those tasks.

In view of the great emphasis on participative management since the publication of this book in 1942, its authors appear particularly perceptive. They understood that employees are not simply interested in greater economic benefits but also in being allowed to make their views known to the management. In recent years, as paternalism has increasingly given way to patterns of consultation with the employees, there has been widespread acceptance, expressed or implicit, of this concept of employee relations as a basic approach for guiding personnel activities. Far from being a single segment of the personnel program, employee relations is a philosophy which underlies all of it. In this sense, everybody with personnel responsibilities is an employee relations agent.

### Relationships with Employee Organizations

The second meaning, relationships between management and employee organizations, is unambiguous. No one seems to question that this is "employee relations," the point rather being that some people regard it as the totality. Undoubtedly, the role and activities of employee organizations constitute today the most dramatic and precedent-shattering aspects of the public personnel scene. Yet it would be arbitrary to assert that only management relationships with organized employees are "employee relations."

During World War II, a work group of the Council of Personnel Administration decided that employee relations referred to "the character and quality of the relationships between employees and their supervisors, between management and employees as a group and among employees themselves." [*313*, pp. 267-68] Accepting this definition, in his treatment of employee relations Norman J. Powell covers such topics as human relations research, supervision, small groups, turnover, absenteeism, grievances, dismissals, leaves, and counselling. He also includes public employee organizations, but devotes relatively few pages to this subject separately considered. [*313*, pp. 267-320] One may not agree with this kind of emphasis, and presumably in view of recent developments Powell would devote more space to employee organizations; however, he is not alone in viewing employee relations as more than simply synonymous with relationships with organized employees. Incidentally, in the present book the term "employee organization" means any organization of employees which has as a primary purpose the improvement of the working conditions of its members. Thus it includes the numerous independent employee associations, as well as those affiliated with the general labor movement. In practice, "employee organization" and "union" are often used synonymously, but some independent associations do not want to be called "unions," a designation they believe should be restricted to the labor-affiliated organizations.

### The Individual Employee and Interpersonal Relationships

The third and fourth meanings of "employee relations" require no detailed explanation in view of the reference above to such treatments as Powell's. He specifically includes both relationships between supervisors and individual workers and those between the workers themselves. Such an interpretation vastly extends the scope of employee relations and could be said to make it almost synonymous with the whole field of personnel administration. On the other hand, it does have the advantage of assuring that consideration is given in the personnel program to the insights and findings of the human relations researchers who have done so much to reorient the activities of scholars and practitioners in so many fields.

### Employee Benefits

The fifth meaning evokes no controversy since the good employer is supposed to provide employee benefits, particularly in view of the strong competition now being offered in this area by many private companies. The first employee relations units in government tended to concentrate on providing services and benefits of different kinds to the employees, and the danger is that some personnel officers may still regard such activities as constituting most of "employee relations." Actually, in public personnel circles today this limited view has now largely disappeared as it becomes clear that the employees want a new relationship with the management, not the mere provision of benefits.

### Scope of Book

This author believes that all five of these meanings of "employee relations" are correct; at least he sees no reason other than a purely arbitrary one for rejecting any of them. In this book we will concentrate upon relationships between management and employee organizations, because it is in this area that some very significant developments have been taking place in recent years. When a preliminary outline of this book was distributed to a representative sample of well-known persons in the public personnel field, their response clearly indicated that they are now most immediately concerned with problems of relationships with organized employees. Although it is not likely that all the different phases of employee relations could be encompassed within the pages of a single volume anyway, the essential consideration was to make a contribution in the area of the most deeply felt current needs.

Because the various parts of employee relations are interrelated, any thorough consideration of dealings with employee organizations will reveal and at least partially include the other aspects listed above. Since one of the major aims of organized relationships between management and the employees is to improve communications and understanding between both parties, this obviously calls for a management approach of taking into account employee reaction to present and proposed policies and the ways in which programs are administered.

Similarly, although no attempt will be made to discuss all relationships between management and the workers, the needs of the individual employee and his relationship to employee organizations will be given appropriate attention. No discussion of employee organizations can leave out the question of what the single employee can gain by becoming a member, nor should the rights of the person who does not want to join be neglected. The broad subject of interpersonal relationships will not be explored, but again any discussion of employee organizations will at least throw some light on the network of contacts between individuals and forces inside and outside them. Finally, although there will be no separate consideration of employee benefit programs, these will necessarily be referred to in the analysis of subjects for collective negotiations.

# 1

# Recent Developments in
# Management-Employee Relations

BEFORE BEGINNING the discussion of specific problems of
management-employee relations, it is advisable to describe
briefly the changes in recent years in the public personnel
function. *Employee Relations in the Public Service,* already
mentioned in the Introduction, was published during World War
II when great strains were placed on the governmental machinery. Merit systems were far from new, but both in the United
States and Canada the era of "modern personnel administration"
was just beginning. The word "modern" has a rather loose
meaning, but in this context it means positive programs of
recruitment, the staffing of personnel offices with technically
trained persons, and in general the expansion of personnel services.

In the United States, the departments and agencies of the
federal government had been required to establish full-fledged
personnel offices only a few years before World War II. In the
Canadian national service, although there had been great progress after passage of the Civil Service Act of 1918, rigidities in
the latter legislation hampered the development of truly adequate personnel programs. [70, p. 6] In 1946, the Gordon Commission found "the existing machinery and procedures for the administration of personnel matters in departments" to be "generally rudimentary in form and routine in operation," and as a
first step recommended the appointment of a competent personnel officer in each department's national headquarters.
[327, pp. 289-90] In both countries few public personnel agencies
had progressed to the point where they could give a high
priority to the employee relations function. Pressing problems
of protecting the merit system and getting acceptance for any
personnel program at all frequently had to be the major concern.
Public employee organizations existed, of course, but within the

context of much more limited concepts of the responsibilities of governments as employers than prevail today.

### The Expanded Concept of Personnel Administration

Although, as is inevitable, practice still lags behind desired accomplishment, public personnel administration is now characterized by an increasing emphasis on understanding and trying to meet the needs of the individual employee. This attention to employee needs is obviously a pre-condition for the promotion of better relationships between management and the employees. If the employer does not understand how the workers react, the only employee relations which will exist will be poor ones. It is not argued that the management should always agree with and yield to the employees, but in general the following findings of human relations research are widely accepted:

1. It is desirable for workers to participate in determining organization policies and work procedures.

2. It is wise for management to take employees into its confidence, as in preparations for program changes, internal reorganizations, and new work flow.

3. It is important to have upward communication (from the workers to the management).

4. "Employee-centered" supervision is superior to job-centered supervision, the former emphasizing worker motivation and the latter putting production quotas first.

5. There is a need to recognize differences in attitudes of individual workers and vary leadership style accordingly.

Although these findings do not necessarily indicate that management should enter into collective negotiations with the employees, rather than dealing with them on an individual basis, they do provide a mental framework which is compatible with the principle of collective dealings. The "human relations approach" can lead to paternalism just as easily as to joint decision-making, because each individual decides for himself how to put human relations into practice.

### Factors Contributing to the
### Drive for Collective Negotiations

Employee organizations' changed conceptions of their role, critical shortages of trained workers in government, industrial labor leaders' new interest in gaining members amongst the ranks of the public employees—all these and other factors have contributed to the drive for collective negotiations. In the eyes of the leaders of employee organizations, the reapportionment of state legislatures in the United States is an example of a fortuitous political event. Witness this statement: [*356*, p. 5]

> The political revolution of the past several years is of more than academic interest to public employees. The more liberal legislatures already have passed legislation providing for collective bargaining in the public sector in several states. The collective bargaining laws passed in Michigan, for example, probably could not have been adopted before redistricting knocked out control by the rural areas. More enlightened measures along this line can be expected from other states in the future.

### Changed Conceptions of Role of Employee Organizations

*Among Leaders of Government Employees.* The desires of many public servants and the pressures of employee organizations have contributed greatly to the acceptance of collective negotiations in a growing number of governmental jurisdictions. As we will see, collective dealings between management and the employees are still far from universal, but the present mood of many government workers suggests that they will do their best to make them so. Any number of statements to this effect by their leaders can be cited, but one will suffice: [*357*, p. 5]

> Democracy means treating all people in society with equal decency with the emphasis on decency. Collective bargaining is not designed to misuse employers. It is the fruit of a dignified democracy. It means that employer and employees sit down and plan their economic and social gains. The only way that public employees can be guaranteed a modicum of decency and dignity is by collective bargaining.

Those are the words of Jerry Wurf, President of the American Federation of State, County, and Municipal Employees (AFSCME), the largest labor-affiliated organization in state and local governments, with a membership estimated at 400,000 and rising. The public employee leaders do not, of course, all think alike, and some do not agree with Wurf that collective bargaining as practiced in industry is essential or even desirable. In both the United States and Canada, however, most of them support the principle of collective negotiations and employee organizations' taking a greater part than they have had in the past in determining policy governing working conditions. They are not satisfied with mere toleration of their existence and want to make it clear that they are seeking this larger role.

*Among Political and Community Leaders.* Since this is their attitude and their strength is growing, legislators, administrators, and influential groups and citizens in the local communities are in turn changing their ideas and paying more attention to public employee organizations. This is the familiar spectacle of groups which interact in terms of the degree of successful pressure which can be exerted, but what is new for public employees is that they have tested their power and found that in many cases they can get what they want. This contributes momentum to their drive for a greater voice, and it is this momentum— obvious in the constant newspaper reports of public employee victories of one sort or another—which suggests that collective negotiations may become the general rule before too long.

This is why Ida Klaus has said that "public employees have been the center of one of the significant areas of social change in this decade." [121] They have broken through traditional ideas which limited them to a relatively passive rather than an active role, particularly in their dealings with department heads and other administrative officials. They have always had strength with legislatures through their lobbying efforts, but in general they were not consulted very widely by the administrators in charge of the day-by-day conduct of public programs. In Miss Klaus' opinion, whereas as recently as 1954 "the subject of labor relations in public employment could not have meant less to more people—in and out of government," today it is a New Frontier. [123] John W. Macy, Jr., Chairman of the United States Civil Service Commission, has stated frankly that "before 1962, federal employee organizations existed on sufferance and by grace, welcomed in some agencies and hardly tolerated in others." [156, p. 5] In Canada, employee organizations initially were stronger than in the United States, but in Canada also the greatest progress towards collective negotiations has come in recent years. J. Douglas Love divides the background into two phases: [154, p. 24]

> In the first of these, the Government was inclined to clothe itself in the doctrine of sovereignty, the employee organizations were relatively weak and badly divided, the relationship between the two was cold and distant and characterized by the occasional presentation of briefs. In the second phase, which began during the Second World War, there has been an emphasis on forms of joint consultation and a slow but certain drift towards a bargaining relationship.

The recent election campaigns provide an interesting illustration of the greater attention being shown public employee organizations. The candidates have been anxious to get the support of government workers, and while this is nothing new, it is much more pronounced. An illustration is Vice President Humphrey's statement at the 1966 convention of the AFSCME that "you have a sympathetic administration, one that recognizes your rights in collective bargaining." [*355*, p. 3] Actually, while President Kennedy's 1962 Executive Order 10988 does provide for the recognition of exclusive bargaining agents and the negotiation of signed agreements, it carefully avoids the term "collective bargaining," and certainly it cannot be said that bargaining on the industry model is taking place. Government workers count for more in the political campaigns, and there is strong competition for their endorsement. Former Premier Lesage of Quebec, in describing progress in that province, said, "we give our civil servants the right to bargain collectively and to strike." [*217*]

*In the Press.* Many newspaper editorials are being written about labor relations in government, and while there is frequent strong criticism of strike threats, there are many statements of support for more adequate attention to employee grievances. An editorial in the *Los Angeles Times,* entitled "End Collective Bungling," criticizes the Board of Supervisors for failure to develop "orderly and effective negotiating procedures" and blames it, along with irresponsible union leaders, for county social worker strikes. [*151*]

The *Times* believes that "greater authority should be given to department heads to conduct meaningful negotiations with employee representatives on wages and working conditions well in advance of budget considerations by the Supervisors." [*150*] The *Times* is a conservative newspaper, so the conclusion must be that it sees nothing irresponsible or undesirable in properly conducted collective negotiations.

### Strength from Increased Numbers and Scarce Supply

Unquestionably, public employees sense their strength from the great increase in the size of their ranks and the fact that in many cases their services are in short supply. A United States Census Bureau survey made late in 1966 showed that there were 11.5 million civilian employees of federal, state, and local governments, comprising about 15 per cent of the civilian labor force. [*94*] Whereas in 1914 the Canadian federal service numbered approximately 25,000, including non-civil service employees

and the many workers in commercial crown corporations, at the
end of 1966 the total was 363,713 civilians. [*86*, p 5] Mere con-
sciousness of size does not necessarily lead to stronger positions,
but in many cases it obviously has. It is difficult to believe, for
example, that school teachers in the United States would be pressing so hard for their rights if they were not aware that their
vastly increased numbers improved their bargaining position.
This is not to imply that their requests are unjustified, but rather
to report the power equation. As governments increase their commitments to the citizens with such programs as hospital and medical insurance, the necessary number of nurses, doctors, and lab-
oratory and other technicians must be induced to stay on the job,
and there are numerous vacancies to fill. Leaders of public employee organizations have generally manifested a responsible attitude, but they naturally have an acute sense of the importance of
the work of their members. Illustrating developments in just one
part of the country, Tom Goff, County Bureau Chief of the *Los
Angeles Times*, writes: [*103*]

> In talking of public employees these days, one no longer refers to a
> small cadre of "dedicated public servants." The growth of public em-
> ployment is fantastic. Federal Bureau of Labor Statistics 10 years
> ago showed one person out of every nine employed in California
> worked for some agency of government. Today that figure is about
> one in six. In another decade it is expected to be one in every 4.5 or 5.
> Unions recognize this. Part of the employee unrest that has been felt
> dramatically in Los Angeles County this year has been symptomatic
> of the struggle that is developing among unions and other employee
> groups to organize and lead this potent force.

### Impact of Changes in Union Strategy

Significant changes in the composition of the labor force have
altered trade union strategy and led the so-called "outside" labor
movement to start major organizing drives among government
workers. Although union membership in the United States
reached an all-time high of 17,892,000 in 1966, this represented
only 28 per cent of the non-farm labor force, the lowest percentage since the period of labor's great growth in the 1930's.
In the previous peak membership year, 1956, there were
17,490,000 members, but they accounted for 33.4 per cent of the
non-farm workers. [*372*] The problem, as stated by William
Kirchner, organizing director of the AFL-CIO, is that "simply
maintaining the numerical total has meant the relative size of
union membership has gradually worsened in the past decade as
the work force grew." [*371*]

As the unions look about for opportunities to gain members, they find that the greatest increase in number of new workers hired has taken place in the "unorganized" industries, meaning retail and wholesale trade, finance, insurance, real estate—and government. In the "unionized industries," where the unions know how to function, the increase has been much smaller, thus greatly limiting the possibilities for attracting very many new members. The unions traditionally have been strong in organizing blue-collar workers, those working in production and maintenance jobs in the industrial plants and in the skilled and semi-skilled trades. Largely as the result of automation, many thousands of production jobs have been eliminated, while at the same time the service industries have been expanding.

"The simple fact," comments James Reston, "is that more and more daily workers in the U.S. are being employed each year in providing services rather than in producing goods in vast industries." [*325*] White-collar are now far more numerous than blue-collar workers, and generally it has been much more difficult for the unions to organize the professionals, managers, and others in the first category. It is no wonder, then, that labor should turn its attention to government, particularly when it is estimated that total public employment in the United States may soon exceed 15 million. This in itself exceeds the 13.5 million membership of the AFL-CIO. The unions never neglected the possibilities in government, but found most of their members in the ranks of the skilled, semi-skilled, and unskilled workers. Now, through necessity, they are making strong overtures to the much larger percentage of government workers who work in offices and in various professional and other white-collar capacities. The same general picture holds in Canada where the comment has been made that "the attitudes of white-collar workers and industrial workers toward unionism and collective action have been growing together in recent years." [*88*, p. 350]

In later chapters of this book, the clash between the approaches of the affiliated unions and the independent associations in representing the interests of government employees will be discussed in detail, but suffice it to say here that organized labor is now in one of its most decisive stages of development. What happens in a small school district or city government, as AFL-CIO locals or other unions try to organize public employees, is more than a purely local issue and it has implications that many employees may not even sense. To them, it frequently is a question of long frustrations and the opportunity now to get better working conditions; to many union leaders, the local battle is part of a sustained effort to put new life into the labor movement.

The governmental administrator who is disturbed or puzzled by evidences of the "union approach" on the part of employees who for years were relatively passive, needs to understand this background of developments in industry. At the same time, he would make a mistake to blame the unions for this new militancy, because the influence of the outside labor movement is only one element in the picture and, furthermore, it operates on other factors, such as discontent with existing conditions. As *Newsweek* commented recently, ". . . civil servants have been the sporadic targets of union organizers for years; their new militancy is a change more in them than in the unions." [*174*, p. 94] It reports that public employees, like farm laborers and the poor of the ghettos, have been left behind in the economic boom and therefore look with much more favor on the unions.

## Present State of Collective Negotiations

In concluding this chapter, an assessment will be given of the picture with respect to collective negotiations at all levels of government in the United States and Canada. A detailed chronology of events will not be attempted, because the older history has already been adequately described by others, and lists of jurisdictions with collective bargaining laws quickly get out of date.

### In United States Federal Government

In the federal government of the United States, the labor-management relations program has definitely entered a second stage. The first period was one of getting the new program under way, with most employee organizations happy that for the first time the federal government was pledged to the principle of affirmative willingness to deal with them. Before the Kennedy Executive Order, some 762,000 persons representing approximately one-third of all federal employees were members of employee organizations. After the Order was issued, employee organization membership began to climb rapidly, and it is now well above the million mark. [*158*, p. 7] Hundreds of agreements have been signed by the employee organizations and the agency managements. The changeover from unilateral to collective dealings with the employees was definitely launched, and the whole complexion of personnel administration has changed greatly as a result. Both management and the employee organizations have admitted to inexperience under the new arrangements, and training programs have been instituted on both sides to prepare their representatives better for the arduous job of negotiations. Early in the implementation of the program, some employee leaders began to express dissatisfaction with certain aspects of it; the criticisms became more widespread, and in September of 1966, Macy commented that "one can hardly pick up a newspaper in Washington these days without reading some broadside allegation—usually attributed to employee organization leaders—that there is extensive dissatisfaction and unrest among government employees." [*156*, p. 2]

The specific reasons for this dissatisfaction will be discussed in detail in later chapters of this book. In general, the employee leaders' criticism is that the program has not really been effective or gone far enough. Obviously, promulgation of the Executive Order raised the expectations of many federal employees: they came to expect a good deal, and fast, rather than slow, progress. At the same time, it is doubtful that very many federal officials understood the implications of the Order in terms of the direction in which it would easily turn labor relations in the government. That direction is towards industry practices, for once exclusive bargaining units are recognized and contracts signed, the procedure is similar enough to the full collective bargaining pattern for some of the employee leaders to want to go the whole way—or as far as one can go in government. Thus, in the second stage, a confrontation is developing, with the employee leaders seeking to make the bargaining more effective from their standpoint and the Civil Service Commission and the departments and agencies anxious to protect the merit system and management prerogatives. A detached observer could, however, conclude that, despite the present uneasiness on both sides, the revolution in management-employee relations had greatly benefited the federal service as a whole. The disagreement basically is over how to make more progress with the partnership program.

### In State and Local Governments in the United States

As to state and local governments, no area of the country is untouched by the growing tendency of public employees to unite efforts and improve their situation. The principle of collective negotiations was accepted in Philadelphia, New York, Cincinnati, and other cities several years before the Kennedy Executive Order, so the federal government was not the leader in this area. Unquestionably, however, the example of Washington did later stimulate many state and local governments to develop formal programs and machinery for dealing with management-employee relationships, but in any case an increasing number of such jurisdictions have agreed to collective negotiations.

It is easy to exaggerate this "trend," because only about one third of the states have passed legislation granting to "state and/or local government employees the right of self-organization for the purpose of collective negotiation." [*407*, p. 5] Some of these laws, however, go well beyond the Kennedy Executive Order and provide for bargaining relationships very similar to those in industry. Furthermore, in hundreds of jurisdictions the employees have what Wurf calls "de facto" bargaining rights even in the absence of statutes. [*358*, p. 5] The right to strike is usually prohibited, but, to compensate for this, systematic procedures are specified to resolve bargaining impasses and generally assure that meaningful negotiation takes place. In these laws, much the same phraseology as that of the Taft-Hartley Act is used, and the existing machinery for regulating labor relations in industry is made to apply to the public sector. The intention of this legislation clearly is to guarantee the employees as large a scope for collective negotiations as is possible in government, with adequate protections at the same time for the management and the public against irresponsible employee actions. Examples of states with such laws are Michigan, Wisconsin, Connecticut, Delaware, Massachusetts, Rhode Island, and Minnesota.

Among the large cities, the labor relations program of New York City, initiated in 1958 by an Executive Order of former Mayor Wagner, is one of the most extensive. Ida Klaus states that it "was the first thoroughgoing code of labor relations for municipal employees anywhere in the country," and that "its history and background and its form and structure parallel very much the National Labor Relations Act." [*123*] Other cities, both large and small, are now negotiating contracts with employee organizations in much the same way as in industry, and the scope of the bargaining includes wages, salaries, and fringe benefits. Of course, the local governing bodies must provide the funds, but many more items are subject to bargaining than in the federal service.

Without question, this wide range of bargaining has in some cases begun to threaten merit principles, a problem discussed in detail in Chapter 2. Kenneth O. Warner and Mary L. Hennessey also point to the fragmentation of personnel programs which unfortunately has taken place in some jurisdictions as the result of piecemeal, uncoordinated negotiations. [*401*, p. 297] How to extend the area of bargaining and yet preserve the integrity and unity of the personnel program is the big problem, but it is capable of solution and is being solved in many cases. Before we leave the field of local government in the United States, it should be noted that teachers and other employees of local school districts have been making intensive efforts to gain bargaining rights. Ida Klaus comments that in public education, "the subject of employee relations has at times taken second place only to problems of integration." [*121*] For this reason, Chapter 9 in this book is devoted particularly to collective negotiations in public education.

### In the Canadian National Government

In Canada, Edward E. Herman believes that "during the last few years a legislative revolution has begun taking place regarding the collective bargaining status of civil servants." [*111*, p. 10] In the national service, the new collective bargaining legislation is the culmination of a long development. Beginning with 1944, a National Joint Council, representing both the staff associations and the government as employer, had been functioning, but both the 1958 and the 1965 Heeney reports cited deficiencies and recommended that the negotiating machinery be strengthened. [*324*, pp. 15-18] The Industrial Relations and Disputes Investigation Act of 1948, providing collective bargaining rights for workers in the private sector and those in certain crown companies, had excluded civil servants, but they apparently did not want to be covered. By 1963, however, their attitude had changed, and the major political parties were on record supporting collective bargaining in government.

The resulting 1967 legislation goes well beyond the Kennedy Executive Order and even permits a qualified right to strike, but, of course, the political institutions in the two countries are different in important respects. Throughout the discussions in the later chapters of this book, references will be made to pertinent aspects of the Canadian experience. Actually, the federal government of Canada, like that of the United States, for many years resisted the idea of collective negotiations. The difference is that some machinery for joint consultations was established much earlier in Canada than in the United States.

### In Provinces and Cities in Canada

In the Canadian cities and in some of the provinces, collective negotiations have been practiced for quite some time. The largest and the most extensive experience has been in the cities, because the provincial labor legislation for industry also applies to the municipalities. Two provinces, Saskatchewan, since 1944, and Quebec, since August 6, 1965, give full collective bargaining rights to their employees, including the strike weapon. In recent years, other provinces have passed legislation providing for consultation or negotiation, "but the emerging pattern of law and practice is neither clear nor complete." [*324*, p. 19]

Recent amendments to the Civil Service Acts of New Brunswick, Manitoba, and Alberta give a "designated staff association in each province the right to negotiate with the government and to enter into collective agreements." In Ontario, since 1963 there has been a ". . . form of collective bargaining in a Joint Council chaired by the Chairman of the Civil Service Commission and composed of representatives of the government as employer and of a staff association named in the legislation."

In British Columbia, the Civil Service Act provides that "an association enjoying the support of a majority of employees may submit disputes relating to terms and conditions of employment to a Board of Reference, which is required to submit its recommendations to the Lieutenant Governor in Council." [*324*, pp. 19-20]

In Prince Edward Island, there is a Joint Council which can hear employee requests but make recommendations only for their disposition. [*111*, pp. 14-15]

In general, collective negotiation in the cities is more widespread than in the United States, but there is, of course, disagreement as to the lessons of the Canadian experience. Some Canadians feel strongly that the collective agreements frequently conflict with merit principles and introduce great inequities in the classification and compensation plans. The problems in collective negotiations tend to be defined in the same way by public personnel workers in both countries, because, in truth, while the pace of developments in each country has varied in certain respects, the issues presented have not differed greatly.

# 2

## Significant Elements in the Environment

Is IT feasible and desirable to adopt industrial labor relations practices in government? Are there significant differences between the private and the public sectors? If so, what are they and what is their bearing on management-employee relations in the public service? Exactly who is the "management" in government? Is there an inherent irreconcilable conflict between merit principles and collective negotiations? It is with these and related questions that this chapter will be concerned.

Traditional practices and institutions have their rationales, imbedded in customs, concepts of the law, and slogans. For them to give way, they must be successfully challenged by new interpretations of what is proper, backed, of course, by successful pressures. Until recently, the almost exclusive mode of dealing with public employees was as individuals, rather than collectively. Employee organizations were sometimes given some encouragement, but with very few exceptions they were not permitted effective negotiation rights. They were not supposed to be entitled to such rights, and in many cases they seemed to agree because they did not demand them. It is not accidental that in the United States both the Wagner (1935) and the Taft-Hartley (1947) Acts have applied only to the private sector and that until very recently in the country as a whole state labor relations agencies had very limited jurisdiction over public employee disputes. [297, pp. 470-71]

In Canada, the Industrial Relations and Disputes Investigation Act of 1948 covers those government workers employed in federal crown companies but not those in the civil service; provincial labor legislation, with the exceptions of Saskatchewan, Quebec, and Prince Edward Island, also excludes civil servants. [329, pp. 12-13] Aside from the Canadian cities, labor relations in the private and public sectors were considered essentially dif-

25

ferent, and the "union" concept of conference-table bargaining with management, representation elections, and written agreements was considered unsuitable for government. The paramount legal doctrine justifying this approach has been that of sovereignty, and it has been referred to so often that it is essential that we take it up immediately.

### The Doctrine of Sovereignty

Basically, this doctrine holds that, as the sovereign employer, the government cannot be compelled to accept any obligation it shuns, or to continue to respect a commitment if it later decides it cannot or should not. In this sense, government is very different from private industry, for businessmen must obey the law and cannot claim to represent a higher force which permits them to define their own responsibilities. The origins of this view of the government's rights are in the English common law doctrines that the king could do no wrong and that no individual could sue the state without its consent.

The American colonists came to reject the king, but they carried over into their legal system those features of the common law they found useful. Alexander Hamilton wrote in *The Federalist* that "it is inherent in the nature of sovereignty not to be amenable to the suit of an individual without its consent." [*109*, pp. 529-30] He sought to assure state governments, fearful of the proposed new Constitution, that their private creditors would not be able to sue them in a federal court. These fears continued even after adoption of the Constitution, and it was found necessary to add the Eleventh Amendment which prevents such suits.

We know, however, that, based on legislation passed over the years by the Congress and the state legislatures, private individuals can sue the government for redress of alleged injuries. Thus, while government is unique in possessing sovereignty, it has voluntarily waived it in many cases. Public agencies enter into many contractual agreements with private parties which in theory the government could fail to respect but in practice always does. To Wilson R. Hart, this makes sovereignty a "meaningless legislative circumlocution," because "a right which will never be exercised is the equivalent of no right at all." [*110*, p. 43] Hart and others believe that sovereignty frequently has been used as an excuse by government officials who do not want to bargain with the unions. It has been considered correct to forget sovereignty and allow the government to be sued by citizens with just claims, but improper to do so when it comes to sharing decision-making with employee organizations. Why is sovereignty insisted upon in the one case and not in the other?

Hart does not challenge the government's right to refuse to enter into collective bargaining agreements or later to repudiate those it does sign. Rather he argues that the government can and should grant its employees collective bargaining rights; in so doing, the essence of sovereignty will be retained because it will have acted voluntarily and could renege on its agreements— although it never will! [*110*, pp. 38-54]

Hart's reasoning is very similar to that of Saul Frankel, the Canadian political theorist who has a strong research interest in employee relations as a problem in constitutional adjustment. Frankel grants that "the idea of sovereignty is a useful legal fiction" because "it provides for an ultimate authority within the state that may be invoked under certain conditions." However, "while it may be that we need the conception of sovereignty to legitimatize the coercive power of the state and to derive some of the principles of political obligation from it, . . . [the] notion of a monolithic, all-powerful sovereign is a thing of the past." [*99*, p. 221]

Like Hart, Frankel stresses that under democratic governments sovereignty resides in the people anyway, so if their representatives in the legislature authorize collective bargaining in the government, this does not violate sovereignty. As we have seen, in fact, legislatures in both the United States and Canada are providing for collective negotiations, and the courts are not objecting. Whatever one's personal beliefs as to the wisdom of such legislation, its existence constitutes clear evidence that sovereignty does not prevent it. While there certainly are some officials who raise the sovereignty argument as an excuse, there also are some who simply are repeating what others have told them. There are numerous discussions of labor relations in government wherein sovereignty is fleetingly referred to as an irremovable obstacle to collective negotiations—and then the person who makes this statement goes on to something else. The same tendency exists when statements are made about how the government cannot delegate its powers to private parties, for example, to outside arbitrators. In fact, public agencies have long entered into construction and other contracts containing arbitration clauses for the settlement of disputes over the contract terms.

### Elastic Nature of the Sovereignty Concept

The argument over sovereignty is now clearly in the realm of "ought" rather than "cannot." The fact that numerous public agencies are entering into contracts with employee organizations shows that they can do so. Whether other agencies should do so is a question of "ought." In Great Britain, since 1925, there has been a system of agreed compulsory arbitration of disputes between the government and civil service workers over questions of pay and other conditions of work. The Canadian Parliament has now provided for a similar process for dispute settlement. In both countries, Parliament retains sovereignty because it can set aside the provisions of any arbitral award, but in Britain it never has, and it is not likely that it will in Canada. In the past, support for compulsory arbitration has been limited in the United States, but two states have provided for it in non-profit hospitals, and increasingly voices are being raised in support of similar arrangements for so-called "essential services." [*297*, p. 399]

In Great Britain and Canada, the government retains sovereignty because it has agreed to the compulsory arbitration. As Frankel explains: [*99*, p. 222]

> It requires only a bit of ingenuity—insertion of a qualifying clause here and there—to provide for the reality of arbitration while preserving the fiction of sovereignty. Thus, the formal document that announced the Civil Service Arbitration Agreement in Britain pledged that, 'Subject to the overriding authority of parliament the government will give effect to the Awards of the Court.'

Similar ingenuity could be shown in the United States, although we want to make clear that we are not recommending compulsory arbitration. Our point rather is that the sovereignty concept is an elastic one, and that it is unbending public officials who will not bend it at all.

### Sovereignty and the Reality in New York City

Speaking about New York City, shortly after his inauguration, Mayor Lindsay announced that the city's fiscal policy had to be "supreme" over the requirements of its contracts with the employee organizations. Since the city was in some financial straits, he apparently was prepared to stop paying the salaries called for in the contracts. The *New York Times* did not question the city's legal right to refuse to be bound by commitments entered into by the Wagner administration, but it warned: [*213*]

> Orderly union-management relations in any field must rest on the
> principle that once an employer and a union sign a contract both are
> under solemn obligation to live up to all its terms. . . . The important
> thing, however, is to decide whether the total good of the community
> can really be served in abrogating contracts by unilateral municipal
> action. Certainly, the transit experience demonstrated that the city
> would be in terrible shape if all its union agreements expired—as the
> subway contract did—just as a new Mayor was stepping into office.
> Equity would be no better served by an arrangement under which
> the unions would be bound but the Mayor was free to tear up any
> part of the inherited contract.

The contracts were not torn up, and the whole incident makes
very clear that hasty recourse to sovereignty will quickly be
challenged. Obviously, if there had been no possibility at all
of the city's finding the funds, the contracts could not have been
respected, but practically speaking, there is no easy way out by
invoking sovereignty. "Sanctity of contract," the title of the
*New York Times* editorial, is just as much a part of the American
legal tradition as sovereignty.

### Arguments Based on the "Public Interest"

Apart from sovereignty, it is frequently argued that the
"public interest" requires special procedures for labor relations
in the government. The employee organizations sometimes make
demands which conflict with the interests of the community
as a whole, and giving them negotiation rights will encourage
them to press these demands. The taxpayer will suffer from the
increased budgets, and the threatened and actual work stoppages
will deprive the citizens of essential services.

The strike question will be discussed in detail in Chapter 4,
but suffice it to say here that the "concept of the public interest
is one that lacks precision." [*99*, p. 223] We never really know
what the public interest is; final decisions are made by the
government after many different groups have argued for their
interpretations of what is best for the community. If the *Los
Angeles Times* is right, the recent county social worker strikes
were against the public interest, but so was the "collective bungling" of the Board of Supervisors. [*151*] Without the "collective
bungling," the strike would not have taken place, so it is clear
that both sides can fail to respect the public interest.

According to Frank P. Zeidler, "it is advanced that public
employees are also a 'public' who have higher claims against the
other 'publics.' " [*422*, p. 9] A former mayor of Milwaukee, he

apparently had contacts with employee leaders who seemed to be taking this attitude. Yet the basic point is that there is plenty of disagreement as to which "publics" should control the government's decisions in specific cases. Some taxpayers may be relatively insensitive to the just requests of the public employees, just as the latter may have no real appreciation of the burdens on these taxpayers. Thus, except for situations such as a subway strike where the inconvenience to the public as a whole is obvious, the public interest argument can take us wherever we want to go.

Even in the case of a subway strike, the public interest does not clearly indicate all of what should be done. There is strong sentiment that such strikes should not be permitted, but just what the government can or should do to prevent them is another question. Was it against the public interest to make the wage settlement finally agreed to by the New York City Transit Authority? What was better for the people of the city, a continuation of the strike or a settlement which inevitably led to an increase in the fare? All of this suggests that, before special curbs are placed on public employees, there should be clear evidence of a situation in government which justifies such restrictions.

## Definition of Management

While it is true that some public officials use the excuse that they cannot legally enter into collective agreements, many others have been genuinely puzzled about just who in government represents the "management." It is at this point that comparisons with industry structure and practice are frequently made. It is sometimes said that everybody knows who represents the management in a private company and that the decision-making is centralized, rather than diffused as in government. Some people seem to have the impression that the bargaining arrangements in industry are relatively simple and not complicated as they must be in the public sector. Actually, this is not so, although, of course, the picture varies from industry to industry.

In some cases, industry-wide bargaining is practiced, which means that the negotiator named to represent all the companies must report back to the directors of each firm, an arrangement which can and sometimes does produce complications. Furthermore, even where, as is the general practice, bargaining is with a single company, there is no one way of assigning responsibilities within the firm for the negotiation and approval of the labor contracts. The procedures within the unions also vary a good deal, with everything greatly complicated by the possibility that certain committees or the rank and file will reject what the union negotiators recommend. Nonetheless, there are peculiar problems in government, as lucidly stated by J. Douglas Love: [*154*, p. 28]

> In coming to grips with the concept of collective bargaining in a public service, one of the most difficult problems is to find management and, having found it, to clothe it with the authority it needs to play its part. In a public service setting, managerial authority tends to be divided between a legislature and an executive, between politicians and bureaucrats, between independent commissions and operating departments. Because badly dispersed, it tends to lack substance and definition and almost, at times, to disappear in a forest of checks and balances. One could almost sustain the thesis that collective bargaining has been slow to establish itself in public services because employee representatives have been unable to identify individuals with whom they could really deal.

### *"Finding" the Management*

There is no one group within the executive branch which represents the management, and usually there is a separation between the fund-recommending and the fund-approving groups. The exceptions are agencies like the New York Port Authority whose board of directors does not have to go to any legislature for the money to meet labor contracts, but this is very rare. Even when the legislature delegates the authority to the executive branch to set pay scales and even pay prevailing rates, it does not relinquish its control of the purse and may refuse to make the necessary funds available. A local school board may not have to get its budget approved by the city council, but if it wants to increase expenditures beyond the estimated yield of the school tax, it must present the issue to the residents of the community in a special referendum. Furthermore, since there is a limit to the money which can be raised locally, it may be impossible for school boards to pay better salaries without an increase in state support.

The possibilities of disagreements between those with important roles in the decision-making process also produce complications. The civil service commission may approve the salary requests, but the budget director may not, or else the mayor agrees with neither—and the city council may be at odds with the mayor. Arvid Anderson relates how the Common Council of the

City of Kenosha voted to reduce the work week of the firemen but the mayor vetoed such action. The firemen then requested mediation, but, comments Anderson, how could mediation be successful without the mayor's participation? [*35*, p. 92] This kind of situation is far from uncommon, and it, of course, illustrates the importance of political factors. (Chapter 3 deals with these political aspects in detail.)

*Under a Parliamentary System.* Yet, to use Love's words, the "management" can be "found" and given the necessary authority. In Canada, this is easier because of the fusion of executive and legislative powers in the cabinet under the parliamentary system. What the cabinet recommends, the parliament is very likely to approve, just as in Great Britain. But even in Canada it was first necessary to designate the employer, that is the agency which should represent the government in its negotiations with the employee organizations. Prior to the passage of the new collective bargaining legislation, working conditions in the national government were based on various statutes, with the Civil Service Commission, the Treasury Board, and a number of department heads and other officials all playing a role. [*324*, pp. 4-6] The management was fragmented, but now the Treasury Board has been named the government's spokesman for all agencies except those designated as "separate employers." In the latter group are a small number of agencies which, because of the nature of their functions, or because of existing statutes or administrative practices, were allowed to retain independence in employment matters. [*350*, p. 28, pp. 52-53] There is now no question as to who negotiates with whom, with the Treasury Board representing the government in negotiations with the great majority of employees. At the same time, legislation was passed expanding the Treasury Board's powers, making it responsible for classification and pay, and otherwise empowering it to negotiate for the government on all matters made subject to collective bargaining. [*352*] Appointments, promotions, and other merit system functions are the responsibility of the new Public Service Commission which replaces the Civil Service Commission. [*351*]

*In The American System.* The American system of separation of powers, and of separate budgetary and personnel authorities within the executive branch, makes the picture very different from that in Canada. The most important difference is that the

President and his Cabinet are not members of the Congress and cannot count upon its support as in a parliamentary system. Even assuming that an agreement could be made within the executive branch to designate a "principal spokesman," past experience strongly suggests that the Congress would not be content with simply ratifying the administration's salary proposals. There is also the question of whether it would be desirable in an administrative establishment as large as that of the United States to attempt to place in a single arm of the chief executive the responsibility for negotiations with employee organizations representing a potential three million workers. Since the Civil Service Commission has been responsible for classification standards and the Budget Bureau for expenditures recommendations, these functions would have to be combined or a bargaining committee established representing both agencies.

Fundamental differences in traditions make it unlikely that the Canadian pattern could be closely followed in the United States, but the principle of fixing responsibility for the negotiations is certainly a good one. The comparison between the United States and the Canadian national governments also has its limitations, because the scope of negotiations in the United States does not extend to pay and fringe benefits. The management has been found for the present bargaining: it is the heads of the individual departments and agencies and their designated representatives. If the bargaining were expanded to include salaries and fringe benefits, then the management empowered to make decisions for the government over that much broader area would have to be found. At present, it appears unlikely that Congress would look with favor on any such expanded negotiations.

The final arrangements for negotiations may seem awkward, particularly in state and local governments with their numerous independent boards and commissions, but they can be made to work. *In no place is it possible to say that there is no one with whom the employees can negotiate, and this is the significant consideration.* Every effort should be made, of course, to simplify the structure and the procedures for negotiation, but the great number of governmental units and the diffusion of authority within and between them impose strict limits on streamlining.

### The Bargaining Timetable

Even the problem of uncertainty as to whether the legislature will have the time to act, and, if it does, actually vote the funds

can be dealt with to some extent at least. One device is to set up
a timetable which assures that negotiations are completed in time
to meet legal and other budgetary deadlines. The City of Milwaukee's agreement with District Council 48 of the AFSCME provides a very good example: [*3*, p. 7]

> *Timetable.* Conferences and negotiations shall be carried on by the
> parties hereto in 1968 as follows:
> Step 1. Submission of Union demands to the City............by Feb.   1
> Step 2. Submission of City's answer (within 6 weeks)........by Mar. 15
> Step 3. Negotiations to begin (within 4 weeks)..............by Apr. 15
> Step 4. Conclusion of negotiations (within 3 months)........by July 15
> Step 5. Mediation, if any, begins..........................by July 15
> Step 6. Fact Finding, if any, begins.......................by Aug.   1
> Step 7. Recommendations issued.............................by Oct. 15

Such a schedule allows ample time to reach agreement prior
to January 1, when the city's fiscal year begins. Each jurisdiction should, of course, make arrangements which meet its
own needs. Arvid Anderson writes: [*35*, p. 95]

> The necessity of adopting budgets and tax schedules also has meant
> that in many instances municipal employers have placed the offered
> increased benefits into effect at the new budget year, regardless of
> whether an agreement has been reached. Aside from the question
> whether such practice could in certain circumstances be considered
> bad-faith bargaining, the impact that such deadlines have on the
> bargaining process is worthy of research. The question of annual
> bargaining and annual budgeting needs to be reviewed. I think it is of
> significance that Milwaukee has entered into a three-year collective
> bargaining agreement. Obviously, the agreement must be implemented
> in each budget year, but the stability of this contract permits more
> realistic preparation for bargaining and better contract administration.

### Clothing the Management with Authority

A re-definition of the responsibilities of the management
representatives in the administrative branch may also pave the
way for legislative acceptance of the contract terms. In recent
collective bargaining legislation, the law plainly holds these
representatives responsible, not only for the negotiations, but
also for doing everything possible to obtain favorable legislative
action. This requirement is intended to satisfy one of the employees' complaints, namely that the bargaining will be meaningless if the administrators refuse to fight for legislative approval
of the pacts. Presumably, it also removes much of the present
justification for the intensive post-negotiations legislative lobbying by employee groups, a frequent source of irritation to the
administrative officials. The Connecticut Municipal Employee
Relations Act provides: [*30*, p. 330]

Any agreement reached by the negotiators shall be reduced to writing. A request for funds necessary to implement such written agreement and for approval of any provisions of the agreement which are in conflict with any charter, special act, ordinance, rule or regulation adopted by the municipal employer or its agents, such as a personnel board or civil service commission, or any general statute directly regulating the hours of work of policemen or firemen shall be submitted by the bargaining representative of the municipality to the legislative body which may approve or reject such request as a whole by a majority vote of those present and voting on the matter. If rejected, the matter shall be returned to the parties for further bargaining.

The above provision is also intended to clear away any existing legislation which impedes carrying out the contract terms. There is no way of guaranteeing that the bargaining representatives will make the strongest case possible before the legislature, but, if they drag their feet, the employees could file a complaint of bad faith bargaining with the State Board of Labor Relations. Furthermore, to resolve any legal doubts which may make the legislature hesitant to act, the Connecticut law provides: [*30*, p. 330]

Notwithstanding any provision of any general statute, charter, special act or ordinance to the contrary, the budget-appropriating authority of any municipal employer shall appropriate whatever funds are required to comply with a collective bargaining agreement which has been approved by the legislative body of such municipal employer.

Some state legislatures may not want to go this far, but it is clear that the Connecticut legislators wanted the municipal employers to have as much freedom as possible in entering into labor contracts. Other state laws, such as in Massachusetts, also obligate the representatives of the employer to request the legislative body to appropriate the funds necessary for carrying out the contracts. [*31*, p. 557] In Canada, the new legislation provides that the agreements, once negotiated by the government's representatives, will be implemented subject to Parliament's agreeing to appropriation of the funds required by the various departments affected by the agreement. No collective agreement may, however, provide for changes in working conditions which "would require or have the effect of requiring the enactment or amendment of any legislation by Parliament." [*350*, pp. 28-29]

### Need for Good Management-Employee Relations in Government

Any discussion of the governmental environment should make

clear why good management-employee relations programs are needed. This makes it possible to compare government and industry in terms of a positive focus: the government's real needs. Sometimes comparisons are made between the private and public sectors which are interesting, but not very useful as guides for action to those concerned with labor relations in the government.

### The Governmental Manpower Crisis

First, employee relations policies have a great bearing on the government's ability to compete with industry and attract larger numbers of qualified persons to the public service. What Senator Muskie of Maine calls the "crisis in governmental manpower" is so well known that this point needs no elaboration. This crisis has reached such proportions that Muskie has introduced unprecedented legislation aimed at substantially improving public personnel administration throughout the United States. ([117]) No new programs, however, will succeed any more than the old ones unless effective management-employee relations policies are developed. Again, as only one example, many school teachers have left public education and taken jobs in industry. Similarly, a great many graduate nurses simply are not interested in working for public employers under present conditions. Obviously, one cannot make exact predictions about how many could be persuaded to return to the government, but certainly many would not have left in the first place if they had been satisfied with their conditions of work.

### Management-Employee Conflicts in Government

Second, it is not true that the absence of the profit motive makes organized dealings between the management and the employees unnecessary. As a matter of fact, some instrumentalities of government do make profits. This manuscript is being written under light provided by the City of Newark, Delaware, which purchases the power from an electric utility company and then charges the customers a substantially higher rate. In this way, the city keeps its taxes down, but still it makes a profit on the transaction. Of course, this is an unusual example, and many better ones, such as bridge authorities and other revenue-producing agencies, could be given. The essential point is that, just as in private companies, friction and misunderstanding can arise between the management and the employees. Furthermore, as mentioned in Chapter 1, much of the conflict has nothing to do with cutting up the "economic pie," meaning the wage and other material benefits. It emerges rather from employee frustrations over inability, as they see it, to participate in the decision-making.

A few individuals are still saying that public employees are so well treated that they should not seek collective negotiation rights, but such statements generally are no longer given credence. On the other hand, there is legitimate fear that the employee leaders will view the governmental administrators in the same light as profit-hungry private entrepreneurs and apply the same pressures as in industry. Therefore, the protective argument is made that the government does not have the same selfish interests as private companies. Everybody, of course, has selfish interests, including the employees and their leaders. The point remains, however, that this attempted distinction between government and industry fails to impress, theoretically or practically, as an argument for denying bargaining rights to public employees. A major grievance of government social workers, largely explaining their recent strikes, is that they are hopelessly overburdened with record-keeping and other clerical work. They feel they cannot perform as true professionals when required to carry out these chores, often under the additional handicap of inadequate space, no desks, and too few telephones. This is one of the more extreme examples, but it does show that conflicts can arise, just as in industry—or for that matter in a labor union itself! Just like unions in industry, the American Federation of Teachers, for example, recognizes and negotiates with an organization of its own employees. [*25*, p. 8] This should be conclusive evidence that there is a need for grievance procedures in non-profit organizations as well.

In fact, some observers believe that governmental administrators may even be tougher than the managers in private enterprise. Witness this statement by an industrial executive: [*337*, pp. 106-07]

> Much has been said about the objectivity and essential fairness of government administrators vis-à-vis employee wages and benefit policies, because they are not subordinate to profit-oriented, unit-cost-conscious corporation boards of directors and not beholden to dividend-hungry stockholders. . . . The electorate, on whose whim and judgment the survival of an officeholder is dependent, zealously protects the pocketbook, peers vigilantly at budget and tax policy, holds accountable the executive or legislative representatives, and blithely tosses them out of office, in marked contrast to the cautious and

restrained actions of stockholders and boards of directors. The public official is subject to continuous scrutiny, accountability and recall, compared to which the corporation manager's life is an idyllic sanctuary . . . the elected public official, in contrast to his private sector counterpart, must cope with an irrepressible electorate, stimulated by an often irresponsible and ill-informed press, radio and TV and a permanently organized opposition of "minority stockholders" who are well financed and led by sophisticated leaders versed in the arts of demagoguery, petard-hoisting and polemics.

The above quotation is particularly interesting, for it is sometimes said that industrial labor relations practices are not applicable because in government there is no owner. But in every public agency there is a group which makes policy and determines working conditions, and the great need exists to develop good relationships between this group and the rest of the employees. If the interests of the supervisors and the non-supervisory employees in government were always the same, no one would worry about putting both in the same bargaining units. This problem is discussed in Chapter 5, but it can be said here that obviously there will be conflicts of interests between employees who have hiring and firing authority and those who do not.

Furthermore, the public constitutes the owner, and, even if it is not as hard on the employees as the preceding statement indicates, still it may not treat them as well as it should. Admittedly, the government is a common enterprise of all employees, but there are different perceptions of how this joint effort should be conducted. Most public employee leaders do not view the government as just the same as any private employer; what they cannot swallow is the contention that the administrators can be trusted faithfully to represent the interests of all the employees. A Canadian public official writes: [*88*, p. 350]

Governments are large institutions with lengthy hierarchy of command like large corporations and . . . unionism is, in part, a function of the size and complexity and degree of impersonality in the decision-making process as it affects ordinary rank-and-file workers . . . . The scope for arbitrary action in government is probably less than in private business because of the protection concerning hiring, promotion and job classification provided by Civil Service Acts, but nevertheless I think there is a good deal of room for the growth of inequality of treatment, not of the conscious sort but of the unconscious sort that develops in any large-scale organization that is complex.

### The Special Problem of Legislative Relations

Third, the area of legislative relations creates special problems and challenges for the employee relations function in government. While industry management and labor cannot dismiss the possibility of legislative intervention, it is a remote one, and they are not dependent on the lawmakers for the funds to implement the contract. Political factors are far from absent in industrial labor relations, because elective officials are very much concerned with public reactions to labor disputes—and with getting votes for themselves and staying in office. But in government the legislature is in the picture from the very start, and the negotiators in the executive branch really are intermediaries between the employee organizations and the lawmakers. Of course, the employees preserve their direct line to the legislature, but, except in small jurisdictions, they ordinarily will not negotiate contract terms directly with the legislators.

The question thus arises as to what strategies and techniques can be employed to make this role of intermediary effective, both in terms of persuading the legislators to accept reasonable employee requests and of counteracting any undesirable pressures by employee organizations which have failed to get what they want in the negotiations. This last sentence is a loaded one, because it is a matter of opinion whether or not the employee requests are reasonable, and the same applies to the efforts by the employee leaders to get more from the legislature than they can obtain in the negotiations. Nevertheless, the problem, peculiar to the public service, is adequately stated: how to function in this "middle" relationship.

Some people feel that legislatures do not support administrative officials in employee relations matters to the same extent that a company board of directors backs the firm's officials. Frank P. Zeidler warns that "public administration officials are relatively powerless before legislatures in opposing the demands of organized public employees because the public administrators do not represent a bulk constituency or voting bloc." [*422*, p. 8] If so, this has serious implications, and Zeidler's comment will be referred to again in Chapter 10. We are concerned here simply with pointing out that good employee relations programs in government are especially needed in view of the legislative complications.

### Removing the Causes of Strikes

Fourth, the fact that public employees generally abstain from using the strike weapon, makes it more imperative that government develop sound management policies and procedures for resolving problems with employee groups. Increasingly this is the conclusion, not simply of the employee organizations, but of many different groups. At a conference sponsored in late 1966 by Columbia University's American Assembly, no agreement was reached on whether public employees should be allowed to strike, but it was decided that "taxpayers must realize that, if they wish to improve the quality of government service and to deal fairly with their employees, they must provide levels of compensation and other conditions of employment equitably related to those prevailing elsewhere." [*257*]

This also is the tenor of editorials in leading newspapers like the *New York Times* and the *Los Angeles Times;* sweeping condemnations of public employee organizations now tend to be the exception. Such provisions as the one quoted below are now found in the authorizing legislation : [*165*]

> . . . Because the paramount interest of the public and the nature of governmental processes makes it necessary to impose special limitations upon public employment, it is incumbent upon governmental agencies to provide orderly procedures for the participation by public employees and their representatives in the formulation of personnel policies and plans to insure the fair and considerate treatment of public employees, to eliminate employment inequities, and to provide effective means of resolving questions and controversies with respect to terms and conditions of employment. It is the public policy of the State of Minnesota that governmental agencies, public employees and their representatives shall enter into discussions with affirmative willingness to resolve grievances and differences. Governmental agencies and public employees and their representatives shall have a mutual obligation to endeavor in good faith to resolve grievances and differences relating to terms and conditions of employment within the framework of laws and charter provisions, and giving consideration to personnel policies, position classification and compensation plans, and other special rules governing public employment.

In industry, the strike weapon is generally considered an essential element in collective bargaining. If work stoppages cannot be permitted in government, what can be done to make collective negotiations so effective that strikes will not take place, whether banned by law or not? Simple solutions, such as firing all striking employees, are neither practical nor sensible. In Canada, arbitration has long been used in the cities and in a few provinces, and now it is available in the national government for employee organizations which have, but give up, the right to strike. In the United States and Canada, most labor groups, both inside and outside the government, are strongly opposed to compulsory arbitration of bargaining impasses. In both countries, the challenge is to show creativeness in developing labor relations policies and practices adapted to the special needs of the government, which will check the growing tendency of public employees to withhold services.

### Protecting the Merit System

Fifth, the transition from traditional employee relations practices to collective negotiations must be guided with great care so as to avoid any damage to the merit principle. The problem in government is one of protecting the great accomplishment of equal opportunity for all and selection based on merit, but at the same time infusing the merit system with the dynamic element of collective dealings. This last matter is so important that the balance of this chapter is devoted to it.

## Collective Negotiations and the Merit Principle

Some of the employee organizations are very critical of the way "civil service" has been administered in the past. They argue that in many cases merit principles really have not been followed and that in general the quality of the recruitment, promotion, and other personnel activities has hardly been as good as the merit system administrators maintain. Above all, they charge that the employee cannot expect an unbiased decision on his requests and grievances by personnel officers and civil service commissioners who basically identify with the "management."

### Issues of Principle vs. Practice

Some employee leaders are unhesitatingly coming out against civil service; most are making no frontal attack but claim that there is no incompatibility between collective negotiations and the merit system. The trouble is that some contract provisions which they justify as true application of the merit principle appear to others actually to contradict that principle. Many public personnel administrators admit that civil service procedures have in certain respects been unduly rigid or otherwise deficient. They recognize that the employee organizations can contribute valuable suggestions towards eliminating these deficiencies *in the administration* of the merit criterion; what they insist cannot be sacrificed is the *principle* of true competition, under which the jobs and the promotions are awarded to the persons who have demonstrated, after application of the best devices available for measuring the abilities of the candidates, that they are the best qualified.

Since there always will be disagreements as to how to measure qualifications and who is the best qualified, the argument as to compatibility of employee organization requests with the merit principle will never end. This author presents evidence below which he believes makes clear that there is a real, not an imaginary, threat to the merit principle in the points of view and demands of some of the employee organizations. However, even in these organizations, the viewpoints of the officials vary, with some not as critical of civil service as others; furthermore, there does not appear to be any fixed, fully elaborated position as such on this issue to which the leadership is irrevocably committed.

Collective negotiations in government are still in a very early stage; the full picture has yet to emerge and all parties concerned have the power to shape the future evolution. Management in government should appraise with an open mind the contentions of the employee leaders that certain existing practices do not contribute to merit, because these criticisms may be well founded. One labor expert writes: "Management in private enterprise years ago feared that unions would weaken *merit*, but in most cases they have instead added equity, uniformity, and more objectivity to management's frequently careless or biased judgments." [*101*]

This, of course, is one man's opinion, but surely everything possible should be done to derive solid improvements in public personnel administration from the collective negotiations process.

### The Delaware Experience

When in June of 1965, the Delaware General Assembly passed "An Act Recognizing the Right of Public Employees to Organize," there was no civil service system for state employees. [*32*] The Levy Court of New Castle County, the most populous area in the state, had, in December of 1964 adopted a merit system, and it was getting under way. The collective bargaining statute applied to the state government and all counties, and to any city or town which by action of its governing body elected to come under it. Employee organizations quickly began to negotiate with state and local government agencies, with the state Department of Labor and Industrial Relations, as provided in the law, passing upon requests for the establishment of bargaining units. The bargaining includes "wages, salaries, hours, vacations, sick leave, grievance procedures and other terms and conditions of employment." In case of bargaining impasses, "any matter in dispute except matters of wages and salaries may be submitted by either party to the State Mediation Service or by agreement of the parties to arbitration." A significant clause reads that "whenever the procedures under the merit or personnel system established by statute or ordinance are exclusive with respect to matters otherwise comprehended by this Act, they shall apply and be followed." Then, in June of 1966, after prolonged efforts, a civil service law for the state service was passed. [*33*]

*The Tax Department Agreement.* In the period between passage of the state collective bargaining and civil service statutes, labor contracts were signed by several state agencies. The first such agreement was between the State Tax Department and Local 1385 of the AFSCME, the exclusive bargaining agent, and it set something of a pattern for the later ones. [*7*] The union shop is provided for all employees, except those hired before January 1, 1940. All new appointees must join the union within 30 days of entrance on duty, and stay in it for the duration of the agreement. Those who do not join the union, except for the small exempt group, must be discharged. Since the union shop is discussed in detail in Chapter 4, the only comment which will be made here is that the principle of equal opportunity for jobs in the government was narrowed by a requirement which also cannot be justified as an objective recruitment standard. Local 1385 includes about two-thirds of the some 155 employees in the Tax Department; the latter principally employs clerks and other whitecollar workers whose skill requirements are not related to any union apprenticeship.

Seniority is the basis for reductions-in-force and re-employment, as well as for temporary transfers. Notices of all vacancies and new positions must be posted on bulletin boards, and "the senior employee making application shall be transferred to fill the vacancy or new position, provided, he has the necessary qualifications. . . ." [*7*, p. 6] If an employee who applies does not get the job but believes he should have, he can appeal through the grievance procedure. The latter covers any grievance whether or not the result of conflicting interpretations of the contract terms, and climaxes in binding arbitration. Thus, the final decision as to who fills the job can be made by the arbitrators.

A true merit system provides for ranking of the candidates according to objective measurements of their qualifications.

Under the above procedure, so long as someone meets the minimum qualifications, he is eligible, and of those eligible the one with the greatest seniority must be named. Furthermore, under these provisions for binding arbitration, a state agency has delegated appointing and promoting authority to the arbitrators without legislative authorization and with no possibility of legislative veto. Since the agreement also permits the union to take to binding arbitration any work rule or regulation established by the employer, any administrative order could be made subject to negotiation and arbitration, and even the collective bargaining contracts in industry do not go that far.

Although an employee is involuntarily separated from the service, he must be paid for all accumulated sick leave, not exceeding 100 work days. The negotiated salary rates and classifications are made a part of the agreement, so presumably the classifications are also subject to binding arbitration. The fringe benefits in the agreement are quite liberal by comparison with those for other state agencies. In Delaware there are no uniform state laws governing sick and annual leave, life insurance, hospitalization, medical, and other benefit rights of state employees. The AFSCME has naturally wanted to sign contracts with the different state agencies as quickly as possible, and, if there had been uniform state laws, these anomalies would not have occurred. All the same, the crazy quilt pattern which has emerged supports the criticism that in a vacuum of this kind, without salary standardization, uniform fringe benefits, and civil service, collective negotiations can create many serious problems.

*Conflicts Between Agreement and Law.* The new civil service law in Delaware states that its purpose is "to establish for the state a system of personnel administration based on merit principles and scientific methods governing the appointment, promotion, transfer, layoff, removal and discipline of employees of the state. . . ." [*33*, p. 2]

The clause in the collective bargaining legislation quoted above makes clear that, in case of conflict with the provisions of any civil service statute, the latter shall prevail. In late 1967, this issue came to a head as progress was being made in the implementation of the civil service act. A private consulting firm employed by the State Personnel Commission was conducting a position classification and pay survey, and the State Personnel Director was looking ahead to June 30, 1968, when he would have to recommend a "uniform pay plan," as required in the civil service statute. Such a plan, based upon the principle of equal pay for equal work, provides that the same pay range apply to all positions in the same job classification.

The AFSCME, which had been negotiating salary rates on an agency-by-agency basis, immediately made known its opposition to implementation of this provision of the law; it announced that it would "tolerate no encroachment by public employers under the guise of a merit system on the bargaining process." The *Wilmington Morning News*, commenting that it was "hard to see how anything uniform could come out of a number of individual (agency) bargaining sessions," could see no reason why "the free exercise of collective bargaining on a pay schedule for the agencies could not be carried out between the State and the union in one formal conference or series of conferences." [*414*]

This was only the beginning of the problems in putting into effect the civil service law after more than two years of signing of collective agreements under the bargaining statute. It was clear that once examinations were given and appointments were made, there would be many other disagreements. In our opinion, the civil service statute should be observed and conflicting contract provisions, such as those providing for binding arbitration of appointments and promotions, should be considered null and void. Ultimately, the courts make the final ruling on conflicts of this kind, but, of course, someone has to start a suit.

*Labor Relations and Civil Service in New Castle County.* In New Castle County, although the Levy Court's resolution calling for civil service did not exclude hourly rated employees—numbering some 260 and mostly in the blue-collar category—it later so provided by ordinance. One interpretation, reflected in local newspaper articles, is that civil service was not considered appropriate for workers most of whom were already union members. [*410*] Local No. 459 of the AFSCME, dealing directly with the Levy Court, negotiated a contract effective July 1, 1966, which provided for the union shop, the same seniority provision for filling promotions and other vacancies as in the case of the state Tax Department, and binding arbitration of all grievances, again including those over work rules and regulations established by the employer. [*5*] The Director of Personnel and the Personnel Commission were given no role at all in the union negotiations.

On January 1, 1967, a new form of government with a County Executive, Chief Administrative Officer, and County Council went into effect. A new Personnel Board replaced the Personnel Commission. The hourly workers were brought under the merit system, and a new contract was negotiated with the AFSCME to cover both hourly employees and those paid on an annual basis.

The intention was to obtain a contract which would meet legitimate union demands, yet preserve merit principles. The original contract with the hourly workers had created certain precedents, and numerous compromises in wording proved necessary, so that the real impact of the new agreement on the county's merit system may very well depend on the arbitrators' interpretations of certain vague provisions. For example, while the agreement states that "positions will be filled from a certified eligible list of the highest three qualified candidates as determined by examination or by other appropriate and valid selection techniques," it also stipulates that "seniority and experience shall receive a very appropriate weight as a promotional factor" —whatever that means. [*6*, p. 7.5] Similarly, although it is agreed that "the continuous overseeing of personnel policies, procedures, and programs by the Personnel Board and the Personnel Director designed to retain and improve the merit system for New Castle County government [are] not subject to collective bargaining," [*6*, p. 8] it is also stated that "classification procedures, discipline, performance evaluations, appointment procedures, ... shall be subject to grievance procedures." [*6*, p. 9]

When they are asked to interpret such provisions, the arbitrators will in effect be making final determinations on the technical personnel program. While it is conceivable that they will always make sound and consistent rulings and that the merit system will be preserved, the dangers are great that they will not.

The contract also contains a provision excluding from collective bargaining only those provisions of the civil service ordinance and those merit system rules and regulations which are not "inconsistent with the terms of this Agreement. . . ." [*6*, p. 9] In other words, if the contract contains a clause which does conflict, then it will be considered to have been properly negotiated; otherwise, the merit system ordinance and rules and regulations remain untouched. In our opinion, this provision of the contract is invalid, because the state collective bargaining law did foresee such conflicts and makes clear that it is the merit system ordinance which prevails, not the "inconsistent" provisions of the contracts. As this is written, there is no indication as yet that a court test will be sought.

*Experience in Other State and Local Governments*

From an analysis of 68 agreements, mostly with the AFS-CME, Coppock concludes that local government units are doing a good job of avoiding conflicts between collective agreements and the provisions of basic law. [*78*, pp. 54-55] Either the wages, fringe benefits, and working conditions provided for by law are made an integral part of the agreement, or it is clearly stated that the law must prevail over any negotiated provision. Coppock, of course, acknowledges that his sample is limited, but his analysis also leaves some unanswered questions.

No one can quarrel with his factual statement that the union shop is "already well established in public agencies." [*78*, p. 57] On the other hand, one can challenge the action of jurisdictions, with or without civil service, which agree to employing only union members. He quotes from an agreement which requires all persons employed under civil service to join the union within one year of their appointment, under penalty of dismissal "under the provisions of the Civil Service System." [*78*, p. 57] As to seniority, he finds that, in the case of layoffs, no problem has arisen in civil service agencies, but only because they usually already use length of service as the criterion. There are, however, some civil service jurisdictions which take merit into account at least to some extent in layoffs, and they are not happy over union pressures for straight seniority. Futhermore, the non-civil service agencies should not be expected to abandon merit practices they voluntarily follow, nor will many citizens be pleased with any coalescence of spoils and union pressures to keep out merit practices. Coppock found that over half of 31 agreements with non-civil service agencies require filling promotional vacancies by the industry practice of bidding, as in the following example: [*78*, p. 58]

> All vacancies shall be posted on the bulletin boards of the public works department. . . . Employees wanting such posted jobs shall sign the posted notice. The employee oldest in point of service in the section whose name is signed as above shall be given the opportunity to qualify for that job. Said employee shall demonstrate his ability to perform the job posted within thirty (30) days and if deemed qualified by the employer shall be permanently assigned the job.
> Should such employee not qualify or should he desire to return to his former job, he shall be reassigned to his former job without loss of seniority. In such event, the man next in line of seniority shall be given the opportunity to qualify until the vacancy is filled.

One-fourth of the civil service agreements in Coppock's sample base promotion on seniority "where two or more employees have relatively equal ability and qualifications." One agency gets around the rule of three provided for in the civil service law by automatically giving the promotion to the person with the highest seniority in the group of three certified. [*78*, p. 58] One-third of the total of 68 agreements require binding arbitration of grievances. In only one-sixth of the total is it provided that the final decision be made by a responsible government body or official, rather than by arbitrators. [*78*, p. 60] Of the 37 civil service agreements, nine call for binding and five for advisory arbitration; only two limit grievances to differences over interpretation of the contract provisions. [*78*, p. 59, p. 61] The conclusion, therefore, must be that in some cases the preservation of the merit system is being entrusted to arbitrators whose decisions are subject to no executive or legislative veto.

### The Merit System and the Grievance Procedure

The grievance procedure clearly will be a major battleground, because many of the employee leaders distrust the present civil service appeals machinery. Wurf states that "the role of the civil service commission is not regarded by the workers as that of a third, impartial party; to most of them the commission is felt to represent the employer." [*306*, p. 52]

In supporting the Brewster bill to transfer jurisdiction over grievances from the United States Civil Service Commission to the Labor Department, John F. Griner, president of the American Federation of Government Employees, which is affiiliated with the AFL-CIO, charged that the commission was "management oriented." [*164*] While they reject the contention that they are not sympathetic to the employees, many of the personnel people themselves will agree with Raymond F. Male that the "average public employee does not look to those of us who are civil service commissioners, merit system directors, or personnel administrators as being wholly their chosen representatives." [*159*, p. 112]

Although he finds little evidence to show that collective negotiations threaten the merit system, Arvid Anderson acknowledges that "efforts will be made by labor unions to amend existing civil service appeal procedures in favor of a grievance and arbitration machinery similar to that which exists in private employment, whereby the arbitrators are impartial persons having no connection with the employer or the employee organization." [*306*, p. 56] He cites the contract between the City of

Milwaukee and District Council 48 of the AFSCME which permits advisory arbitration of disciplinary cases, but the usual procedure in industry is for binding arbitration of grievances.

*The Brewster Bill.* This bill is a grim example of the danger to the merit system. [*91*] Not only does it define grievances very broadly, but it also permits binding arbitration by three-member boards of arbitrators. "Grievance" means any employee complaint about the "effect, interpretation, application, claim of breach, or violation of any law, rule or regulation governing conditions of employment, which the head of the department or agency has the authority to correct." "Condition of employment" includes:

> . . . such factors as working conditions, work schedules, work procedures, automation, safety, transfers, job classifications, details, promotional procedures, demotions, rates of pay, reassignments, reductions in force, hours of work, disciplinary actions, and such other matters as may be specified by law, rule, or regulation.

Although the bill includes a "management rights" section as well as a proviso that contract agreements must conform with existing and future laws and agency regulations, the grievance provisions open up a Pandora's box. Conceivably, the agency budget itself could be arbitrated, because "conditions of employment" depend upon funds available. Interpretation of the meaning of civil service and other statutes could become the responsibility of arbitrators, and they could also define the nature and the extent of the agency administrators' discretion. The United States Civil Service Commission, the Budget Bureau, and the General Accounting Office would be constantly contesting the legality of the arbitral awards, since the bill is far from clear as to its intent. In important respects, it is very similar to the Rhodes-Johnston bills, supported by the union leaders, which were so severely criticized by Wilson R. Hart, himself a strong advocate of collective bargaining in the federal service. [*110*, pp. 140-73]

### The Situation in Canada

Since it limits negotiations to matters not requiring enactment or amendment of any legislation, the new federal legislation in Canada protects the merit system which, of course, rests upon statute. [*350*, pp. 28-29] As stated at the end of the previous chapter, some of the contracts entered into by the Canadian municipalities have been criticized as violating merit principles.

Peter M. Thompson reports that the negotiation of pay scales with bargaining agents representing employees in different occupational groups results in inequities, owing to the greater pressures of the more powerful employee organizations; he says that the unions take advantage of "both the public service and legalistic background of the merit system protection" and the industrial-type bargaining emphasis on the "full prevailing wage rate." [*363*, p. 239]

George W. Noble reports that "while municipal councils are generally in favour of all municipal employees being given the same fringe benefits, conciliation and arbitration boards are more inclined to grant the fringe benefits currently provided in the trade or profession." [*296*, p. 256]

This results from the practice of dealing with unions which represent certain groups or classes of employees, which means that municipal employees in certain lines of work want the same wages and fringe benefits as their counterparts in industry. According to Noble, Canadian municipal employers have in the past paid general laborers wages 5 to 10 per cent higher than in industry. [*296*, p. 255]

The collective bargaining agreements "leave much to be desired from the management viewpoint," as evidenced in one contract which provides that "members of the Force shall have a choice of work strictly on a basis of seniority." [*296*, p. 257] Another agreement reads:

> The Corporation shall retain in its employ only members of the Union in good standing. The Union shall be the sole judge of the good standing of its members, and any employee who shall hereafter cease to be a member in good standing shall on notice to the Corporation be discharged immediately.

Noble understandably comments: [*296*, p. 258]

> The municipal corporation agreeing to the inclusion of the foregoing clause has waived part of its management prerogatives—namely, the right to hire and discharge. This clause could place management in an untenable position in the event that an employee lost his good standing in the union because of reasons not related to his employment.

The new federal legislation, however, makes agreements of this type impossible in the national government.

*Management and Employee Definitions of Merit.* A study made by M. Z. Prives, entitled *Unionism and the Merit System in Municipal Relations in Canada,* is very revealing. Reproduced in 1958 by the Canadian Federation of Mayors and Municipalities, it makes clear that management and the employee organizations simply do not define merit in the same way. This is illustrated in their respective views on promotion policy. Management wants the best-qualified man promoted, whereas to the employee organizations, "the opportunity of progress and promotion to every member or employee who could perform the duties of a given position, is the governing principle." They believe that "every employee who might possibly attain to the level needed in order to fulfill the functions of a position should be given the chance," and that "only the obviously inadequate individual" should be eliminated from consideration. [*316*, p. 39] Furthermore, even if the senior employee's qualifications are doubtful, he should be given the promotion on a conditional basis, being required to serve a probationary period, usually of six months' duration. If he proves unsatisfactory, then he should be demoted and replaced by the next senior candidate.

A very interesting argument is made against awarding the promotion to the best qualified candidate, without regard to seniority. The contention is that the remuneration is based on the duties of the position, not the qualifications of the incumbent, and that it is not correct to place a superior employee in the job unless the management is prepared to reclassify the position immediately and give the individual the higher pay he deserves. While compensation plans based on equal pay for equal work can be criticized for failing to provide adequate recognition for persons of outstanding ability, what is overlooked here is that "superior" persons will qualify for the next promotion much faster than those who barely meet the qualifications for the higher rated job under immediate consideration. The solution is not to hold back the "superior" persons, but to give them appropriate increases within the salary range, and promote them to the next higher class of position as rapidly as their abilities and the circumstances as to vacancies permit.

The Canadian employee organizations also maintain that there is no true merit system if the morale of the workers is adversely affected, such as by management's "disregard for seniority in pursuit of a theoretical advantage of a quest for the top candidate available." [*316*, p. 51] Prives sympathizes with this point of view, for he believes that: [*316*, p. 53]

> The task which faces present day management is one of tempering the theory of merit by insights gained in its practice . . . [and that] . . . solicitous care for the welfare of the employee force, servicing their needs and providing satisfaction at work are as important as any part of management.

Public personnel administrators, leaders of civic organizations, and many others in both Canada and the United States strongly disagree that the "quest for the top candidate available" represents only a "theoretical advantage." Without this insistence on the best-qualified, civil service in both countries would never have accomplished as much as it has in recruiting and retaining great numbers of very competent public employees. Prives states: "The pent up feelings of resentment on the part of individuals with long and meritorious service records, who might be passed over when a junior is promoted or when an outsider is recruited, would obliterate any possible gain to the organization." [*316*, p. 53]

If those passed over are really as well-qualified as the "juniors" or the "outsiders," this would be true. In appraising morale and worker satisfactions, a distinction should be made between "resentments" caused by unfair treatment, and the sense of disappointment naturally experienced by the unsuccessful candidates. For the organization as a whole, most employees will be more satisfied, and the public better served, when recognition is on a merit basis, rather than on time-serving.

# 3

# Impact of Political Factors

THIS CHAPTER deals with a very broad area, because basically politics is the process by which influence in forming and executing public policy is acquired and exercised. The chapter will be divided in two parts: (1) A general discussion of the political factors; and (2) A case history of the New York City subway strike as an illustration of the politics in labor disputes in government.

## Political Activities of Public Employees

The governmental environment is intensely political, because political parties, elective officials, pressure groups, the press, and the millions of voters all struggle to control public policy. Labor relations in industry fall directly within the political arena, as anyone who follows the news knows: the President himself is poised to take action if there is a possibility of a major strike. The AFL-CIO, the Canadian Labour Congress, and the rest of the labor movement are very much involved in politics, as their lobbying, voter registration, and political action programs make obvious. Chester A. Newland makes the point that "public employee unions are *primarily* political organizations, differing in that respect (at least in degree) from employee unions in the private economy." [*173*, p. 586] He explains: [*173* p. 609]

> The outstanding cnaracteristic of public employee unions which is basic to understanding of governmental labor-management relations is their heavy dependence upon political power and methods to accomplish their goals. This is partly due to the absence of effective economic sanctions, such as the strike. It may be even more the consequence of the political environment. Organized public employees represent potential voting blocs, and politicians cannot ignore them. Local governmental employee unions are often among the most informed on bond elections, charter referenda, and other local political issues. With traditionally

small voter participation in these elections public employees, in cooperation with central labor councils, may exercise decisive power.

### Public Employee Unions and State and Local Trades Councils

In recent years, the affiliated public employee unions have augmented their political power by forming closer ties with the state and local trades councils which support them in representations before elective officials. A sign of the closer relationship is that in some cases the government unions are using "locally experienced union leaders" from the private sector as their business agents. [*173*, p. 602] The independent organizations are far from powerless politically, as evidenced by the accomplishments of the California State Employees' Association (CSEA) in the 1965-66 legislative session. Sixteen of the bills it sponsored were passed and 14 signed by the governor, while 48 of the 50 it opposed were defeated. [*338*] Recent research at Michigan State University showed that the state education association was the most powerful lobby in California, New Jersey, Ohio, and Tennessee, and the Executive Secretary of the National Education Association was "sure that the findings would be similar elsewhere." [*52*, p. 12]

### Ways of Influencing Candidates

Despite the legal restrictions on partisan political activities, government workers have effective ways of influencing candidates for political office. Mike Causey writes: [*57*]

Unlike many unions, whose power is limited to big city or urban areas, the government organizations have a broad base.

There are federal meat inspectors, customs employees and border inspectors in some of the most remote areas of the country—areas where there aren't many longshoremen, or garment workers, or truck drivers. Places which don't have sidewalks, or mailmen, still have rural letter carriers and postmasters. And they all have wives and families, most of them voters.

What the employees, and their unions, can't do directly for political friends because of the Hatch "no politics" Act, their wives can do through ladies auxiliaries. They are especially influential in nonurban areas.

Within the last couple of weeks, several key members of Congress have been honored at banquets in their home states by government unions. One member was given a cake for his birthday, and another got a cake—commemorating the birthday of a union. . . .

"We keep in touch with members of Congress on a friendly basis, and it pays off," a union legislative aide said. And many top union officials will be watching key races tonight to see how their man comes out.

A *Washington Post* editorial expressed little regret over the defeat in the Democratic primary of Representative James H. Morrison, long a member of the House Post Office and Civil Service Committee and a strong supporter of the employee organizations. According to the *Post*, Morrison made "open appeals for money at the convention of the American Federation of Government Employees," in conflict with the spirit, if not the letter of the Hatch Acts. [*404*] Morrison's case is probably exceptional, and it is also true that congressmen are hard-pressed to obtain campaign funds. Many people question the desirability of the political activity restrictions anyway, and some local jurisdictions have recently liberalized them.

No matter what happens to the Hatch Acts and similar legislation, it is obvious that public employee organizations will continue to be strong in politics. In federal elections, the law permits the unions to collect voluntary political contributions from their members, so a government local of the AFL-CIO benefits from the financial support that the latter gives to various political candidates and committees. The pre-election issue of the *American Teacher* carried a list of ". . . candidates who have proven themselves friends of labor and education, and who have received the endorsements of the American Federation of Teachers and in most cases, of the state and district committees of the AFL-CIO as well. . . ." [*26*, p. 14]

In state and local elections, although public employees frequently are prevented from being active themselves in political campaigns, they can obtain the desired result through their unions. In Philadelphia, where there is a rigid restriction on political activity, the local AFSCME Council is a member of the Committee on Political Education (COPE), representing the AFL-CIO unions in that city. In a recent mayoralty campaign, COPE probably raised more than half a million dollars. For the municipal union member, there was no need for political activity violations, and none was reported.

### Public Employee Organizations in Canada

In Canada, the public employee organizations have also emphasized political action. Many of the departmental components of the Public Service Alliance, which is the largest organization in the federal service, have for some time been affiliated with the Canadian Labour Congress.

Some of the provincial and municipal organizations have also long been affiliated with the labor movement. The same effective lobbying techniques have been employed as in the United States; for example, passage of the new collective bargaining legislation is largely attributable to the pressures of the employee organizations. For many years, the law has prohibited federal employees from engaging in partisan activity in national and provincial elections, a ban which is continued in the new Public Service Employment Act. [*351,* pp. 13-14]

There is a similar prohibition in most of the provinces, but in 1963 the Ontario legislature amended its Public Service act to allow most provincial employees considerable freedom in political activities. [*353*] Because it strengthens the employees' role in negotiations within the administrative branch, the new collective bargaining legislation may reduce the need for lobbying with the Canadian Parliament, and the same may be true in the provinces with similar laws. It is very unlikely, however, that the employee organizations will de-emphasize political activity, for there is always the need for increased appropriations and new legislation to provide additional benefits.

### Public Employees and the "Boss"

While labor relations both in industry and government have political implications, public employees wield indirect power over the "boss." With their votes, they can retain or kick out members of the "management"—the legislators and elective administrative officials who make decisions on their salary and other requests. Industrial workers must put up with the management of the company and instead try to influence legislators and politicians to support policies that will strengthen labor's hand with management. The distinction is a significant one, because since government is the "boss," labor relations in the public sector are highly charged with politics: [*310*, p. 4]

> Teachers have at least one very important advantage in negotiations with school boards that employees in private industry do not have with their employers. . . . If working conditions are intolerable and grievances cannot be resolved through cooperative negotiation, teachers can exercise their political rights to secure the election of a better board by the community. This has been done successfully by many *A. F. of T.* locals.

Of course, the other side of the coin is that taxpayers and other groups can elect school boards which favor their interests as against the teachers. Failing everything, public employees can, in some states, use initiative petitions or charter revision proposals to put on the books the legal provisions they want.

Louis J. Kroeger reports that in San Francisco the employees obtain their benefits mostly through charter amendments. There is no comparable way in which workers in private companies can go over the head of the management. Their primary weapon is the strike, and even here some people think government workers have an advantage. Peter M. Thompson believes that Canadian municipalities are weak in their bargaining with the employee unions because of their fear of strikes which would inconvenience the voting public. [*363*, pp. 239-40]

Of course, the same criticism is made of public officials who could at least try to prevent strikes in industry but hold back, apparently not wanting to antagonize labor. In a standard work on industry labor relations, [*297*, pg. 280] it is stated that

> In Rhode Island the director of the Department of Labor is apparently always selected from the top ranks of organized labor in the state; and the state mediators, who are under his jurisdiction, are former associates. Some employers in Rhode Island appear to regard the Rhode Island state mediation service as a virtual adjunct of organized labor and therefore do not welcome its services.

In Delaware, some people believe that the State Department of Labor and Industrial Relations is clearly biased in favor of the unions in representation elections and other matters under that state's collective bargaining law for public employees. It is also claimed that politically appointed and elective state department heads, anxious for voter support, have sometimes extended themselves to please the unions in the negotiations.

Country-wide, however, there is no indication that the government workers will sweep the negotiations, because they are held back by strong countervailing forces. The funds must be appropriated to meet any new contract obligation, and there frequently are strong indications of negative legislative reactions. Moreover, the tax rate, on which the compensation of state and local government workers depends, is much more visible to, and potentially subject to influence by, the citizen than the inflationary consequences of liberal wage settlements in industry. These settlements might eventually take more money from his pockets through inflation than a small increase in the local tax levy, but he generally is not interested in this kind of fine analysis.

### Rivalries Between the Employee Organizations

Politics is a struggle for power, and the employee organizations themselves are locked in combat. Perhaps the best example

of this is the fight between the "unions" (labor-affiliated) and the
independent associations. They employ different strategies and
approaches, and they seek to shape public policy to their ends.
A most interesting development is the tendency of the associations, under pressure from the competition of the "unions," to
take positions which bring them close to the labor viewpoint.

A recent example is the action of the Los Angeles County
Employees' Association in dropping its 55 year old no-strike
pledge. [149] Reporters commented during the welfare workers'
strike that the Association's president sounded as bitter about
the County Board of Supervisors as the "union," meaning AFL-
CIO County Employees Local 434 which had frequently denounced the Association as a "tool of the county government."
[147] Although the associations may modify their positions, they
do not necessarily warm up to the unions, as demonstrated by
the National Education Association's coolness towards the American Federation of Teachers. The latter in turn uses all its
political power to outrank the NEA in the eyes of legislators,
administrators, and the general public. They are rival pressure
groups with strong political action programs.

From time to time, the management in government is
accused of being partial to one of two or more rival unions,
as happened recently in New York City. Teamsters Local 237
picketed Metropolitan Hospital, slowing the delivery of food and
drugs, but the supplies were soon brought in by hospital trucks
driven by non-union drivers. Nearly 100 employees, most of them
kitchen workers, walked out of the hospital to join the Teamster
picket lines. The Teamsters charged that one of their members
had been arbitrarily transferred, but the hospital administrator
said the employee had been suspended for refusing to obey a work
order. The real reason for the picketing was the Teamsters'
belief that city officials had favored the AFSCME in a representation election where the AFSCME emerged as the bargaining
agent for the hospital's nurses, messengers, and clerical personnel, and the Teamsters for the cooks. The president of the
Teamsters' local charged the city with "union-busting." [245]

### The Complicated Political Struggle in New York City

When, in late 1966, the New York City Council was considering a bill to establish a new Office of Collective Bargaining,
since passed in the summer of 1967, the proposal was favored
by some of the employee organizations but opposed by others.

One contention was that the proposal discriminated against the smaller organizations and contained "the seeds of company unionism." [260] Earlier the Council had held extensive hearings at which Wurf, speaking for the AFSCME which represents the largest block of organized workers in the city, termed the bill "the most forward-looking plan, the most decent mechanism public employees have ever had." Yet spokesmen for the Social Service Employees Union and two Teamsters locals argued that it would weaken collective bargaining and prevent some employees from being represented by the union of their choice. [249] In addition to the opposing union pressures, there was the partisan conflict between Republican Mayor Lindsay who supported the bill and the Democratic-controlled Council. In this atmosphere, small incidents flared up into sharp controversies. The Council majority leader, Bronx Democrat David Ross, accused Deputy Mayor Timothy W. Costello of publicly demanding action on the bill within a two-week deadline but privately asking the Council to hold it up for more amendments. "I resent any two-week deadline to the Council by the Lindsay administration to pass a bill that is not yet ready," Ross declared. From the very start, there had been friction between the new administration and the Council, which was to be expected with divided political control of the city. A spokesman for the Lindsay administration soothingly commented: "The Mayor's office wants to cooperate in every way with the City Council. It has great respect for the Council." [260]

### The Rochester Controversy

How the competition both between rival employee organizations, on the one hand, and political parties, on the other, can embroil a city in long controversy is seen in the case of Rochester, New York. After the November, 1961, elections, the Democrats, who had pledged themselves to "recognize the legal bargaining representatives of public employees when properly designated," won control of the City Council from the Republicans. The outgoing Republican administration encouraged the employee organizations to start organizing drives, which displeased the Democrats who wanted to see the organizing delayed until they assumed control. They were even more nettled when the Republican lame-duck Council authorized a dues checkoff for municipal employees, followed by an ordinance giving the employees representation rights.

The mayor-designate announced that the ordinance would be repealed, and it was, in the summer of 1962, by the new Democratic-controlled Council. Organizing activity started again, with the AFSCME signing up employees in the Department of Public Works and the Democratic County Chairman saying it was "an intelligent, responsible union." The city manager later told the Council that he was satisfied that the AFSCME represented a majority of the employees, and in September it passed an ordinance authorizing him to "recognize a duly organized union or employee organization as the bargaining agent for an appropriate unit of city employees upon submission to him of satisfactory proof that such union or organization is representative of the unit."

The Teamsters and the Civil Service Employees' Association were in competition with the AFSCME, and the Association charged the city manager with favoring the AFSCME. The latter retaliated that the Association was "a phony organization, an insurance company, not a true representative of the city employees of Rochester."

The Association went to court in an unsuccessful attempt to have the ordinance declared unconstitutional on grounds of vagueness and to set aside what it considered arbitrary action by the city manager in selecting the AFSCME as the exclusive bargaining agent. The city manager signed an agreement with the AFSCME in October of 1962, but serious bargaining could not take place until the court test was finally decided in the city's favor in March of 1963. Thus, for many months Rochester was the scene of intensive maneuvering by the politicians and the employee leaders, a situation of multiple conflict. [*178*, pp. 55-64]

### The New York City Subway Strike

The New York City subway strike illustrates many of the special characteristics of major labor disputes in government. The workers' claims of wage inequities, the Transit Authority's financial difficulties, its inability to bargain knowing exactly how much money it could offer, the absence of effective procedures for settling the bargaining impasse without a strike—these and many other elements were in the picture. The account below relates the entire story, but pays special attention to the political aspects.

## Quill's Demands

On November 3, 1965, the day after he won the mayoralty election, John V. Lindsay received a telegram of "sincere congratulations" from Michael V. Quill, president of the Transport Workers Union (TWU), AFL-CIO. At the same time, Quill sent the mayor-elect a copy of the 76 proposals the TWU and the Amalgamated Transit Union (ATU) planned to make to the Transit Authority in the joint negotiations of the unions for a new contract to replace the one terminating on December 31. (The ATU represented 1,800 bus drivers in Queens and on Staten Island, and the TWU the 33,000 subway workers.) On the following day, the two unions made their proposals to the Transit Authority, an autonomous agency established by the state legislature and headed by a three-man directorate, with one member appointed by the governor, one by the mayor, and the third, serving as chairman, named by the first two. "Chairman Joseph E. O'Grady, declaring himself 'flabbergasted,' estimated that these demands would cost the Authority $250 million over two years. 'There isn't enough gold in Fort Knox to pay this bill,' he told reporters.' " [*48,* p. 50]

The TWU requested: a 32-hour, four-day work week instead of 40 hours; retirement at half pay after 25 years of service; and six weeks vacation after a year on the job. The ATU made the same demands, except it asked for a five-day 30-hour work week.

## Negotiations Begin

Negotiations began, with little promise of success and both Lindsay and outgoing Democratic Mayor Robert F. Wagner unwilling to take any initiative. Since he had not yet assumed office, Lindsay felt that all he could do was closely follow the negotiations. Wagner did not want to make any commitments binding his successor. The author, Thomas R. Brooks, commented that ". . . the mayor and the mayor-elect engaged in a kind of pantomime, each trying to suggest that the other was responsible for settling matters." [*48,* p. 50] All three members of the Transit Labor Panel named by Wagner in 1963 resigned because they doubted the mayor-elect would be satisfied with a carry-over mediation board. As the negotiations dragged on, Lindsay began to take more interest. On November 18, he announced that he was "in" the picture and that he would confer with Wagner about establishing a new mediation panel. By this time, O'Grady had re-estimated the cost of the union demands at $680 million.

The big problem from the city's standpoint was where to find the money to be able to offer the unions any terms they might accept. Either the 15-cent fare would have to be increased or Lindsay would have to find additional funds from some other source. The Transit Authority by law had to be self-sustaining and meet all operating expenses from its revenues, but it had already incurred substantial deficits, expected to total $43 million by June, 1966, not taking into account the increased labor costs of a new contract. Two years previously, at the request of Governor Rockefeller and Mayor Wagner, the state legislature had passed a law making it clear that the Authority would be "self-sustaining" when it had sufficient funds on hand from *any* source to meet its current expenses. This permitted the city to give it various subsidies, such as for bond payments, police protection, and electrical power, totalling as much as $40 million in 1965, and this help enabled the Authority to reach an agreement with the unions.

In his campaign, Lindsay had promised to keep the 15-cent fare. Abraham D. Beame, the defeated Democratic candidate for mayor, now suggested that the surplus revenues of the Triborough Bridge and Tunnel Authority be used to avoid a fare increase. Earlier the same week, Robert Moses, chairman of the Triborough Authority, had expressed his opposition to any such plan in a statement he sent to the Triborough stockholders. A spokesman for the Automobile Club of New York supported Moses, arguing that the motorist should not be required to help meet the costs of a service not directly related to motor vehicle use. [*181*]

### Difficulties in Naming New Mediation Panel

At the end of November, Lindsay presented a list of ten possible mediators, but Quill rejected it, claiming that none of the persons suggested knew anything about New York City transit problems. The list omitted the name of Theodore W. Kheel, who had been a member of Wagner's panel and in whom Quill had confidence. According to Brooks, "Kheel was the broker who arranged trades under which the union got security and the Authority got greater efficiency and labor stability." [*48*, p. 51] Relations between Lindsay and Quill became increasingly unfriendly and, when he received a telegram from the mayor-elect charging him with not bargaining in good faith, Quill threatened a walkout on December 15. [*183*]

Mayor Wagner now felt compelled to intervene. He requested the Transit Authority and the two unions to meet with him at City Hall to "discuss the current negotiations . . . with particular emphasis on the announced possible strike of the transit system on Dec. 15." [*183*] Meanwhile, the Transit Authority obtained a State Supreme Court order directing the TWU to show cause why it should not be enjoined from striking in violation of the state's Condon-Wadlin Act. This law, to be discussed in detail in the next chapter of this book and finally repealed with the passage of new legislation in April of 1967, had long been a major political issue in New York State, and the controversy over it now flared up again. It provided that striking public employees must be dismissed, and that, if subsequently rehired, they could not receive pay increases for a three-year period.

Wagner now moved to end the delay in naming a new mediation panel. He asked Kheel if he would serve, and Kheel said he would if also invited by Lindsay. Wagner and Lindsay then agreed upon a three-man panel consisting of Wisconsin law professor Nathan P. Feinsinger, Sylvester Garrett, the permanent arbitrator for U.S. Steel and the United Steelworkers, and Kheel. Quill acquiesced and called off the December 15 walkout. The mediators immediately went to work, but the days passed without a settlement, and the December 31 contract deadline loomed closer and closer. John J. Gilhooley, the Republican member of the Authority, who had been appointed by Rockefeller, charged that Wagner was "playing politics with the [15 cent] fare, something, of course, no Republican would do." [*48,* p. 51] The *New York Times,* which published many editorials condemning Quill, complained that "waiting until a crisis arises before setting up peacemaking panels, as the city had done in the Board of Education, the Welfare Department and other disputes, infuses a deplorable blend of politics and appeasement into the bargaining process." [*184*]

Christmas passed, with still no agreement and not even an offer by the Transit Authority. There was nothing they could offer, because Lindsay had given them no word of financial assistance from the City. John O'Donnell, the TWU attorney, told Brooks, "if you think a Democratic controlled Transit

Authority is going to relieve a Republican mayor-elect of the responsibility of a fare increase by raising it themselves, you're crazy." [*48*, p. 52] Chairman O'Grady and the third member, Daniel T. Scannell, were Democrats.

### Lindsay Directly Participates

On December 27, Lindsay directly participated in the negotiations for the first time and met with both sides. He indicated to the press that he had been exploring the possibilities of financial aid from the state and federal governments, and he reported that Governor Rockefeller was "deeply concerned." The one definite statement he made was that as soon as he assumed office, he would set in motion steps for merging all the city's transportation agencies, as a permanent solution to the Transit Authority's financial difficulties. [*185*] The Authority made plans to secure an injunction to prevent the subway and bus strike Quill had scheduled for 5 a. m. New Year's Day. [*186*] Quill was undaunted, and he wisecracked that "injunctions make very poor trackwalkers." [*187*]

On December 30, the union representatives walked out of the negotiations and announced they would not return until Lindsay agreed to participate on a continuing basis. Appearing on television, Quill tore up court papers served on him to show cause why the TWU should not be enjoined from calling the strike. Lindsay, who was to be sworn in at 6 p. m. on the following day and assume his duties as mayor at midnight, said that he would meet with the unions at 10 in the morning. The members of the Transit Authority announced that they would stage a "sit-in" until the union negotiators returned. Wagner bowed out, saying that "from now on, it's the responsibility of the Transit Authority, the mediators, the unions and the mayor-elect." [*189*]

### Some of the Political Factors

Emanuel Perlmutter of the *New York Times* now reported that a strike was likely. He quoted one member of the Transit Authority as saying, "We're like players in a stud poker game facing an opponent without knowing what's in our hole cards." [*304*] According to Perlmutter, there were numerous political factors, involving Lindsay, Wagner, Rockefeller, President Johnson, the mediators, and the labor movement. Rockefeller was willing to propose a merger of the city's transportation agencies to the legislature, but he had said publicly that the state would not give the city direct financial help. In previous negotiations, the mediators had known what money they could count on from Wagner, but now he was virtually out of the picture, and Lindsay was not making any commitments. Neither Feinsinger nor Garrett, who is from Pittsburgh, had a political base in the city. Kheel, a former labor adviser to Wagner, did, but Lindsay had appointed him only because Quill wanted him; thus Kheel could not serve as the go-between with City Hall as in the past.

Harry Van Arsdale, Jr., president of the New York City Central Labor Council and a Wagner supporter, had no role in the negotiations. He had helped break the negotiation impasse two years earlier, at 3 a. m., January 1, 1964, two hours before Quill's strike deadline. The labor leaders most influential with Lindsay were David Dubinsky, president of the International Ladies' Garment Workers Union, and Alex Rose, president of the United Hattery, Cap and Millinery Workers Union. They controlled the Liberal party which had backed Lindsay for mayor, but they were cool to Quill. Not only did Quill lack the old relations with City Hall, but he was also subject to strong pressures within the TWU to do better for them than the $39 million package he had obtained the last time.

### Negotiations on New Year's Eve

On Friday, December 31, Lindsay met with both the mediators and Quill, but to no avail. He left the negotiations to be sworn in as mayor, and then at 7:45 p. m. State Supreme Court Justice George Tilzer issued an order temporarily enjoining the two unions and their officers from striking. Quill repeated previous statements to the effect that he would ignore the injunctions. Wagner left for a vacation trip to Acapulco, Mexico. Rockefeller was scheduled to return from the Virgin Islands, where he had been vacationing. Quill also appeared briefly on a radio program in which he bitterly assailed the *New York Times* which he said had published 17 editorials on the transit dispute since Lindsay's election, more than it had written on Vietnam. [*190*] Without doubt, the *Times* was engaged in an all-out effort to whip up public resentment against Quill.

### The Strike Begins

At Lindsay's request, on Friday evening the Transit Authority made its first offer, a $25 million package in wages and fringe benefits, but it was immediately rejected by Quill as "peanuts."

The union negotiators walked out again, and the strike began at 5 a.m., January 1, 1966. [*191*] The new mayor was now confronted with the problem of avoiding chaos when business resumed in the city on Monday, January 3. He urged New Yorkers to stay at home unless engaged in essential services, or required to work by their employers, or too poor to risk losing a day's pay. To avoid paralyzing traffic jams, he asked them not to drive their cars into congested business districts. He said it would help to take hotel rooms near one's place of work, and he asked employers to request only those who were absolutely essential to come to work. [*191*]

On Sunday, January 2, Quill suddenly made a new offer, the estimated cost of which was $180 million. Quill pronounced, "If they want to bargain, and roll the subways and buses tomorrow morning, they are dealing with a union that has yielded 80 per cent." But O'Grady's reaction was that the offer apparently was not made in good faith and that the Authority would not make a counter offer. [*192*]

The following day the Transit Authority asked the State Supreme Court to cite Quill and the other union leaders for civil contempt in ignoring the injunction. Worried that New York might become a "labor injunction city," the New York City Central Labor Council sent Quill a telegram expressing its strong support for the strike. On the other hand, the New York Chamber of Commerce praised Lindsay for his "decisiveness and vigor in the face of the present intolerable and economically near-disastrous transit strike." A White House spokesman said that the President was following the developments but not considering federal intervention. [*193*]

### Quill is Jailed

Quill and his associates were jailed on Tuesday noon, January 4. Ed Townsend, labor correspondent of the *Christian Science Monitor*, [*369*] wrote:

> Mr. Quill's arrest has tightened not only union ranks but also the ranks of most of New York's powerful labor movement against what one official called "the return of a labor injunction state." If there's ground-giving now, it will have to be more by the transit authority and city than by the union.

The *New York Times*, branding Quill with representing the " 'last hurrah' of a cynical Old Guard type of unionism," found it "shameful and shocking" that the national leaders of the AFL-

CIO and the Liberal party in New York were unwilling to condemn the strike. It found "even more disgusting" the support given Quill by the city's AFL-CIO Central Labor Council, and resolutely stated, "New York will not cave in under the TWU assault." [194] An hour and a half after he was jailed, Quill suffered an apparent heart attack and was removed to a hospital.

Negotiations resumed, with Douglas L. MacMahon and James F. Horst, both international vice-presidents of the TWU, taking over for Quill. The press now reported that the Lindsay administration, recognizing that there were pay inequities between the transit workers and other city employees, was prepared to increase its package offer to $32 million. [194] State legislative leaders began to get into the act. Frank G. Rossetti, Manhattan Democrat and chairman of the Joint Legislative Committee on Labor, announced he would call public hearings to consider measures to prevent public service strikes. Senator Joseph Zaretzki, Manhattan Democrat slated to be Senate minority leader, claimed that the Transit Authority would have had more "leeway" in dealing with Quill if Rockefeller had not vetoed a Democratic-sponsored bill softening the penalties of the Condon-Wadlin Act. [194] When the legislature convened on January 4 and Rockefeller said nothing about the strike in his annual message, Democratic legislators strongly criticized him. [196] President Johnson, in his State of the Union message, said he would recommend legislation to deal with strikes that threaten "irreparable damage to the national interest."

### Wirtz Visits New York

On January 6, Lindsay called President Johnson and asked him to send Secretary of Labor W. Willard Wirtz to New York to help try to settle the strike. Taking a shuttle flight, Wirtz arrived in a couple of hours. The same day Van Arsdale and 24 members of the New York City Central Labor Council visited City Hall to urge Lindsay to obtain the freedom of Quill and the other jailed strike leaders. Meanwhile, it was reported that MacMahon was proving more inflexible to deal with than Quill who, despite his truculence, had not been considered uncompromising in the past by the labor experts. [197] Not only did the Transit Authority refuse to request the release of the union leaders, but also it asked the State Supreme Court to assess the striking unions $322,000 in damages for every day of the strike. Wirtz returned to Washington on January 7, saying the situation remained "uncertain and serious." Senator Robert F. Kennedy, newly elected Democratic Senator from New York, termed the strike a "catastrophe" and urged negotiations on a 24-hour basis, without recesses, until a settlement was reached. [*198*]

Richard Witkin in the *New York Times* wrote that Governor Rockefeller was now in close touch with Lindsay and "busily countering any impression that he was not sufficiently alert to the magnitude of the crisis." Witkin speculated that the Governor might be delaying any move to aid the city until the unions reduced their demands to "something that might be considered reasonable by both city and state officials." Although his political popularity had recently risen somewhat, Rockefeller had to weigh his moves in terms of his chances for re-election in November. Furthermore, there were many cities in the state besides New York with serious transit problems, and, if he helped New York, they would "almost inevitably want comparable help." At the same time, however, "the Governor could improve his political image in the New York metropolitan area if he became the hero in a transit settlement." [*420*]

Assembly Speaker Anthony J. Travia, Brooklyn Democrat, and Senate Majority Leader Earle W. Brydges, Niagara Falls Republican, told the press that they were willing to consider seriously Lindsay's proposal to merge the Transit Authority and the Triborough Bridge and Tunnel Authority. Asked if he thought the subway fare should be raised, Brydges replied that he did not think there was any alternative. [*198*] Businessmen "urged the state to intervene." [*367*] Although they blamed Lindsay and the Transit Authority for the strike, union leaders, worried about the wage losses of workers unable to get to their jobs, appealed for action. Some progress was reported in the negotiations, but the parties were still said to be far apart. On January 9, the *New York Times* reported that "the belief was growing among those involved in the transit talks, as well as those in political power, that an increase in the 15-cent fare might be necessary to pay for the union contract." [*199*] Zaretzki, the Democratic Senate minority leader, was now of this opinion; he also claimed that Rockefeller could if he wanted to find $10 million to help settle the strike. [*200*] Business surveys showed that the strike was costing the economies of the state and the city hundreds of millions of dollars. Midtown merchants appealed to the President to intervene. [*368*]

*Lindsay Assails the "Power-Brokers"*

In a televised news conference on January 10, Lindsay condemned the "handful of men" who had "consigned a city of eight million people to paralysis." He made clear that his administration would not "allow the power-brokers in our city, or any special interest, to dictate to this city the terms under which it will exist in New York." The union negotiators, he said, were making demands that were in clear violation of the national wage-price guidelines and would require an increase in the fare to 30 cents. [*201*] The *New York Times* praised Lindsay for his "bold speech" and called attention to MacMahon's remark that "Lindsay doesn't know what he's doing; it was a sad day when Bob Wagner left town." [*202*] With the strike still on, it was now reported that Rockefeller, who in the opinion of some political analysts was "wary of newcomer Lindsay in New York's Republican politics," would be forced to intervene. [*366*] Rockefeller, however, refused to seek an immediate state appropriation to end the strike, as proposed by Raymond R. Corbett, president of the New York State AFL-CIO. Meanwhile, the TWU denied the truth of an article in the *New York Herald Tribune* alleging that MacMahon was attempting to build up his political power within the union, by taking a hard line in the negotiations and not following Quill's wishes. [*203*]

Another well-known political leader, Adam Clayton Powell, then Chairman of the House Education and Labor Committee, entered the picture by sending two Committee aides to New York to investigate the strike and prepare a report which might serve as the basis for remedial legislation. Calling attention to the low income levels of his constituents, Powell warned that, unless the strike was ended soon, he would ask the President for emergency assistance to Harlemites unable to get to their jobs. [*204*] Robert Kennedy flew in from Washington on January 12 to confer with Lindsay who had now directed the mediators to give him their views on how to settle the strike. The meeting between the two men, widely considered "presidential possibilities," was friendly, but Kennedy told the press that the mayor should have asked the mediators for their opinions 48 hours sooner. Pointing out that they could not make actual recommendations for settlement without the consent of both parties, the mediators did submit a report to the mayor with their "views." [*204*]

### The Strike Is Ended

On January 13, the strike was settled, on the basis of terms suggested by the mediators. The *New York Times* wrote, "the city's subways and buses never looked so good as they did yesterday after twelve days in dead storage." [*206*] The two-year cost of the new contract was estimated at $52 million by the mayor; $60 million by the Transit Authority; and $70 million by the jubilant TWU. The *Times* thought this was fair to the city and the workers, and Feinsinger said it was within the wage-price guideposts. President Johnson, however, disagreed and denounced the agreement as inflationary. In a public statement, Gardner Ackley, chairman of the Council of Economic Advisers, charged the TWU with insisting on an inflationary agreement, unlike "most other labor unions which, in the past five years, have been willing to act with restraint in the public interest." [*205*] The President had been criticized for moving back recent aluminum and steel price increases, but doing nothing about the subway strike.

Lindsay, who was generally being praised for his handling of the strike, replied to the President's criticism by referring to Feinsinger's statement on the guideposts. Van Arsdale, who certainly had not supported Lindsay in the strike, now defended him and said the mayor had emerged from the controversy "much bigger in the city and nationally." [*205*] In an editorial entitled, "Politics, the LBJ Way," the *Times* assailed the President for not having denounced the strike when it was on and for not giving Lindsay any help. It wrote: [*207*]

> Such help from Mr. Johnson would have been doubly meaningful in the light of attempts by some elements in the old-time Democratic-labor cabal in this city to exploit the strike as an instrument for humiliating the new Republican-fusion Mayor, thus hoping to kill his future political career.

### The Aftermath of the Strike

In the aftermath of the strike, Townsend of the *Christian Science Monitor* expressed a commonly held opinion when he wrote, "labor nationally has been hurt." The Commerce and Industry Association estimated that the strike had cost New Yorkers $1 billion, of which less than 25 per cent would be recovered. It recommended the fare be increased to help pay for the settlement, and said it would request Rockefeller to sponsor tougher anti-strike legislation. [*370*] Meanwhile, in accordance with the recommendation of the mediators, the Transit Authority had asked the courts not to invoke the Condon-Wadlin Act penalties against the strikers. Lindsay announced that his administration was developing improved machinery, including factfinding and advisory arbitration, for preventing similar strikes. At the same time, Rockefeller named a five-man study group to make recommendations for improved state legislation. [208] He also obtained and signed legislation giving the city $100 million to help the transit system; $51 million was in accelerated payments that the city would have received after April 1, and $49 million represented a long-deferred payment of state school aid. [211]

A complication arose when, on January 21, the State Supreme Court vacated an order prohibiting the Transit Authority from punishing the strikers, thus opening the way for taxpayers' suits to invoke the Condon-Wadlin penalties. One such suit, brought by George Weinstein, a lawyer, and viewed with sympathy by many business and civic organizations, was already pending against the Authority. [212] Frank D. O'Connor, the Democratic city council president and a leading candidate for his party's nomination for governor, made a speech upstate charging Rockefeller with having contributed to the subway strike by vetoing a Democratic-sponsored measure in the past session to repeal the Condon-Wadlin Act. [214] Van Arsdale, pointing out that this statute had proved ineffective, warned that labor would oppose any new anti-strike measures. [215] After three weeks in the hospital, Quill made a public appearance in which he accused President Johnson of "cheap politics," said Lindsay had done all he could to prevent the strike, described the settlement as "fair," and denied rumors that MacMahon had sought to undermine his leadership. [216] "On January 28, 1966, fifteen days after the end of the strike, he died of heart failure in his sleep." [48, p. 55]

### The "Forgiveness Legislation"

Shortly thereafter, a State Supreme Court judge ruled the strike settlement illegal and ordered the Transit Authority to withhold any wage increases pending hearing of the Weinstein suit. The *New York Times* aptly expressed the dilemma: if the judge's order were made final, it would probably mean another shutdown, but, if the legislature passed retroactive legislation exempting the strikers from Condon-Wadlin, this would be no permanent solution and it would encourage disrespect for the law. [*218*]

Rockefeller decided to request such legislation, and it was quickly passed by the legislature, but with many misgivings. [*223*] Many legislators were against the bill in principle but voted for it to avoid being branded anti-labor in an election year. A disturbing fact was that similar "forgiveness" had not been shown the ferryboat captains and welfare workers who had been on strike earlier. Majority Senate Leader Brydges expressed concern that "if we pass this bill gratuitously, civil service groups may feel that it's better to get a special bill every time they strike rather than seek an intelligent overhaul of Condon-Wadlin." Mrs. Judith Mage, president of the Social Service Employees Union, said, "the only way we can view the bill is that the government gives special treatment only to public employees who can put the city in a mess, but not to those whose strikes affect only a few people." [*221*]

A Democratic-sponsored amendment to include the 8,000 welfare workers was defeated. The Democrats did not include the ferryboat captains in the amendment, because the captains, who had been involved in a jurisdictional strike, had not directed their action against the city as such. Gilhooley, the Republican member of the Transit Authority and an old friend of the Governor's, "roamed the chambers and corridors of the Capitol . . . trying to round up votes for Mr. Rockefeller's bill." In the Republican-controlled Senate, all 16 nay votes were cast by Republicans; in the Democratic-dominated Assembly, the 39 negative votes were cast by Republicans and three upstate Democrats. [*223*] Many upstate legislators could not see why the state should bail out New York City to preserve a transit fare lower than that charged in cities in their part of the state. The *New York Times* called the special act "the latest triumph for *Realpolitik* at Albany." [*220*]

The story still continued, however, for another lawyer brought a suit claiming that the exemption for the subway workers violated the equal protection clauses of both the federal and state constitutions. [*224*] On March 24, a State Supreme Court judge denied the suit, arguing that the legislature could reasonably make a distinction between transit and other public employees, just as it had granted exclusive privileges and immunities to railroad workers. [*228*] Many people were not convinced by the reasoning, but they accepted the decision as a realistic one.

The subway drama was now concluded, but, as a postscript, the fare was raised to 20 cents on July 1, 1966. In May of 1967, Governor Rockefeller signed into law a transit unification bill which provided for the Metropolitan Commuter Transportation Authority (MCTA) to assume responsibility for the Long Island Rail Road (of which it was already in charge), the Transit Authority, and the Triborough Bridge and Tunnel Authority. Under the unification plan, which was effective March 1, 1968, the MCTA board was expanded and the boards of the other two authorities were dissolved. The new legislation also gave the city the legal authority to provide operating subsidies for the transit system, so the fare was expected to remain at 20 cents indefinitely. [*289*]

### Resume of Political Factors in Subway Strike

Let us now briefly summarize the political factors in the strike. First of all, the change in city administrations unfortunately coincided with the expiration of the contract. The old agreement terminated, and a new mayor came in, right after midnight, January 1, 1966. The city had suffered a harrowing experience two years before, but veteran Mayor Wagner, who had been re-elected to a third four-year term, was on hand to deal with union officials he had known in his official capacity for a long time. This is why some observers joked that Wagner and Quill were rehearsing an old script. Many people suggested that in the future the contract deadlines be so arranged that the negotiations take place under a mayor who would still have part of his term to complete. There is no suggestion that the TWU prefers the present arrangement simply in order to be able to intimidate a new mayor, but apparently no change is going to be made in the future contract expiration dates. In industry, the same ownership and management are usually on hand to conduct the new contract negotiations, but in democratic governments the people have the right to change administrations.

### *The Thin Line Between Bargaining and "Politics"*

Lindsay had run as a vigorous, young Republican-Fusion candidate who would revitalize a city administration dominated too long by the Democrats. Some attribute his early unwillingness to participate in the negotiations to inexperience but others believe it was deliberate and reflected his disapproval of past "political back door" dealings between Quill and City Hall. There was no question that Wagner had played an important role in previous settlements, but the *New York Times* and other critics charged that there had been no real bargaining, simply some theatrics by Quill and then a private deal between him and Wagner.

Actually, it is unrealistic to expect bargaining of this importance to take place in any city with the mayor not deeply involved, particularly when the workers have deep grievances and impasses develop. While Lindsay made no private deals with the TWU, by mid-November he was squarely in the negotiations, and he got the strike settled by requesting the mediators to present their "views." It is really impossible to say when true bargaining ends and unwarranted political intervention begins in situations of this type. So long as government is the employer, politics, to a lesser or greater extent, will always be present.

*Cross Currents Between the Politicians.* Lindsay faced a hostile, Democratic-controlled City Council, and he could not count on warm support from Rockefeller because of the rivalry between them in the Republican party. The governor had to weigh his moves in terms of his chances for re-election, upstate resentment over the efforts to preserve the uneconomical 15-cent fare, and pressure from the Democratic Assembly to soften, and from the Republican Senate to tighten, the Condon-Wadlin Act. Neither could Lindsay expect great friendliness and encouragement from a Democratic President; his relations with Johnson were hardly like those between Franklin D. Roosevelt and Fiorello LaGuardia. Johnson naturally wanted the strike settled, but he had been charged with being tough on business and easy on labor in interpreting the wage-price guideposts. By criticizing the settlement, he embarrassed no Democrats in New York and could win praise for a firm stand against inflationary wage agreements.

Freshman Senator Robert F. Kennedy felt compelled to do what he could to help settle the strike, as did a host of other politicians. Some sought narrow partisan advantage; most responded to what they considered a challenge to their public service responsibilities. The New York City politicians in particular were very anxious to maintain the 15-cent fare, in the interests of the numerous low-income families who depend so much on the subway. In fact, one suggestion seriously made was that the subway service be offered free, like schools and playgrounds.

*The Internal Union Struggle.* Lindsay was not without friends in organized labor, but, once court injunctions were served, labor's support went to Quill. That labor leaders' public acts have nothing to do with their private sentiments was revealed when Quill refused to criticize Lindsay after the strike, and Van Arsdale even praised him. Merely being identified with the same political party did not guarantee full agreement or anything like it: Quill, an AFL-CIO union leader, found the President a "cheap politician." Overlooked by most people was the political situation in Quill's own union. Pictured by some as a labor baron, in actual fact his hold on the union members was in some respects tenuous. Some of the agreements he had made with the Transit Authority in the past had made him unpopular, and he had even helped break a wildcat strike of the motormen in December of 1957.

*Lindsay's Historic Twelve Days.* New Yorkers were greatly inconvenienced during the 12-day strike, the business and other losses were enormous, and the whole nation was concerned over the paralysis of activities in New York City. There was much more than partisan politics in the situation, and what stood out more than anything else was the complexity of the problem of avoiding public service strikes. As usual, simple solutions were abundantly proclaimed, but John Lindsay could truthfully have said that, in his first days as mayor, he had gotten the most valuable political experience of his lifetime.

Lindsay's actions in the summer and early fall of 1967 indicated that he had resolved to inject himself into the picture early when negotiation of the next contract began. A newspaper article, dated September 25, 1967, reported that he had been "meeting quietly with officials of the TWU and the Transit Authority for the last seven weeks in an effort to avoid another transit strike next New Year's day." [*294*] He was hopeful that the city's new labor relations procedures, adopted with the ordinance establishing the new Office of Collective Bargaining, would put it in a much better position to prevent such strikes.

# 4

# Key Policy Issues

D URING THE DISCUSSION of the governmental environment and of the political factors, brief references were made to
some of the basic policy issues surrounding labor relations in
government. In this chapter, these controversial questions will
be discussed in detail, but with emphasis upon realistic courses
for future policy. It is futile to spend much time deploring the
developments summarized in Chapter 1; it is much wiser to
analyze the problems, benefits, and dangers in collective negotiations with a view to establishing sound programs.

## The Right to Organize

Legislators and administrative officials now usually accept
the right of public employees to form organizations of their
own. In most jurisdictions, public employers recognize that the
employee organizations are here to stay.

### In Canada and the United States Federal Government

That this was not always so, however, is seen in the fact
that at one time in Alberta, Canada, any employee who requested
a salary increase was considered to have resigned his job! Yet
the same employee leader who reminds us of the former "absolutely negative attitude of officialdom" states that "to the best
of my knowledge I know of no instances in Canada where there
has been any positive prohibition on freedom of association by
government employees." [135, p. 356] In the United States the
first federal employee unions met with considerable opposition,
reflected in Van Riper's reference to "the anti-union actions
of Post Office Department officials and other heads of executive
agencies." [396, p. 216] Presidents Theodore Roosevelt and Howard Taft issued so-called "gag orders" prohibiting the employees
from making requests to Congress except through the depart-

ment heads, so the unions were not only held down within the executive agencies but also denied a recourse of appeal to the legislature. The Lloyd-LaFollette Act of 1912 prohibits the removal or reduction in rank or compensation of any postal employee for joining any organization not affiliated with an outside body imposing an obligation to engage in, or support, a strike against the United States. It also guarantees the right to petition the Congress, and, although it mentions only the postal employees—at that time the ones mainly concerned in the confrontations with the administrators—it has been held ever since to protect the organization rights of all federal employees. [*378*, p. 2.05]

### United States State and Local Governments

In most state and local governments in the United States, either the law specifically grants public employees the right to organize, or else this is protected by judicial decisions, opinions of attorney generals, or custom. Some people claim that legislation is unnecessary because to join employee organizations is to exercise the right guaranteed in the First Amendment of the United States Constitution to assemble peaceably and to petition the government for redress of grievances. It is pointed out that [*399*, p. 6]:

> Although the framers of the Constitution had no thought of the present-day professional association, employee organization, or labor union either in private or in public employment . . . the colonists knew about the guilds in England and, had the question arisen at the time, it is inconceivable that the framers of the Constitution would have denied the guilds the right to assemble and to petition the government for a redress of grievances.

Some state court decisions have cited the First Amendment, but the United States Supreme Court has never made such an interpretation binding on the states. [*394*, p. 7]

The courts have, however, upheld the right of a governmental employer to refuse to allow all employees, or certain groups of them, to organize or to affiliate with outside organizations. In Alabama, if state government employees join a labor union, they forfeit benefits under the merit system. [*399*, p. 19] In North Carolina, all public employees are prohibited from joining labor organizations. [*399*, p. 32] In South Carolina, although there is no legislation on the subject, the attorney general has ruled that municipalities may pass ordinances prohibiting their employees from joining labor unions. [*399*, p. 36] Usually, however, where a prohibition exists, it applies to specified kinds of employees, in most cases policemen and firemen but sometimes school teachers. [*348*, p. 26]

In 1963, the United States Supreme Court refused to review a case arising in Michigan where the Muskegon Police Department had issued a "rule prohibiting police officers from becoming members of any organization identified with any federation or labor union which admits to membership persons who are not members of the Muskegon Police Department." The Michigan Supreme Court had ruled that the policemen were not deprived of any constitutional rights, and that the municipal officials had acted within their authority in promulgating a rule they deemed necessary "in the interest of a fair and impartial administration of the law by those entrusted with its enforcement, without discrimination or partiality." [*15*, pp. 155-56]

Actually, prohibitions of the kind cited above are exceptional, and there even are plenty of AFSCME locals composed entirely of policemen. Public employees have now been organized for so long that it is very unlikely that state legislatures and local governing bodies will move in the other direction.

Before leaving this subject, it should be noted that in a few cases state right-to-work laws, six of which apply to public as well as private workers, have had an unexpected effect. The intention of these laws is to ban the union shop, but—once the individual is guaranteed the right to join or not join a union —then how can the state or one of its subdivisions refuse to allow him to join a union? In Texas, a state court which, ten years previously, had upheld the legality of a Dallas ordinance forbidding union membership by city employees, declared the same ordinance unconstitutional because in the meantime a right-to-work amendment had been added to the state constitution. [*79*, p. 3]

### Attitude of Government Towards Union Membership

Some people argue that the government should not only permit but also encourage its personnel to join employee organizations. The word "encourage" needs clarification here, because, from one point of view, legislation such as the Lloyd-LaFollette Act constituted encouragement even though it did not state the principle that federal employees should join the unions. Many people feel that the government should be neutral when it comes to personal decisions of this kind by the individual employees, and that it goes as far as it should when it removes any impediments in the way of the employee's free exercise of his will. Clearly, employee organizations are "encouraged" when the government establishes their legality, and the federal unions were in a better position after rather than before the Lloyd-LaFollette Act. But their real strength dates from the issuance in January, 1962, of Executive Order 10988 which states [*400*, p. 349]:

> The efficient administration of the Government and the well-being of employees require that orderly and constructive relationships be maintained between employee organizations and management officials.

This is an affirmative statement of the desirability of employee-management cooperation which goes well beyond the Lloyd-LaFollette Act's protection of the bare right of organization. The "encouragement" given the employee organizations is evidenced by the very substantial increases in their membership since issuance of the Order in January of 1962. No place in the Order, however, does the government give its blessing to union membership, and the Civil Service Commission has accordingly advised the agencies that they may neither encourage nor discourage the employees from joining. [*378*, pp. 5.03, 5.04] The Brewster bill, referred to in Chapter 3, would dispense with this neutrality in no uncertain terms [*91*, p. 1]:

> Participation of employees with management, through employee organizations or unions, in decisions which affect them, contributes to the effective conduct of the public business. Therefore, strong democratically run employee organizations or unions are in the public interest and their development should be encouraged by lawful means.

Wilson R. Hart, who has his disagreements with the unions, does believe that the federal government should encourage its employees to become union members. His argument is that this is essential for proper implementation of the objective stated in the Executive Order of encouraging "participation of employees in the formulation and implementation of personnel policies affecting them." [*110*, p. 53] To participate effectively, the unions must be strong, and this depends upon the size of their membership. If the management really wants the unions to have an important role, it is obliged to do what it can to encourage union membership.

### *TVA Agreement*

This is the philosophy of both the Tennessee Valley Authority and the Bonneville Power Administration which granted their employees collective bargaining rights long before issuance of Executive Order 10988. The agreement between the TVA and the Tennessee Valley Trades and Labor Council, negotiated as early as 1940 and continued ever since, provides [*102*, pp. 3-4] :

> Membership in unions party to this agreement is advantageous to employees and to management, and employees are accordingly encouraged to become and remain members of the appropriate unions. Such membership is a positive factor in appraising relative merit and efficiency. Accordingly, within the limits permitted by applicable laws and federal regulations, qualified union members are selected and retained in preference to qualified nonunion applicants or employees.

The supplementary schedules for trades and labor employees establish that "membership in a union affiliated with the Council is a positive factor of merit and efficiency which is considered in determining relative qualifications" for both appointment and promotion. [*102*, pp. 23-24] Similarly, the agreement with the Salary Policy Panel, which represents the white collar employees, states that membership and participation in one of the unions represented on the Panel will be "recognized as improving relations between management and employees and promoting employee efficiency and understanding of TVA policy, thereby contributing to the accomplishment of TVA objectives," and that these "are among the positive factors of merit and efficiency to be considered in selecting employees for promotion, transfer, and retention." [*39*, p. 35]

John E. Massey, TVA Director of Personnel, sums all this up as follows [*160*, p. 131] :

> The members of the TVA board and its personnel advisers believed in organized labor. They looked on strong unions as the most practical way for management to deal with large numbers of employees and as the best way for employees to channel their thinking into an enterprise in which they had as much stake as their supervisors.

### *Bonneville and the Columbia Power Trades Council*

The accord between Bonneville and the Columbia Power Trades Council reads [*73*, p. 19] :

> It is recognized that membership on the part of employees covered by this agreement in the unions affiliated with the Council is helpful in accomplishing the purposes of this agreement and the purposes of the Administration.

The Bonneville Power Administration comes under the Civil Service Act; the TVA, although not under the Civil Service Act, has a strong merit system of its own based on a provision

in the statute creating it. Both agencies regard union membership and activity as evidence of "merit," and the Bonneville
agreement provides that each signatory union "will assist the
Administration by directing qualified eligibles to the sources
through which employees are obtained." [*73*, pp. 28-29] Obviously, it is a strong inducement for the employee to become a union
member if the management rates this a plus factor in his record.
At present, TVA and Bonneville are exceptions in this respect,
but, since they both have maintained merit principles, this raises
the possibility that a management policy of offering incentives
for union membership may under proper safeguards be a desirable one.

The ordinance of the City of Philadelphia authorizing the
mayor to enter into an agreement with the AFSCME specifically
encourages "expanded union representation," but this appears
to be an unusual provision. [*38*, p. 2] Legislators and administrative officials in state and local governments who approve
collective negotiation arrangements may regard this as sufficient
encouragement for the unions; they may also fear that they
will be accused of favoring a particular union, although this
criticism is sometimes made anyway. Actually, union membership can be encouraged without any officially stated policy to
that effect, and it is often said that this is what is happening
in jurisdictions where labor is strong politically. On the other
hand, many of the public employee leaders believe that most
state and local jurisdictions are in fact hostile towards employee
organizations.

It is interesting to reflect on the experience in the private
sector with "neutrality." While the Wagner Act "did not affirma-
tively promote union organization of employees," it did "state
that the policy of the government was to encourage unionism." [*297*, p. 44] The Taft-Hartley Act protected the right of
the workers *not* to join a union, and thus "appeared to place the
government in the position of a neutral." [*297*, p. 70] The entire
experience in the administration of both Acts, however, shows
clearly that the definition of neutrality depends in part upon
who happen to be the members of the National Labor Relations
Board at a particular time. This bears out the point just made,
namely, that public employee organizations will be given as
much encouragement as the administrators in a particular place
want to give them.

## Checkoff of Union Dues

Any services the government renders the unions could be considered encouragement, and one of these is checkoff of union dues. A common practice in industry, "it is widely regarded as an important means of ensuring the stability of employee organization membership, freeing the organization leaders for more important duties." [*315*, p. 21] Some people have argued that it is improper for the government to become a collection agency for any organization, and, besides, this makes it seem that union membership is compulsory.

In a report made in 1960, a majority of the members of the National Civil Service League's Special Committee on Employee Organizations took this stand, but the other members could see nothing wrong with the checkoff if the employee gave his consent in writing, could withdraw it at any time, and the union paid the administrative costs. [*89*, p. 2] President Kennedy's Task Force on Employee-Management Relations in the Federal Service also approved of the checkoff under the same conditions, but it did think that authorizing legislation was necessary. [*315*, p. 21] The Comptroller General later ruled that the necessary legal authority did exist, and on January 1, 1964, voluntary checkoff systems were begun in the federal agencies. In industry, the Taft-Hartley Act bans the compulsory checkoff, but in government this issue has fortunately not arisen since the unions are usually satisfied with the voluntary arrangements. [*297*, p. 222]

The AFSCME estimates that half its collective bargaining agreements provide for the checkoff. The International City Managers' Association reports that the checkoff is voluntary in most cities and can be revoked at will by the employee, although in some municipalities he must wait a calendar year or until the end of the fiscal year, or until the contract is terminated. The employer may or may not make a charge for the service; the ICMA found that most cities do not. [*118*, p. 6] In the Canadian municipalities, "only New Brunswick and Manitoba make no provisions for checkoff for municipal employees." [*400*, p. 61]

## Bargaining Rights

Employee organizations can be permitted and even encouraged but still not have a very strong role. The big question in recent years has been whether or not to grant them bargaining rights, and, if so, to what extent. In Chapter 1, it was related how a growing number of jurisdictions are entering into collective negotiations, but at this point we need to clarify our terms.

### Meaning of Collective Negotiations and Collective Bargaining

Collective negotiations refers to any arrangement in which the employer recognizes an employee organization, or organizations, and meets with their representatives to come to agreement on conditions of work. The employer may or may not deal with an exclusive bargaining agent, meaning an employee organization, or a council of employee organizations, which represents the majority of the employees in the bargaining unit. The exclusive bargaining agent, as in the case of the TVA, may also be a council of employee organizations which represents all bargaining units of a certain kind, such as craft or white collar. Purely consultative arrangements cannot be considered negotiations, because the employer is under no obligation to work out a joint agreement with the employee organizations. Some collective agreements block out areas for negotiation and others for consultation. The essence of collective negotiations is that, for their mutual benefit, the employer and the employees engage in joint decision-making.

Public employee unions that are affiliated with the labor movement insist that collective negotiations do not mean much without recognition of exclusive bargaining agents. The Taft-Hartley Act, itself an amendment of the Wagner Act, continues the provisions of the original legislation which empower the union representing the majority of the workers in the bargaining unit to negotiate agreements with the employer binding on *all* employees in the unit. In the private sector in Canada, the same picture holds [*88*, p. 347] :

> Most collective bargaining acts require that the union represent a majority of the employees and that the organizational unit for which the union bargains be specifically defined before requiring that an employer bargain with the union.

Those opposed to the recognition of several different organizations for negotiation purposes argue that this smacks of a policy of divide and rule, and that it may produce several different agreements for workers in the same bargaining units—or none at all because of the disputes between the organizations. To labor leaders in the private sector, there is no such thing as collective bargaining without exclusive bargaining units, which is one reason why in the previous chapters of this book the term "collective negotiations" has been frequently preferred. Another reason is that the strike weapon is considered an essential part of the collective bargaining process in industry, whereas in government no right to strike is recognized.

Nonetheless, some of the recent state legislation governing public employee relations provides for "collective bargaining" but at the same time bans the strike. The definition of collective bargaining in the Taft-Hartley Act [*132*, p. 8] is picked up almost word for word, as, for example, in the Michigan statute [*344*, p. 25]:

> To bargain collectively is the performance of the mutual obligation of the employer and the representative of the employees to meet at reasonable times and confer in good faith with respect to wages, hours, and other terms and conditions of employment, or the negotiation of an agreement, or any question arising thereunder, and the execution of a written contract, ordinance or resolution incorporating any agreement reached if requested by either party, but such obligation does not compel either party to agree to a proposal or require the making of a concession.

The same law requires the public employer to bargain collectively, but in other states, such as Wisconsin under its Municipal Employer-Employee Labor Relations Law, it is simply authorized to do so, yet the terminology used is "collective bargaining." [*415*] The term is being used without its precise meaning in private enterprise where bargaining is mandatory and "the exclusive representative of the workers in a plant or an employment unit sits at the bargaining table as a full equal with the employer or his representative, who together 'bargain' in good faith until an agreement or impasse is reached." [*100*, pp. 45-46]

There are other essential aspects of collective bargaining in the private sector in the United States and Canada, and they will be referred to in the later chapters of this book.

### The Bargaining Alternatives

The possible courses of action in government are: (1) to recognize no employee organization for bargaining purposes; (2) to provide varying forms of recognition without allowing exclusive bargaining agents; (3) to follow industry practice and give the employees the opportunity by majority vote or other proof to select an exclusive representative.

In her *Report on a Program of Labor Relations for New York City Employees,* published in June, 1957, Ida Klaus, summarizing extensive research, wrote that "group participation of any kind in the formulation of terms and conditions of employment for the civil servant is not yet the prevailing fashion." There were very few cases of recognition of employee organizations for bargaining purposes, although some public employers had "established some form of collective contact with their employees." [*122*, p. 17] Why are many more jurisdictions now engaging in collective negotiations, in some cases closely resembling the pattern in industry? Apart from the employee pressures, why have they considered it good public policy to do so?

### *Reasons for Granting Bargaining Rights*

This raises the question of why people join unions, and the reader will remember the interpretation of a Canadian official, quoted in Chapter 2, to the effect that unionism is a response to the impersonality of large-scale organization in both the private and public sectors. No matter how benevolent the employer may be, the workers will not be satisfied if he makes the decisions unilaterally. Mere consultation with the employees, erroneously considered "collective bargaining" by some people, is not enough, because it does not satisfy the employees' basic psychological needs. Unions in industry are considered hard-headed, just like the management, but a labor expert writes [*82*, p. 9] :

> Although some workers are certainly coerced into unions and others join out of apathy, it is well established that many, if not most, workers join unions because they are dissatisfied with having the employer unilaterally decide all questions concerning their conditions of work. This worker discontent can be described in mystifying psychological jargon; it can be justified by noting the countless irritations that arise everywhere between those who give orders and those who must take orders; the expression of this discontent can even be protected by society in laws such as the Wagner Act. However it is phrased, the simple fact is that millions of workers have joined unions in order to satisfy, among other needs, the desire to share in decisions about their jobs.

He relates how, when a company president found entirely reasonable, and agreed to, all the union's initial requests, the workers, instead of being happy and cooperative, did not produce as much and even went out on wildcat strikes. The apparent explanation is that "the employer *gave* the workers a contract; they did not *win* it." True bargaining had not taken place; the "kindly employer simply waved his magic wand." [*82*, p. 10] This jibes with Miss Klaus' opinion [*122*, p. 84] :

> Human nature is such that paternalism, no matter how bounteous its gifts, may be of less real satisfaction and advantage to both sides

than the process of reasoning together around the family table, no matter how meagre the fare.

President Kennedy's Task Force on Employee-Management Relations in the Federal Service stated [*315,* p. 11]:

> Responsible, active employee organizations contribute to the efficient and harmonious performance of government functions. Experience within the Federal Government and on other levels of government in the United States has abundantly demonstrated this fact. Wherever any considerable number of employees at their own initiative manifest their desire to establish formal dealings with management officials, there should be no question of the willingness of the agency to enter such relations.

John J. Carson, Chairman of the Canadian Public Service Commission, making a family analogy, says:

> I would suggest that we shuck off our immature notions about the pathology of conflict and accept it as a normal and potentially developing process. Admittedly conflict can bruise in irreparable ways, but those of you who have survived a number of years of marriage or have raised teenagers will surely agree that conflict faced in mature fashion can provide the basis for a strong, enduring, and mutually respectful relationship.

To him, labor relations should be accepted "as a dynamic, volatile group extension of everything we know about human relations." [*53,* p. 48] T. J. Plunkett emphasizes the value of collective negotiations as a stimulus for innovation [*308,* pp. 10-11]:

> Traditionally, public service management has sought for a degree of certainty in such matters as budget preparation, precedent in dealing with decision-making and legislation to establish an operating framework for any new undertaking. These characteristics of public service management have led some to conclude that these have established a degree of inertia in public management in dealing with the new and more challenging problems emanating from the community at large. The advent of collective bargaining may therefore establish a new and more invigorating climate for public management by helping to overcome built-in inertia and permitting public management to become a little more venturesome instead of seeking precedent and certainty with respect to every action and decision.

### Legal Status of Collective Negotiations

Apart from what should be done, there is the problem of what can be done legally, and in Chapter 2 we saw that "sovereignty" is being redefined to permit collective negotiations. In the past, the prevailing view of legal authorities was that there must be express authority in the form of a constitutional provision or state statute, but in some cases collective dealings are now being sanctioned by legal opinions of the state attorney-generals, court rulings, and even administrative action.

Although there is no state authorizing statute, the Indiana attorney general ruled in October of 1966 that public employee organizations in the state had negotiation rights. [*359*, p. 5] Similarly, although there is no legislation in Illinois allowing or prohibiting collective bargaining for teachers, such bargaining is taking place because of a circuit court judge's ruling, sustained by the Illinois Appellate Court on November 9, 1966. [*142*, pp. 188-98] Although the New York State courts had held that the provision in the state constitution granting collective bargaining rights did not apply to public employees, long before passage in April of 1967 of the Public Employees' Fair Employment Act [*317*], New York City had been negotiating extensive collective agreements under sanction of Mayor Wagner's 1958 Executive Order.

Since in most states, the law is silent on collective negotiation rights of public employees, it is possible that such negotiations will spread in the future as much by court rulings and unchallenged administrative action as by passage of authorizing legislation. In a few states, the law prohibits collective negotiations, and, in these states as well as some of those without any legislation, the attitude of the attorney generals, the courts, and administrative officials is that the employees are decently treated and that giving them bargaining rights might encourage them to go out on strike.

### Rationale for Recognition of Exclusive Bargaining Agents

The management justification for designation of an exclusive bargaining agent is the same as in industry: it avoids having to deal with several different unions representing the same kinds of workers. Negotiations are time-consuming, and a single agreement applying to all workers in the bargaining unit is much better than several accords containing different terms. A New York state legislative committee concluded [*177*, p. 43]:

> As other public employers and the legislature have discerned, the advantages of exclusive recognition are substantial. Public employees get enhanced power for their representative. It can speak authoritatively for them, as a number of organizations, each representing splintered segments of the work force, could not. When public employers negotiate with many unions, the pattern is typically one of polite attention by the employing agency, with little or no effective power in the employee organizations involved. . . .
> The increased power that exclusive representation permits has correlative advantages for the public employer. The morale of employees is frequently improved by an awareness that an effective

organization is looking after their interests. In addition, an exclusive representative can be held responsible in a way that it could not if it were merely one of many. Moreover, when its understanding of the public employer's problems require it, an exclusive representative can go along with proposals that may be unpopular with those it represents. Where multiple representation is involved, each organization may well fear to agree to such proposals, lest competing unions gain an advantage among the employees represented.

Most of the new state laws granting bargaining rights to public employees provide for exclusive bargaining agents, but Governor Rockefeller's Committee on Employee Relations recommended further study of the question. Although it could see many advantages in exclusive bargaining agents, including the possibility that they would show responsibility in restraining the membership from strike action, the committee felt that all of this depended upon *"prior solution of the unit problem."* They said, "We do not believe that the problem is sufficiently clarified in the public sector at this time, nor has there been sufficient experience in solving it to permit wise legislation on this matter at this time." It did propose that in the meantime public agencies in the state be permitted to enter into agreements with the employee organizations for exclusive representation. [*107*, p. 39]

In Canada, the new collective bargaining legislation provides for exclusive bargaining agents based on majority representation; it permits certification of a council of employee organizations as the exclusive representative, provided that "each of the employee organizations forming the council has vested appropriate authority in the council to enable it to discharge the duties and responsibilities of a bargaining agent." [*350*, p. 17] In the United States, arrangements of this type are found in TVA and Bonneville, and in shipyards, arsenals, and space centers where joint councils of the metal and building trades exist. In the Oregon state service, "a council of organizations" may be recognized as the bargaining agent. [*301*]

*Protection of Minority and Individual Rights.* Granted the conveniences of recognition of exclusive bargaining agents, citizens have the "constitutional right to petition their government" and "to be heard over and beyond the rights established by collective bargaining statutes in public and private employment." [*36*, p. 41] In industry, "the individual employee has no right to negotiate directly with the employer if he is dissatisfied with the contract made by his union representatives." [*297*, p. 163] A purpose of the Bill of Rights section of the Landrum-

Griffin Act of 1959 is to make the union leadership more responsive to the desires of the rank and file membership in negotiating contract terms and otherwise managing union affairs. Muriel M. Morse, General Manager of the Los Angeles City Civil Service Commission, believes that, if collective bargaining means recognition only through a group, then the individual is denied the right to speak for himself; furthermore, "the right of representation of more than one group is equally fundamental to a merit system in representative government." [*167*, p. 242]

Where exclusive bargaining agents are authorized in government, there often is a provision guaranteeing the right of individual employees, whether or not union members, to present their views and grievances to the management. For example, the Michigan Public Employment Relations Act, paralleling a provision in Taft-Hartley [*132*, p. 10] states [*344*, p. 24]:

> Any individual employee at any time may present grievances to his employer and have the grievance adjusted, without intervention of the bargaining representative, if the adjustment is not inconsistent with the terms of a collective bargaining contract or agreement then in effect, provided that the bargaining representative has been given opportunity to be present at such adjustment.

The agreement between the City of Winnipeg and the Canadian Union of Public Employees makes clear that at any time an individual employee can present a grievance directly to "the Head of the Department in which he is employed." [*10*, p. 36] Apart from individual grievances, the right of any employee or group of employees to meet with the management is also frequently protected, but contract terms as such can be negotiated only with the exclusive bargaining agent. The Kennedy Executive Order states [*400*, p. 351]:

> Recognition, in whatever form accorded, shall not . . . preclude any employee, regardless of employee organization membership, from bringing matters of personal concern to the attention of appropriate officials in accordance with applicable law, rule, regulation, or established agency policy, or from choosing his own representative in a grievance or appellate action.

Some laws and agreements make no mention of the right of minority groups and individual employees to meet with the management, and the new federal legislation in Canada states [*350*, p. 42]:

> An employee is not entitled to present any grievance relating to the interpretation or application in respect of him of a provision of a collective agreement or an arbitral award unless he has the approval of and is represented by the bargaining agent for the bargaining unit to which the collective agreement or arbitral award applies.

This does not affect the privilege which civil servants have had for 20 years to appeal directly to the Civil Service Commission (now the Public Service Commission) in the case of promotions, demotions, suspensions, dismissals, transfers, and salary increments—a privilege that became a right under the Civil Service Act of 1961.

Undoubtedly, the advent of collective negotiations makes essential careful consideration of the rights of minorities and of the individual worker to assure that the grievance and other procedures are consistent with the constitutional and legal protections enjoyed by public employees. Collective negotiations should represent a clear gain to government workers, without loss of any existing rights.

### Other Forms of Recognition

The Kennedy Executive Order provides for formal and informal, as well as exclusive recognition. [*400*, pp. 350-53] The Bureau of Programs and Standards of the United States Civil Service Commission explains [*378*, p. 5.08]:

> In the private sector of the economy, management is not obliged to deal with employee organizations which do not represent a majority of the employees of the bargaining unit. In government, however, the varied development of employee management relations among agencies and within agencies, the inherent limitations on collective bargaining in the public service, and established federal policies and practices in employee consultation combine to make differentiation in levels of dealing desirable.

Informal recognition is provided for employee organizations that do not have enough members in the bargaining unit to entitle them to formal or exclusive recognition. It confers the right to meet with the management and express views on matters of concern to its members, but management is under no obligation to accept these opinions or to consult with the organization before formulating personnel policies. Basically, it gives minority groups the opportunity to be heard. Formal recognition is granted organizations which, although not qualified for exclusive recognition, have a stable membership of 10 per cent or more of the employees in the unit. It guarantees that the management will "consult with such organization from time to time in the formulation and implementation of personnel policies and practices, and matters affecting working conditions that are of concern to its members." [*400*, p. 352] It does not confer bargaining rights; these are reserved for organizations which can show that they represent more than 50 per cent of the employees in the unit. When an organization is granted exclusive recognition, none other can be given formal recognition, no matter what its membership; if a group already has formal recognition, it loses it and receives informal recognition instead.

This three-stage recognition formula, recommended by President Kennedy's Task Force on Employee-Management Relations in the Federal Service, is an interesting adaptation to the government environment, but it is not being generally imitated in state and local governments. In Minnesota, formal recognition, available to any employee organization which represents a majority of the employees in the bargaining unit, gives "the right to meet with, confer and otherwise communicate with the governmental agency . . . with the object of reaching a settlement applicable to all employees of the unit." Informal recognition, given to any employee organization "regardless of the recognition granted to any other . . . organization," bestows the "right to meet with, confer and otherwise communicate with the governmental agency . . . on matters of interest to its members." [*165*]

A proposed employee relations ordinance for Los Angeles County, rejected by the Board of Supervisors in the summer of 1967, provided for three forms of recognition, exactly as in the Kennedy Order, but using the terminology, "nominal," "secondary," and "majority" recognition. [*90*]

Those who would like to see the federal government follow industrial practices closely criticize the Kennedy Executive Order for "making deliberate allowances for competition among unions simultaneously representing different minority groups of employees within a single bargaining unit." [*339*, p. 199] Conversely, the Order has been criticized by groups such as the National Federation of Federal Employees, which is not affiliated with the AFL-CIO, because it does provide for recognition of exclusive bargaining agents. [*397*, p. 76] Actually, the experience with the three-level plan of recognition has not proved satisfactory as far as many agency officials themselves are concerned. When, in the fall of 1967, President Johnson appointed a committee to evaluate the federal employee-management cooperation program, Civil Service Commission Chairman John W. Macy, Jr., listed the recognition arrangements as one of the major areas of concern expressed to the Commission by some of the agencies,

Their contention was that the multiple recognitions were becoming burdensome and a source of friction, and that informal and formal recognition tended to perpetuate "fragmentary, nonsignificant and overlapping relationships" which might no longer be justified in view of the extensive amount of exclusive recognition already granted. [*95*]

Some people favor proportional representation of employee organizations according to their membership strength, without any exclusive bargaining agent, but, as the Rockefeller committee commented, this is an "alternative filled with operational complexities." [*107*, p. 38] One state, California, recently adopted the proportional representation scheme, but for its teachers only. The American Federation of Teachers is very much opposed, as will be elaborated in Chapter 9, and "evidence to date on the operation of the law . . . is inconclusive." [*409*, p. 120] It is up to the policy-makers to determine what kinds of recognition to grant; the experience shows that in any case substantial protections can be given minority groups and individual employees.

### The Union Shop

In Chapter 2, it was mentioned that union shop agreements are being signed in government, in jurisdictions both with and without civil service. The AFSCME claims to have negotiated dozens of such agreements, and it obviously rejects Spero's judgment that the union shop "is not an essential element of collective bargaining in the public service." [*342*, p. 3] Organizations affiliated with the AFL-CIO, like the AFSCME, tend to believe, as the unions in the private sector do, that compulsory union membership is essential. They reason that it is only fair for the employees in the bargaining unit to become members of a union which, as the exclusive bargaining agent, negotiates benefits for all of them. Non-members are "free riders" who get the benefits without even paying dues. Furthermore, union membership goes up with the union shop, and labor must use all legitimate means of making itself a real equal with management in the tough bargaining sessions. The Taft-Hartley law permits the union shop except in states which elect to pass laws prohibiting it. Nineteen states now have such "right to work" legislation. [*60*]

### *The Issue of Individual Rights*

Wherever the union shop is permitted, the issue of individual rights arises, because any organization enjoying compulsory membership can abuse its power and treat the captive members unfairly. Accordingly, the Taft-Hartley Act provides that under union security agreements, the union can require the employer to discharge a worker only for failure to pay the regularly required initiation fee or dues. This does not protect the person's right to belong to a union; rather, it guarantees his holding his job in a union shop so long as he pays the normal union fees or dues. [*132*, p. 6] Union shop adherents want it made clear that, under this provision of the law, the union cannot take a member's job away for any reason other than non-payment of the dues, even if it expels him from the union.

### The Union Shop and the Merit System

The fundamental assumptions of the merit system are these:

1. Any person interested in a government job who meets the minimum qualifications should be allowed to participate in the competition.

2. Selection of the successful candidates shall be based on their competence only.

3. Once appointed, they should be evaluated for retention and other purposes solely in terms of their performance on the job.

The union shop meets none of these criteria for the following reasons:

1. Someone who does not want to join the particular union, or any union, will not apply.

2. Those who, for whatever reason, do apply, will enjoy restricted competition owing to failure of others to do so because of the union shop requirement.

3. Both new and old employees who drop out of the union must be dismissed, no matter how competent they are.

The counter argument is that none of this will happen because all applicants and employees will want to join the union, but this is highly theoretical. Government blue collar workers have wanted to join the unions, but this has not been true of the much more numerous white collar workers. Many of the latter are now joining, but many others are not. Furthermore, members of employee organizations which lose in the representation election usually do not want to change their affiliation, yet the union shop would require them to do so.

It is significant that the TVA and Bonneville, despite their encouragement of union membership, do not have the union shop; since they are under merit systems, they cannot have it. The Kennedy Task Force stated "its emphatic opinion that the union shop and the closed shop are contrary to the civil service concept upon which federal employment is based, and are completely inappropriate to the federal service." [*315*, p. 25] Under the closed shop, only union members can be hired, whereas under the union shop, the new employee is usually given 30 days to join.

Arvid Anderson suggests that the way out may be to suspend the union membership requirement until the employee completes his probationary period. [*34*, p. 146] The reasoning here apparently is that in merit systems union membership cannot be made a "condition of hire," but it can be made a requirement for retention. Civil service administrators would reject such an interpretation as inconsistent with the merit concept, nor would this be a helpful suggestion for making the probationary period really effective in weeding out misfits. The Kennedy Executive Order is so worded as to prohibit the union shop in the federal service, and union shop agreements in state and local governments, while not rare, are the exception rather than the rule.

### Legislative and Judicial Status of the Union Shop

Several states have laws banning the closed and union shops, and, where right-to-work legislation applies to public employees, this has the same effect. The other states have no legislation on this subject, so it is up to those who do not believe such agreements are legal to challenge them in the courts. In December of 1966, the Delaware State Highway Commission announced that it would not sign a union shop agreement with the AFSCME because its attorney had found that courts in other states had declared them illegal. Several other state agencies had already signed such agreements. [*413*]

Actually, there are very few recent court decisions on the subject. [*399*, pp. 9-10] The traditional court view has been that the union shop has "no place in public employment in the absence of specific statutory authorization," but such agreements are now being signed anyway. One can only agree that "predictions of future trends in judicial views are not only dangerous but may serve little purpose." [*348*, p. 32] In the Canadian municipalities, union shop agreements are legal, although in some cases existing employees do not have to join the union. [*329*]

### The Modified Union Shop

The so-called modified union shop, in effect in the City of Philadelphia since March, 1961, gives the individual somewhat more leeway. The ordinance authorizing the agreement with District Council 33 of the AFSCME, covering some 12,000 of the city's total of 18,000 civilian employees, provides for three categories of union membership: mandatory, voluntary, and prohibited. The city and the union, by mutual agreement, assign all classes of positions under the municipal civil service system to these three categories, except for uniformed and investigatory personnel. When a majority of the incumbents in a given class of positions are union members, the class is placed in the mandatory category.

All new employees in the mandatory group are required to join the union upon completion of the six-month probationary period; existing employees in this category did not have to join. Those in the mandatory group can withdraw from the union in the period between June 15 and June 30 of *any* year. Employees in the voluntary group may, or may not, join as they see fit, but, if they do so, they can withdraw at any time. Those in the prohibited category may not become union members. [*375*] In August of 1967, of a total of about 1,200 classes, there were 266 in the mandatory group, 529 in the voluntary, and 404 in the prohibited categories.

This is not the union shop as it functions in industry, but new employees are required to join the union and remain in it for at least a time. Foster Roser, city personnel director of Philadelphia, does not believe that this agreement has damaged the merit system. Annually, about 75 to 100 employees drop out of the union; their complaint is not about violation of merit principles, but rather that the union has not done anything for them. In his opinion, the union has obtained more members than it would have otherwise, and he reports that very few members are in the white-collar ranks.

Critics of the modified union shop in Philadelphia point out that the city's contributions for health and welfare insurance go directly to District Council 33, which has built a hospital for its members and uses the money to meet expenses of operating the hospital and to pay hospital-medical-surgical benefits to the members. Someone who does not become a union member cannot participate in this plan, so he is penalized for failing to join. The Philadelphia example is being studied carefully and may be used increasingly as a model in the future.

AFSCME Municipal Employees Local 1635 in Rochester, New York, recently signed an agreement with the city which is similar in some respects to the one in Philadelphia. [*359*, p. 10] The University of Delaware, not covered under the state's civil service law, has an agreement with the AFSCME which requires all new employees to join the union after 90 days but permits them to withdraw during the first 15 days of the last month of the contract. [*13*, p. 5]

### The Agency Shop

Under the agency shop, declared legal in industry by the United States Supreme Court, non-union members are required to "pay a fixed sum monthly, usually the equivalent of union dues, as a condition of employment, to help defray the union's expenses in acting as bargaining agent for the group." [*399*, p. 14]

In 1965, the Wisconsin legislature passed a bill permitting the municipalities to sign contracts providing for deductions from the pay of *all* employees in a bargaining unit to cover the union's costs in representing them in the negotiations. Before any such agreement could be made, two-thirds of the employees voting would have to give their approval, and this two-thirds would have to constitute a majority of the employees eligible to vote in the unit. The state attorney general ruled that such agreements would be constitutional and serve a public purpose [*346*], but Republican Governor Knowles vetoed the bill, his objection being that the employees would be required to contribute money to organizations whose policies they might not like. He said he would not support such legislation unless it were clearly shown that these obligatory employee payments were in the public interest. [*307*, p. 6] Democratic Lt. Governor Lucey supported the efforts of Wisconsin City and County Employees Council to persuade the legislature to override the governor's veto, arguing that it was unfair for the union members "to foot the bill for the union to represent people who pay no union dues." [*354*, p. 9] The Wisconsin senate, by just two votes, failed to override the governor's veto.

At public hearings conducted in early 1967 to consider changes in the municipal labor relations law, the Wisconsin League of Municipalities strongly criticized a proposed agency shop provision, arguing that local officials were still very much opposed. The League disputed the contention that, if employee organizations were allowed to negotiate agency shop provisions, this would deter them from sanctioning illegal strikes, among the penalties for which would be cancellation of the dues deductions. [*133*, pp. 1-2]

In October of 1966, the Minnesota AFL-CIO Federation, following the proposals of Council of State Employees 6, included a provision for the agency shop in its recommendations for amendments to the state's collective bargaining law for public employees. [*359*, p. 12] The AFL-CIO's Postal Clerks recently went on record in favor of the agency shop. [*125*] The agency shop impresses some merit system advocates as an acceptable compromise, namely, to avoid the union shop. As phrased by one of them, "it permits the union to work for everyone, but it preserves the right of the individual not to join the union if he doesn't want to." [*311*]

## The Strike Issue

In the United States, the courts have long ruled that public employee strikes are illegal, whether or not prohibited by statute, the reasoning being that such statutes are merely declaratory of the common law. The dominant court view is that such strikes are against the people themselves and therefore cannot be tolerated.

### Court Decisions

A case frequently cited is *Norwalk Teachers Association* v. *City of Norwalk,* in which the Connecticut Supreme Court ruled [*116*, pp. 3-4]:

> Under our system, the government is established by and run for all of the people, not for the benefit of any person or group. The profit motive, inherent in the principle of free enterprise, is absent. It should be the aim of every employee of the government to do his or her part to make it function as efficiently and economically as possible. The drastic remedy of the organized strike to enforce the demands of unions of government employees is in direct contravention of this principle. . . .
>
> In the American system, sovereignty is inherent in the people. They can delegate it to a government which they create and operate by law. They can give to that government the power and authority to perform certain duties and furnish certain services. The government so created and empowered must employ people to carry on its task.

Those people are agents of the government. They exercise some part of the sovereignty entrusted to it. They occupy a status entirely different from those who carry on private enterprise. They serve the public welfare and not a private purpose. To say that they can strike is the equivalent of saying that they can deny the authority of government and contravene the public welfare.

On occasion, the employees have argued that there is a right to strike against proprietary activities of government, such as electric power systems, on the grounds that these are commercial-type enterprises similar to those in industry. With very few exceptions, the courts have denied this contention; furthermore, it has been pointed out [*100*, p. 22] :

The people have infinitely more at stake in the uninterrupted service of some public proprietary services (e.g. transportation) than in some strictly governmental functions (e.g. the maintenance and operation of a recreation center or an art gallery) and that if a logical distinction is to be made, it will have to be along some other line than lies between governmental and proprietary operations and services.

Actually, there are situations under which strikes in the private sector are unlawful; for example, the Taft-Hartley Act prohibits strikes for a closed shop or to force the employer to recognize or bargain with a union when another union is the certified bargaining agent. [*132*, p. 7]

Since some of the public employee leaders now say that the right to strike is essential, the question arises as to how the courts would rule on legislation specifically granting such a right. No such laws now exist, but, to show how thinking has changed, in a recent address to the League of Municipalities in Atlantic City, New Jersey, Attorney General Sills is reported to have said that "times and conditions change and perhaps the time has come to consider whether or not public employees engaged in non-public safety functions should or should not have the right to strike." The *Shield*, official organ of the New Jersey Civil Service Association, believes that Governor Hughes apparently wants the issue opened to public discussion, and comments that Sills' statement "may turn out to be one of the more important utterances of a generation in New Jersey's history." [*362*]

In the 1966 elections, the Democratic Party in Michigan adopted a platform plank calling for the right to strike for public employees, the only exceptions to be "in cases of clear and present danger to the public safety, such exceptions to be confined to policemen and firemen." [*358*, p. 12] In 1951, a Minnesota lower court, rejecting the contention that public employees have no right to strike simply because they are employed by the government, said that the right to strike is rooted in the freedom of man, and " . . . may not be denied except by clear, unequivocal language embodied in a constitution, statute, ordinance, rule, or contract." When this decision was upheld by the Minnesota Supreme Court, the state legislature passed a law barring public employee strikes. [*399*, p. 10]

In 1957, the New Hampshire Supreme Court, although upholding an injunction prohibiting a teachers' strike, said that "there is no doubt that the legislature is free to provide by *statute* that public employees may enforce their right to collective bargaining, by arbitration or strike." [*399*, p. 10] These court opinions are exceptions, however, and it is doubtful that the courts in most states would look with favor on permissive strike legislation. Of course, no predictions can be made about exactly how they would rule, because this depends on state constitutional provisions and many other factors.

### Anti-Strike Legislation in the United States

Before the end of World War II, the only known anti-strike legislation consisted of local ordinances and some statutes applying only to particular classes of employees. In the post-war period, there was a rash of public employee strikes, and this led to "enactment of a federal statute and several state laws of general application forbidding public employee strikes." [*116*, p. 6]

The federal legislation referred to here is section 305 of the Taft-Hartley law; it made it illegal for any federal employee to strike, under penalty of immediate removal, loss of civil service status, and a three-year ban against re-employment. The only previous legislation on the subject was the Lloyd-LaFollette Act of 1912, the protections of which, it will be remembered, did not extend to employees joining unions affiliated with outside organizations claiming the right to strike. The Taft-Hartley Act provision was repealed by Public Law 84-330, passed on August 9, 1955, which makes it a felony for federal employees to strike or assert the right to do so, or knowingly to belong to an organization which claims such a right. The penalty is a fine of not more than $1,000 or imprisonment of not more than one year and a day, or both.

Beginning with Virginia in 1946, some states have passed anti-strike legislation; the number fluctuates and has never been very large, although it has increased recently to 18 [*286*] because most of the new laws providing collective bargaining rights contain offsetting anti-strike provisions. The "prevalent pattern is to secure compliance by a threat of discharge"; later reinstatement is permitted, but the employee must serve a substantial period of time under a new probationary period and without salary increases. The federal law, the only one with criminal penalties, apparently does not contemplate the reinstatement of *any* striking employee. [*116*, p. 7]

### Legal Status of Strikes in Canada

In Canada, there has been no legislation of general application prohibiting strikes in the federal government. Canadian federal employees have been free to belong to organizations which advocate the right to strike, although under the 1961 Civil Service Act, those absent for more than seven days without a good reason risked having their jobs declared vacant. This penalty was not applied, however, during the postal strike in the summer of 1965. [*111*, p. 17] Under the new collective bargaining legislation, they have the right to strike, although they relinquish it if they agree in advance to come under binding arbitration. In any case, however, no employee may strike whose position has been previously designated as "necessary in the interest of the safety or security of the public." [*350*, p. 38]

Under the Canadian Industrial Relations and Disputes Investigation Act of 1948, Crown corporation employees have the right to strike except where expressly excluded by Order in Council. Only the National Research Council and Canadian Arsenals Limited have been excluded, the latter only partially; employees of such government corporations as the Canadian Broadcasting Corporation and Air Canada have for many years had the right to strike and occasionally exercised it. This leads to the wry remark that "one must deduce that the attitude of the Government of Canada is that services rendered by the employees of many Crown corporations are not of such a high degree of essentiality that the strike weapon must be denied to them." [*97*, p. 136] The attempt to distinguish between essential and non-essential workers will be discussed in detail later in this chapter.

At present, only New Brunswick prohibits strikes by provincial government employees. Quebec and Saskatchewan expressly permit them, except for those in essential services. In the municipalities, strikes are permitted, although in some provinces the right is withheld from workers in essential services, such as police and fire protection and hospitals. [*329*, pp. 12-13] Teachers are prohibited from striking in Manitoba only, and in Alberta and Quebec the law grants them the express right to strike. [*24*, p. 13] Concluding on Canada, it should be noted that on occasion the federal and provincial governments have passed *ad hoc* legislation to stop particular strikes.

### The Reality of Strikes in the Public Service

Despite anti-strike legislation and the court view that public employee strikes are illegal under the common law, such strikes are taking place in the United States, as any reader of the newspapers knows. In Canada, although the Heeney committee in its July, 1965, report had expressed confidence that the federal government would be able to cope with strike threats, in the following month the postal strike took place. Furthermore, even where the law bars strikes of essential workers in the provincial and municipal governments, work stoppages take place anyway, as evidenced by the mass resignations of public school teachers in Toronto recently.

In the United States, where unlike Canada the law has never granted government workers the right to strike, much of the public is shocked by the recent public employee strikes, walkouts, demonstrations, picketing, work stoppages, sick-call boycotts, mass resignations, slowdowns, and absences for "rest purposes." Actually, while many more employees are asserting the right to strike than in the past, "before 1940 there already had been more than one thousand authenticated cases of actual strikes by public employees, some strikes successful, some failures, some of short duration, others fairly long, with average length of six days." [*100*, p. 26] The Bureau of Labor Statistics reports that there were at least 743 government strikes during the years 1942-61, and all of this is before the accelerated strike activity of the past few years. [*387*]

*Recent Strikes in the United States.* Apart from disputes in the public schools, the year 1966 saw the following: the twelve-day New York City subway strike; a strike of firemen in Atlanta —the first in the United States in 25 years [*237*]; threatened mass resignations of almost half the registered nurses in New York City municipal hospitals and of three-fourths of the city's public health nurses [*231*]; a doctors' walkout causing shutdown or curtailment of service in New York City's 232 health centers, stations, and special clinics [*240*] ; a 17-day strike of nearly 1,000 social workers in Los Angeles County's Bureau of Public Assistance—the first ever officially called by a public employee union in Southern California—followed by a second walkout of several days' duration [*146*] ; threatened mass resignations of some 2,000 nurses in the San Francisco Bay Area, and a 24-hour sick call-in of virtually all staff nurses in three San Francisco city hospitals [*153*] ; a two-day strike of 600 New York City welfare investigators [*255*] ; a walkout by firemen in Kansas City, Missouri, and another in St. Louis [*152*] ; municipal employee strikes in Dayton, Ohio, Duluth, Minnesota, and Lansing, Michigan [*61*] ; a two-day "sick" strike of police in Pontiac, Michigan [*411*] ; a one-day walkout of 3,500 of Rhode Island's 11,000 state employees to "rest" [*258*] ; resignation of almost the entire police force in Frankfort, Kentucky [*412*] ; a strike of nearly 100 kitchen workers in New York City's Metropolitan Hospital [*256*] ; and a year-end, two-day strike in Toledo, Ohio, of more than 500 municipal workers, mostly laborers and refuse collectors. [*273*]

In public education, an area of intense employee activity, some of the 1966 developments are as follows: a two-day strike of about 1,500 teachers in Newark, New Jersey [*219*] ; a three-day strike of several hundred teachers in New Orleans [*226*] ; a one-day "professional protest" of Kentucky's 29,000 teachers [*59*] ; a four-day strike of 363 teachers in the Plainview-Old Bethpage School District of Long Island [*50*] ; a six-day strike of 150 teachers at Henry Ford Community College in Dearborn, Michigan—the first union walkout by college teachers [*247*] ; teacher walkouts of several days in four Detroit suburbs and nearby Flint, and in Traverse City, Michigan [*236*] ; a week-long strike of about 300 teachers in Youngstown and Hubbard, Ohio [*265*] ; a two-day wildcat strike of more than 200 teachers in Denver [*266*] ; a seven-day teachers' strike in Richmond, California—first of its kind in that state [*26*, p. 4] ; a strike of the faculty of the entire Chicago junior college system, largest professors' strike in the nation's history [*27*, p. 3, 14] ; and a massive one-day teacher walkout in Kansas City, Missouri. [*26*, p. 4]

### Changed Views of Employee Organizations

The two listings above are not by any means complete, and, furthermore, there were many threats of walkouts, some of which were prevented only a few days or even hours before the strike deadline. In Chapter 1 of this book, we discussed the employee organizations' changed conception of their role, but their position on the strike question was deferred for detailed treatment in this chapter. Except for the United States federal government, in both Canada and the United States public employees are now much less willing than in the past to commit themselves to a policy of *never* striking.

*In Canada.* The change is more marked in the United States, because public employee strikes have never been legal, as in the Canadian municipalities. Yet in Canada, although in 1964 Robertson G. MacNeill, then Chairman of the Civil Service Commission, reported that the majority of federal employees had "repudiated the right to strike" [*155*, p. 5], on August 26, 1965, the 80,000 member Civil Service Federation of Canada adopted a resolution opposing any legislation denying civil servants the right to strike. [*111*, p. 17] On February 3, 1966, William Kay, the President of the Postal Union, threatened a strike vote if the proposed collective bargaining legislation denied the employees the right to strike. [*111*, p. 17]

S. A. Little, national president of the Canadian Union of Public Employees, the largest employee organization in Canada, has said [*143*, pp. 56-57] :

> While we do not expressly advocate strikes, we think it is important that the "right to strike" be maintained as a right. . . . I am sure we can all agree that this does not mean that such strikes are a desirable method of settling disputes. In the public service, as in private industry, a strike is the very last resort when all other methods have failed.

In 1966, besides other public employee strikes, there was a week-long railroad strike, closing service on the government-owned Canadian National Railways, [*244*] and a ten-day walkout of more than 5,000 machinists, preventing operations of the publicly-owned Air Canada, the country's principal domestic airline. [*261*]

*In United States State and Local Governments.* In state and local governments in the United States, not only do the AFSCME, AFT, and other AFL-CIO affiliated groups claim the ultimate right to strike, but this is also becoming the position of some of the independent organizations. After the first of the two welfare workers' strikes in Los Angeles County in the summer of 1966, the 33,000-member Los Angeles County Employees Association (LACEA), largest organization of its kind in the country, dropped its 55-year-old no-strike pledge. The LACEA, strongly criticized in the past by the AFL-CIO affiliated employee unions as being management-dominated, explained that the county had refused "to create a fair and reasonable procedure for collective negotiations" and, therefore, "a posture of greater militancy" was necessary. [*149*]

In August of 1966, the 13,000 member California Nurses' Association endorsed the use of the strike, despite the long-standing anti-strike policy, adopted in 1950, of the parent national organization, the American Nurses' Association. A representative of the national organization, present at the meeting when the California group adopted its new policy, was quoted as saying that the "state association was obliged to take note of the circumstances of the times and to watch the attitude of the nurses." In the American Nurses' Association, decisions on economic security matters are taken at the state level. The Associate Executive Director of the California affiliate commented [*243*]:

> My understanding is that there has been a militancy in a few other organizations around the country in recent months, so that other state associations may well take a step similar to ours, and the A. N. A. may well review its position.

In October of 1966, the Pennsylvania Nurses' Association rescinded its no-strike pledge adopted 20 years previously. [*254*]

The Newark school teachers' strike mentioned above was called by the National Teachers' Association, an affiliate of the National Education Association. Until recently, the NEA favored sanctions instead of strikes, a major point of contention with the AFL-CIO affiliated American Federation of Teachers, but some of the NEA affiliates, like the one in Newark, used the strike weapon anyway, apparently to meet the AFT competition by becoming more "militant." Then, in July of 1967, the NEA announced a new policy of providing funds and giving legal advice and support to affiliates which use the strike "under conditions of severe stress." [*292*] Some of the teacher strikes at the beginning of the school terms in September, 1967, were by NEA affiliates, as in Michigan, which received the help of the national organization. [*326*] The independent Fire Fighters' Union, Inc., authorized the strike in Atlanta. Furthermore, wild-cat strikes, like the one by teachers in Denver, seem to be becoming more frequent.

In general, the justification for the strike is that it is necessary, because abstaining from using it has in the past not brought fair treatment for the employees. The International

Executive Board of the American Federation of State, County, and Municipal Employees included the following in a policy statement adopted on July 26, 1966 [*400*, p. 403]:

> AFSCME insists upon the right of public employees—except for police and other law enforcement officers—to strike. To forestall this right is to handicap free collective bargaining process. Wherever legal barriers to the exercise of this right exist, it shall be our policy to seek the removal of such barriers. Where one party at the bargaining table possesses all the power and authority, bargaining becomes no more than formalized petitioning.
>
> The right to strike, however, is not something to be exercised casually. It should be exercised only under the most extreme provocation or as a final resort if an employer acts in an irresponsible manner. . . . It is beyond the authority of any officer of this Federation or of the International Executive Board to call a strike. The decision to strike or to accept an agreement to end a strike can be made only by the members of a local union involved in a dispute.

At the AFSCME 1966 convention, President Jerry Wurf, commenting on a presentation by Secretary of Labor W. Willard Wirtz, said [*355*, p. 2]:

> I, and I am sure hundreds of people in this room, have sat at the negotiating table and had a board tell us, "Take it or leave it. If you don't like it, take another job...." We have found that when the boss thinks he can really step on our necks, it is much easier to tell us "No," than to have the guts to tell the city council that they have to raise some taxes to pay the employees decently.

After the New York City subway strike, both Mayor Lindsay and Governor Rockefeller named task forces to make recommendations for avoiding such strikes in the future. In some respects, their proposals were quite similar, but, whereas the Lindsay group did not call for an express prohibition of strikes, the Rockefeller panel recommended replacing Condon-Wadlin with a new law containing strike sanctions it believed would be more realistic. [*107*] The AFL-CIO-affiliated unions supported the Lindsay proposal, but vigorously opposed the Rockefeller plan. They believe that statutory anti-strike legislation, because of its punitive nature actually leads to strikes; Wurf has said, "every repressive law that has ever been passed to prevent us from striking has led to a strike." [*355*, p. 2]

Angered by a *New York Times* editorial of May 25, 1966, supporting the Rockefeller plan, H. R. Newman, Vice President of New York State Employees Council 50, AFSCME, wrote a letter saying [*235*]:

> No scroll of punishments, whether fines or rack, decertification or thumbscrew, can stop public strikes. Only collective bargaining in good

faith and recognition that public employees are not a species different from those in the private sector can.

The unaffiliated Civil Service Employees Association, whose membership includes most state employees as well as some 42,000 county and municipal workers, supported the Rockefeller proposal "because it gives to public employees valuable rights and asks only for a commitment of continued uninterrupted governmental services in return." [230] In early 1967, delegates at the Association's convention unanimously voted to rescind its 19-year old, voluntary no-strike pledge. The reason given was failure of the state legislature to vote salary increases and provide a workable procedure for contract negotiations [284], but the Association was also plainly convinced that it had suffered from its policy of observing Condon-Wadlin while other employee organizations successfully flouted it. [283]

When, in April of 1967, the state legislature repealed Condon-Wadlin and replaced it with a statute continuing the prohibition of strikes and providing for stiff fines for employee organizations violating this provision, the labor-affiliated and some of the independent unions were very much opposed. In New York City, AFSCME District Council 37, the Transport Workers Union, and the United Federation of Teachers held a mass protest meeting at Madison Square Garden. Their leaders argued that the new law would make it impossible for the employee organizations to bargain on equal terms with the public employer, and that actually its effect would be to increase, not decrease, strikes. [291] Earlier these same three organizations had announced that they would raise more than a million dollars to meet any anti-strike penalties and to work for the defeat of legislators who voted for the law. [290] A detailed analysis of the new legislation is given later in this chapter.

As to the firemen, in accordance with a resolution adopted at its 1966 annual convention, the 120,000 member International Association of Fire Fighters named a study group to reconsider the no-strike clause in its constitution from the very time it was chartered by the American Federation of Labor in 1918. William D. Buck, its president, explained [272]:

The new generation of men who have entered the ranks of fire departments have often felt, with considerable justification, that they are being exploited by public officials and administrators. In this era of an expanded role for collective bargaining between government employees' unions with federal, state, and city agencies, we have felt the need for a fresh, hard look at our union's entire realm of negotiating

procedures—including the question of whether changes in our traditional no-strike policy should be seriously considered.

*Strike Talk in the United States Government.* Although federal law makes it a crime to strike in the national government,
recent months have seen some strike talk there also. At the
1966 annual convention of the AFL-CIO's 160,000 member Postal
Clerks, a resolution, sponsored by several locals, to eliminate
the no-strike clause in the union's constitution was defeated.
[*55*] The 70,000 member independent National Postal Union,
although rejecting a resolution to eliminate the no-strike clause
from the constitution of its national, state, and local units, did
instruct its officers "to thoroughly investigate the feasibility
of testing the constitutionality of laws forbidding the postal
worker the right of free men to strike against their employer,
and, if feasible, the national officers are instructed to institute
such testing." [*126*]

Some Congressmen, agency officials, and others fear that
strikes may take place in the near future, but the prediction is
also made that, as in the past, the strikers will be dealt with
severely. In August, 1962, some 80 TVA sheetmetal workers
were discharged for participating in a jurisdictional strike. A
work stoppage threatened in December of 1964 by teachers in
military dependents' schools in Europe "was averted only after
firm action by the Defense Department." [*157*, p. 4] The United
States Supreme Court refused to hear the appeal of two San
Francisco postal employees fired in 1948 for walking out and
picketing the office there. Jerry Kluttz writes [*127*]:

> But only a few hotheads believe strikes by federal employees are
> the answer to their problems. There is general agreement among
> Federal officials and union leaders that strikes against Uncle Sam
> would set back labor-management relations in Government for years
> and lead to punitive actions by the President and Congress.

The constitutions of most federal employee unions forbid
strikes, and the Kennedy Executive Order prohibits recognition
of any organization which advocates or assists in any strike
against the federal government. [*440*, p. 350]

### The Foreign Analogy

Although not the principal justification given, employee organizations both in Canada and the United States stress that public service strikes are permitted in many countries of the world.
S. A. Little, quoted earlier in this chapter, states [*143*, p. 56]:

In Great Britain, there is no law forbidding Civil Servants to strike. Several highly developed countries as different as France, Norway, and Sweden, have come to the conclusion that strikes are the last recourse and right of the public servants against the general public.

A few examples of strikes during 1966 by public employees abroad were: postal employees and workers on nationalized railways in France; school teachers and other public employees in Sweden; and the personnel, including senior staff officials, of the European Common Market, the Coal and Steel Community, and the Atomic Energy Community. [*225*] In July of 1964, there was a strike of thousands of postal workers in Great Britain, the first strike in that government "since negotiation and arbitration procedures were instituted just after World War I." [*333*, p. 27]

While Little's statement is correct, an International Labour Office publication reports that in some countries government employees do not have the right to strike, and in others while they do, "because of their long-term engagements and conditions of service, they would commit a breach of contract by going on strike and would run the risk of loss of seniority or even dismissal." [*119*, pp. 93-94] Nonetheless, public service strikes are legal and do take place in quite a few countries, and while the foreign examples need not be followed, they are informative. Most people, however, are not likely to be solely influenced by them one way or the other.

### The Accident of One's Employment

The employee leaders also point to the inconsistency in allowing or forbidding strikes of the same kinds of workers where they are employed both by government and private firms rendering the same service [*321*]:

In New York Transit, the drivers of buses on the old Fifth Avenue and Third Avenue systems had an unquestioned legal right to strike until 1962 when the city took over the franchise on their routes. Now they belong to the same local of the same union and drive the same buses over the same streets, but they are lawbreakers when they strike.

Nurses and hospital workers are frequently in the same position, a situation difficult to explain because it obviously is just as important to keep patients alive in the private as the public hospitals. While admitting that this is illogical, some people argue that strikes should be prevented in all "essential" services, whether publicly or privately offered. This brings us to the detailed discussion of "essential" workers, promised earlier,

### Difficulty of Defining "Essential Workers"

For many years, proposals have been made to resolve the strike question by allowing strikes in non-essential activities. Some of the public employee unions are now in effect taking the same line, but, as we saw above, the AFSCME limits essential services to police and fire protection, and this is also the stand of the AFL-CIO Executive Council. [*22*, p. 16] Many people agree with the *New York Times* that this definition of essentiality is so "narrow that it would expose the public to endless hardship." [*267*]

In any case, it is very difficult to make distinctions of this type; indeed, some people think it impossible. Secretary of Labor Wirtz told the AFSCME that a strike of teachers was the same as one by policemen. Wurf disagreed, saying the community could take strikes by teachers but not by the police. [*355*, p. 1] To some citizens, a strike of the garbage collectors may be even more intolerable than one by teachers or the police. Obviously, as noted earlier, few people are affected if a government art gallery closes down and many more if the subway trains do not run. Home-owners and many taxpayers will generally define essential services much more broadly than the unions.

The Rockefeller panel came to the conclusion that "a differentiation between essential and non-essential government services would be the subject of such intense and never-ending controversy as to be administratively impossible." [*107*, p. 19] Similarly, in Illinois the Governor's Advisory Commission on Labor-Management Policy For Public Employees was convinced that "any attempt to draw lines between critical and non-critical public strikes would bristle with unmanageable difficulties and would be likely to undermine the strike prohibition in those areas where the consequences of a strike might be intolerable." [*106*, p. 26]

*Experience in Canada.* Yet the Canadians do not consider impossible the attempt to distinguish between essential and non-essential services, and they have been willing to experiment with legislation along these lines. In Quebec, municipal police officers and firemen may not strike under any circumstances, but all other kinds of employees, including those in the provincial government, may do so, provided that arrangements for maintaining essential services have been made "by prior agreement between the parties or by decision of the Quebec Labour Relations Board." [*329*, p. 89] This is a flexible arrangement, but it may lead to vacillation by the political leadership. In August of 1966, Jacob Finkelman, then Chairman of the Ontario Labour Relations Board, commented [*97*, p. 135]:

> We have just witnessed a three-week strike by some 32,000 hospital employees in the Province of Quebec where hospital employees do have the right to strike. It is worthy to note that, until the strike had gone on for some time, not only did the government not make any move to threaten the employees with legislation curtailing the right to engage in a strike, but, what is even more interesting, the government did not resort to the remedies that are provided for in existing legislation to deal with strikes in essential services.

The experience in Quebec and other provinces with similar legislation needs to be studied in detail before any definite conclusions can be reached. Finkelman reports that strikes have been no more numerous in jurisdictions which expressly permit them than in those where they are prohibited. He estimates that, in the period from January 1, 1957, to December, 1965, an average of slightly over three strikes a year took place in Ontario, where the municipalities have had the right to strike for over two decades. Finkelman concludes that "at the municipal level in Ontario, the recognition that municipal employees do have the right to strike has not on the whole had serious repercussions," and that this is also true in Saskatchewan, where both provincial and municipal workers have had the same right since 1944. [*97*, p. 134]

The new collective bargaining legislation for Canadian federal government employees will provide a real test of the feasibility of trying to distinguish between essential and unessential services. Employee organizations must specify, before they can be certified as bargaining agents, which of two procedures for disputes settlement they have selected: binding arbitration or conciliation. If they choose binding arbitration, they give up the right to strike; under conciliation, they may strike except for those workers in the bargaining unit who have been named "designated employees," meaning that their "duties consist in whole or in part of duties the performance of which at any particular time or after any specified period of time is or will be necessary in the interest of the safety or security of the public." [*350*, p. 38]

No conciliation board may be appointed until the parties have agreed upon the list of designated employees, and, failing agreement, the Public Service Staff Relations Board (on which both sides are represented) will make the decision. The employee organizations would not be indefinitely committed to the procedure they choose, because they can review the situation and make a new decision every three years. Herman comments: [*111*, p. 21] :

> The implementation of this section at the administrative level undoubtedly will give insomnia to many an administrator. There are quite a few gray areas, where the essentiality of services is blurred, and is dependent not only on the services performed, but also on the period of time the public can do without them. It seems that the only way the task of the administrators in this area can be facilitated is through the efforts of a good staff of researchers, who would initiate research projects before crises develop.

Finkelman, now the first chairman of the Public Service Staff Relations Board, believes the lawmakers would have difficulty resisting the pressures "generated by screaming headlines, and complaints from merchants about the loss of business and from voters about the inconveniences they are suffering." [*97*, p. 137] He states that, while in Ontario the government has consistently refused to order striking municipal employees back to work and "some of the strikes have probably caused only slight inconvenience and annoyance to the public," there have been some with "substantial effect." His examples are a 19-day strike in January of 1952 of some 5,000 municipal transport employees in Toronto, one lasting 69 days by 135 stationary engineers in Hamilton in 1961, and a 16-day walkout of 420 garbage disposal and street cleaning employees in Etobicoke in 1964. The government of Ontario did pass *ad hoc* legislation in 1965, however, to prevent a threatened strike of employees of the Toronto Hydro-Electric System. [*97*, pp. 137-38] There always will be pressures for such *ad hoc* legislation; both in 1950 and in the summer of 1966, the national Parliament passed laws ordering striking railwaymen back to work. [*242*]

### Anti-Strike Legislation Considered in Detail

So far in this chapter, no detailed analysis has been made of legislation prohibiting all strikes. Of course, the case study in Chapter 3 of the New York subway strike is illuminating in this respect, but thorough discussion of Condon-Wadlin and similar laws was deferred for this chapter.

*The Question of Civil Liberties.* The American Civil Liberties Union (ACLU) believes that "prohibitions on the right to strike do weaken the First Amendment guarantees." Admittedly, some strikes cause "public discomfort," but, as to the private sector, "the conclusion has been reached in this country that such disadvantages are a price well worth paying for the freedom reflected in the right to strike." Some governmental services are "so basic that their even momentary interruption might irreparably weaken the social fabric," but this is also true of some private ones. A blanket prohibition of all public employee work stoppages is both unjustified and unnecessary. As to essential services, limitations can be placed on the right of both public and private workers to strike, but even this is "fully defensible only if and when adequate machinery for handling employer-employee relations has been established." [*17*, pp. 2-3]

Some employee leaders emphasize the strike as a "basic freedom." For example, in a recent issue of the *American Teacher*, it was noted that "the right of teachers to strike was upheld once again by representatives of some 80 countries who met in Paris this fall in the final meeting of the Intergovernmental Conference on the Teachers' Condition." [*27*, p. 14] The reminder that the strike right protects the employees' freedom to "decide what working conditions should govern their employment" is a desirable one, particularly for those who would act hastily to curb strikes, but, as the ACLU grants, some strikes should not be permitted. [*17*, p. 2] Thus, while the argument provides a useful general orientation, it cannot give a specific solution to the strike problem.

*Experience with Anti-Strike Legislation.* It is generally agreed that anti-strike legislation in the United States local and state governments has been ineffective. The Condon-Wadlin Act, already referred to several times in this book, is a prime example. Following a teachers' strike in Buffalo, it was passed in 1947 at the request of Governor Dewey, who told the legislature, "Strikes against government are wholly unlawful. This bill places upon our own statutes a clear statement of the principles involved and provides effective penalties in case of violation." [*176*, p. 31] Any employee who strikes thereby abandons his position and all rights in it. If later re-employed, "his compensation shall in no event exceed that received by him immediately prior to violating the law; his pay may not be increased until three years after re-employment; and he must serve a new probationary period of five years." [*176*, p. 30]

Although Dewey considered these penalties "moderate but

firm," the employees and many others thought them much too severe and inflexible, and, in view of the failure to invoke them except in a very few cases, it could hardly be said that they proved "firm." Despite passage of Condon-Wadlin, there were strikes of teachers, welfare workers, sanitation employees, ferryboat officers, and, of course, subway workers, but only the ferryboat officers and subway motormen "suffered penalties of short duration." [*179*] A four-week strike in January of 1965 of some 5,000 New York City welfare workers, the longest by public employees in New York State, was settled only after the city agreed to hold up any penalties pending a final court determination of the constitutionality of Condon-Wadlin. [*373*] On December 14, 1965, the New York State Supreme Court did rule it constitutional, but the question of penalties against the welfare workers is still in the courts.

The ferryboat strike, in May of 1965, involved 139 deck and engine officers; they were dismissed but all were later rehired. [*188*] This is the only instance in the history of Condon-Wadlin where the strikers have suffered loss of employment. Although, as related in Chapter 3, the legislature did not include the ferryboat officers in the "amnesty legislation" for the subway strikers, it did later pass a law exempting them from the penalty provisions. The subway motormens' strike is the one mentioned in Chapter 3; it lasted eight days and four officials of the now defunct Motormen's Beneficial Association were jailed. In the 1965 welfare workers' strike, 19 union officials were jailed, but this was for contempt in refusing to obey a court injunction to stop the strike, just as happened to Quill and his associates during the subway strike. In both cases, the courts enjoined the strikes as illegal, but did not invoke the Condon-Wadlin penalties against the strikers.

In 1963, in an effort to make the penalties more realistic, the legislature at Governor Rockefeller's request amended Condon-Wadlin on a two-year, trial basis. Strikers were subject to mandatory salary deductions equal to twice their daily compensation for each day on strike, up to a maximum loss of 30 days' pay, with other possible punishments, including a reprimand, a two-month suspension or demotion. If re-employed, they served on probation for one year, instead of five, and their salaries could be increased after six months, rather than three years.

These were the penalties in effect during the welfare strike, but not the subway strike, because the amendments lapsed on July 1, 1965. In June of 1965, Rockefeller vetoed a Democratic-sponsored bill which would have kept the anti-strike ban but reduced the penalties to ordinary misconduct under the civil service rules, ranging from simple reprimand to dismissal. The governor argued that these amendments would remove the deterrents against strikes.

The experience in other states with anti-strike legislation has been about the same. When municipal workers in Warren, Ohio, went out on strike, Mayor Raymond Schryver at first threatened to invoke the state's Ferguson Act but then changed his mind. He explained, "All the law does is declare the strike illegal and allow us to fire the employees. It doesn't force them to go back to work, which is the thing we're after." [*357*, p. 3] As any newspaper reader knows, the employees can give other reasons than "strike" for not showing up for work. No matter how carefully the law is worded, it is very difficult, probably impossible, to make it airtight.

*Attempts to Make Anti-Strike Legislation Effective.* Some of the laws make no attempt to define "strike"; others like Michigan's Public Employment Relations Act do. The Michigan law states [*344*, p. 23]:

> Any person . . . who, by concerted action with others, and without the lawful approval of his superior, wilfully absents himself from his position, or abstains in whole or in part from the full, faithful and proper performance of his duties for the purpose of inducing, influencing or coercing a change in the conditions or compensation, or the rights, privileges or obligations of employment shall be deemed to be on strike. . . .

Condon-Wadlin contained similar language, but also defined a strike as the "failure to report for duty, the wilful absence from one's position, the stoppage of work, . . . ." [*176*, p. 29] The Rockefeller panel said [*107*, p. 61]:

> We should make it clear that we intend to treat as a strike any concerted work stoppage or slowdown by public employees for the purpose of inducing or coercing a change in the terms or conditions of their employment,—in other words, that the definition be broad enough to include any concerted interferences with service for the purpose indicated.

Even if the employees were placed in a position where they dared not strike, there is always the slowdown, actual but denied if necessary. Usually, where slowdowns are threatened or take place, the provocation is grievances over working conditions.

The Rockefeller panel believed that the way to prevent irresponsible strikes was to remove the ". . . $250 per day maximum fine in criminal contempt proceedings set forth in Section 751 of the Judiciary Law with respect to the enforcement of restraining orders or injunctions issued against strikes of public employees."

Furthermore, it believed that, to protect against any "forgiving" attitude by the employing agencies, the law should make it obligatory for "specified law officers to initiate court action for injunctive relief before any such strike breaks out and as soon as it can be proven that it is about to occur, and if the resulting order or decree of the court is violated to institute a criminal contempt proceeding promptly." [*107*, p. 62] These fines would be levied against the union, the approach long recommended by the *New York Times*, which had expressed its opinion that "no deterrent is more persuasive than an assault on a union's treasury." [*233*]

As to dealing with striking employees, instead of automatic dismissal, a penalty so drastic as to be in practice unusable, the flexible punishments provided under the misconduct provisions of the existing civil service law, ranging from reprimand, fine, demotion, and suspension to dismissal, could be employed. Employee organizations seeking recognition for bargaining purposes would have to pledge themselves not to use the strike, and, if they broke their promise, they would be de-certified.

*The New York Public Employees' Fair Employment Act of 1967.* For a long time after release of the recommendations of the Rockefeller group, no legislation to change Condon-Wadlin could be passed; the Republican-controlled Senate approved a bill with stiff strike penalties and the Democratic-dominated Assembly passed one of its own with much milder penalties. [*238*] Passage of the Public Employees' Fair Employment Act of 1967 in the final hours of the legislative session was apparently attributable, to some extent at least, to the concern of some legislators over threats of picketing and work slowdowns by New York City policemen and firemen, then in a contract dispute with the City. [*287*]

On how to make the strike prohibition effective, the new law follows the suggestion of the Rockefeller panel and shifts

the main weight of the penalties from the employees to the
employee organizations. Employees who violate the law are made
subject to the "disciplinary penalties provided by law for misconduct, in accordance with procedures established by law."
[*317*, p. 5]

If it appears that public employees or an employee organization have violated or are about to violate the anti-strike provision, the "chief executive officer of the government involved"
must notify the "chief legal officer" of such government, and
the latter must "forthwith apply to the supreme court for an
injunction against such violation." If the supreme court's order
"enjoining or restraining such violation" is not complied with,
the chief legal officer must request it to "punish such violation"
by invoking the financial penalties called for in the law. For
each day of the strike, the court may levy a fine against the
employee organization equal in amount to one week's dues collections from its members, or $10,000, whichever is less.

Employee organization leaders who fail to observe the court's
orders are subject to a fine of not more than $250 or to im-
prisonment for not more than 30 days, or to both. The chief
legal officer of the government involved, or the Public Employment Relations Board created by the statute, are required to
institute proceedings before the Board to determine whether the
alleged violation of the law has taken place. If the Board after
a public hearing so finds, it must order termination of the employee organization's dues deduction privileges for a specified
period, not to exceed 18 months. [*317*, pp. 6-7]

The first test of the new legislation came with the 14-day
strike of the New York City school teachers in the fall of 1967.
The United Federation of Teachers had already made known its
intention to circumvent the law by calling for mass resignations
which it maintained could not legally be deemed strikes, and
which, incidentally, are not defined in the statute.

That most of the city's teachers did not report for duty and
were absent for two weeks was clear indication that the law
had not in this case been effective. There was no indication that
fear of the new penalties was a factor influencing the UFT to
come to terms. Although the city's corporation counsel, in accordance with the law, requested the State Supreme Court to punish
the UFT and its officials, and although Supreme Court Justice
Emilio Nunez rejected the UFT's contention that a strike was

not in progress, the court hearings were recessed several times in order to allow UFT President Albert Shanker to return to the bargaining table. At this point, Nunez obviously thought the important thing was to get the strike settled, not to punish Shanker and the UFT. All of this bore out the predictions of those who had said that the supposed more "realistic" penalties of the new legislation would not prevent strikes any more than Condon-Wadlin had. [*293*]

After the teachers returned to work, Nunez did find Shanker guilty of criminal contempt for refusing to obey the court's order to prevent the walkout, and Shanker was fined $250 and sentenced to 15 days in jail. Calculating that the UFT had been in violation of the law for 15 days, Nunez fined the UFT $150,000. This amounted to about $3 a member, or a little less than three weeks' dues collections. [*295*]

While this was being written, the UFT announced that it would appeal, and the prospect was that the final decision on the case would be long delayed. As to the dues checkoff privileges, the city had, in accordance with the new law, requested the Public Employment Relations Board to revoke these privileges for the UFT, and the Board has scheduled a hearing to ascertain the facts. Here again the likelihood was that the UFT would appeal to the courts any adverse ruling of the Board.

Some opinion was expressed that the teacher walkout was not a test once and for all of the effectiveness of the "new approach," since the new legislation went into effect on September 1, 1967, which was too late for it to be invoked successfully in the teacher controversy. Some said it surely would work against smaller employee organizations without the UFT's substantial financial resources. Only the future would tell the complete story, but the weight of the evidence strongly suggested that penalties as such would not prevent public employee strikes.

*Absences for Legitimate Reasons.* Another problem in writing anti-strike legislation is to protect the employee absent from duty for legitimate reasons. Under Condon-Wadlin, any person absent without the "lawful approval of his superior" was presumed to be on strike, although he could file an appeal with the "office or body having power to remove" him, within 10 days after his compensation has ceased. Such "office or body" had within 10 days to "commence a proceeding" to determine whether the employee had violated the law. [*176*, p. 30] No prior notice to the employee was required; furthermore, although the hearing after discharge had to be conducted in accordance with the legal provisions governing removal of any public employee, there was no further right of appeal. [*177*, p. 33] A joint legislative committee, in recommending that striking be considered misconduct within the meaning of Section 75 of the civil service law, stressed that this would also remove the "various special procedural handicaps . . . imposed upon alleged strikers by Condon-Wadlin." [*177*, p. 49]

The Michigan law follows Condon-Wadlin closely in the "punishment" provisions, but, besides contemplating other penalties besides dismissal, it permits any individual losing his appeal in the "proceeding" before the employer to take his case to circuit court. The latter determines whether the employer's action "is supported by competent, material and substantial evidence on the whole record." [*344*, p. 23] Some people who favor anti-strike legislation think that, upon the balance, it is better not to try to define "strike"; they point out that it is not defined in the federal law which has been effective.

### The Ultimate Solution

The ultimate solution, of course, is to create conditions where public employees will not want to strike. Since at present disputes settlement machinery is non-existent or limited in many places, the present wave of strikes and strike threats could easily prove transitory. Realistically, however, as Ida Klaus stresses, there is no sure preventive for strikes both in government and industry. She has some common-sense suggestions for deterrent measures, and they make an excellent conclusion for this chapter [*121*, p. 16]:

> *First,* the accent must shift from a mere negative prohibition to an affirmative legislative program of fundamental rights of organization and collective bargaining and fair procedures for their enforcement—as in Michigan, Wisconsin, and Connecticut.
> *Second,* collective bargaining must be given a fair chance to work and objective ways must be provided for the resolution of just grievances.
> *Third,* fair procedures for the peaceful resolution of a *true* impasse in bargaining must be devised, i.e., acceptable mediation and failing that, fact finding with recommendations by a neutral body, such as a state agency; or any other device that holds promise for peace in any particular situation.
> A *fourth* deterrent may lie in providing by law for reasonable and realistic sanctions against the strike if it should occur. Such sanctions may be imposed either directly by court action followed by fines and

penalties or by withdrawal of recognition (as in the Federal Order) and discontinuance of the checkoff. But more important, whatever sanctions are provided, government must be prepared to enforce them so that strike action will be taken only as a last resort with full knowledge of its serious consequences. If government cannot or will not invoke the penalties it has threatened, then it is defeating its purpose. It may actually be encouraging strikes and even making them pay off. The integrity of government is threatened when government provokes disrespect for its own processes.

It is far better to have no law and no sanctions.

# 5

# Framework for Collective Negotiations

I N THIS CHAPTER we will be concerned with the administrative arrangements and the ground rules for collective negotiations. Specifically, this includes: the allocation of responsibilities for administering the program; the mutual obligations of the public employer and the employee organizations; the determination of bargaining units and holding of representation elections; and the provision of agency time and facilities to employee organizations.

## The Administrative Machinery

The scope of the labor relations program will obviously have a great bearing on the kind of administrative machinery created to carry it out. Ida Klaus' proposals, presented at the end of the preceding chapter, assume a comprehensive plan similar to the industrial model but adapted to the peculiarities of the government environment. With few exceptions (the principal ones being the Canadian municipalities and certain governmental proprietary activities in Canada and the United States), until recently public jurisdictions did not adapt labor relations techniques from industry. There was little interest in doing so, because the principle of joint decision-making with employee organizations—the cornerstone of collective bargaining in industry—had few advocates.

Miss Klaus' plan is still ahead of the thinking for the United States as a whole, because, as noted in Chapter 1, relatively few states have passed comprehensive legislation of the type she has in mind. The administrative machinery required for such a program will include certain elements not yet found in many jurisdictions where collective negotiations, including recognition of an exclusive bargaining agent, already take place. There are many gradations of collective negotiations and thus a variety of possible administrative arrangements. The first part of this chapter will present some examples of the newer programs adopted by jurisdictions which were dissatisfied with previous practices. The reactions, both favorable and unfavorable, to these programs will be reported; of course, it is up to the reader to make up his own mind.

### The Kennedy Executive Order

In the preceding chapters, various references were made to the Kennedy Executive Order, but nothing was said in detail about the responsibility for administering it. Basically, each federal agency is responsible, because Section 10 provides [*400*, p. 355] :

> Not later than July 1, 1962, the head of each agency shall issue appropriate policies, rules and regulations for the implementation of this order, including: A clear statement of the rights of its employees under the order; policies and procedures with respect to recognition of employee organizations; procedures for determining appropriate employee units; policies and practices regarding consultation with representatives of employee organizations, other organizations and individual employees; and policies with respect to the use of agency facilities by employee organizations. Insofar as may be practicable and appropriate, agencies shall consult with representatives of employee organizations in the formulation of these policies, rules, and regulations.

Accordingly, each agency defines the bargaining units and determines, "by an election or other appropriate means," whether a majority of the employees in each unit want an exclusive bargaining agent and, if so, which employee organization it shall be. Upon the request of the agency or of a qualified employee organization seeking exclusive recognition, the Secretary of Labor may nominate, "from the National Panel of Arbitrators maintained by the Federal Mediation and Conciliation Service one or more qualified arbitrators" to render advisory opinions as to the "appropriateness of a unit for purposes of exclusive recognition" and/or which employee organization, if any, should be the exclusive agent.

The United States Civil Service Commission is charged with establishing and maintaining a "program to assist in carrying out the objectives" of the Order. The Labor Department and the Commission were required jointly to propose both a set of Standards of Conduct for Employee Organizations and a Code of Fair Labor Practices in the Federal Service, promulgated by

President Kennedy on May 1, 1963. [*381*] Details of the Standards and the Code will be given later in this chapter; the Standards are the requirements which employee organizations must meet to qualify for recognition, and the Code "prohibits certain conduct on the part of agencies and unions very similar to the unfair labor practices" banned under the Taft-Hartley Act. [*16*, p. 132]

The individual agencies are responsible for the enforcement of the Standards and the Code, the role of the Civil Service Commission being to provide advice and information to the agencies as to their application and enforcement. [*380*, 711-24] Respecting the Standards, each agency makes the final decision as to whether to grant, deny, suspend, or withdraw recognition. Before denying a request for recognition, the agency head must consult with the Secretary of Labor, and he must also do so before withdrawing recognition already granted. As to the Code, the agency makes final and binding decisions as to whether complaints of violations are justified. If the agency head finds that an employee organization has engaged in a prohibited practice, he is expected to order corrective action, and, if it is not forthcoming, he may suspend recognition. "There is no provision in the Code for consultation with the Secretary of Labor on this determination; and there is no appeal from this decision of the agency head." [*380*, 711-29] If he decides that the agency itself is guilty of a prohibited practice, the agency head is required to "take necessary action immediately . . . to remedy the situation." Likewise, there is no appeal from these decisions of the agency head. [*380*, 711-29]

Under the Taft-Hartley Act, the National Labor Relations Board decides disputes as to which union shall be the bargaining agent, what subjects can be included in the bargaining, and whether complaints of unfair labor practices can be sustained. The rationale behind the Standards and the Code, however, was that "care should be taken to avoid imposing on the federal service some of the extremely detailed and complex requirements governing labor relations in the private sector of the economy," and that the "necessity of establishing a separate agency with elaborate proceedings for its [the Code's] administration and for the resolution of disputes" should be avoided. [*381*, 711-2 (2)]

*Attitude of AFL-CIO Unions.* After several years of experience with the federal labor-management relations program, the AFL-CIO affiliated unions in particular are dissatisfied with these administrative arrangements. They charge that some agency managements have refused to bargain in good faith and even to recognize qualified employee organizations, and that, being judge and jury when it comes to Code violations, they can conveniently excuse their own misconduct. They also say that the Civil Service Commission has been ineffectual in trying to get the agencies to respect the Order and treat the employee organizations fairly.

Some of the unions want an agency similar to the NLRB, with real enforcement powers, one which, unlike the Commission, is not "management-oriented." Specifically, they are supporting the Brewster bill, already referred to in Chapter 2. Under this bill, the Secretary of Labor would issue rules and regulations to be followed by the agencies in their dealings with the employee organizations. If he found that an agency had "failed to develop an adequate labor-management program" or had "permitted administrative violations to occur," he would be required to assume direct responsibility for the administration of its program until it had given "satisfactory evidence" of elimination of the "deficiency." The Civil Service Commission and the Department of Labor would jointly prepare standards of conduct for employee organizations and a code of fair labor practices, and presumably the Secretary of Labor would be responsible for their enforcement. [*91*, p. 12] Agency heads would be authorized to suspend, remove, or otherwise discipline administrative officials who interfere with the right of officers or representatives of employee organizations to "present grievances in behalf of their members without restraint, coercion, interference, intimidation, or reprisal." [*91*, p. 2]

Civil Service Commission Chairman John W. Macy, Jr. said recently, "So far we have been unable to see any necessary or really useful purpose a central authority would serve except in rare situations. Conversely, there is good indication that if there were free access to such a body it would weaken the bilateral relationships that have been established in the departments, which have been the main emphasis and value of the program as it has developed so far." [*157*, p. 67]

The Commission's attitude may be influenced in part by this desire of some of the employee organizations to remove it from the picture. In its 1966 report, the American Bar Association's Committee on Law of Government Employee Relations saw little chance for passage of the Brewster and similar bills. It did think, however, that establishment of a federal labor relations board might stop the "pyramids of regulations now being established by each and every government agency for the regulation of employee-management relations" under the Kennedy Order. They reported [*16*, pp. 137-38] :

> It is a common fact, for example, after the Department of Defense issues a regulation . . . that each department, that is, the Navy, Army and Air Force, issue regulations interpreting the original regulations, then each branch of the service, that is, for example, in the Department of the Navy, the Bureau of Ships, Bureau of Yards and Docks, Bureau of Weapons, Bureau of Personnel, issues regulations interpreting the regulation that was issued by the Department of the Navy. Then each and every installation under the various departments issue regulations. The fact of the matter is that you would not recognize the original regulation issued by the Department of Defense.

The Committee recommended that "some action be taken either by legislation or executive order to establish uniform policies for labor relations in government." [*16*, p. 138] It also proposed that, since there were no penalties in the Code of Fair Labor Practices against agency refusal to correct its violations, there be none against the employee organizations, and that, "at the very least," the agencies be required to consult with the Secretary of Labor before suspending an employee organization's recognition for an alleged Code violation. [*16*, p. 134]

### The Canadian Public Staff Relations Board

The Canadian Preparatory Committee on Collective Bargaining elected to follow industrial patterns more closely than the Kennedy Task Force. Although it was "conscious of the constitutional forms and responsibilities that make it impossible to draw a direct parallel between the Government of Canada and a private employer," its view was that "as far as possible, the system of collective bargaining and arbitration in the Public Service of Canada should be rooted in the principles and practices governing employer-employee relations in the Canadian community at large." Its examination of the private sector in Canada showed that "third-party functions," such as certifying bargaining agents and providing concilation services, are usually divided between a minister of labour and a labour relations board. This was satisfactory in industry, where the government can function as a neutral between the employer and the employees, but not in the public service because "the Government *is* the employer and the Minister of Labour is a member of the Government." [*324*, pp. 24-25] Accordingly, the Committee "concluded that the administrative responsibility for the system, including responsibility for the provision of all 'third-party' services, should be concentrated in an independent body." [*324*, p. 26]

> The Preparatory Committee recommends that an independent Public Service Staff Relations Board be established to regulate the system of collective bargaining and arbitration: to determine bargaining units and certify bargaining agents; to provide for the conciliation and arbitration of disputes arising out of the negotiation of collective agreements and for the adjudication of grievances and the resolution of disputes arising out of the administration of agreements; and to provide such supporting services as the system may require.
>
> The Board should consist of a Chairman and four members, two chosen to be representative of employer and two to be representative of employee interests. All should be appointed by the Governor in Council for a fixed period and should have a secure tenure.

The new collective bargaining legislation follows this recommendation, although it provides for a chairman and a vice-chairman and "not less than four nor more than eight other members to be appointed as being representative in equal numbers of the interests of employees and of the interests of the employer respectively." The chairman and vice-chairman are appointed by the Governor in Council "to hold office during good behaviour for such period, not exceeding ten years," as he determines, "but either may be removed at any time by the Governor in Council upon address of the Senate and House of Commons." Each of the other members is appointed by the Governor in Council for a period not exceeding seven years, subject to his right to remove them at any time for cause. [*350*, p. 8]

The legislation also creates a Public Service Arbitration Tribunal, consisting of a chairman appointed by the Governor in Council upon the recommendation of the Board, and of ". . . two panels of other members, one panel to consist of at least three members appointed by the Board as being representative of the interests of the employer and the other to consist of at least three persons appointed by the Board as being representative of the interests of employees." [*350*, p. 30]

These provisions for equal representation of employer and employee interests, and removal of board members for cause only, presumably forestall any charges of "employer-domination." Yet, as the history of the NLRB in the United States shows, the kinds of appointments made by the administration in power will inevitably influence many of the decisions made by the "impartial board" on bargaining units, scope of negotiations, and other matters which cannot, and should not, be spelled out in the legislation in great detail.

When we contrast the United States and Canadian plans, we find that, under the former, implementation and enforcement rest with the individual agencies whereas, under the latter, there is a central, independent body to supervise the program. The Canadian federal service is much the smaller, but some will argue that this is no justification for the decentralized arrangements in the United States when one considers the vast field of industry labor relations regulated by the NLRB and its regional offices. This issue, however, will most likely be decided on grounds other than the size of the enforcement problem, the real question being, as Macy says, whether an independent agency would serve a "useful purpose." Incidentally, if we accept the reasoning of the Preparatory Committee in Canada, the Brewster bill in the United States does not provide for "impartial" administration. The Department of Labor represents the government even more directly than the Civil Service Commission, since the Secretary of Labor, although appointed with the Senate's confirmation, can be removed at any time by the President.

### Some of the New State Plans

As noted in Chapter 1, several states utilize existing state machinery for regulating labor relations in industry. Among them are Connecticut, Massachusetts, Michigan, Wisconsin, and Delaware.

*Connecticut.* Connecticut's Municipal Employee Relations Act provides for the State Board of Labor Relations, in contested cases, to determine the exclusive bargaining agents and to enforce, through cease and desist orders and otherwise, the section of the statute dealing with prohibited practices. If the board finds that either party has refused to bargain in good faith, it can order fact-finding and assess the full cost against the guilty party. If they are unable to come to an agreement, either party, or both jointly, may ask another state agency, the Board of Mediation and Arbitration, to initiate fact-finding. The services of the latter agency are also "available to municipal employers and employee organizations for purposes of mediation of grievances or contract disputes and for purposes of arbitration of disputes over the interpretation or application of the terms of a written agreement." [*30*, p. 329]

The Connecticut plan can be characterized as a state-local government arrangement, with state agencies providing the enforcement and "third-party" functions. Municipal employers and the employee organizations do the bargaining under such arrangements as they mutually determine, with conflicts referred to the above-mentioned state agencies for resolution. In one respect, however, "third-party" machinery is contemplated at the municipal level, for both parties may also make their own arrangements "for the use of other arbitration tribunals in the resolution of disputes over the interpretation or application of the terms of written agreements between municipal employers and employee organizations." [*30*, p. 329]

*Massachusetts.* The Massachusetts law is very similar, but it specifies that "the municipal employer shall be represented by the chief executive officer, whether elective or appointed, or his designated representative or representatives." It also states that, in "bargaining with an employee organization for school employees, the municipal employer shall be represented by the school committee or its designated representative or representatives." In Massachusetts, the state agencies providing "third-party" services are the Labor Relations Commission and Board of Conciliation and Arbitration. [*31*, pp. 556-57]

*Michigan.* Administration of the Michigan Public Employment Relations Act, which not only covers all political subdivisions of the state but also state government employees not under the merit system, is the responsibility of the State Labor Mediation Board. Determination of the bargaining unit, direction of representation elections, enforcement of the ban on unfair labor practices, and provision of mediation services are all entrusted to it. [*344*, pp. 22-28] An interesting provision is that the Board must provide for separate administration of the "labor relations and mediation functions." [*344*, p. 28]

*Wisconsin.* In Wisconsin, where state as well as municipal

employees now have collective bargaining rights, it is the Wisconsin Employment Relations Board which certifies bargaining units, prevents prohibited practices, and provides mediation services. The Delaware legislation—which covers state, as well as county and municipal, employees—authorizes the State Department of Labor and Industrial Relations to determine the bargaining units, supervise representation elections, and make regulations necessary to "administer" the act. In case of bargaining impasses, the services of the State Mediation Service are available. [*32*]

*Oregon.* In Oregon, 1965 amendments to the original 1963 legislation provide that "any board or commission which, pursuant to state law, administers a civil service system for public employees, shall establish, by rule, procedures for the selection and certification of the collective bargaining representative of the classified employees under such system." [*300*] The Oregon Civil Service Commission administers the legislation in the state service, but, in accordance with the 1963 law, mediation services are available through the State Conciliation Service.

*Washington.* In the state service of Washington, where collective negotiations take place on the basis of Section 15 of the Civil Service Act of 1960 (approved by the voters as Initiative 207), the Personnel Board, through the Director of Personnel, administers the program. [*361*, p. 11] He certifies bargaining units and tries to mediate bargaining impasses, with the appointing authority or the exclusive bargaining agent having the right to take cases he cannot resolve to the Personnel Board. The Board's findings are final and binding in disputes in areas falling under its jurisdiction and advisory in those coming under the appointing authority. [*405*]

What these examples make clear is that there are a variety of possible administrative arrangements. Those in Oregon and Washington, since they assign an important role to the civil service agency, presumably do not meet with the approval of the AFSCME and similarly minded unions. The Connecticut, Massachusetts, Michigan, Wisconsin, and Delaware plans are more acceptable, but not completely so, to the AFSCME, for in a recent statement it claims that "in all instances fact finding and/ or mediation boards are employer boards and do not represent an impartial body." [*359*, p. 6] The AFSCME, however, does thoroughly approve of the plan, originally adopted in the form of a Memorandum of Agreement between the City of New York and seven signatory employee organizations, and then adopted by ordinance, effective September 1, 1967. [*144*]

### The New York City Plan

The essential element in this plan is that it provides for a labor relations program directed by "an agency that is independent of either party." [*144*, p. 9] Specifically, an Office of Collective Bargaining (OCB) is created, the director of which is the chairman of a seven-member board of collective bargaining, which board is a part of the OCB. The board has two kinds of members, "impartial" and "partial." Two of the "partial" ones are "city members," named by the mayor to serve at his pleasure, and the other two are "labor" members, appointed by the mayor from "designations" by the Municipal Labor Committee (MLC). (The latter committee consists of representatives of the different municipal employee organizations.)

The city and labor members, by unanimous vote, elect the three impartial members, designating one as chairman. The partial members serve without compensation; the director of the OCB receives a salary for his services as director; and the two other impartial members receive per diem fees for services rendered. All seven members are reimbursed for expenses incurred in carrying out their duties. Half the cost of the disbursements for salary, per diem, and expenses is met by the MLC, being allocated among its members in accordance with rules and regulations issued by the board of collective bargaining. [*144*, p. 1] Thus, the impartial members have no reason to regard the city as their "boss," a vital point in view of the previously mentioned suspicions of the employee organizations that presently constituted merit system and labor relations commissions and boards are fundamentally management-oriented.

Within the OCB, there also is a board of certification, consisting of the impartial members only, with the chairman of the board of collective bargaining also serving in the same capacity for the board of certification. The latter board's functions are as follows:

1. To make final determinations on bargaining units.

2. To determine the "majority representative" of the employees in the unit, by conducting a secret-ballot election

or by "utilizing any other appropriate and suitable method."

3. To determine "the length of time during which such certification shall remain in effect and free from challenge or attack."

4. To decertify any exclusive bargaining representative "which has been found by secret-ballot election no longer to be the majority representative" or which otherwise is found to have become ineligible for certification under the ordinance. [*144*, pp. 3-4]

The full board, meaning the board of collective bargaining, is responsible, upon the request of one of the parties, for investigating the charge that the provisions of the collective bargaining ordinance are not being properly interpreted, enforced, or complied with, and for reporting its "conclusion to the parties and the public." Upon the request of an "employer or certified public employee organization engaged in negotiations," it also makes final determinations as to whether a "matter" is negotiable under the ordinance, and as to whether a "dispute is a proper subject for grievance and arbitration procedure" under the ordinance. [*144*, p. 3]

The OCB maintains a register of mediators, whose names are approved for listing by the board of collective bargaining, and two other registers, one of impasse panel members and one of arbitrators, "approved for listing thereon by a majority of the entire board . . ., including at least one city member and one labor member." The board of collective bargaining, upon the request of both parties, or of the director of the OCB, is authorized to instruct the director to appoint an impasse panel if it agrees that this is desirable. The OCB director, "with the advice and guidance" of the same board, determines when the report of the impasse panel should be released to the public. [*144*, pp. 5-6] As to arbitration, the OCB establishes "procedures for impartial arbitration which may be incorporated into executive orders and collective bargaining agreements between public employers and public employee organizations." [*144*, p. 6]

The OCB director, in addition to his other responsibilities, carries out the rules and regulations both of the board of collective bargaining and of the board of certification. He also maintains "communication with public employers and public employee organizations engaged in collective bargaining negotiations"; at their request, furnishes them with "such data or information as may aid them"; and, "if he determines that either party is remiss in its obligations," he "communicates this information as he deems appropriate." [*144*, p. 4]

Some hard thinking went into the development of this proposed administrative machinery, providing as it does for two policy-making groups: the board of collective bargaining, consisting of all board members, and the impartial members as a subunit with full authority to act in designated areas where impartiality is considered essential. In truth, it is hard to see how decisions of either the entire group or the impartial members could be challenged as being stacked in favor of either the city or the employee organizations, although realistically no one expects both parties would be pleased with these decisions all of the time. These may not be the best administrative arrangements, but they certainly represent a commendable effort to develop solutions geared to the peculiar problems in government.

## Recognition Policy

Once a decision has been made on the administrative machinery, one of the first questions to resolve is that of the policy to follow in acting upon employee organization requests for recognition.

### Definition of Employee Organization

The Kennedy Executive Order states [*400*, p. 350]:

> When used in this Order, the term "employee organization" means any lawful association, labor organization, federation, council, or brotherhood having as a primary purpose the improvement of working conditions among federal employees, or any craft, trade, or industrial union whose membership includes both federal employees and employees of private organizations; but such term shall not include any organization (1) which asserts the right to strike against the Government of the United States or any agency thereof, or to assist or participate in any such strike, or which imposes a duty or obligation to conduct, assist or participate in any such strike, or (2) which advocates the overthrow of the constitutional form of government in the United States, or (3) which discriminates with regard to the terms or conditions of membership because of race, color, creed or national origin.

This definition of "employee organization" disqualifies from recognition social, fraternal, religious, and other organizations not primarily concerned with obtaining better working conditions for their members. This does not mean that the agency managements may not consult with such organizations; the whole tenor of the Order is that they should hear the views of every group and every employee. Rather it means that bargaining may take place only with employee organizations which concentrate on improved working conditions.

The new Wisconsin State Employment Labor Relations Act uses the term "labor organization" and defines it to mean [*345*, p. 2-3]:

> Any employee organization whose purpose is to represent state employees in collective bargaining with the state, or its agents, on matters pertaining to terms and conditions of employment; but the term shall not include any organization: (a) which advocates the overthrow of the constitutional form of government in the United States; or (b) which discriminates with regard to the terms or conditions of membership because of race, color, creed, or national origin.

The Massachusetts and Connecticut statutes simply define "employee organization" as "any lawful association, organization, federation or council having as a primary purpose the improvement of wages, hours and other conditions of employment." [*30*, p. 555], [*31*, p. 325]

Evidence that the petitioning organization sometimes fails to meet this standard is seen in the refusal of the Connecticut State Board of Labor Relations to recognize the Bridgeport Police Officers Association, because it was not convinced that the Association had as a "genuinely primary purpose the improvement of working conditions." [*77*, p. 8]

The Delaware law defines "bargaining representative" as "any lawful organization which has as a primary purpose the representation of public employees in their employment relations with the public employer." [*32*, p. 2]

The Oregon statute defines "labor organization" as "any organization which includes public employees and which has as one of its primary purposes representing such employees in their employment relations with the public employer." [*299*] The rules of the Oregon State Civil Service Commission require that a "candidate for representative," in requesting a representation election, submit a statement "pledging nondiscrimination in regard to race, color, creed, age and political affiliation." [*301*, 98-200]

The Michigan Public Employment Relations Act authorizes public employees to join "labor organizations" and "bargain collectively with their public employers through representatives of their own free choice," but it does not define "labor organization." [*344*, p. 23] It does state that the bargaining will cover "rates of pay, wages, hours of employment or other conditions of employment," so obviously "labor organization" is one representing the employees in such matters. [*344*, p. 24]

### Standards of Conduct for Employee Organizations

In any jurisdiction, of course, the agency which passes upon requests for certification must be sure that the employee organizations are "lawful" ones. Any additional requirements must be consistent with the provisions of the collective bargaining statute and clearly within the agency's discretion. The Kennedy Executive Order is distinctive, because it called for the prompt development of comprehensive Standards of Conduct for Employee Organizations. [*400*, p. 356] In this, the Kennedy task force was influenced by the inclusion of a Bill of Rights section in the Landrum-Griffin Act of 1959, and by the fact that many of the trade unions themselves had developed codes of ethical practices. The federal Standards of Conduct provide as follows [*381*, pp. 711-2 (5)]:

> No agency shall accord recognition to any employee organization unless the employee organization is subject to governing requirements, adopted by the organization or by a national or international employee organization or federation of employee organizations with which it is affiliated or in which it participates, containing explicit and detailed provisions to which it subscribes calling for the following:
>
> (a) The maintenance of democratic procedures and practices, including provisions for periodic elections to be conducted subject to recognized safeguards and provisions defining and securing the right of individual members to participation in the affairs of the organization, to fair and equal treatment under the governing rules of the organization and to fair process in disciplinary proceedings;
>
> (b) The exclusion from office in the organization of persons affiliated with Communist or other totalitarian movements and persons identified with corrupt influences;
>
> (c) The prohibition of business or financial interests on the part of organization officers and agents which conflict with their duty to the organization and its members; and
>
> (d) The maintenance of fiscal integrity in the conduct of the affairs of the organization, including provision for accounting and financial controls and regular financial reports or summaries to be made available to members.

*Enforcement of the Standards.* Since these same standards are provided in the AFL-CIO Codes of Ethical Practices, all the

AFL-CIO affiliates have to do is to establish their identity in a letter and state that they subscribe to these codes of the parent organization. In any case, recognition may not be denied or withdrawn for failure to adopt or subscribe to the standards without first notifying the "organization and the national or international organization with which it is affiliated of such alleged deficiency" and giving the "organization a reasonable opportunity to make any amendments or modifications or take any action that may be required." The agency is not required to hold any formal hearings before it makes its final decision. [*38*, 711-2 (6) (7)]

Once recognition is granted, and the agency has reason to believe that the employee organization no longer respects the standards, it must hold a hearing if one is requested by the employee organization. Furthermore, upon request it must ". . . make available to the employee organization for use in the hearing a concise and accurate summary of the facts on which the agency intends to rely in reaching its decision, together with a statement of the reasons for the agency action."

Representatives of the employee organization, including counsel, have the right to be present at the hearing, to testify and to offer documentary evidence for the record. [*381*, 711-2 (8) (9)] These procedural requirements are essential since the agency head's decision, as noted earlier in this chapter, is final. The Civil Service Commission has warned that: "the agency should not start proceedings against an employee organization on the basis of unsupported or fragmentary allegations; and it should avoid being drawn into a challenge against an employee organization based on irrelevant or unsupported charges stemming from competition between organizations or factional disputes within an organization." [*381*, 711-2 (11)]

Although the state laws referred to above do not say so specifically, it could logically be argued that the labor relations agency is obligated to hear appeals against an agency head's refusal to recognize an employee organization for alleged misconduct. The basic question here is whether the employee organization meets the definition in the statute of "labor organization," and it would not be consistent with the other provisions of these laws to allow an agency head's decision on such a matter to be final. Furthermore, if there is provision for appeal to the courts from the determinations of the labor regulatory agency itself, this logically should include recognition cases of this type. In any event, the employee organizations are not apt to be satisfied with unreviewable decisions of agency heads on such matters. As the American Bar Association's Committee on Law of Government Employee Relations commented in its first report on the federal program: "The agencies, therefore, face a major test of their ability to be detached about problems concerning which their managers, as employers, feel deep, even emotional concern.Agencies have not always met the test of detachment." [*15*, p. 143]

### Requirements of New Canadian Legislation

Before leaving this subject, it is in order to summarize the pertinent provisions of the new Canadian legislation. [*350*, pp. 21-22] The Public Service Staff Relations Board may not certify any employee organization:

1. in the formation or administration of which the employer has participated, or is participating, to such an extent as to "impair its fitness to represent the interests of employees in the bargaining unit."

2. which receives from its employee members, handles or pays in its own name on their behalf, or requires as a condition of membership, the payment of "any money for activities carried on by or on behalf of any political party."

3. which "discriminates against any employee because of sex, race, national origin, colour or religion."

### Fair Labor Practices

If collective negotiations are to be successful, both management and the employee organizations must observe certain rules, commonly referred to as "fair labor practices." This terminology comes from the Wagner and Taft-Hartley Acts; under the Wagner Act, only unfair practices by the employers were listed, but Taft-Hartley balanced this by adding a section on unfair practices by the unions. Since the federal Code of Fair Labor Practices, as well as the new state laws referred to above, define unfair labor practices in much the same way as the Taft-Hartley law, a brief summary will be given of the latter's pertinent provisions.[*132*, p. 6] As to the employers, it is an unfair labor practice for them:

1. To interfere with, restrain, or coerce employees in the exercise of the rights guaranteed to them by the law. These

rights are "to form, join or assist labor organizations, to bargain collectively through representatives of their own choosing, and to engage in other concerted activities for the purpose of collective bargaining or other mutual aid or protection," and "to refrain from any or all of such activities."

2. To dominate or interfere with the formation or administration of any labor organization or contribute financial or other support to it.

3. To encourage or discourage membership in any labor organization, by discriminating in regard to hire or tenure of employment or any term or condition of employment.

4. To discharge or otherwise discriminate against an employee because he has filed charges or given testimony under the Act.

5. To refuse to bargain collectively with the representatives of his employees duly chosen under the procedures specified in the Act.

### Unfair Practices by Labor Organizations

The comparable list of unfair practices for labor organizations, omitting only one or two items not of great importance to the governmental environment, is as follows [*132*, pp. 6-7]:

1. To restrain or coerce the employees in the exercise of their right under the law to join unions and to bargain collectively through representatives of their own choosing, as well as to refrain from such activity except where the union shop exists as permitted by law.

2. To cause an employer to discriminate against an employee for non-membership in a union unless there is a legally authorized union shop contract.

3. To refuse to bargain collectively with the employer.

4. To force the employer or any other person to "cease using, selling, handling, transporting, or otherwise dealing in the products of any other producer, processor, or manufacturer, or to cease doing business with any other person."

5. To force or require any employer "to recognize or bargain with a particular labor organization as the representative of his employees if another labor organization has been certified as the representative of such employees."

6. To force or require any employer to assign certain work to employees in one union or craft rather than to those in another union or craft, unless "such employer is failing to conform to an order or certification of the Board determining the bargaining representative for employees performing such work."

If upon investigation the NLRB decides that a complaint of unfair labor practices has been sustained and the guilty party refuses to desist from the practices in question, it issues a cease and desist order, enforceable in federal court. With respect to prohibited union practices (4) and (5) above, it is required to seek an injunction against the union if it has reasonable cause to believe the charge is true.

### The Federal Code of Fair Labor Practices

The Code of Fair Labor Practices under the Kennedy Executive Order prohibits the agency managements from:

1. Interfering with, restraining, or coercing any employee in the exercise of his rights under the Order;

2. Encouraging or discouraging membership in any employee organization by discrimination in regard to hiring, tenure, promotion or other conditions of employment;

3. Sponsoring, controlling or otherwise assisting an employee organization, except for providing routine facilities such as billboard space;

4. Disciplining or otherwise discriminating against an employee because he has filed a complaint or given testimony under the Order or the Standards of Conduct for Employee Organizations or Code of Fair Labor Practices;

5. Refusing to accord appropriate recognition to an employee organization qualified for such recognition;

6. Refusing to hear, consult, confer, or negotiate with an employee organization as required by the Order.

The employee organizations are prohibited from:

1. Interfering with, restraining or coercing any employee in the exercise of his rights under the Order;

2. Attempting to induce the agency management to coerce any employee in the enjoyment of these rights;

3. Coercing or attempting to coerce, or disciplining, any member as punishment or reprisal for, or for the purpose of hindering or impeding the discharge of his duties as an officer or employee of the United States; calling or engaging in any strike, work stoppage, slowdown, or related picketing engaged in as a substitute for any such strike, work stoppage or slowdown, against the United States government;

4. Discriminating against any employee with regard to the terms or conditions of membership because of race, color, creed, or national origin;

5. If it has exclusive recognition, denying membership to any employee except for failure to meet reasonable occupational standards uniformly required for admission, or for failure to pay initiation fees and dues uniformly required as a condition of acquiring membership. [*381*, 711-2 (13) through (21)]

As noted previously, the agency sanction against unfair practices is to withdraw recognition; in case of strikes, the offending employees can be dismissed and otherwise punished under the 1955 law referred to in Chapter 4. The agency is required to try to settle unfair labor practice complaints, brought by either party, through informal means. If this fails and the agency is convinced that there is a "substantial basis" for the complaint, it is to hold a hearing presided over by hearing officers whom it selects.

Since the agency itself determines what is a "substantial basis for complaint" and also chooses the hearing officers, in the opinion of an American Bar Association Committee this tends "inherently to create the feeling among the parties that a fair and impartial review of the charges cannot be obtained under the code." Therefore, they recommend that "substantial basis" be changed to "reasonable basis," "thus lessening the burden of the charging party as well as the broad discretion of the agency to deny a hearing." [*16*, pp. 134-135] They also propose that ". . . the code be amended to give both agencies and unions the option of choosing an outside arbitrator or hearing officer or an inside hearing officer, in either event the designee to be the choice of both parties." [*16*, p. 133]

The Department of Labor has "adopted a procedure whereby

the agency chooses one member of a three-man panel, the union chooses the second member and those two members choose an impartial third person." [*16*, p. 132] Civil Service Commission Chairman Macy has suggested advisory arbitration to solve this problem of possible conflict of interest on the part of the hearing officer. Actually, very few cases have come up under the Code, although, as the Bar Association Committee says, "it may well be . . . that these procedures have discouraged the filing of charges." [*16*, p. 133]

In late February, 1967, in the first finding of its kind, charges of unfair labor practices against a high-ranking federal official were partially upheld by the Treasury Department. These charges were made in late 1966 by the National Federation of Federal Employees against James J. Saxon, then Comptroller of the Currency in the Treasury Department. According to the NFFE, its local in New York City had been denied formal recognition although it met the 10 per cent membership requirement. Saxon's view was that the NFFE did not have the necessary number of members; the problem was complicated by doubt over whether or not to count certain employees temporarily assigned to the New York office. Both parties requested one of Macy's assistants to count the NFFE members; he found the NFFE had the necessary membership, and recommended formal recognition to which Saxon agreed.

Shortly thereafter, Saxon again asked the NFFE "for proof of its 10 per cent membership, implying it didn't have sufficient members to warrant continued formal recognition," and, according to NFFE President Nathan Wolkomir, threatened to withdraw recognition, which action he later took. In its complaint, the NFFE also claimed that the first president of its New York local had been summarily ordered transferred to Billings, Montana, and that "NFFE members the agency could identify as such had not been given grade promotions."

Saxon, "an independent-minded official," flatly denied these charges. A formal hearing to determine the facts was held on November 10, 1966 in New York City by a hearing officer for the Treasury Department, and, in accordance with the present procedures, he was not authorized to make any recommendation but simply to turn over the evidence to Treasury Secretary Fowler.

When Acting Secretary of the Treasury, Joseph W. Barr,

handed down the decision, there was a new Comptroller, William B. Camp, because Saxon's term had expired and he was not a candidate for reappointment. The Treasury Department agreed with the NFFE that Saxon had erred in withdrawing formal recognition and ordered that it be restored. It also supported the examiner's finding that two NFFE members active in its New York local had been victims of "arbitrary and punitive transfers which were not justified." These transfers were cancelled and the Treasury promised that, if they were transferred in the future, it would be "in accord with the procedures and criteria applicable to all employees."

Although the decision made no mention of the NFFE contention that grade promotions had been capriciously withheld from its members, Wolkomir expressed general satisfaction with the outcome. [128] Nonetheless, some of the employee organizations still remain suspicious of the entire procedure, despite the outcome in this case.

One of the complaints made by the employee organizations is that, when impasses develop in the negotiations, the agency officials declare the matter closed. This is the contention of John F. Griner, head of the American Federation of Government Employees, who claims that "some federal agencies and officials have resisted entering into good-faith collective bargaining with properly-recognized unions." [163] The problem of impasses is considered in detail in Chapter 7; it is clear from the federal experience that the absence of disputes settlement machinery encourages the feeling that the bargaining is not meaningful.

### Prohibited Practices in the Canadian Federal Government

The new legislation [350, pp. 7-8] provides that no person:

1. . . . who is employed in a managerial or confidential capacity, whether or not he is acting on behalf of the employer, shall participate in or interfere with the formation or administration of an employee organization or the representation of employees by such an organization.

2. (shall) refuse to employ or to continue to employ any person, or otherwise discriminate against any person in regard to employment or any term or condition of employment because the person is a member of an employee organization or was or is exercising a right under this Act.

3. shall impose any condition on an appointment or in a contract of employment or propose the imposition of any condition on an appointment or in a contract of employment that seeks to restrain an employee or a person seeking employment from becoming a member of

an employee organization or exercising any right under this Act; ...or ... seek by intimidation, by threat of dismissal, or by any other kind of threat, or by the imposition of a pecuniary or any other penalty or by any other means to compel an employee...to become, refrain from becoming or cease to be, or . . . except as otherwise provided in a collective agreement, to continue to be a member of an employee organization, or to refrain from exercising any other right [under this Act, except that] no person shall be deemed to have contravened this subsection by reason of any act or thing done or omitted in relation to a person employed, or proposed to be employed, in a managerial or confidential capacity.

If upon investigation, the board finds that there has been a violation of these requirements, it may order corrective action. If the order is not complied with, the board is required to make a full report to the minister through whom it reports to Parliament, and the minister is to forward all the documents in the case to the Parliament. Apparently, it is anticipated that the possibility of exposure before Parliament will deter violations.

### Prohibited Practices in Recent State Laws

Most of the new state laws specify prohibited practices very similar to those in Taft-Hartley, using almost identical language. The Michigan Public Employment Relations Act, however, lists no unfair practices by labor organizations "on the theory that they are not necessary, as a public employer may discipline or discharge a striking employee." As Robert G. Howlett, head of the Michigan Labor Mediation Board points out: "This legislative concept with respect to labor organization unfair labor practices is not consistent with reality, for unfair labor practices may be directed against other employees, as well as employers; and employees have used means other than strikes to exert pressure on an employer, while refusing to engage in collective bargaining." [*114*, p. 7]

However, since the statute does define bargaining in good faith as a "mutual obligation of the employer and the representative of the employees," Howlett adds that "perhaps the union's obligation to bargain in good faith (a duty, but *not* an unfair labor practice) is enforceable in equity." [*114*, pp. 7-8]

The Delaware law contains no list of prohibited practices, simply stating that "no public employer, or other person, directly or indirectly, shall interfere with, restrain, coerce, or discriminate against any public employee in the free exercise of any right under this chapter." [*32*, p. 2] The feeling that the law is heavily weighted in favor of labor has discouraged some public officials in this state from making any statements to the employees which could in any way be interpreted as anti-union. The advantage of the law's listing unfair labor practices *on both sides* is that it should prevent misunderstandings of this type. In the private sector, there is a long history to this question of the employers' rights to free speech, but suffice it to say that the Taft-Hartley Act permits them to express their views about the unions without fear of being charged with an unfair labor practice unless they make an "actual threat of reprisal or force or promise of benefit." [*297*, p. 77]

The Connecticut and Massachusetts statutes authorize the state labor relations board, when it concludes that there has been a refusal to bargain collectively, to order fact finding and charge the full costs to the guilty party. [*30*, p. 328], [*31*, p. 559]

The Wisconsin law providing for collective bargaining in the municipalities authorizes fact finding "where an employer or union fails or refuses to meet and negotiate in good faith at reasonable times in a bona fide effort to arrive at a settlement." [*415*, p. 111-70] Not all the state statutes *require* the employer to bargain collectively; for example, the Wisconsin Employment Relations Board has ruled that under the 1962 statute, bargaining is voluntary with the municipal employer. [*36*, p. 30]

Actually, as experience in the private sector shows, it is very difficult to establish clearly that one of the parties has refused to bargain in good faith. As we saw in Chapter 3, the New York Transit Authority did not believe that Quill was bargaining in good faith when he reduced his original demands from an estimated $680 to $180 million. The city had offered $25 million, but ended up by agreeing to more than twice that amount. Perhaps at this stage, Quill was not bargaining in good faith, but his supporters will stoutly maintain that he was maneuvering in an effort to break a pattern of unfair treatment by the city of the members of his union. Of course, if one of the parties simply refuses to sit down and negotiate with the other, this clearly is an unfair labor practice. Industry experience may be no guide here, but, interestingly, a recent study of more than 1,000 cases closed by the NLRB during the five-year period ending June 30, 1962, shows that most employers "abide by their legal duty to bargain." [*253*] Particularly since collective negotiations are so new in the public service, a program of educating both sides as to their responsibilities is in order and should help avoid some of the complaints of unfair labor practices.

*The Enforcement Process.* Under the state laws, the process for enforcing fair labor practices is similar to that under Taft-Hartley, but the exact procedures vary depending on the state. In Michigan, complaints are made to the Labor Mediation Board which holds a hearing. If on the basis of the testimony it finds no justification for the complaint, it closes the case; if it concludes that a violation has taken place, it orders the guilty party to "cease and desist from the unfair labor practice, and to take such affirmative action, including reinstatement of employees with or without back pay, as will effectuate the policies of this act." If necessary, the Board may "petition the court of appeals for the enforcement of the order and for appropriate temporary relief or restraining order," and the court is to consider the Board's findings of fact conclusive "if supported by competent, material and substantial evidence on the record considered as a whole." At the same time, any person "aggrieved" by a final order of the Board can request the court of appeals to review the order, but again the Board's findings of fact must be accepted by the court on the same basis. [*344*, pp. 25-28]

Unlike the NLRB, the Michigan Labor Mediation Board does not itself investigate the charges; rather it weighs the evidence presented by the contending parties. It adopted this policy, not only because it lacks the funds to employ the necessary staff of trained investigators but also to avoid having to serve as both prosecutor and judge. [*114*, p. 11] This charge was repeatedly made of the NLRB until with the passage of Taft-Hartley, "the prosecuting function was removed from the Board and vested in a General Counsel who in this respect was made completely independent of the Board." [*297*, pp. 70-71] The NLRB has no mediation functions; this is the responsibility of the Federal Mediation and Conciliation Service.

The Wisconsin Employment Relations Board deals with unfair labor practice complaints in the same way as Michigan. Arvid Anderson reports that "under the Wisconsin procedure it is necessary for the parties to prosecute their own cases. This is distinct from the practices under the NLRB, where the government investigates the charge and, if it finds that such charge is meritorious, issues a complaint and prosecutes the case. If we were to adopt such a procedure, we could not at the same time retain the effectiveness of our mediation and informal fact-finding settlements in the same agency." [*136*]

There are really two issues here, (1) the need to separate the functions of judge and prosecutor, and (2) the problem of how to make acceptable the mediation services of an agency which also makes decisions on unfair labor practice complaints and thus inevitably alienates both labor and management from time to time. On the latter point, the problem in the states is that the volume of "labor relations board cases does not seem large enough to support separate agencies from a taxpayer point of view." [*297*, p. 255] Northrup and Bloom believe that "the work of multipurpose agencies like the Wisconsin Employment Relations Board would seem to indicate that conflicts [between the mediation and labor relations functions] are easily avoided by good administration, and an agency which is charged with various responsibilities can do all quite well." [*297*, p. 255]

### Bargaining Unit Determination

Far from being a routine question, determination of the bargaining unit is a matter of great concern to both the management and the employee organizations. Each wants the unit defined in that way it deems best serves its interests in the particular situation. Management sometimes prefers a large bargaining unit, perhaps to reduce the number of unions with which it will have to deal, or even in the hope that no union will have enough members in it to be declared the exclusive bargaining agent. On other occasions, it may prefer craft or occupational units. Similarly, the unions seek large or small units, depending on which arrangement suits their strategy. Since the employer and the union may not be in agreement on the unit, in the private sector, both in the United States and Canada, the final decision on this question is made by the labor relations agency.

As to public employers, they often prefer larger units for reasons of "administrative convenience, orderliness and effectiveness." The quoted words are from the report of the Rockefeller panel which, while it recognized that the employees' desires had to be considered, argued that governmental administrators could not ignore "this criterion of appropriateness" any more than private employers could escape the "compulsion" to "have the kind of administrative structure that contributes to their profit-making mission." [*107*, pp. 35-36] Fragmentation into numerous small bargaining units can also lead to jurisdictional fights between the different employee organizations and consequent unstable labor conditions which hamper the agency in its work.

Too, the more organizations the management has to negotiate with, the greater the danger that it will be pressured into granting more favorable terms to some groups of workers, thus alienating the others. The Rockefeller group warns against separate bargaining units requested by employee organizations that want to negotiate, for the "special benefit" of their members, "modifications or supplementations to the terms which are supposed to apply to a more comprehensive group of employees such as all employees of the State, or a city, or town, or county." This can produce a "crazy quilt of salary and wage and welfare benefits." [*107*, p. 28]

They believe that the "union" approach means "fragmentation" of the units of representation, whereas under civil service there is a "unitary rule system of job classification," with various occupational groups included in the same salary classifications. Thus, in their opinion, the "multiple-unit negotiation" favored by the unions not only is disorderly, but also carries a grave threat to the merit system. [*107*, pp.5-7]

From the employee organizations' standpoint, what is at stake is, first of all, the chance of having *an* exclusive bargaining agent and, second, of being designated as *the* agent. The individual workers, of course, also have an interest, because they may not want any exclusive representative or they may prefer a particular one. As to the Rockefeller panel's fear of "fragmentation," the employee leaders argue that this is unfounded and that the wages and other benefits which are negotiated can be fitted into the pattern of equal benefits for the same kinds of workers.

The employee organizations do not by any means always prefer small units, but this is the tendency during early organizing efforts when, as in the public service, their membership is relatively small. If, on the other hand, they command a sizeable membership, they may press for a large unit, in the expectation or hope that they will emerge as the bargaining agent for all these employees. Their strategy obviously will be adapted to the situation, and in some cases at least, the public employer may prefer a smaller unit than that sought by some employee organizations.

A very large unit increases the power of the exclusive agent, and the management may also deem it inappropriate for negotiating terms of employment for so many different kinds of workers. Furthermore, just as in industry, craft and professional groups tend to prefer separate units and to object to installation-wide and other large bargaining units in which they would be engulfed along with production, maintenance, and other workers.

### Experience in the United States Federal Government

The early experience under the federal program revealed a management preference for larger units, because most of the disputed unit cases "resulted from the tendency of some agencies to favor the largest possible unit, generally an entire installation." [*15*, p. 134] Either party may request the Secretary of Labor to nominate an arbitrator or arbitrators from lists maintained by the Federal Mediation and Conciliation Service, to investigate the facts and render advisory opinions as to what the bargaining unit should be. [*400*, p. 355] In its first report, the Labor Department's newly-created Office of Federal Employee-Management Relations stated that "the arbitrators in 15 of the 18 decisions found the units requested by the employee organizations to be appropriate. Agencies in each of the cases sought installation-wide or agency-wide units." [*392*, p. 3] These opinions, accepted in every case by the agency managements, "had a meaningful impact" on the evolution of the federal program, because other agencies which initially favored installation-wide units decided to accept "blue collar, white collar, pattern makers, inspectors and technical units where the facts support this type of unit." [*392*, p. 4]

The general picture is, however, still one in which the agencies usually prefer installation-wide units and the "unions continue to press for recognition in smaller and smaller units so as to increase the possibility of obtaining exclusive recognition." [*138*] In practice, activity-wide units, such as Air Force bases, shipyards, Veterans Administration hospitals, and Internal Revenue Service district offices, are very common, although smaller units are also frequently-established. [*379*]

TVA's agreement with the Tennessee Valley Trades and Labor Council provides that the director of personnel shall try to settle disputes "as to the employees who constitute an appropriate unit  or as to who is the duly authorized representative of a unit." If he fails to obtain agreement, "either party may invoke the services of an arbitrator secured through the Federal Mediation and Conciliation Service whose recommendation shall be accepted by all parties to the dispute."[*102*, p.5] The agreement with the Salary Policy Panel states that the "Director of Personnel resolves questions concerning the appropriateness of a proposed bargaining unit." Supplementary Agreement 1 deals with the classes of positions included in each unit, and makes clear that "disputes with respect to the assignment of new classes to defined bargaining units, the establishment of classes not assigned to any bargaining unit, or the designation of excluded positions will be resolved by the Director of Personnel." [*39*, p. 2, p.8]

### The Program in the Canadian Federal Government

Earlier in this chapter, it was noted that in Canada the Public Service Staff Relations Board will define the bargaining units. The new legislation states in detail the procedure to be followed by the Board. Bargaining units are to comprise all positions in given occupational groups throughout the "central administration" (the reader will recall from Chapter 2 that this includes all agencies except the few "separate employers"). The first step is for the Public Service Commission, within fifteen days of the Act's becoming effective, to "specify and define the several occupational groups within each occupational category . . . in such manner as to comprise therein all employees in the Public Service" to be represented by the Treasury Board as the employer, and for the PSSRB to specify, for each occupational category, the "day on and after which an application for certification as bargaining agent for a bargaining unit comprised of employees included in that occupational category may be made by an employee organization, which day shall not . . . be later than the sixtieth day" after the Act goes into effect. [*350*, p. 15]

"Occupational category" means the following, besides any others the Board finds necessary: (1) scientific and professional; (2) technical; (3) administrative and foreign service; (4) administrative support; and (5) operational. [*350*, p. 4] "In determining whether a group of employees constitutes a unit appropriate for collective bargaining, [the Board must consider the] duties and classification of the employees in the proposed bargaining unit in relation to any plan of classification as it may apply to the employees in the proposed bargaining unit." No one may be included who holds a position in a different occupational category from that represented by the other employees in the unit, but at any later date the Board will, "on application by the employer or any employee organization affected," decide any question "as to whether any employee or class of employees is or is not included therein or is included in any other unit." [*350*, pp. 18-19] During the "initial certification period," notices to bargain collectively may be filed only after the day specified for the occupational category in a staggered time schedule contained in the legislation. [*350*, p. 16, p. 53]

This is an interesting contrast with the United States federal government, where the installation so often is the bargaining unit. The Preparatory Committee did not think the industrial practice in Canada of recognizing units "local in character, encompassing employees in a particular 'plant' or 'establishment' in a particular community" was appropriate for the kind of government it has. "In the 'central administration,' the distribution of authority and responsibility dictated by Parliamentary control of funds and the collective responsibility of the Cabinet for expenditures would make it virtually impossible to establish an effective collective bargaining relationship on this basis. We have therefore come to the conclusion that the 'central administration' should be regarded as both a single employer and a single establishment." [*324*, p. 30] Its judgment was that "bargaining unit boundaries consistent with the occupational groups on which the new system of classification and pay is being based ... would make good sense." Furthermore, "they would assist the parties to relate rates of pay and conditions of employment in the Service to those prevailing outside, and would tend to ensure a concern for equitable relativities within the Service." [*324*, p. 31]

In comparing bargaining unit determination in the United States and Canadian federal governments, it should be remembered that in the United States the scope of bargaining does not include compensation, whereas in Canada it does. The activity-wide units in the United States thus do not lead to the "serious inequities in rates of pay and conditions of employment" the Canadian Preparatory Committee was anxious to avoid. This illustrates why unqualified statements cannot be made about the superiority of installation-wide over occupational bargaining units, or vice versa. The kind of government (presidential as against parliamentary), number of employees, scope of permissible negotiations, the structure and the ideologies of the employee organizations—all these and other factors have to be considered. Jurisdiction-wide bargaining with unions representing very large numbers of employees in certain occupations takes place in New York City, so it obviously has application in the United States also.

### Procedures Under the New State Laws

In collective negotiations in United States state and local governments, the public employer also often prefers the larger bargaining units. Under the new state laws, the employer must accept the bargaining unit as defined by the state agency which certifies the employee organization for representation purposes. This again illustrates the difference from the federal program under which each agency is the ultimate final authority, although none has ever rejected the arbitrator's decision in a unit case.

When the state labor relations agency receives a petition for the establishment of a bargaining unit and recognition of an exclusive agent, it holds a hearing, listens to the presentations of both parties, renders its decision on the bargaining unit, and orders the representation election. For example, on January 2, 1963, the Wisconsin Employment Relations Board, in ordering an election among employees of the Lincoln County highway department, stated that one of the "issues raised by the Municipal Employer" [the county] was whether the highway department constituted a separate division or department. The Board said: [416, p. 3]

> The evidence indicates that the County Highway Department is under the administrative supervision of the County Highway Commissioner, subject to the control of the County Highway Committee. The employees in the Department are under the supervision of no other executive officer of the Municipal Employer and engage in a separate and distinct function of the Municipal Employer. They perform work substantially different than work performed by other employees of the Municipal Employer. The Board concludes that the Highway Department is a distinct and separate department of the Municipal Employer and that employees in such department have a common interest in wages, hours and working conditions distinct and separate from the other employees of the Municipal Employer.

An interesting feature of the new Wisconsin legislation requiring collective bargaining in the state service is that the WERB can, if it so decides, permit the "employees involved" to "determine for themselves whether they desire to establish themselves as an appropriate collective bargaining unit." [*345*, p. 2]

The Connecticut law uses language quite similar to the Taft-Hartley Act in providing that the State Board of Labor Relations ". . . shall decide in each case whether, in order to insure to employees the fullest freedom in exercising the rights guaranteed by this act and in order to insure a clear and identifiable community of interest among employees concerned, the unit appropriate for purposes of collective bargaining shall be the municipal employer unit or any other unit thereof. . . ." [*30*, p. 327]

In Oregon, which is distinctive because the State Civil Service Commission certifies the bargaining agents, the Commission has adopted a rule providing that "all classified employees who are under the same appointing authority" shall constitute the unit, except that he "initially may consider requests for and, if justified by professional, geographical, organizational unit or other consideration affecting employment relations, authorize negotiating units on other than a total agency basis." The appointing authority is required to "post appropriate notice of his decision" on such requests, and "any affected employee or employees or their representatives" may appeal to the Civil Service Commission which "may sustain or set aside the decision." [*301*, 98-100]

In most cases, agency-wide units have been established, but smaller ones have been approved for such employee groups as radio technicians in the forestry department, nurses at the state hospital, engineers in the highway department, physical and occupational therapists employed by the Workmen's Compensation Board, and electricians and plumbers at the University of Oregon. [*139*] Some observers believe that an unsuccessful court challenge by the AFL-CIO of the constitutionality of the 1965 collective bargaining statute was largely motivated by this Commission rule which does encourage the concept of total agencies as negotiating units. The Oregon State Employees Association has been winning the representation elections because of its substantial membership superiority over the individual AFL-CIO unions.

*Criteria Followed.* The criteria used by the NLRB in defining bargaining units—the history of collective bargaining between the parties, if any, and the mutuality of interest of the employees—are being used as a general framework of reference.

The Delaware law, for example, states that the Department of Labor and Industrial Relations "in determining, modifying or combining the bargaining unit, [shall] consider the duties, skills, and working conditions of the public employees; the history of collective bargaining by the public employees and their bargaining representatives; the extent of organization among the employees; and the desire of the public employees." [*32*, pp. 2-3]

The Connecticut State Board of Labor Relations, in a very clear presentation of the issues involved [*77*, p. 2], states that it takes into account the following factors:

1. *Agreements by the parties.* Since the study group which drafted the law believed that "questions of this nature should be governed by agreement of the parties where agreement can be had," the Board will ratify such agreements "unless the resulting unit clearly contravenes the policy of the Act."

2. *The similarity (or dissimilarity) of work and working conditions.* "Whether the work is clerical or manual (white collar or blue collar); whether there is common supervision; whether the work is performed in a single location; are examples of the sort of things the Board will look for and try to weigh. Obviously these considerations may sometimes pull in opposite directions. Employees in the same department may, for instance, perform different kinds of work, and work classifications often cut across department lines."

3. *The convenience of the municipal employer* in the light of its personnel and other relevant policies and practices. The Board rejected a blue collar unit alone in the Greenwich public works department, "when the Town showed that this would disrupt its policy of uniform treatment for all employees in the work classifications involved, many of whom were in other departments, and where there appeared to be no countervailing consideration."

4. *Past bargaining history, if any.* While the "municipal employer's past practices and patterns of negotiation and recognition" are not legally binding, "nevertheless they have some tendency to show what the parties themselves have considered appropriate and feasible and what they are used to." The Board also gives some consideration to the

"patterns worked out in other cities and towns," and also to "the employee organization's over-all pattern [in this country] . . . since it has at least a slight tendency on pragmatic grounds to show something about feasibility and about the kind of unit which the organization can effectively represent."

5. *The desires of the members of a group* to be associated together for bargaining purposes.

6. *The desirability of keeping the unit as broad as possible,* "where that is consistent with the need for community of interest, and respect for legitimate special interests." This is one of the guidelines set forth by the interim commission which drafted the statute. [*323*, p. 15]

*Special Problems of Police and Fire Personnel.* In some cases, the law itself prescribes separate units for certain kinds of employees; for example, the Connecticut statute provides that uniformed and investigatory employees of the fire department and uniformed and investigatory employees of the police department shall each be in separate units. [*30*, p. 327] Even here, however, the Connecticut Board had to decide whether this prevented putting clerical and non-uniformed employees in the same unit as the uniformed and investigatory personnel. Its decision was to approve a department-wide unit where "sought by the employee organization filing the petition," but also to confine the unit to uniformed and investigatory personnel where "that is what those members or their representatives seek." [*77*, pp. 3-4]

The Maine Fire Fighters Arbitration Law states that the bargaining unit recognized by the state Commissioner of Labor and Industry shall include "all of the members of the municipal fire department." [*343*, 672-2] The definition of "employee" contained in the statute also has a bearing here, as in the case of the Wisconsin law applying to municipalities, which includes all municipal employees "except city and village policemen, sheriff's deputies, and county traffic officers." [*415*, p. 2120] This may prevent the establishment of any department-wide unit in departments employing such personnel.

### The Problem of Professional Employees

The size and nature of the bargaining unit also depend upon the decision as to where to place professional employees. Industry experience has provided a general guide; under Taft-Hartley, the NLRB may not place professional and non-professional employees in the same unit unless a majority of the former vote for such inclusion. [*132*, p. 10] The governing consideration here is that there may not be "mutuality of interest" between the two kinds of workers.

The Kennedy Order stipulates that, "except where otherwise required by established practice, prior agreement, or special circumstances," no unit shall be established for exclusive recognition which includes "both professional employees and nonprofessional employees unless a majority of such professional employees vote for inclusion in such unit." [*400*, pp. 352-353]

The United States Civil Service Commission points out that the definition of professional employees should not be difficult in the case of those holding positions under the Classification Act of 1949, since the Commission's *Handbook of Occupational Groups and Series of Classes* can be consulted. Most of the professional positions not under the Classification Act are easily identified, such as the physicians, dentists, and nurses in the Veterans Administration. For doubtful cases, the Commission suggests that the agencies may find helpful the definition contained in the Taft-Hartley Act: [*378*, 5. 17-5. 18]

> (a) ... any employee engaged in work (i) predominantly intellectual and varied in character as opposed to routine mental, manual, mechanical, or physical work; (ii) involving the consistent exercise of discretion and judgment in its performance; (iii) of such a character that the output produced or the result accomplished cannot be standardized in relation to a given period of time; (iv) requiring knowledge of an advanced type in a field of science or learning customarily acquired by a prolonged course of specialized intellectual instruction and study in an institution of higher learning or a hospital, as distinguished from a general academic education or from apprenticeship or from training in the performance of routine mental, manual, or physical processes; or (b) any employee, who (i) has completed the courses of specialized intellectual instruction and study described in clause (iv) of paragraph (a), and (ii) is performing related work under the supervision of a professional person to qualify himself to become a professional employee as defined in ... (a).

In the Canadian federal service, since the new law initially prohibits placing positions with different occupational content in the same bargaining unit, professional workers will not be intermingled with any others. Ultimately, the composition of a bargaining unit will depend upon the decisions of the Public Service Staff Relations Board, and it is conceivable but unlikely that the

Board could include subprofessionals with professionals in the same bargaining unit.

The Connecticut and Massachusetts laws use the Taft-Hartley definition word-for-word, except that the Massachusetts law omits section (b), and both laws provide that a majority vote of the professional employees is required to include them in a unit with nonprofessionals. In the other states with collective bargaining legislation, the state labor relations agency takes into account the desires of the professional employees in determining the negotiating units.

Illustrating again that the words of the statute seem almost always to make different interpretations possible, the Connecticut State Board of Labor Relations had to decide whether *all* professionals had to be polled together, or the members of *each profession* had to be polled separately. It decided that the legislature must have intended separately, because, as one example, it could not have meant that doctors should be put in a unit including nonprofessionals because they were outvoted by nurses and librarians. [*77*, p. 4]

On the other hand, the law is sometimes criticized as inflexible. In Wisconsin, in determining bargaining units in municipal governments, the Wisconsin Employment Relations Board cannot under the law include craft employees in a unit with other workers. The WERB has defined craft employees to include professional workers, such as teachers, nurses, and engineers. Arvid Anderson believes that this provision of the law has led to excessive fragmentation of bargaining units and created "unnecessary union competition." [*37*, p. 6] Significantly, the new Wisconsin law applying to state employees provides that the Board will determine "whether the employees engaged in a single or several departments, divisions, institutions, crafts, professions, or occupational groupings, constitute an appropriate collective bargaining unit," and that it need not ascertain the wishes of the employees involved. [*345*, p. 2]

In the federal service, most professionals have voted not to join units which include nonprofessionals, but they frequently have affiliated with national unions which have nonprofessional members. The American Federation of Government Employees (AFL-CIO) has many professional employee members, some in combined units, and others in separate units. Professional employees may, of course, form their own organizations and ask to be represented through them only, and at all levels of government the advent of collective negotiations is spurring formation of such groups and strengthening their role.

### Inclusion of Supervisors in Bargaining Units

Since there inevitably will be differences of opinion between the management and the employees to resolve, the question arises as to whether supervisors should be included in the bargaining unit, and who is a "supervisor" as distinguished from the other employees. If supervisors are indiscriminately allowed in the unit, they may conceivably end up negotiating with themselves, depending on their policymaking role within the management. Even if they have no direct role in determining management attitudes towards employee organization requests, they may be suspected of sympathizing with the management and even being its "stooges." Another question is whether supervisors should be allowed to form their own unions, or to join *any* employee organization.

In industry, supervisors from the foreman level up are usually excluded from the bargaining units when the issue is decided by the NLRB, but by mutual agreement between unions and managements in the skilled trades, such as construction, printing, and metal trades, first line foremen are commonly included. In maritime and transportation occupations a variety of supervisors are represented by unions, usually of a craft nature. Such similar examples exist in motion pictures, newspapers, radio, and television as directors' guilds or unions.

In considering this problem, the Canadian Preparatory Committee on Collective Bargaining in the Public Service "... found itself in largely uncharted seas. There are few industrial precedents to which it could turn with any sense of assurance, for in private industry the most deeply-rooted and widely accepted practices governing managerial exclusions are those applying to production and maintenance operations of one kind or another. Practices applying to large-scale organizations in which office employees are predominant, and in which supervisory relationships form a complicated and continuous spectrum, have yet to fall in a clearly discernible mould." [*324*, p. 32]

The same comment can be made about the United States; Wilson R. Hart writes [*110*, pp. 184-185]:

> The dividing line between labor and management or between workers and supervisors is much more clearly drawn in industry than

in government. Civil-service laws, rules, and regulations generally apply without differentiation, to both workers and supervisors. Both are covered by the same leave systems, the same pay systems, the same pension plans, and the same operating rules.

Industry is more likely to accentuate the dividing line between the two categories of personnel by assigning them to different systems and subjecting them to different company rules. Perhaps as a result of the different relationship which exists in government, government employee unions have not generally followed the normal trade-union practice of restricting eligibility for membership to non-supervisory workers. The only eligibility requirement laid down by most government employee unions is that the member or applicant for membership must be on the federal pay roll. Presumably even the President of the United States could qualify. While no presidents have ever joined, there have been instances where high-ranking presidential appointees, including the heads of independent agencies, have become government employee union members. To satisfy oneself that this situation differs radically from the practice which prevails in industry, one need only reflect upon the probable reaction if Henry Ford or one of his vice presidents were to apply for membership in the United Automobile Workers.

This, of course, does not mean that there is no problem of possible "conflict of interest" in including supervisors. Rather it means that in government it is much more difficult to identify the positions in which such conflicts might arise.

*In the United States Federal Government.* The Kennedy Executive Order provides that "except where otherwise required by established practice, prior agreement, or special circumstances," no unit for exclusive negotiations may include managerial executives, employees engaged in personnel work in other than a purely clerical capacity, and "both supervisors who officially evaluate the performance of employees and the employees whom they supervise." [*400*, pp. 352-353] The right to be included in a bargaining unit and the right to join an employee organization are separate matters; the Order protects the right of all employees, including supervisors and other management officials, to join organizations which include rank and file workers.

The Civil Service Commission has advised the agencies that there should be very few exceptions to this policy of not including executives, supervisors, and personnel workers in exclusive bargaining units. As a general guide for defining "managerial executive," it offers the following: *"persons who make or recommend management policies or who direct, control, or supervise Government operations or personnel, and those associated with or assisting in such direction or control."* [*378*, p. 5. 12] For help in identifying "supervisory" positions, it suggests the agencies consult the Supervisory Grade Evaluation Guide in the first volume of the Commission's *Position Classification Standards*. These standards stress responsibility for assigning work to, and making personnel action recommendations concerning subordinate employees. [*378*, p. 5. 18] If they disagree with agency decisions as to excluded positions, the employee organizations can request advisory arbitration, but up to now this has been a minor element in their petitions for such arbitration.

*Policy on Conflicts of Interest.* The most difficult problem has been in making decisions under section 1 (b) of the Kennedy Order, which provides that "the rights described in this section [to "form, join, and assist any employee organization"] do not extend to participation in the management of an employee organization, where such participation or activity will result in a conflict of interest or otherwise be incompatible with law or with the official duties of an employee." [*400*, p. 350]

Since such conflicts arise when someone active in the management of an employee organization also has a part in determining agency policies, the Civil Service Commission logically concludes that "the most likely groups to be affected" are managerial executives, as defined above. However, regardless of the nature of the position, the agency must be convinced that an actual or potential conflict of interest exists.

Actually, conflicts of interest may also be found in some nonsupervisory positions, such as "budget analysts, manpower planners, management analysts, and internal investigators and auditors." Participation in the management of the employee organization "clearly includes holding office" in it or serving as its representative; otherwise "there are many other activities to consider," and the agency should distinguish between "ordinary membership activities and activities associated with leading, organizing, policy making, and representing employee groups." [*378*, p. 5. 12, 5. 13] Even though a supervisor cannot be included in the same bargaining unit as the workers whose services he officially evaluates, he can participate in the management of the union if "his supervisory duties do not involve sufficiently significant management responsibilities to lead to a conflict of interest between his role in the union and his role as a supervisor." [*378*, p. 5. 19]

In its regulations, the United States Department of Health, Education and Welfare provides that the decision as to whether conflicts of interest exist "shall be made on a case-by-case basis by management after discussion with the official concerned." Conflicts are deemed to exist when an official of an employee organization or one who actively represents it "either (a) has continuing responsibility as a management official for making administrative decisions or formal recommendations on cases or policies advocated by the same or a similar employee organization," and the conflict is "immediate and real, not remote and theoretical" or (b) has continuing responsibility as a management official for dealing with officers and representatives of the same or a similar organization. [*386*, 711-1-20, p. 3]

John Macy, chairman of the Civil Service Commission, believes that the agencies have generally been consistent in their conflict of interest determinations and that "differences in organization, in delegation of authority, and in the type of work properly account for most variations." He grants, however, that it is a "knotty question," and in fact some of the most severe criticism of the federal program has been directed at this phase of it. [*157*, p. 65]

Nathan T. Wolkomir, president of the National Federation of Federal Employees, claims that thousands of federal employees are being deprived of their right to hold office in employee organizations. He considers the conflict of interest precautions a "borrowed private-sector union concept which is inappropriate to the government relationship," and for this and other reasons he recommends creation of a three-man independent review board, appointed by the President, to issue rules and regulations guaranteeing uniform administration of the labor-management relations program. [*162*] A bill introduced in 1965 by former Representative Morrison of Louisiana would have required "management at all levels" to "exercise utmost concern to the end that no employee will be excluded or discouraged from holding an employee organization office unless the likelihood of his being 'placed in a position of bargaining with himself' is real and proximate, not merely hypothetical or remote." [*92*, p. 4]

*Organizations of Supervisors.* Under Taft-Hartley, supervisors can form unions of their own, but the prohibitions against employer interference with the rights of "self-organization" and collective bargaining do not apply in this case. The reasoning is that supervisors, as official representatives of the management, should not put themselves in a position where they are pitted against it. Although the Kennedy Order does not say anything specifically about exclusive recognition rights for units made up entirely of supervisors, they have been granted in some agencies. General practice, however, is to give such units formal recognition and consultation privileges only. Macy comments that there is "doubt as to proper policy" on this matter, and it is one of the items for clarification in any revision of the federal program. [*157*, p. 66]

### Canadian Federal Government Practice

Although with respect to "managerial exclusions" the Preparatory Committee could find no sure guides in industrial experience, it did not dismiss as inconsequential the conflict-of-interest problem. It recommended that all individuals with significant management responsibilities, or serving in confidential capacities to management, be excluded from the bargaining units. [*324*, p. 32]

Its specific proposals are incorporated in the new legislation which, in excluding persons employed in a managerial capacity from bargaining units, enumerates the following: [*350*, pp. 4-5]

1. Those serving in positions confidential to the Governor General, any Minister, judge of the Supreme or Exchequer Court, or deputy department head or "the chief executive officer of any other portion of the Public Service;"

2. Legal officers in the Department of Justice;

3. Any other person in the service "who in connection with an application for certification of a bargaining agent... is designated by the Board, or who in any case where a bargaining agent... has been certified by the Board is designated in prescribed manner by the employer, or by the Board on objection thereto by the bargaining agent, to be a person" who: (a) has executive duties; (b) whose responsibilities include those of a personnel administrator or directly involve him "in the process of collective bargaining on behalf of the employer;" (c) is required to "deal formally on behalf of the employer" with grievance cases filed under the Act; (d) is employed in a position confidential to any person described in (2) through (3) (c) above; and (e) who is not described in (3) (a) through (d) but "who in the opinion of the Board should not be included in a bar-

gaining unit by reason of his duties and responsibilities to the employer."

Rates of pay and conditions of work for those excluded from bargaining units will be established by the employer, with the managerial personnel having access to some sort of consultation machinery to be provided outside the framework of the Public Service Staff Relations Act.

While managerial employees, under the terms of the Act, share in its guarantees to every employee of the right to join employee organizations, they cannot be members of a bargaining unit. Furthermore, as previously stated in this chapter, it is a prohibited practice for "managerial employees," as defined, to participate in the formation or administration of employee organizations, or in the representation of the interests of their members. It should be noted that this Act does not exclude supervisors, as such, from bargaining units.

*Under the New State Laws.* The Connecticut law [*30,* p. 327] provides that the State Board of Labor Relations, in the event of a disagreement between the municipal employer and an employee organization, shall decide whether supervisory or other positions are covered by the Act. It specifies that the Board shall consider among other criteria whether the principal duties of the position are concerned with: (a) such management duties as assigning and reviewing the work of subordinate employees; (b) doing work which is distinct and dissimilar from that performed by the subordinates; (c) exercising judgment in adjusting grievances, applying personnel policies and procedures, and enforcing collective bargaining agreements; and (d) "establishing or participating in the establishment of performance standards for subordinate employees and taking corrective measures to implement" them. These criteria, however, "shall not necessarily apply to police and fire departments."

So far, there have been few disagreements on this matter between the parties, and, where they have occurred, they have usually involved the police and fire departments. The Board's policy is to include in the unit officers below the rank of chief and deputy or assistant chief if the petitioner so requests, and there is no evidence that the officers themselves object.

The reasoning is that it is the chief or the chief and the police commissioners who exercise "ultimate disciplinary authority," and the officers and the men have undergone the same experience and "share the traditions of the department." All officers move up through the ranks on the basis of seniority, and they often work together with the patrolmen, exposing themselves to the same dangers. On occasion those of lower rank are even required to perform the same duties as their superiors. "In the case of firemen, officers live, sleep and eat with the men. All this has led to departmental *esprit de corps*, and to a strong feeling of community of interest among officers and men. Every patrolman has a very real chance to become an officer; every officer has been a patrolman." [77, p. 6] Moreover, throughout the country organizations of policemen and firemen have traditionally included both the officers and the men.

The Michigan law excludes "executive or supervisory positions" from the bargaining units, with the State Labor Mediation Board defining the jobs which fall in this category. The statute does specifically state that in fire departments, "no person subordinate to a fire commission, fire commissioner, safety director, or other similar agency or administration shall be deemed to be a supervisor." [344, p. 25]

Although the Wisconsin law covering municipalities does not define "employee" to exclude supervisors, the Wisconsin Employment Relations Board has so ruled, arguing that "should supervisors be included in the same bargaining unit with employees they supervise, said individuals would be in a position either to prefer the interest of employees over that of the municipal employer or to prefer the interest of the municipal employer as the agents thereof over that of the employees." Furthermore, the ballots of the supervisors could affect the results of representation elections, and, as "supervisors," presumably even the chief executive officers of the municipality would have a right to be in the same bargaining unit as other employees. [417, pp. 4-5] The Wisconsin State Employment Labor Relations Act does exclude "employees who are performing in a supervisory capacity, and individuals having privy to confidential matters affecting the employer-employee relationship, as well as all employees of the board." [345, p. 3]

In Oregon, the Civil Service Commission's rules read that "a negotiating unit shall not include those employees who otherwise would be in the unit but who are (a) management and supervisory employees designated by the appointing authority to represent, assist or advise him in collective negotiations; (b) employees who occupy a position of special trust and confidence involving matters of a confidential nature; and (c) temporary and emergency employees."

When a representation election is announced by the civil service director, the appointing authority must post a list of proposed excluded positions. Any affected employee can appeal to the civil service director, who conducts a "fact-finding" hearing and submits his recommendation to the Commission, whose decision is final. [*301*, p. 1] The Commission believes that this rule has generally worked out well, although it has had to restrain some appointing officers who wanted to exclude practically all supervisors. It considers that the following memorandum to all section supervisors by the chairman of the State Tax Commission is a very good interpretation of the rule: [*302*]

> Attached for your information is the list of excluded positions from the proposed negotiating unit. The Commission carefully considered each supervisory position for exclusion but we believed each supervisor and employee should have the right to participate in the negotiating unit *unless the individual would be directly involved in negotiating with the elected employee representative.* Your inclusion within the unit does not mean you are not an integral part of management. Your inclusion does mean that even though you are a supervisor and part of management, you can participate fully in the negotiating unit.

*Participation in Employee Organizations.* The Wisconsin State Employment Relations Act provides: "It shall not be a prohibited practice, however, for an officer or supervisor of the state employer to remain or become a member of the same labor organization of which its employees are members, when they perform the same work or are engaged in the same profession, provided, that after 4 years from the effective date of this subchapter said supervisor shall not participate as an active member or officer of said organization." [*345*, p. 5]

The Connecticut State Board of Labor Relations has ruled that an employee organization which permits supervisors excluded from the bargaining unit to be officers or active members is not a "lawful association" under the Act. The Board grants that this is not a prohibited practice on the part of employee organizations under the law, but it argues that, in using the words "lawful association," the legislature must have meant an organization "which is so constituted and organized that it is fully capable of serving the law's policy to have a disinterested and independent bargaining representative for employee units which want representation." An organization which "acquiesces in or permits voting membership or office-holding by supervisors excluded from the bargaining unit" simply does not meet this standard. [77, p. 9]

In Oregon, where some management officials have also been leaders in the state employees' association, the latter has amended its constitution so that, as explained by Executive Secretary Thomas C. Enright: [140]

> If at any time a competent tribunal or court holds that our right to represent employees is curtailed by membership in the association of management personnel, these people will automatically be shifted to "associate" membership, without the right to vote or hold office.

The associations have traditionally included supervisors and other management officials in their membership, whereas most labor-affiliated employee organizations follow the "union" approach of denying most such persons membership. The decision in Connecticut cited above relies heavily on industry precedents. So, in addition to the disagreements between the public employer and the employees, there is again the complicating factor of the differing approaches of the "associations" and the "unions."

### Representation Elections

Throughout this chapter, frequent references have been made to representation elections. Here again there are many policy questions to resolve, such as: Should such elections be held and, if so, under what circumstances? Should a space for "No Union" be on the ballot, along with the names of the employee organizations qualified to participate in the election? What percentage of the votes should be required for designation as the exclusive bargaining agent? Should decertification elections be permitted and on what grounds? How often should representation elections be allowed? These are the principal questions, but there are many others concerned with the detailed conduct of the elections which will be mentioned later in this chapter.

### *In the United States Federal Government*

In Chapter 4, mention was made of the provisions in the Kennedy Order for formal recognition, dependent on a stable membership in the unit of at least 10 per cent, and for exclusive recognition, based on selection by a majority of those in the unit. [400, pp. 351-353] Since the Order itself makes no mention of elections, this is a matter for determination by the individual agencies, in accordance with the advice of the United States Civil Service Commission.

Elections are never held to determine formal and informal recognition, because the determination here is upon the basis of membership, not votes. Memberships naturally rise and dip, presenting some problem in defining "stable membership," and the Commission's view is that "nothing limits management from asking for re-verification at any time if it wishes; however, the organization should not be arbitrarily or capriciously asked to demonstrate that it meets the requirement." [*378*, p. 5. 10]

The Commission leaves to the agencies the selection of the means of verifying employee organization claims as to membership. The agencies examine such evidence as: certified copies of the payment reports of employee organizations to their national headquarters; affidavits from these national headquarters; reports of audits made of the organization treasurer's records; and data secured by any other method acceptable to the employee organization. The Commission warns that "when the majority determination is made by other means than an election, management must assure itself that a majority of all the employees of the unit wish to be represented by the employee organization." [*378*, p. 509]

The Department of Health, Education, and Welfare requires a secret ballot election when two or more employee organizations are seeking exclusive recognition in the same unit, but if only one organization is involved, it permits "secret ballot, authorization card check, membership list check or other means acceptable to the official who would accord recognition." [*386*, p. 711-3-40]

*Labor Department Rules and Procedural Guide.* As stated at the beginning of this chapter, either the agency or the employee organization can request the Secretary of Labor to arrange for advisory arbitration of disputed representation cases. Using the authority granted him in the Kennedy Order, the Secretary of Labor has promulgated rules for the nomination of arbitrators which "require both agencies and employee organizations to process requests for exclusive recognition and the nomination of arbitrators in an expeditious and orderly manner." For example, these rules set deadlines for employee organization requests for the nomination of arbitrators and also for agency action on requests for exclusive recognition.

The Department of Labor's Office of Federal Employee-Management Relations, created to carry out the functions vested in the Secretary by the Order, has issued a *Procedural Guide for Majority Status Determination under Section 11 of the Order*. While it need not be followed by the agencies, in practice it is—particularly when there are disagreements between the management and an employee organization, or between competing employee organizations. Essentially, the Guide establishes standards and procedures to guarantee fair elections. Requests for advisory arbitration are rejected if the agency has conducted elections in conformance with these requirements, because the Labor Department does not believe that it should provide arbitrators "for the sole purpose of reexamining election procedures or redetermining majority status simply because an employee organization did not agree with the particular procedures used."

Specifically, the Guide provides for election agreements to cover the following: (a) schedules for release of employees from work for voting; (b) determination of position on the ballot; (c) mail balloting, where necessary; (d) appointment of observers for each party; (e) thorough check of voter eligibility lists; (f) challenge ballot procedure; (g) period for posting notices prior to the election; (h) notice of election; (i) safeguarding of ballots and ballot box before and after election, and during recesses or intervals; (j) procedures for the tally of ballots; and (k) a period after the election during which objections may be filed.

All of this is explained, and there are numerous appendices including a sample election agreement and sample ballots. [*392*, pp. 5-6] Where more than one employee organization seeks recognition, in addition to listing them over separate squares the ballot also has a "No Union" square.

*Election Problems.* In the private sector, the NLRB will not hold elections unless there is a "showing of interest;" specifically, evidence must be presented, usually through authorization card checks, that at least 30 per cent of the employees in the unit want an election. The purpose is to avoid wasting time with elections in which no employee organization stands a chance of getting a majority vote. The NLRB originally ruled that the word "majority" in the Wagner Act meant the majority of those eligible to vote, but, when it found that some employers were coercing the workers not to vote, it re-defined it to mean a majority of the votes cast. Neither the Civil Service Commission nor the Labor Department requires the agencies to follow the NLRB rule on "showing of interest," but some departments have incorporated it into their regulations.

The disagreements in the federal service have been over (1) the so-called "60 per cent rule," and (2) whether or not runoff elections should be permitted. When the program went into effect, the employee organizations argued that NLRB practices should be followed and that, for an election to be valid, no set percentage of eligible voters need participate. The Kennedy Temporary Committee on the Implementation of the Federal Employee-Management Relations Program disagreed and instead recommended that 60 per cent of the eligible voters be required to participate.

The Civil Service Commission endorsed the 60 per cent rule, but not on an inflexible basis, because its guidelines state that "in particular situations, an agency might determine that a percentage slightly less than 60 per cent is representative." Furthermore, the rule does not apply if an absolute majority of the employees in the unit votes for one organization; using the Commission's example, "if only 52 per cent voted of those eligible to vote, the agency still should grant exclusive recognition if 51 per cent [of those who voted] voted for one union." [*378*, p. 5. 11] In industry, the voter turnout is usually heavy, so the danger of a union's winning the election with very small support is not very great. Nonetheless, some of the employee organizations are strongly opposed to the 60 per cent rule, because from their standpoint it is an obstacle to their growth and strength.

The Temporary Committee also opposed use of runoff elections as under the NLRB where, if none of the choices on the ballot receives a majority of the votes cast, a second election is held between the two front runners. The Committee's reasoning was that the disappointed organizations could qualify for formal recognition, not available in industry. But in its first report on the Kennedy program, the American Bar Association revealed: [*16* p. 137]

> At least four elections in which two unions were on the ballot have resulted in such close finishes that a relatively small number of "no union votes" has prevented either union from winning a majority. Analysis of two of these cases shows that in one of them 86% of the employees wished exclusive representation by one of the unions, 5%

wanted neither union, and 9% did not vote. In the other case, 92%
of the unit members wanted exclusive representation, 5% wanted no
union, and 3% abstained. . . . The unions involved . . . have preferred
to gamble on exclusive recognition, and in nearly all cases have
sought run-offs.

The Civil Service Commission later changed its policy, and
runoff elections are now permitted. However, the question then
arose as to whether the 60 per cent rule applied to runoff elections. In a later report, the Bar Association pointed to " . . . two
elections in which sixty per cent of the employees voted and
there was a valid election. There were three choices on the ballot,
two employee organizations and no union. The two employee organizations received the most votes but did not receive a majority of the eligible voters. . . . In both instances the agencies
involved contended that for the second election to be valid there
was a necessity of having a sixty per cent vote; on the other
hand, one of the labor organizations contended that . . . this
would in essence be giving the employees who voted non-union
another opportunity to cast such a ballot for no union by not
voting." [*16*, p. 136]

In one of these cases, the agency refused to hold the runoff
until the 60 per cent problem was solved, and one of the employee organizations requested a ruling from the Commission.
On May 23, 1966, the Commission advised the agencies that the
60 per cent rule was not needed in a "runoff election situation
when such election is held following an initial election in which
60 per cent or more of the employees present and eligible voted."
Its reasoning was that "in the previous election the question of a
representative vote had been settled." [*383*]

In accordance with Section (3) (b) of the Kennedy Order,
the Commission's guidelines provide that elections need not
be held more than once in any twelve-month period; this also is
the NLRB policy. The reasoning is to avoid fruitless elections
requested by over-optimistic employee leaders. Decertification
elections are provided for in the agencies' regulations; in the
Department of HEW, the regulations provide: [*386*, 711-3-20]

Redetermination of an employee organization's continued eligibility
for exclusive recognition shall be made by secret ballot when:

1. A petition signed by 30 per cent of the employees in the unit
   requesting a redetermination election is received, and
   a. one year has elapsed since a determination was made as to the em-
      ployee organization's eligibility for exclusive recognition and a basic
      agreement has not been signed at the installation, or

b. when a basic agreement has been signed and the redetermination petition is received between the 90th and the 60th day prior to the terminal date of the agreement or two years, whichever is earlier, or

2. Unusual circumstances exist which will substantially affect the unit or the majority representation.

### In the Canadian Federal Government

In Canada, the Public Service Staff Relations Board will certify exclusive bargaining agents when it is "satisfied that a majority of employees in the bargaining unit wish the employee organization to represent them." In verifying majority membership, the Board may: (1) examine evidence submitted to it by the employee organizations; (2) itself "make or cause to be made such examination of records or make such inquiries as it deems necessary;" (3) review documents relating to the constitution or articles of association of the petitioning organization; and (4) "in its sole discretion," direct that a representation vote be taken.

If the Board decides an election is necessary, it determines which employees are eligible to vote and makes "such arrangements and gives such directions" as it finds appropriate for the conduct of the election. [*350*, pp. 19-20] Thus, presumably it will directly hold, or supervise, the elections. Decertification elections are contemplated, because the Board's regulations will cover applications not only for certification, but also for revocation of certification of bargaining agents. [*350*, p. 12]

Since the bargaining units are to be established on a staggered time basis, no employee organization may request exclusive bargaining status before the date on which the employees in the unit became eligible for collective bargaining. If a collective agreement or an arbitral award applying to the unit is in effect and is to last not more than two years, the request can be made only within the last two months of the duration of such agreement or award.

If the duration is more than two years, the request must be made during the twenty-third and twenty-fourth months, or during the last two months preceding the end of each year it continues to operate after the second year, or after the beginning of the last two months of its operation. If the collective agreement provides for automatic continuation for a "further term or successive terms if either party fails to give the other notice of termination," an employee organization may apply to represent "any of the employees in the bargaining unit to whom the collective agreement applies" at any of the times specified above, or "during the two-month period immediately preceding the end of each year that the collective agreement continues to operate after the term specified therein." [*350*, pp. 17-18]

The Canadians obviously anticipate some agreements of fairly long duration. In the United States federal service, more than 90 per cent of the agreements are for one year, subject to automatic renewal for an equal period.[*388*, p. 11]

### In United States State and Local Governments

In Connecticut and Massachusetts, if the state labor relations agency finds that "a question of representation" exists, it is required to direct a secret ballot election or use "any other suitable method" to determine the exclusive bargaining agent. It may not direct an election in the same bargaining unit or "subdivision thereof within which in the preceding twelve-month period a valid election has been held," nor during the term of a collective agreement "except for good cause."

Both laws make no specific mention of de-authorization proceedings, but presumably the same requirements would apply. If none of the choices receives a majority, a runoff election between the two highest choices is mandatory. [*30*, p. 327; *31*, p. 556] The Connecticut State Board of Labor Relations, using its administrative discretion, has adopted not only the NLRB 30 per cent "showing of interest" requirement before the election can be held, but also its rule that no union may appear on the ballot unless it has at least 10 per cent of the membership in the unit. [*77*, pp. 10-11]

The Michigan Act makes secret ballot elections mandatory if the Labor Mediation Board decides that there is a representation question, but it specifies the 30 per cent showing of interest requirement and also makes clear that the issue in dispute may be that the currently recognized bargaining agent no longer commands majority support. Elections may be held only once in every twelve-month period, and may not be directed in any bargaining unit where a fixed-term collective agreement is in force "which was not prematurely extended," except that "no collective bargaining agreement shall bar an election upon the petition of persons not parties thereto where more than 3 years have elapsed since the agreement's execution or last timely renewal, whichever was later." Runoff elections between the two highest choices are mandatory. [*344*, pp. 24-25]

The Delaware statute requires the Department of Labor and Industrial Relations to hold secret ballot elections upon the request of any employee organization which gives written proof of at least 30 per cent membership in the unit. The ballot must contain the name of any organization which can show a membership of at least 10 per cent, and also a space for a marking of no representation. A new representation election may not be held until one year has passed since the last one. Runoff elections are not mentioned, but up to now the Department has not had to make an administrative determination on this since the name of only one organization has appeared on the ballot in the elections held to date. [*32*, pp. 3-4]

In Oregon, the Civil Service Commission's rules provide that, upon receipt of a "valid request," the Civil Service Director must hold a representation election if an employee organization obtains the signatures of 30 per cent of the employees in a proposed unit on petitions saying that they want it to represent them and request an election; names of all organizations proving 10 per cent membership must be placed on the ballot.

If no organization gets a majority, a runoff is required, with the ballot providing for a "choice between the two candidates for representation receiving the largest and second largest number of votes ... as well as the choice of no representation." If no one wins, 12 months must pass before a new election. If there is a winner, it is recognized as the exclusive bargaining agent "for at least 12 months except that the Civil Service Commission for proper cause may call for a new election."

After the successful organization has served for at least 12 months, its recognition may be challenged in a petition to the director signed by at least 30 per cent of the employees in the unit. A new election is held, with the ballot containing "only the choice of continuing or discontinuing" the existing bargaining agent. If a majority votes against continuing the latter, its recognition must be withdrawn. [*301*, 98-300; 98-600] The Oregon provision that the "No Union" choice must be on the runoff ballot in any case departs from NLRB procedure and obviously will not please the unions.

*Unusual Provisions of New Wisconsin Law.* The new Wisconsin State Employment Labor Relations Act provides another

variant. The Wisconsin Employment Relations Board must place
on the ballot the names of all qualified "persons, having an
interest in representing state employees, submitted by a state
employee or group of state employees participating in the election," as well as a "No Union" choice. If no one wins a majority,
the Board may conduct a runoff, in which case it "may drop from
the ballot the name of the representative that received the least
number of votes at the original election," or it shall "drop from
the ballot the privilege of voting against any representative
when the least number of votes cast at the first election was
against representation by any named representative."

There is no limit on frequency of elections: "the fact that
one election has been held shall not prevent the holding of another
election among the same group of state employees, if it appears
to the board that sufficient reason therefor exists." [*345*, pp. 4-5]

### Use of Agency Time and Facilities

To function effectively, employee organizations require certain facilities, and the question arises as to how far the management should go in giving them help. The matters to be mentioned
below may seem like trivia, but from the organizations' standpoint they are important, and in fact they can lead to major
issues with the management or with rival organizations.

#### *In the United States Federal Government*

The Kennedy Order requires that the solicitation of memberships and dues and all internal employee organization business
must be conducted during nonduty hours. "Officially requested
or approved consultations and meetings" between the management and the employee organizations are, "whenever practicable," to be conducted on official time, except that the agency may
request that negotiations with an exclusive bargaining agent take
place "during the nonduty hours of the employee organization
representatives involved." [*400*, pp. 354-355] This latter provision
follows the recommendations of the Kennedy task force which
stressed that the negotiations could prove time-consuming and
pointed out that the TVA had such a policy. [*315*, p. 20]

As to travel and overtime expenses of employees serving as
employee organization representatives, Civil Service Commission
recommendations, approved by the Comptroller General, provide
[*384*] :

1. Travel expenses should be paid for activities such as joint employee-management committees when the activity is primarily in the government's interest;

2. They should not be paid to attend employee organization meetings, conferences, or training sessions;

3. Although as a general rule, they should not be paid to attend negotiation sessions for the purpose of negotiating an agreement, the agency may pay them for consultation or special consultation meetings it calls if it determines that the circumstances justify such payments; and

4. No overtime compensation may be paid.

The Civil Service Commission's advice to the agencies is as follows: [*378*, p. 5.23]

1. Permit employee organization meetings on government property, but caution that "this privilege should not be loosely granted";

2. Ban such meetings on government time;

3. Permit union representatives to solicit members during the lunch period;

4. Allow use of agency bulletin boards;

5. Disapprove of the use of intra-office messenger systems for the distribution of union publications but leave this decision to the agency, with the proviso that "there should be a clear understanding in advance as to the kinds and classes of materials to be distributed";

6. Permit unions to place notices of meetings or other notices in agency "house organs"; and

7. Oppose giving them free office space on government premises, except under unusual circumstances such as in a "remote place ... where other facilities are not reasonably available."

The agencies in their regulations specify in detail the privileges which may be granted, and the collective agreements contain provisions specifying the commitments made in this respect to the exclusive bargaining agent. The Post Office agreement provides for separate bulletin boards, for the exclusive use of each organization party to the accord, to "be placed in each installation in all swing rooms and work areas if space is available and it is otherwise feasible." If separate bulletin boards are not possible, one will be made available for all the organizations at each "appropriate location." The installation head determines their number and location, passes upon the suitability of material for posting if any such question is raised, and otherwise "governs use of the boards." Before removing any posted material, he must consult with the craft representative, and, if no agreement is reached, he must send the craft representative a copy of the bulletin in question with his initials, the date, and his reason for the removal. [*12*, p. 8]

Indicative of the kind of dispute which can break out, in some agencies the bargaining agents demanded that no postings be allowed for organizations without exclusive recognition, and in December of 1966 the Civil Service Commission, addressing itself to this problem, advised the agencies to limit the bulletin board privileges to exclusive representatives only, except that an organization with informal recognition be allowed to post notices of meetings of its members to be held off agency premises. [*385*] The Bonneville agreement provides for the names of shop stewards to be posted on appropriate bulletin boards. [*73*, p. 20] These are only some of the matters dealt with in this area of employee organization privileges; numerous others arise.

### In the Canadian Federal Government

The only provision on this subject in the new legislation is that, "except with the consent of the employer, no officer or representative of an employee organization shall attempt, on the employer's premises during the working hours of an employee, to persuade the employee to become or refrain from becoming or to continue to be or to cease to be a member of an employee organization." [*350*, p. 8] Detailed questions such as those discussed above presumably are covered in the regulations issued by the Treasury Board (the "employer").

### In United States State and Local
### Governments and the Canadian Cities

The union contracts cover these matters, and a few random examples will be given. The agreement between the Delaware State Department of Health and the Laborer's International Union of North America states: [*4*, pp. 3-4]

1. The Department will recognize any authorized union official and permit him to visit the Hospital for the Mentally Retarded (the bargaining unit), provided that on each visit the union representative identifies himself to the hospital superintendent, and that there is no interference with patient care and the employees' performance of their duties;

2. Shop stewards, seven in number, will be recognized as representatives of the local union, along with the president and business agent;

3. The union will be given office space and telephone on the grounds of the hospital; and

4. A designated union official will be granted leave with pay, for not to exceed two days per week, to administer union business.

The agreement between the Oregon State Treasury Department and the Oregon State Employees' Association provides: [*11*, p. 4]

1. Employees shall conduct Association internal business during nonduty hours only, "unless by special permission of the employer in limited instances involving the mutual benefit of the agency and employees;"

2. When available, the facilities of the agency may be used for Association chapter or committee meetings during nonduty hours of the employees involved;

3. The employer will provide the Association with "reasonable bulletin board space;"

4. It will advise employees in the bargaining unit of the Association's status as their representative and provide "each new employee with a piece of literature furnished by the Association, containing a notice that the Association is the collective bargaining representative and other pertinent information, including information as to how the employee may become a member of the Association."

Cincinnati's agreement with the AFSCME stipulates: [*9*, p. 2]

1. Union representatives will be permitted reasonable access to city work areas in order to conduct legitimate business, but only with advance approval of the agency head;

2. "A reasonable number of shop stewards for each agency" will be allowed;

3. No union business may take place on city time, other than that required to represent union members in administrative procedures;

4. The stewards will be given a "reasonable time to investigate and process grievances;"

5. "The union must secure permission from the agency head or his authorized representative . . . to contact any employee on city time."

Milwaukee's contract with the AFSCME specifies that no union business shall be conducted on city time, "except as specified in this Agreement," and it defines carefully the kinds of union notices to be permitted on bulletin boards, prohibiting "anything political or controversial, or anything reflecting upon the city, any of its employees, or any labor organization among its employees." [*3*, p. 10]

The Winnipeg agreement with Local 500 of the Canadian Union of Public Employees permits leaves of absence without pay to undertake full-time union work or to attend union conferences as official delegates. Such leave to attend union conferences may not be granted to more than twelve city employees at any one time. Leaves for full-time union work may be given for periods of not less than six or more than twelve months, subject to automatic renewal unless either party gives six months' prior notice of its desire to terminate the leave. [*10*, pp. 41-42]

These illustrations, not typical in any sense because there is such a variety of practices, at least indicate some of the items which are negotiated.

# 6

# Scope and Conduct of Negotiations

THE PURPOSE of the arrangements discussed in the preceding chapter is to make possible productive collective negotiations. We now turn to the negotiations themselves, the following aspects of which will be covered in this chapter: (1) Subjects appropriate for negotiation; (2) Joint bargaining by employee organizations; (3) Selection and training of the negotiating team; (4) Preparations for negotiating individual contracts; and (5) Conduct of the negotiation sessions, including bargaining strategy.

Because of its importance, attempts to settle bargaining impasses will be dealt with in depth in Chapter 7.

## Subjects Appropriate for Negotiation

To the employee organizations, the "bargaining" is virtually meaningless if the scope of the negotiations is very restricted. When they compare what can be negotiated in the private sector with the more limited sphere in government, many public employee leaders feel cheated. Conversely, the comparison with the private sector makes the public employer apprehensive, because he fears that the industrial experience will be duplicated in government, namely that many management prerogatives will go by the boards and become agenda items for bargaining sessions with the employee organizations.

### Content of Negotiations in Industry

Since the Taft-Hartley Act, like the Wagner Act before it, speaks only of bargaining over "wages, hours, and other terms and conditions of employment," [*132*, p. 8] the NLRB and the courts have had to decide exactly what could be negotiated. The employers' opinion initially tended to be that "conditions of

177

employment" meant only matters directly affecting the workers, such as wages, hours, and safety, but the unions maintained that it included much more because nearly every management decision "directly affects" the worker.

In general, the NLRB and the courts have supported the employees' side of this argument, because the scope of the mandatory bargaining has been progressively widened to include such items as paid vacations, holidays, merit increases, incentive-pay plans, Christmas bonuses, pensions, group health and accident insurance, stock purchase plans, the rental of company houses, the price of meals in company cafeterias, automation, and subcontracting. As Cullen points out, although "no court or the Board has said it would go this far, . . . *all* decisions in an enterprise are potentially open to bargaining (since all affect the workers)." [*82*, p. 46]

The reader will recall the reference in Chapter 2 to the Brewster bill; its very broad definition of "working conditions" reflects the thinking of organized labor, based upon its negotiating experience in industry. This may explain the AFSCME's statement that the "scope of the bargaining is greatly limited" where there is "a flat stipulation that the results of bargaining may not conflict with existing civil service or charter provisions." [*359*, p. 6] If anything affecting the employees is a proper subject for negotiation, the whole personnel program logically can be included. This would mean that decisions of legislative bodies, embodied in laws, could be annulled by collective agreements entered into by certain public officials and certain unions.

The way collective bargaining functions in industry a company can voluntarily give up management prerogatives by agreeing to make them subject to bargaining. Civil Service administrators and many other people do not see how a public agency, created by the legislature, financed by the tax-payers, and functioning under civil service, budgetary, and other laws, can agree to the same wide scope of negotiations as in industry. Roch Bolduc, a member of the Quebec Civil Service Commission, expresses this very well when he criticizes the view that the "collective agreement is the one and only rule that must regulate personnel administration in the civil service. As if the whole statute of the civil service could be summed up in a contract between the government and its employees. That is, in my opinion, a false principle because it denies any responsibility to the Parliament. In a democratic political system, ... public personnel administration is also a matter of public policy and as such its major orientation must be defined by the Parliament." [*47*, p. 15]

### Management Rights

It is true, however, that, if the public employer is constantly thinking about its "rights" and "prerogatives," it will refuse to negotiate about many matters which do not conflict with civil service and other laws and in no way impede the efficient conduct of the government's business. Indeed there is much room for improving personnel programs and the government's entire operations through collective agreements providing for new work procedures and employment relationships which are more satisfactory to the workers. Furthermore, as stressed in Chapter 4, the employees are stimulated to greater endeavors, because they are given a voice in decisions affecting them. There is still a question of which decisions, and it is here that some employee leaders are pressing for a change in traditional concepts. Witness this statement by S. A. Little, national president of the Canadian Union of Public Employees: [*143*, pp. 54-55; 60]

> Another of the basic concepts behind our collective bargaining system is that of the "residual rights." That is to say, the idea that all rights belong to management unless specifically modified by law or by a collective agreement. The labor movement feels it must fight for a 20th century viewpoint for labor-management relations which will replace this theory of residual rights with one based on a concept of equality between two partners. . . .
> In studying one of the recommended books for this seminar, I noted an extract from a report presented to President Truman about management rights. This quote . . . said that "labor members are convinced that the field of collective bargaining will in all probability continue to expand into the field of management." This is . . . exactly the philosophy which we are advocating today. . . . Let me make it clear at this point that I am not advocating the traditionalist syndicalist approach but a recognition that in modern society the trade union has a greater role to play than just that of an economic bargaining agent for the employees.

If this concept of equality were accepted, the scope of the negotiations would be broadened greatly, but just how much it is not clear. What is certain is that public employee organizations, just like those in industry, want to negotiate more than just wages, hours, and fringe benefits. Speaking of Canadian municipal employees, T. J. Plunkett points to their "increasing de-

sire to include, for example, such questions as the introduction of automation and the conditions of contracting out certain
services or operations in the collective agreement," a development which he predicts "will no doubt also occur in other public jurisdictions as well." [*308*, pp. 8-9] Should this question
of the scope of the negotiations be resolved by developing "statutory definitions of bargainable matters and statutory descriptions of management rights"? Plunkett thinks not, for "taken
together these have the effect of virtually nullifying each
other." His reasoning is stated thus: [*309*, pp. 188-89]

> The collective agreement which has been arrived at by mutual
> consent of the parties at any one time contains the appropriate defini-
> tion of management rights and bargainable matters, even if the agree-
> ment is silent on what constitutes management rights. If one starts
> with the assumption that management first of all had all rights
> and is only limited by the matters set out in the agreement, then
> it reserves all residual rights. In the future, though, it may qualify
> these residual rights by consenting to the addition of other items
> to the agreement. *It is clear that management's objectives will be to
> narrow the list of subjects for negotiation, while union and association
> leadership, on the other hand, will inevitably be attempting to expand
> these. This is, of course, the very core of collective bargaining, and
> it is doubtful that these matters can be statutorily set out for all
> time to come.*
> The desire for a clear-cut definition of the bargaining area and the
> rights of management stems, I suspect, from the traditional require-
> ment of public management for clarity and definition. But we are
> dealing here with a highly volatile area of human relations which
> in the social and economic change and flux of modern society cannot
> really be rigidly defined. Moreover, if collective bargaining is going
> to have any meaning, flexibility must be the keynote. There must
> be a good deal of free wheeling at the bargaining table if agree-
> ments are to be arrived at which have any potential for acceptability.

It is appropriate to refer to the experience in private enterprise with "management rights" statements in union contracts,
because such provisions now frequently appear in the agreements with public employee organizations. The Bureau of Labor
Statistics of the United States Department of Labor recently
published a report on this subject, based on an analysis of virtually all contracts covering 1,000 or more workers in effect in
1963-64, exclusive of railroad, airline, and government agreements. A little less than half of the total of 1,773 agreements
studied were found to contain formal statements of management rights, either of a general character or much more
frequently in the form of a list of enumerated functions reserved to the employer.

Each of these two kinds of management rights provisions has its advocates. Those in favor of general statements feel that this gives a blanket protection to the management, whereas, in any list of enumerated rights, important ones might be overlooked, and the arbitrators could reason that the omission of a particular right evidenced management's agreement to give it up. Those who believe it better to list the rights argue that this will make it clear to the arbitrators that the management is retaining control over the functions enumerated. [*391*, pp. 1-24]

The public employer has the same decision to make: whether to insist on a management rights statement and, if so, what kind of statement it should be, general or detailed, and, if the latter, which points it should include. Detailed references to management rights statements in government will be made below, but it must be emphasized that, just as in industry, the entire agreement must be read, because in other provisions the management often accepts limitations on rights it professes to maintain. For example, the contract may open by stating categorically that the management reserves the right to "direct the employees," but later clauses may require supervisors to make work assignments in certain ways only, as in the skilled trades.

### Scope of Bargaining in the United States Federal Government

In accordance with the recommendations of the Kennedy task force, Executive Order 10988 stipulates that all agreements shall expressly state: [*400*, p. 354]

1. In the administration of all matters covered by the agreement officials and employees are governed by the provisions of any existing or future laws and regulations, including policies set forth in the Federal Personnel Manual and agency regulations, which may be applicable, and the agreement shall at all times be applied subject to such laws, regulations and policies;

2. Management officials of the agency retain the right, in accordance with applicable laws and regulations, (a) to direct employees of the agency, (b) to hire, promote, transfer, assign, and retain employees in positions within the agency, and to suspend, demote, discharge, or take other disciplinary action against employees, (c) to relieve employees from duties because of lack of work or for other legitimate reasons, (d) to maintain the efficiency of the

Government operations entrusted to them, (e) to determine the methods, means and personnel by which such operations are to be conducted, and (f) to take whatever actions may be necessary to carry out the mission of the agency in situations of emergency.

Since Congress by law establishes pay policies and the pay ranges for classified employees, as well as fringe benefits, this removes all "economic" considerations from the negotiations, except for a few agencies like the Tennessee Valley Authority and the Bonneville Power Administration which have the authority to set their own rates. (As discussed later in this chapter, the pay of the some 800,000 wage board employees, most of whom are in the Defense Department, is set administratively, not by Congress.)

The merit system, veterans' preference, and various other personnel policies are also provided for by statute, so these also may not be contravened by any provisions in collective agreements. The United States Civil Service Commission, however, issues its own rules and regulations implementing such legislation, and increasingly it has been delegating to the agencies the responsibility for deciding the details of personnel programs, in accordance with Commission guidelines and subject to later post-audit by the Commission.

As Harold H. Leich, of the Commission's staff, has said: [*134*]

> In the programs where the Congress or Commission has given flexibility to Agency heads for developing their own programs within broad policy guidelines, a wide field is thrown open for consultation between union representatives and agency management. In other words, unions *can* influence management to an appreciable extent in these areas where management of the agency has the right to shape its own personnel programs.

Furthermore, agency regulations, as for example in the Post Office Department, cover numerous work procedures which the agency can also open to negotiation.

*Employee Organization Complaints of Restricted Bargaining.* Some of the employee organizations have from the very start complained, however, that the agencies were using the strong statement of management rights in the Order to refuse to negotiate, terminating the conversations with the employee representatives by saying the matters in question were already covered in the agency regulations. The phrase ". . . or future laws and regulations . . ." in Point (1) of the Kennedy Order, quoted in the foregoing, makes it possible to avoid bargaining over a particular item by simply adopting a regulation to cover it. Furthermore, the employee leaders complain that, with agency regulations already adopted to cover the entire agency, local and other subdivision managers have little discretion to bargain.

Otto Pragan of the AFL-CIO said in May of 1966: [*314*, pp. 38-39, 42]

> Contrary to the intent of the Task Force and the President, the experience of 3 years of collective bargaining shows that the gulf between bilateral collective bargaining and unilateral regulations has narrowed only very little. The main reason for this . . . is that by far the greatest number of agreements is negotiated on the local level where the local manager can only negotiate such matters that fall within his administrative discretion. . . . In the two cases of agency-wide bargaining [the Post Office Department and the Railroad Retirement Board] the unions can successfully participate in the formulation of personnel policies and, thus, restrict the power of management in issuing unilateral regulations relative to subject matters that can be negotiated.

Section 7 of the Kennedy Order requires that "any basic or initial agreement entered into with an employee organization . . . must be approved by the head of the agency or any official designated by him." [*400*, p. 353] Pragan also reiterated the union contention that the agencies were insisting upon such approval even for supplemental agreements, thus further limiting the authority of the local managers.

The agencies have contended that these complaints are exaggerated and that sincere efforts are being made to make the bargaining meaningful, within the framework of the Order. As to approval of the supplementary agreements, they point out that the Order does not require the agency head to delegate this. In its first report on the federal program, the American Bar Association stated, "most agencies are much too devoted to their own regulations. They must learn that regulations are not Holy Writ. They can be changed or modified—and they can also be discussed or negotiated." [*15*, p. 143]

Charles Rehmus, co-director of the Institute of Labor and Industrial Relations of the University of Michigan, reports that some agency officials initially announced they had no authority to negotiate on anything—although in fact, as Rehmus sees it, there is much of importance which can be negotiated at local levels. [*341*, pp. 26-27] Reviewing the total picture, however, he believes that the employee organizations now participate in agency

decisions to a greater extent than they did before the Order. He
disagrees with those who say that "collective bargaining in the
federal service must essentially come to little or nought because
there are so few 'gut' issues about which the parties can negotiate," because much "genuine and creative problem-solving . . . is
taking place . . . which is not reflected in the language of the contracts that have been negotiated." From personal experience, he
knows of cases where "policies were clarified and administrative
problems resolved simply because of the urgent pressure exerted
by the unions in the course of collective bargaining," resulting in a
"major change in personnel administration." [*322*, p. 55]

The Civil Service Commission guidelines state flatly that
"over-restrictive agency-wide regulations which would prevent
cooperative dealings at subordinate echelons would clearly be contrary to the intent and spirit of this program." [*378*, p. 5.21] Unlike the NLRB, however, the Civil Service Commission cannot
issue decisions spelling out the matters on which the agencies
must bargain, so any amount of exhortation by the Commission
on this subject will not satisfy those who want a "little NLRB."

Actually, the initial reaction of the unions was that, although
the area for bargaining was much more restricted than in industry, there was a good deal of significance to negotiate about.
David L. Perlman, Assistant Editor of the *AFL-CIO News*,
wrote: "It would be a mistake to underestimate the significance
of such matters as meaningful grievance procedure, job-bidding
rights, promotion procedures and safety regulations. They are as
important in the federal employment area as in the private
sector." [*303*]

The unions are understandably repeating the pattern in the
private sector, namely, trying to obtain the right to bring new
items to the bargaining table.

*Examples of Negotiable Items.* The Commission lists the following illustrative policy areas in which negotiations can take
place: [*378*, p. 5.21]

1. Grievance and internal agency appeals systems;
2. The work environment (light, heat, ventilation, cleanliness
   and sanitation, and safety practices and equipment);
3. Design and scheduling of work (tours of duty, rotation
   assignments, joint employee-management cooperation committees, meal periods, and vacation scheduling);
4. Career policies and procedures (promotion plans, training

programs, reduction-in-force procedures, and disciplinary practices and procedures) ;

5. Employee benefits and services (lunch rooms, snack bars, coffee breaks, check-cashing services, recreation facilities, and parking arrangements) ;

6. Implementation of pay legislation, where permissible under the law, such as in conduct of wage surveys for employees paid local prevailing rates;

7. Services to employee organizations, such as bulletin boards and use of intra-office distribution system.

Paul M. Camp, Deputy Director, Office of Personnel, Public Health Service, has prepared a checklist of Subjects for Consultation or Negotiation under the Kennedy Order which includes more than a hundred items. (See Appendix A.) Examination of this list shows many matters which administrators and personnel officers had traditionally considered important and none of which could be considered inconsequential to the employees. Union and management officials in industry have often observed that it is these erroneously labelled "little things" which on a year-round basis produce more conflicts than the publicized disputes over wages and fringe benefits. A Department of Labor study [*388*], summarizing findings as of late summer 1964, showed that the agencies were negotiating agreements in most of the areas shown on the Camp list and this continues to be the case.

*The TVA Approach.* Obviously, the management's philosophy on labor relations will determine how far it goes in opening areas for negotiation. To demonstrate the willingness of the Tennessee Valley Authority to negotiate with the unions just as far as it legally can, TVA General Manager Louis J. Van Mol uses the following example: [*395*, p. 90]

TVA must apply federal law and regulations in taking certain adverse actions against employees who have veterans' preference. Management could have drawn a line here and said to the unions: "We will not negotiate with you on matters involving adverse actions because part of this area is controlled by federal law." Instead, we told the unions: "We must follow federal law with regard to certain adverse actions involving employees with veterans' preference, but we will negotiate adverse action provisions to cover nonpreference employees and to cover preference employees in areas to which federal law does not extend. . . ." This kind of approach has assured our unions that we are ready to talk about *any* area where we have some maneuverability. Union representatives have responded with an understanding that has helped us through many a tight spot when we have hit an issue involving a major management responsibility.

In using the authority in its enabling legislation to pay prevailing wage rates to trades and labor employees, the TVA also provides for maximum union participation. Not only are these rates negotiated annually in a wage conference presided over jointly by the director of personnel and the president of the Tennessee Valley Trades and Labor Council, but there also is a continuing Joint Classification Committee with an important role. Composed of four TVA representatives appointed by the director of personnel, and an equal number of council representatives named by the council's president, its functions include the following:

1. Approval of requested classification changes in the wage schedules, such as establishment or elimination of classes and changes in titles and the relative level of a class;

2. Approval of qualification and classification standards for trades and labor jobs; and

3. Settling problems concerning clarification of the duties and responsibilities of trades and labor classes.

The committee's decisions are binding upon the TVA and the Council if approved by the director of personnel and the president of the Council. Assignment of individual positions to scheduled classes, and grievances concerning classification matters, are not, however, within the province of this committee. Management allocates the positions to classes; if the individual employee is dissatisfied with his classification, he can invoke the grievance procedure. [*102*, pp. 14-15] Under the latter, to be discussed in greater detail in Chapter 8, the Council can insist on final resolution of the grievance by binding decision of an impartial referee. [*102*, pp. 52-53]

Striking evidence of the TVA's willingness to share decision-making is the inclusion in the agreement with the Council of a mutually-agreed upon definition of the word "vicinity," as used in the section of the TVA Act calling for payment of prevailing rates. The exact geographic boundaries of the TVA "vicinity" are carefully set forth, such as "the boundary of the power service area from Memphis to the southeastern tip of that area" [only one part of the demarcated area]. [*102*, pp. 21-22] In effect, the unions shared the TVA's discretion in interpreting the statute.

Pay rates for white-collar employees are negotiated with the Salary Policy Employee Panel, which represents various unions of such workers. Assignment of new classes of positions to salary schedules is the responsibility of a Joint Salary Schedule Committee consisting of five representatives of the TVA and a like number from the panel. In cases of disagreement, the director of personnel may make a tentative assignment until resolved by the TVA and the panel. [*39*, p. 20]

As to position classification, requests for new classification standards may be initiated by the TVA, or by the appropriate employee organization which contacts the personnel division directly. Before any such standards are officially adopted, the employee organization representing the positions involved is asked to review and approve them. Unresolved disagreements are referred to the panel and the director of personnel for resolution, but if they cannot agree, the final decision is that of the director of personnel. [*39*, p. 9] Management allocates the individual positions to classes, with classification appeals handled through the grievance procedure, again terminating in the binding decision of an impartial referee. [*39*, p. 53] All agreements on wage and salary rates and other policy matters are made subject to approval by the TVA board of directors. [*378*, p. 3.04]

The TVA agreements with both blue-collar and white-collar workers are also distinctive because they require joint training programs and an elaborate system of labor-management cooperation. The contract with the Trades and Labor Council calls for establishment of a central joint council on apprenticeship, equally representing both the TVA and the Trades and Labor Council, with the responsibility of developing "an adequate system of apprenticeship." Upon the request of one of the unions represented on the council, a joint training committee consisting of representatives of that union and the TVA must be formed to plan and administer other training programs for "placement or promotion in trades and labor classifications."

The TVA and the council are pledged to establish and support a central joint cooperative committee and local joint cooperative committees to ". . . give consideration to such matters as the elimination of waste; the conservation of materials, supplies, and energy; the improvement of quality of workmanship and services; the promotion of education and training; the correction of conditions making for misunderstandings; the encouragement of courtesy in the relations of employees with the public; the safeguarding of health; the prevention of hazards to life and property; and the strengthening of the morale of the service." [*102*, pp. 8-9]

Similarly, the agreement with the salary policy employee panel calls for joint committees to plan and carry out training programs if the unions so desire. [*39*, p. 63] It also provides for creation of a central joint cooperative conference and of local joint cooperative conferences to "provide an orderly means through which the contribution of employees and management to the program of the TVA can be promoted and maintained." These cooperative conferences deal with the same kinds of problems as the joint committees, but also with "improving communications between employees and management" and "encouraging good public relations." [*39*, p. 56] As Van Mol states, while these committees and conferences do not handle negotiable items, "they do work in areas where employees and management can pool their ideas and come up with ways to improve job efficiency, working conditions, and working relationships." [*395*, p. 93]

*The Post Office Agreement.* Illustrating just how broad the scope of the bargaining can be under the federal program, the Post Office department-wide agreement with seven unions provides that "to the extent provisions of the Postal Manual which are in effect on the effective or renewal date of this Agreement are in conflict with this Agreement, the provisions of this Agreement will govern." [*12*, p. 106]

The agreement is 109 pages long and includes numerous provisions in which the management accepts limitations upon its right to make work assignments, such as a lengthy section on the principles to be followed in reassigning workers in case of closing or consolidation of installations, reductions-in-force, and introduction of centralized mail processing, and another on "Assignment of Ill or Injured Regular and Substitute Employees." [*12*, pp. 53-73]

Machinery for labor-management consultations is substantial. Departmental representatives must meet with those of the unions, not less than once a month and as often as necessary, to "confer, but not negotiate, with respect to nationwide personnel policies and practices and matters affecting working conditions, matters affecting the basic agreement, supplements there-

to and interpretations and disputes arising out of the adminis-
ration of local agreements." Furthermore, the agenda for these
monthly meetings includes the "status of current projects and
new programs." [*12*, pp. 11-12]

Similarly, regional directors are required to hold meetings at
least quarterly with the regional representatives of the unions
"to announce new or to confer on the status of current projects,
programs, and other activities of interest to the employees."
State representatives of the unions may be invited to these
regional meetings when the agenda includes "major problems or
plans such as the Christmas operation or a national emergency."
[*12*, p. 14] Finally, in all except the "very smallest" post office, the
installation head must hold similar meetings at least once quarterly, and, in the largest ones, more frequent meetings are
expected. [*12*, pp. 15-16]

Illustrating again the pattern of declaring management
rights and then immediately qualifying them, another section
reads, "while the Department retains the right to determine
the methods, means and personnel by which operations are conducted, a mechanization committee shall be established." This
committee, consisting of union representatives and designates
from "appropriate bureaus in the Department," is "primarily
concerned with the effects on personnel of proposed and
adopted mechanization." Specifically, it is to be "consulted about
proposed implementation, identify and discuss problems resulting from mechanization, propose solutions to problems" and "be
advised of the results of research when appropriate." [*12*, p. 106]

It is the very breadth of these negotiations and consultations,
however, which worries some Congressmen. Representative Steed
of Oklahoma, who in the past has managed the postal budget in
the House, recently charged: [*54*]

> I don't know of a single modern plan Post Office has started that
> postal unions have ever supported. They don't like the Zip Code,
> mechanization, work measurements. . . . It seems to me they're com-
> pletely obsessed with the idea that Post Office operates solely for
> the employees and not to give mail service to the public.

Whatever the truth of these criticisms, Mike Causey sen-
sibly states that "the advance of federal employee unions . . .
will depend, to a great extent, on keeping Congress and the
public convinced that union members are government employees
first and union men next." [*54*]

*Union Role in Wage Surveys and Position Classification.* Since the pay of the some 800,000 federal blue-collar employees, amounting to about one fourth of the total work force, is fixed by the agency heads on the basis of data on prevailing rates collected by local wage boards, this leaves room for union participation. In late August, 1964, 55 of 209 agreements covered in the Labor Department study included statements on wage board procedures, typically providing for union participation in one or more of the following: "notification of survey, observers on survey committees, nomination of individuals to be data collectors, and the right to recommend the inclusion or exclusion of firms or jobs to be surveyed." In 26 of these agreements, the union was given the right to request new wage surveys, and in six, to appeal if it felt the data had been compiled or collected incorrectly. [*388*, pp. 28-31]

The AFL-CIO, which represents most federal blue-collar workers, regards this as "token participation" and is asking for "complete bilateral procedures on the local and national levels for selecting the firms, the key jobs and the geographical area to be surveyed as well as for determining the rates of pay." Pragan, quoted earlier, cites an agreement between the Morgantown, West Virginia, Research Center, Bureau of Mines, and the American Federation of Government Employees, calling for the parties to negotiate basic hourly rates, using the wage survey findings as the basis for discussion. [*314*, pp. 46-47] In the fall of 1967, when the Senate Post Office and Civil Service Committee favorably reported on a bill introduced by Senator Monroney of Oklahoma, the purpose of which was to make extensive changes in the system for determining the pay of wage board employees, the Committee said in its report that, except for the Navy Wage Board, there was no employee participation in "development of wage board policies and the determination of rates." [*96*]

With respect to positions covered by the Classification Act, Pragan believes the agency managements "should provide a role for the union to participate through collective bargaining in developing the policies for a fair and just grade determination," which, he says, is being done only in a few cases, citing as one example the agreement between the Labor Department and the AFGE. [*314*, p. 46]

This raises a crucial point: can the integrity of the classification and pay plans be maintained if the bargaining includes classification of individual positions? The federal Classification

Act of 1949, like similar state and local legislation, provides for an orderly system of classifying positions according to approximate similarity in duties and responsibilities in order to make possible "equal pay for equal work." Since the classes of positions are assigned to pay grades, the allocation of an employee's job to one class instead of another may put him in a different salary bracket.

Civil service administrators argue that in just which class a position belongs is a determination to be made upon the basis of the evidence, namely, the job content, not through the pull and haul of negotiations. They know that classification experts will disagree about the level of individual positions, but they remind that the employees can appeal through the established administrative machinery. Since bargaining is the exercise of power by each party, with the outcome usually determined by compromise, they fear that the more powerful employee organizations would obtain inflated classifications for individual positions.

Others argue that the employee leaders can be counted upon to show restraint and to respect the principle of equal pay for equal work. Presently, the agreements in some agencies allow an employee who is not satisfied with his job description to be assisted and represented by the union in taking up the matter with the management.

*Negotiable Items in Canada.* The Preparatory Committee on Collective Bargaining recommended that there be no limitations on the "subject matter of discussion at the bargaining table," but that arbitration be restricted to "rates of pay, standard hours of work, leave entitlements and directly related conditions of employment." It also proposed that employee rights to superannuation, death benefits, and accident compensation continue to be governed by statute, and that it "be made clear that the subject-matter of arbitration may in no circumstance extend to the processes governing appointment, transfer, promotion, demotion, lay-off, discharge, discipline and classification." [*324*, p. 34] The committee's viewpoint was that "agents of the employers" should be empowered to "bargain about most basic conditions of employment and to give effect to changes agreed upon, or awarded by arbitration, without seeking amendments to particular statutes." [*324*, p. 33]

These recommendations were followed in the collective bargaining law and the two companion statutes establishing the new Public Service Commission and redefining the powers of the Treasury Board respectively. The law amending the Financial Administration Act authorizes the Treasury Board to "determine and regulate the pay to which persons employed in the public service are entitled for services rendered, the hours of work and leave of such persons and any matters related thereto." [*352*, p. 3] The employee relations law states that "nothing in this Act shall be construed to affect the right or authority of the employer to determine the organization of the Public Service and to assign duties to and classify positions therein." [*350*, p. 7]

It also provides that "no collective agreement shall provide, directly or indirectly, for the alteration or elimination of any existing term or condition of employment or the establishment of any new term or condition of employment, (a) the alteration or elimination of which, or the establishment of which, as the case may be, would require or have the effect of requiring the enactment or amendment of any legislation by Parliament, except for the purpose of appropriating moneys required for its implementation, or (b) that has been or may be, as the case may be, established pursuant to any Act specified in Schedule C." [*350*, pp. 28-29]

Since this schedule includes not only the Superannuation Act, but also the new Public Service Employment Act, the merit system is removed from the bargaining table. The section dealing with "Subject Matter of Arbitral Award" does add "standards of discipline" to the Preparatory Committee's list, but it excludes ". . . the standards, procedures or processes governing the appointment, appraisal, promotion, demotion, transfer, lay-off or release of employees, or with any term or condition of employment of employees that was not a subject of negotiation between the parties during the period before arbitration was requested in respect thereof." [*350*, p. 34]

Because it includes pay and some fringe benefits, the scope of the bargaining is wider than in the United States national government, but the merit system appears to be about as well-protected and the classification of positions is clearly stated as a management responsibility.

*Canadian Provinces and Cities.* As to the two provinces which grant full collective bargaining rights, in Saskatchewan the agreements cover not only salaries and working conditions, but also civil service procedures, such as the following: "For example, written examinations are limited to those specifically enumerated, and the right of the Association [Civil Service Association] to appoint an observer on promotion or selection panels is guaranteed. The only limitation to the scope of the agreements is Section 50 of the Civil Service Act, which guarantees that the Civil Service Commission shall have complete authority over the classification plan and job specifications, and a refusal by the government to bargain on superannuation, which is controlled by statute." [*330*, p. 389]

In Quebec, negotiation does not extend to "such issues as job classifications, appointments, promotions, transfers, and training programs, all of which are still the responsibility of the Civil Service Commission." [*111*, p. 12] In the cities, since they are under the general labor relations acts, the scope of the bargaining is as wide as it is in industry.

### Range of Bargaining in United States State and Local Jurisdictions

As already indicated in Chapter 1, quite a few state and local governments are negotiating pay rates and fringe benefits with the employee organizations. The new state laws either use the language of the Taft-Hartley Act, namely, "wages, hours, and other terms and conditions of employment," or they define the scope as "employment relations."

The Wisconsin State Employment Labor Relations Act differs from the others in two respects: it specially lists the "subjects of collective bargaining"; and it excludes pay and fringe benefits. The negotiable items are:

1. Grievance procedures;

2. Application of seniority rights to "matters contained herein";

3. Work schedules and shift assignments;

4. Use of sick leave and scheduling of vacations and "other time off";

5. "Application and interpretation of established work rules";

6. Health and safety matters;

7. Intra-departmental transfers; and

8. "Such other matters consistent with" the above and the "statutes, rules and regulations of the State and its various agencies."

It also provides that "nothing herein shall require the employer to bargain in relation to statutory and rule provided prerogatives of promotion, layoff, position classification, compensation and fringe benefits, examinations, discipline, merit salary determination policy and other actions provided for by law and rules governing civil service." [*345*, p. 8]

Exclusion of examinations and other merit system processes is not unusual; the reader will remember the reference in Chapter 2 to the section in the Delaware statute on this. In Connecticut, the law stipulates: [*30*, pp. 331-32]

> Nothing herein shall diminish the authority and power of any municipal civil service commission, personnel board, personnel agency or its agents established by statute, charter or special act to conduct and grade merit examinations and to rate candidates in the order of their relative excellence from which appointments or promotions may be made to positions in the competitive division of the classified service of the municipal employer served by such civil service commission or personnel board. The conduct and the grading of merit examinations, the rating of candidates and the establishment of lists from such examinations and the appointments from such lists and any provision of any municipal charter concerning political activity of municipal employees shall not be subject to collective bargaining.

The Interim Commission which prepared the legislation wanted the bargaining to "include the entire spectrum of conditions and benefits which apply to public employment," including "seniority in promotions, transfers and layoffs, discipline and discharge and grievance arbitration provisions." [*323*, p. 14] Since the excluded merit system area in the law mentions only appointments, promotions, eligible lists, and political activity, the employee organizations may be able to bring transfers, layoffs, and other personnel matters to the bargaining table.

Illustrating the differences in the provisions of these state laws, whereas the Massachusetts law provides that contract provisions are invalid if they conflict with "any law, ordinance or by-law," the Connecticut law states [*31*, p. 557; *30*, p. 331]:

> Where there is a conflict between any agreement reached by a municipal employer and an employee organization and approved in accordance with the provisions of this act on matters appropriate to collective bargaining, as defined in this act, and any charter, special act, ordinance, rules or regulations adopted by the municipal employer or its agents such as a personnel board or civil service commission, or any general statute directly regulating the hours of work of policemen or firemen, the terms of such agreement shall prevail.

The Connecticut law is the only one with such a provision. *Negotiations in Cincinnati and Tacoma.* Not to limit the examples to states with statutes expressly granting public employees negotiation rights, on April 6, 1960, the Cincinnati City Council passed a resolution stating that its future policy would be "through the City Manager and his designated assistants, to bargain collectively with city employees . . . on all matters pertaining to wages and working conditions before any final determination is made by City Council." [*67*, p. 1] The agreement with AFSCME District Council No. 51, the exclusive bargaining agent, states that: [*9*, pp. 1-2]

Wages, fringe benefits, and working conditions for employees covered . . . shall be in accordance with the ordinances from time to time passed by the City Council, which are herewith made a part of this agreement. . . . the union has the right to negotiate the establishment or modification of agency personnel regulations within an agency in which the union represents a majority of eligible employees, but no such regulation shall be effective until approved by the City Personnel Officer. It is understood that all agency personnel regulations will be in conformity with any law, ordinance, Civil Service Commission rule, or with the personnel policies as agreed to by the City Manager and the union.

The August, 1966 resolution of the City of Tacoma, Washington, providing for collective bargaining with the unions over "wages and working conditions," also includes the following in its statement of general purposes [*349*, p. 3] :

1. "Stability of employment" and "satisfactory tenure";

2. "Improvement and betterment programs" for the employees;

3. "The highest degree of efficiency, morale, and responsibility in the performance of the work and the accomplishment of the public purposes of the City"; procedures for the "prompt adjustment of all disputes"; and "systematic labor-management cooperation."

The agreements must conform with the "provisions of applicable State laws, the City Charter, City Ordinances," and are void if they conflict. [*349*, p. 5]

*"Management Rights" in New York City.* In New York City issues have arisen which go to the heart of the question of management rights. There are plenty of disputes about salaries, hours, and fringe benefits, but increasingly much of the worker dissatisfaction has been attributable to excessive work loads, too much clerical work for professional employees, and differ-

ences of opinion about individual work assignments and the adequacy of the particular agency's services to the public.

Just as teachers in many parts of the country are now able to negotiate over class size, a topic to be elaborated in Chapter 9, so have social workers in New York City and elsewhere won the right to bargain over caseloads. Among the unsatisfied demands of the Social Service Employees Union which led to a strike in January of 1967 were: an individual caseload reduction from 60 to 45; the establishment of a reserve staff to handle workloads of employees on temporary leave; improved physical facilities; and elimination of much required paper work. [*279*] The new element in the union's requests, however, was a long list of proposals to improve Welfare Department services to its clients, including: a 25 percent increase in welfare budgets; revision of family budgets in accordance with the Consumers' Price Index; and creation of a "workload committee" of four union and four city representatives, to meet weekly "to discuss, review, and study all questions relating to any aspect of the work load affecting staff," with the Welfare Commissioner *required* to implement the committee's decisions. [*49*, p. 72]

The union also sought to "force the department to join it, *by contract*, in demanding far-reaching changes ... from the state and Federal government" aimed at revising grant-in-aid requirements in the interests of more simplified procedures. The position of the Welfare Department and of the Lindsay administration was that this was a policy area reserved to the management. Welfare Commissioner Ginsberg said: "We ought to create a channel for suggestions and discuss them, but that doesn't mean we should negotiate them. I am the one who is legally responsible for the direction of the welfare program, not the union or a joint union-management committee." [*49*, p. 73]

The issue here, in blunt terms, is who runs the department, but it is a much more complex question than it seems when put this way. If teachers can, as they have, obtain agreements allowing them to participate in curriculum matters and in the selection of textbooks, welfare workers reason they should also have the right to negotiate "professional" matters. There are bound to be differences of opinion over just how far a public agency can go in sharing its administrative discretion with the employee organizations.

*Arbitrator's Decision on Work Assignments.* The memorandum of agreement between the city and seven employee organizations, referred to in Chapter 5, reads: [*131*, pp. 4-5]

> It is the right of the City, acting through its agencies, to determine the standards of services to be offered by its agencies; determine the standards of selection for employment; direct its employees; take disciplinary action; relieve its employees from duty because of lack of work or for other legitimate reasons; maintain the efficiency of governmental operations; determine the methods, means and personnel by which government operations are to be conducted; determine the content of job classifications; take all necessary actions to carry out its mission in emergencies; and exercise complete control and discretion over its organization and the technology of performing its work. The City's decisions on these matters are not within the scope of collective bargaining, but, notwithstanding the above, questions concerning the practical impact that decisions on the above matters have on employees, such as questions of work load or manning, are within the scope of collective bargaining.

In the summer of 1966, the Patrolmen's Benevolent Association and the Uniformed Firemen's Association, negotiating jointly with the city, made a number of demands relating to work assignments of firemen and policemen. The firemen wanted at least six firemen and an officer assigned to every truck; a fixed number of men always to be available in a given area and not to be moved around; and a clear departmental listing of all job duties (firemen were not to be required to perform maintenance chores). The policemen sought a guarantee that patrol cars be staffed with two men, and that policemen required to make early appearances in court be taken off late shifts the night before. [*241*]

The background behind the firemen's request was that Commissioner Robert O. Lowery had started a new policy of shifting companies from lower Manhattan to night-time duty in heavily-populated areas like Brownsville, East New York, and the Bedford-Stuyvesant section of Brooklyn. The reasoning here is that after business hours some of the fire equipment can be spared and used to make fire protection more effective in other parts of the city. The *New York Times* wrote: [*248*]

> At the root of their reluctance to have companies shifted is moonlighting, the off-duty employment permitted to firemen below a certain salary level. Commissioner Lowery has taken an initial step toward ending this highly questionable practice, which makes men unwilling to leave the neighborhood in which they have established part-time jobs.

As to the patrolmen, they were concerned that the Police Department might return to the practice of assigning only one man to each patrol car, a practice "abandoned many years ago after the police had fallen easy prey to thugs in some neighborhoods." [251]

The Lindsay administration refused to negotiate on these matters, the mayor saying that "it is not a proper issue of collective bargaining that unions should control the location of manpower." He argued that "the safety of the people" should not be "bargained away at the negotiating table." Lindsay later reversed his position and agreed to submit to binding arbitration the question of whether the memorandum of agreement quoted earlier intended that the bargaining cover such matters. [241]

The arbitrator ruled that it did not, because the "city, exclusively, determines what programs and services shall be furnished; what equipment shall be utilized; what employees shall perform the services; and when, where and under what conditions they shall be performed." He also said, however, that if the unions found the city's decisions on staff assignments to be "unreasonable" or "unduly burdensome," they could require it "to bargain with respect to demands as to the existence of undesirable working conditions." While the city was obligated to determine whether this condition existed and, if so, what could be done to alleviate it, it did not have to bargain "on the specific method, means or manner in which such change or alleviation shall be effected." As to the list of job duties for firemen, the arbitrator thought the city should submit one, but that the determination of the duties was the responsibility of the Fire Department and therefore not negotiable. [251]

The *Times* applauded the decision, commenting: "Under the arbitrator's broad construction of the clause preserving certain management rights . . . it is plain that he applies the philosophy to all municipal services . . . . Unquestionably, the limitations the award puts on the scope of bargaining will heighten the objections many unions of public employees have raised to ratification of the code by the City Council. These unions would like to make every aspect of job assignment a matter of co-determination." [252] The "code" refers to draft legislation (later passed) to make the memorandum of agreement a matter of law.

### *"Professionalism" and "Co-determination"*

Although the immediate cause for the two Los Angeles County

social worker strikes in the summer of 1966 was a dispute over salaries, the broader issue was "professionalism," threatened by "the mounting administrative complexity that has gotten in the way of case work and preoccupied professionals with paper work they say should be handled by a larger clerical staff." [*239*] The employee organizations do not see how bargaining can be effective in improving working conditions if the agenda may not include work load and job assignments.

Analyzing the reasons for the threatened mass resignation of New York City hospital nurses in the spring of 1966, Martin Tolchin in the *New York Times* referred to "the mounting frustration over working conditions in which rookie nurses sometimes found themselves in charge of 200 patients during the midnight-to-dawn shifts." [*364*] In the settlement with the city, the nurses secured its promise to try to stop giving them non-nursing chores, such as messenger work. [*232*]

There is a good deal of sympathy for this and other forms of "co-determination" which improve the employers' ability to attract and retain competent personnel. The *Times* wrote enthusiastically about a recently-signed contract between the city and the AFSCME providing for a training program for some 17,000 hospital aides to relieve critical shortages in the supply of hospital technicians and other subprofessional employees. Pointing out that most of the workers benefited would be Negroes and Puerto Ricans holding unskilled, low-paid jobs, the *Times* said that those with ability would ". . . receive on-the-job training to equip them for duty as inhalation therapists, ambulance technicians and a variety of subprofessional services in operating and delivery rooms . . . . To the extent that it takes the dead-end out of the most menial of hospital jobs, the training plan will help attract better employees to the municipal institutions at the same time that it counteracts the pressure on physicians, nurses and other professionals." [*263*]

## Joint Bargaining

Turning to the conduct of the negotiations, joint bargaining, as by the policemen and firemen in New York City, although now the exception, may become more common. The employee leaders in government astutely borrow tactics which have proved effective in the private sector, and they may be impressed with such developments as the "coordinated bargaining" of a coalition of unions, led by the International Union of Electrical Workers, with the General Electric Company. [*234*] Requesting a "joint contract package of wage increases and fringe benefits" estimated at $200 million for one year, the Patrolmen's Benevolent Association, representing 24,000 policemen, and the Uniformed Firemen's Association, speaking for 10,500 firemen, announced that "neither would settle until both were satisfied." Mayor Lindsay said he had no objection to the joint negotiations "if they choose to do it in this fashion and their members agree." [*229*] After the city had made an offer acceptable to the policemen but not to the firemen, the dispute was referred to a three-man fact-finding panel to hold hearings and make recommendations.[*275*]

Joint bargaining on an area-wide basis, covering workers under separate governing bodies, may even be a possibility. In a move unprecedented in teacher unionism, the Long Island Council of the American Federation of Teachers voted in January of 1966 to start a drive for joint bargaining by its locals with *all* the school districts on Long Island. Presumably such bargaining would take place between a negotiating committee of the union locals and one representing all the school districts.

Nathan Feinstein of the AFT said that such an arrangement would "...allow teachers to act together on salaries, instead of allowing ourselves to be divided against each other by school boards who reach their own concerted agreements on teacher salaries while publicly pretending they are defending local option." [*20*, p. 5]

The AFT wants to stop "salary-hopping" from one district to another by teachers who are attracted by small increases offered by the school boards in what the union believes is a "subtle practice ... of inching up the salary scale in a pattern that is basically depressed and only superficially competitive." [*214*] If the AFT is successful in starting area-wide bargaining by teachers, other unions with members employed in different local government units, for example, in the same metropolitan area, may try to do the same thing.

### Cooperation by Canadian Municipalities

Joint bargaining by municipalities has for some time existed to some extent in Canada, specifically by the three municipalities of Vancouver, Burnaby, and New Westminister in British Columbia. The background here is that in 1955 nine cities in the lower mainland of the province, including these three, joined to form a Metropolitan Municipal Personnel Advisory Committee, the objective being to improve their position in union negotiations and to cooperate on personnel matters.

The committee quickly proved its value in collection of wage and other data for the bargaining sessions, and in 1959 Burnaby proposed that all nine cities bargain jointly through a single negotiator. Vancouver and New Westminster concurred, and the three municipalities established a Joint Labor Relations Committee and together hired a counsel to represent them in the negotiations. All nine cities still continue on the Metropolitan Municipal Advisory Committee, but up to now the six others have preferred to stay out of the joint bargaining. In 1964, the Joint Labor Committee, convinced that it needed more help, established a Labor Relations Bureau with a full-time director and a staff to help him prepare for and conduct the negotiations.

The three cities have been more effective in the negotiations as the result of their joint bargaining, but disadvantages have been noted. It is said that the director of the bureau cannot possibly have the same detailed knowledge of contract problems as that possessed by personnel and other officials in each of the three cities. Furthermore, his workload is held to be excessive, since, in addition to entering into the negotiations with the unions, he has to be present at the numerous conciliation board hearings which prove necessary. [*400*, pp. 66-67]

For these reasons, the opinion is advanced that it would be better for a big city to negotiate separately, but it is not clear why it should not be possible to staff for joint negotiations in such a way as to solve the workload difficulty and also give proper attention to the problems of each cooperating city. After all, in some industries numerous large-sized employers find it advantageous to bargain jointly with the unions through a negotiating committee or even a single negotiator.

Perhaps general agreements applying to all the cooperating cities could be entered into on some matters such as wages and fringe benefits, with individual contracts negotiated to cover each municipality's "local" problems. This is the arrangement in some industries where both national and individual plant contracts are negotiated. In any event, the initiative may come from the employee organizations, because S. A. Little, president of the Canadian Union of Public Employees, in an address at the 1965 Annual Conference of the Canadian Federation of Mayors, said [*400*, pp. 243-44] :

> We have got to move toward some form of collective bargaining on a regional basis. . . . for you, as employers, it means that you must be prepared to cede some of your autonomy to a central bargaining committee, and we for our part are going to have to forego the pleasure of playing you off against the other.

Little's union had a reported membership in 1966 of 89,409 in 535 locals of crown corporations, provincial, municipal, and other local government employees. [*400*, p. 38]

Whether or not the municipalities bargain jointly, George W. Noble, personnel officer for the Municipality of Metropolitan Toronto, believes it is essential that they cooperate closely in labor relations matters. His argument is that the Canadian municipal unions are operating on a national basis, with annual conventions at which they "decide just what amendments [to collective agreements] they will seek from their municipal employers." The unions have area offices in most of the provinces, and they "furnish the local unions with organizers, negotiators, research assistance, publications, and assistance in the preparation and presentation of briefs to conciliation boards." Noble says: [*296*, p. 260]

> Compare this situation to that facing the municipalities. Until recently there was not even a central location where a municipality could obtain current wage rates and working conditions prevailing in other municipalities. . . . It is essential that a reliable source of information be developed, to which all participating municipalities would have access, so that municipalities will at least be as well informed as the municipal unions before they enter into bargaining.

The Canadian Federation of Mayors and Municipalities now has a plan to compile and disseminate pay data on a nation-wide basis. [*400*, p. 245]

### Councils of Employee Organizations

Within a single governmental jurisdiction, negotiations may take place with councils of employee organizations. The public employer does not have to bargain separately with numerous employee organizations, a process which is not only time-consuming but also may terminate in separate agreements providing unequal benefits for employees who should be treated alike.

*The Tacoma Example.* In August of 1966, the City of Tacoma, Washington, adopted a resolution providing for an arrangement of this kind. In that city, there is a Joint Labor Committee which represents unions that are members of, or are affiliated with, the Pierce County Central Labor Council and/or the Tacoma Council of Teamsters. The resolution states that this committee will "exclusively represent" its unions in "all collective bargaining negotiations involving issues and matters common to all member unions"; however, it must ". . . establish adequate procedures whereby the authorized and official bargaining representatives of each individual union may, if it so desires, collectively bargain in respect to all issues and matters that are not common to all unions, but are peculiar and specific to the union involved."

The Committee is ". . . recognized by the City as the exclusive bargaining agency for all employees of the City where said union represents or has in its membership a majority of those City employees concerned in a Bargaining Unit; provided, that such employee representatives establish to the satisfaction of the City that such union represents a majority of the City employees in a classification or other employee bargaining unit; provided, however, that nothing herein contained shall be construed as prohibiting the right of any union to utilize the procedures set up by the Joint Labor Committee as above provided to negotiate with the authorized bargaining representatives of the City in respect to all matters peculiar and specific to the particular union in question."

Any employee organization, not a member of the Pierce County Central Labor Council or the Tacoma Council of Teamsters, which is named an exclusive bargaining agent may, with the consent of the Joint Labor Committee, become a member; or it may elect to "negotiate directly with the representatives of the City in collective bargaining in the same manner" as the Joint Committee. [*349*, pp. 1-2]

City Manager David D. Rowlands points out that

In highly unionized cities like Tacoma, where there are a number of craft and industrial unions, in addition to fire and police unions, and the American Federation of State, County, and Municipal Employees, the process of negotiating with 17 to 22 functioning labor unions and employee organizations becomes quite complicated and cumbersome.

Thus, it is advantageous for the city to be able to negotiate with the Joint Labor Committee on "those questions pertaining to salaries, wages, fringe benefits, or working conditions which are, in general, applicable to all city employees."
[*360*, p. 6] From the unions' standpoint, joint bargaining in
some cases is not only more convenient but, by uniting their
forces, it strengthens them in the negotiations.

*Councils Within Agencies.* Individual agencies may also negotiate with councils of employee organizations. As indicated
in Chapter 4, in the case of blue-collar workers, the TVA
bargains with the Tennessee Valley Trades and Labor Council,
which represents all craft bargaining units, and, for white-
collar workers, with the Salary Policy Employee Panel. As TVA
General Manager Louis J. Van Mol stresses, this approximates
the advantages of agency-wide bargaining units, and at the same
time it flexibly permits separate negotiations with the individual
unions on matters which concern them alone. Furthermore, it
"requires the unions to maintain stable interunion relationships
so they speak to management with one voice," which "assures
that TVA will become involved in a minimum of interunion
disagreements." [*395*, pp. 90-91]

In its advice to the agencies on the Kennedy Order, the
Civil Service Commission notes that "joint councils exist at such
places as TVA and Bonneville Power Administration, with excellent results in terms of time saved, minimized competition for
benefits, and comprehensiveness and consistency in treatment of
like groups," but cautions that "if the employee organizations
involved cannot establish satisfactory working relationships with
each other, attempts to conduct joint dealings may not be as
successful." [*378*, 5.16]

Illustrating one agency's response, the Department of Health,
Education, and Welfare permits installation heads to require
employee organization representatives to consult or negotiate
with them in joint meetings, provided they all at least have
formal recognition and that none of them objects that they
claim overlapping jurisdictions and compete for members. Only
organizations with exclusive recognition may participate in
joint negotiations, with either joint or separate agreements
resulting from such negotiations. Similarly, a council of employee organizations at a single installation may ask to consult or
negotiate; it may consult if all its members at least have formal

recognition, and negotiate only if they all have exclusive recognition. Furthermore, councils representing employees in more than one installation may also ask to consult or negotiate, and "such a request will be evaluated on the same basis as a request for a unit larger than an installation." [*386*, 711-1-80] District offices of the Social Security Administration and Public Health Service hospitals are examples of HEW installations.

*The Problem in the Canadian Federal Service.* Since under the new legislation the boundaries of the bargaining units will correspond with occupational groups, Saul Frankel's warning about the "large number of independent, or semi-independent, associations competing with each other for the same membership in some cases, and representing identical classes in almost all cases" must be taken seriously. [*98*, p. 34] When Frankel published *A Model for Negotiation and Arbitration Between the Canadian Government and its Civil Servants* in 1962, the three major employee organizations were the Professional Institute, the Civil Service Association of Canada, and the Civil Service Federation. He characterized the first two as "unitary organizations whose spokesmen represent their respective constituencies with apparent authority," the third as "essentially an organizational structure that seeks to coordinate the activities and represent the interests . . . on issues of service-wide concern" of the some 16 national departmental affiliates. [*98*, p. 35] His analysis was that "any process of achieving effective representation of the staff side as a whole would require two stages of integration—one within the Civil Service Federation and the other among the three major groups." [*98*, p. 36] In July, 1966, the Federation and the Civil Service Association merged into the new Public Service Alliance.

The Preparatory Committee on Collective Bargaining in the Public Service recommended that a "council of two or more employee organizations be able to gain and hold certification so long as it is able to meet the test of majority representation and satisfy the Public Service Staff Relations Board that appropriate constitutional and administrative arrangements have been made for the discharge of its responsibilities." [*324*, p. 33]

The new Public Service Staff Relations Act authorizes the certification of councils of employee organizations as bargaining agents, provided the Board is satisfied that "each of the employee organizations forming the council has vested appropriate authority in the council to enable it to discharge the duties and responsibilities of a bargaining agent." [*350*, p. 17] When the law is put into effect and the bargaining units are defined, the council of employee organizations device may prove very useful in integrating union bargaining efforts and in obtaining more uniform general working conditions than otherwise would be possible.

## The Negotiating Team

Turning to the actual negotiations, the first matter to decide is the composition of the negotiating team. This, of course, is a problem for the employee organizations as well as the public employer, and each party has legitimate concern over the competence, integrity, and other qualities of the other side's negotiators. The rest of this chapter will be primarily concerned with how the employer carries out its role in the negotiations, but this, of course, takes place in dynamic interaction with the employee organization representatives at the other end of the conference table.

Since collective negotiations are so new in government, no very clear patterns have emerged as to the membership of the negotiating team. There seem to be some general areas of agreement, such as the desirability of including the personnel and finance directors and some representatives of the line departments, but in many jurisdictions the discussions as to who should be included are basically in their very early stages. This does not mean that the matter is being handled on a haphazard basis, although this may be true in some places, but rather that desirable experimentation is taking place until the most workable patterns are found. Sometimes the public employer is caught unprepared by an employee organization that initiates negotiations under authority of a law providing for mandatory bargaining, and the public jurisdiction or agency, whichever it is, must put together a negotiating team almost as hurriedly as a bucket brigade.

### Representation of "Three Elements"

Summarizing a Seminar on Collective Bargaining in the Public Service held in Scarborough, Ontario, in the summer of 1966, T. J. Plunkett said that the composition of the bargaining team "can be broken down into a consideration of three elements in public management concerned primarily with (1) central financial control, (2) centralized personnel management, and (3) operating management. Somehow these three elements have to be embodied in the government bargaining team and, if the responsibility is assigned almost completely to one, the others must be closely associated with it." [*309*, pp. 189-190] At the same seminar, D. G. Pyle, Consultant to the Central Ontario Industrial Relations Institute in Toronto, recommended a small permanent committee to include "the senior spokesman of personnel, a financial or treasury official, an operational manager, and, perhaps, either legal counsel or a consultant." [*318*, pp. 70-71]

Both men had in mind principally the negotiating team for an entire jurisdiction, such as a municipality, but the same general prescription can, and has been, suggested for individual agencies. Stressing that the "size of the negotiating committee usually depends upon the size of the establishment and the variety of functions within it," the United States Civil Service Commission states that "normally the membership is designed to provide representation of top management, the personnel office, and the managers of the principal operating divisions concerned." [*378*, p. 6.01] The agency personnel officers have a major role in the negotiations, with other management officials also participating. [*376*, p. 14]

In the TVA, the director of personnel is the chief negotiator for the management; in bargaining with the Salary Policy Employee Panel, he is assisted by a Salary Policy Negotiating Committee made up of top management officials from organization units which include a large proportion of the white-collar workers. In negotiations with the Trades and Labor Council, he is aided by a similar committee representing the parts of the organization in which most of TVA's trades and labor employees are employed. [*378*, p. 3.04]

### Role of the Civil Service Commission and the Personnel Director

This raises the question of possible conflict of loyalties, because the personnel officers, whether in the central personnel agency or in the line agencies, are supposed to protect the employees' interests as well as represent management. In the past, personnel men have often successfully walked the tight rope by carrying out efficient recruiting and other programs in the interests of the management, but also intervening on behalf of employees with just complaints. With few exceptions, they have not been in the open position of trying to whittle down the employees' requests for improved economic and other benefits; this unpleasant task has fallen to budget officers, department heads, chief executives, and legislators. When a personnel director is a member of the management bargaining team, he emerges clearly as one of the "bosses," no matter how sympathetic he may seem by comparison with others on the team. This new role of his convinces some employee representatives even more how "management-oriented" the personnel man is. At the same time, those who have been saying all along that personnel officers should face the reality that they are above all representatives of the management are vindicated.

In his treatise quoted above, Frankel wrote, "in theory, at least, it seems difficult to reconcile the notion of the Commission as impartial administrator of the merit system with that of the Commission as partisan negotiator. Because the federal Civil Service Commission has managed, on the whole, to maintain its independence and impartiality, it would seem inadvisable to saddle it with a necessarily partisan task." [*98*, p. 27] The Parliament followed this line of reasoning, because, as previously related, it has made the Treasury Board responsible for negotiations and transferred to it from the old Civil Service Commission the position classification and pay functions. The new Public Service Commission is in charge of recruitment and the merit system in general, and while it has no formal role in negotiations with the employee organizations, it is expected to provide data on recruitment-retention problems to the Treasury Board negotiating team.

In the United States, where there seems to be little support for merging classification and pay with general finance functions, this solution is not likely to be available. What may become common is an arrangement whereby the personnel director of the jurisdiction serves as a member of the bargaining team and keeps the civil service commission informed of developments in the negotiations. The commission retains its classification and pay functions, and serves in an advisory capacity to the chief executive and the legislature on the terms of collective agreements. It may disagree with the bargaining team and, for that matter, with the personnel director. He is obliged to listen to their views and keep them informed, but may take an independent course in the negotiations.

In New Castle County, Delaware, the director of personnel is appointed by the county executive, upon the recommendation of the personnel board, whose three members are appointed by the county executive with the approval of the county council. The civil service ordinance provides that the director of personnel shall serve as a "participating member in negotiations and other proceedings in labor-management relations," and that the board "shall advise the County Executive in labor-management relations." [*171*] Of course, this will not cause employee leaders to change their minds about the management sympathies of the civil service commission and the personnel director. The commission does maintain a posture of independence, and it is available as one of the reviewing bodies within the administrative branch to weigh the negotiating team's proposals. From the practical standpoint, members of a part-time board cannot be expected to have the time anyway to spend on negotiations which can easily stretch over a long period of time. In the province of Saskatchewan, though, the chairman of the Public Service Commission is the government's chief negotiator, and the results appear to have been good. [*99*, pp. 29-30]

In the city of Philadelphia, the bargaining team consists of the personnel director, managing director (equivalent to city manager), finance director, and labor relations consultant; pursuant to a civil service regulation, the personnel director is authorized to negotiate and sign agreements with the exclusive bargaining agent, District Council 33 of the AFSCME. The personnel director, Foster B. Roser, feels strongly that there is no conflict in the administrator of the merit system being one of the negotiators. He puts it this way:

> When he [the personnel director] is on the negotiating team, he may haggle, bargain, and compromise. But it is part of his job to discuss and consider employee requests presented by their representatives. When he administers the merit system, the grievance procedure, or any other part of the labor-management agreement, his job is to find out *what* is right, not *who* is right. He can wear all these hats and still be respected by employees and their representatives.

Roser further believes that the personnel director should take advantage of the new developments and assume a leading role in labor relations, because in this way he strengthens the personnel function and his own role in the management. He points out that "in industry the personnel men with the highest salaries and the greatest prestige are those who function mainly in the area of labor relations and union negotiations." [*328*, pp. 80-81]

*Specific Reasons for Including Personnel Director.* Since the personnel director usually is responsible for making pay plan recommendations to the civil service commission and/or to the chief executive, he can judge the impact of employee organization proposals on the existing salary scales and convey his reactions to the other members of the bargaining team. If proposals are made to raise the scales for certain pay grades, or to assign certain classes of positions to higher grades, and he is convinced that this would upset the balance in the classification and compensation plans and do damage to the principle of equal pay for equal work, he is the expert in the municipal administration to say so. Many of the employee organization proposals will deal with appointment, promotion, and other personnel policies and procedures, and he has a heavy responsibility for identifying points of conflict with the civil service law and regulations and explaining to the other management, as well as the employee representatives, why he thinks these conflicts exist. Suffice it to say, that if the personnel director, and the civil service commission in its advisory role, are not on the alert to protect the merit system, it may be seriously damaged as the employee leaders press the argument that their proposed contract will give superior protections and benefits to the employees.

This, of course, is a very difficult role for the personnel director, because the employees' negotiators may equate protection of the merit system with blind defense of the status quo. He must do his best to try to convince them that personnel improvements can and should be negotiated, including changes in the civil service rules and even the law, but in accordance with the legal procedures for making such changes and without replacing the merit system completely with industry-type labor contracts. This is not an anti-union posture, but it may be so regarded, and the personnel director may have to struggle to preserve his basic attitude of sympathetic response to employee organization requests for improved working conditions and substantial areas of joint decision-making.

Another important reason for having the personnel director on the bargaining team is that he necessarily will have an important role in the administration of the labor contracts once signed. Questions as to the employees' rights to overtime pay, sick and annual leave, and other benefits provided for in the agreement will be referred to him for interpretation because these are matters customarily dealt with by the personnel office. He will be in a good position also to evaluate the *real* impact of various contract provisions on the merit system, and he will, of course, be vitally concerned with the grievance procedure. Furthermore, his knowledge of how previous contracts have worked out in practice will make him all the more valuable to the management team. It is hard to see how the jurisdiction can afford to leave him off the team, but, to do a good job in this new role, he must re-tool, so to speak, because personnel administration under collective negotiations is quite different from what it has been under traditional concepts.

Because it may take the personnel director too long to become effective in negotiations, some jurisdictions may prefer to hire full-time labor relations experts and place them directly on the chief executive's staff, as was done recently in New York City. [*298*] Another solution is to create such a position, with subordinate staff, in the personnel department. In industry, the responsibilities for industrial relations, on the one hand, and the remaining personnel functions, on the other hand, may be kept separate or be combined. As will be elaborated in the final chapter of this book, some public personnel people feel strongly that the labor relations function is an integral part of personnel administration and should, therefore, be under the personnel director.

On occasion individual agencies may have strong reasons for limiting the role of the personnel office. In the Bonneville Power Administration, because it was not considered "one of the stronger divisions" and had "been plagued by a procession of directors," "in 1945 all dealings with the crafts as such were removed from the Personnel Division and placed in the hands of a labor relations adviser" who reports directly to the administrator. [*393*, p. 64] Some of the employee leaders are against the personnel officers' representing management in dealings with the unions. This opinion was expressed by John Griner, President of the American Federation of Government Employees, at a Society for Personnel Administration round table; his reasoning was that their role should be limited to giving objective, impartial interpretations of the regulations. [*340*, p. 6]

212 Management-Employee Relations

### Other Members of the Team

The reason for including the finance director is, of course, to make it possible for the management team to determine quickly the relationship of any proposed agreements on pay and economic benefits to the city's financial resources. The chief executive and the legislature will decide what benefits to grant, but they will expect the finance director to give them accurate estimates of the cost to the city.

Because the negotiations will deal with some matters affecting the entire administrative establishment, it is desirable to include some line department representatives. They must live with the contracts, and they have detailed knowledge of both working conditions and work requirements which such staff people as the personnel and finance directors may not have. When the negotiations are with an employee organization whose members are employed in a certain department only, as in the case of social workers, then there is a logical justification for representing that department on the bargaining team.

When it comes to including the jurisdiction's chief legal officer, opinion is more divided. Within both management and employee organizations, there may be objection that lawyers become bogged down in technicalities, and in addition usually have little of value to contribute in substantive policy-making in labor relations. Nevertheless, there often are important questions of law to be resolved before the management team can accept the wording in a proposed contract and before those authorized to sign for the jurisdiction can feel safe in putting their signatures to it. One suggestion is to have a legal representative sit in on the negotiations as an adviser to, but not a member of, the management team. Failing this, someone on the team can be in touch with the legal department, and, of course, the latter should review the contract document before it is signed. The opinion has been expressed that, in time, public service, like private enterprise, may develop specially trained lawyers who can make good contributions in the bargaining sessions themselves.

*Role of Appointive and Elective Chief Administrators.* In some cities, the city manager himself does the negotiating or participates directly in it. In Cincinnati, the manager represents the city, except in the bargaining with the independent boards and commissions. Illustrating the point that he will need help, particularly in a large city, the Cincinnati manager has given the personnel officer the "primary responsibility for negotiations on city-wide issues, including all wage matters." [68]

In Tacoma, "the City Manager and the Director of Utilities, jointly or on behalf of General Government or the Department of utilities, as the case may be," are "the exclusive representatives of the City in all collective bargaining negotiations." [349, p. 2] Since the manager is an appointive, professional administrator, there is no reason why he should not participate in negotiations and be present at all the bargaining sessions if he has the time. The same holds true of city administrators in mayor-council jurisdictions and of chief administrative officers in counties.

As for elective chief executives, like mayors and county executives such as in New Castle County, Delaware, there is a good deal of opinion to the effect that, particularly in large jurisdictions, it is probably better that they stay out of the negotiations. They likely would prefer to do so, because of the pressures on their time and the realization that as political figures they would inevitably carry at least the appearance of politics to the bargaining table. In the event of deadlocked negotiations, they can intervene as the ultimate arbiters within the administrative branch, which gives the management team the opportunity to hold off on those employee demands it feels should be resisted and granted only if the chief executive decides to make the concessions. Industry experience, as explained by Paul M. Berthoud, Employee Relations Director, Ground Employees, United Airlines, may be useful here: [46, p. 54]

> . . . the union usually wants to involve the top decisionmaker of the company because he is used to making decisions, will make them, and from then on the issue is settled. But such a man usually does not have the patience of the professional negotiator who realizes that the timing of a concession is probably more important to the progress of the negotiation than the concession itself. If the company spokesman is at a level lower than top management, the negotiator has the opportunity to say, "We will have to study your proposal a little more and review it within the company." A more thorough consideration of the proposal can then take place. . . . Additionally, at least in large corporations, top management could not devote the amount of time that is necessary to conduct negotiations.

From Canada, D. G. Pyle also opposes having chief executives and other elective officials at the bargaining table. He says, "we have had our experience not only with elected representatives intervening in our municipal negotiations but, indeed, elected personages at the federal and provincial levels, both in disputes in private industry and in those having more overtones of a public interest. Seldom have the results been regarded by management personnel as rewarding to anyone but the union and the employees. All in all I am satisfied that unions must relish these developments with real glee when they see these political novices take over." [*318*, p. 72]

Showing that no one formula can decide questions like these, the Connecticut Municipal Employee Relations Act reads: "except as hereinafter provided ... the chief executive officer, whether elected or appointed, or his designated representative or representatives, shall represent the municipal employer in collective bargaining with such employee organization." Where "the municipal employer is a district, school board, housing authority or other authority established by law, ... such district, school board, housing authority or other authority, or its designated representatives, shall represent such municipal employer in collective bargaining." [*30*, pp. 330-331]

The nature and size of the jurisdiction obviously have a great bearing on whether elective administrative officials should participate directly in the negotiations. The interim commission which drafted the legislation said in its report: [*323*, pp. 16-17]

> We recognize that the administrative structures of some Connecticut communities suggest that the chief executive will want to appoint an administrative officer and/or a committee of municipal representatives to act for the city in dealing with employee organizations. In some municipalities, a committee composed of members of the budget authority, the legislative body, and the executive branch of the municipal government may be the most appropriate representatives of the municipality. The responsibility for representing the municipality, however, vests in the chief executive, and we are providing that he should sign any agreement as a ministerial act.

*Use of Outside Consultants.* Instead of naming one of their own full-time employees, some jurisdictions are contracting for the services of an outside labor relations specialist to serve as their negotiator for individual contract negotiations. They may do this simply because they have no one available for the task, or it may be a conscious decision to bring in someone experienced in "hard" bargaining techniques.

Others argue that, sooner or later, the jurisdiction will have to use its own people to do the negotiating and that it should start to do so without delay. They also maintain that, although the consultant is skilled in negotiating techniques, as a stranger to the community he cannot possibly know enough about its labor relations problems. Furthermore, because most of these consultants have developed their reputations in industry, the fear exists that they will not appreciate the differences in the government environment and will see nothing wrong with such things as the union shop and binding arbitration which have long been accepted in the private sector. Still others contend that this background of the consultant is advantageous, because it will make him more acceptable to the employee organizations than, for example, the "management-oriented" personnel director.

All of these arguments have to be weighed in terms of the characteristics of the particular consultant. He may turn out to have a very good understanding of governmental problems since in recent years his "public" business may have understandably expanded. Everything considered, employment of outside negotiators may prove an excellent short-range solution, but, of course, there is also the problem of having to pay the fees their reputations command.

*Advisability of Councilmanic Representation.* Some people strongly feel that the bargaining team should include a representative of the city council or other local governing body. The argument here is that, since the lawmakers have the final say, the management team negotiates in a vacuum if it has no idea of what they will approve. Others believe that this problem is better dealt with by establishing a liaison relationship between the team and the council. They see the danger that the councilmanic representative may react in the negotiations in accordance with his political commitments and that, through his personal contacts with other council members, he may quickly involve the whole body in the bargaining process. There is also the point just made above: the management team is better off when no one on it has final decision-making power or a share in it, as in the case of a council member.

Based on their experience in Hartford, Connecticut, as city manager and executive secretary to the manager, respectively, Carleton F. Sharpe and Elisha C. Freedman give three reasons why "the city council should stay clear of negotiations until the city manager-union discussions end":

1. The council preserves objectivity by not "teaming up with the manager versus the unions," "it can get the feel of public opinion" by "sitting back and letting the manager and the unions discuss the issues openly," and such a pro-

cedure "can shield councilmen from making premature commitments before all the facts are digested";

2. "By remaining independent of both the manager and the unions during the discussions," it "can serve as a kind of arbitration board," thus discouraging union requests for calling in outside arbitrators; and

3. "Political considerations, which are the council's, and the technical-administrative considerations, which are the manager's, should not be intermingled."

They believe that "an internal two-step procedure in the bargaining process with a reasonable time lapse between union-manager discussions and city council review provides a built-in cooling-off period and a safety valve ... needed to avoid hasty and drastic actions." [*336*, p. 101]

Although admitting that "a city council surely is a most unlikely negotiating agency," D. G. Weiford, former city manager of Eau Claire, Wisconsin, believes that "we have no choice but to be pragmatic, for it is an inescapable fact that only the city council can make final decisions in financial matters." He says that "for this reason, it has been determined in Eau Claire that, difficult or not, the city council *must* perform an active role in labor negotiations," and that, while in "very large cities this may not be practical ... in most council-manager cities, and in some mayor-council cities, it does ... offer possibilities."

He recommends that, about two months before the negotiations, wage and other data be collected and submitted to the council, together with the union requests and an estimate of their cost. Arrangements should then be made "for the full city council and the bargaining units to meet at least once and preferably twice in order to clarify all requests," to be followed by more informal meetings between the union designates and the "chief executive (either mayor or manager), along with his staff and ... a few designated council representatives." The full council should receive the minutes of each meeting and, if the negotiations bog down, be prepared to "re-enter the bargaining process and seek to find areas of agreement."

Weiford reports that in Eau Claire the full council now participates in all negotiations, but he believes "the large size of most city councils in Wisconsin will no doubt sharply limit the general adoption of this practice." Although Hartford is a much larger city than Eau Claire, it is clear that Weiford does not accept the strategic and other arguments advanced by Sharpe and Freedman against direct involvement of the council in the negotiations. [*406*, pp. 23-24]

Recently in the same state of Wisconsin, one of the aldermen in Madison resigned from the council bargaining committee in protest over a full council vote on firemen's overtime pay which disregarded the committee's recommendations. He wrote the mayor:

> I do not feel it is justifiable to me or my family to be forced to attend protracted bargaining sessions lasting until 2 a.m. or 3 a.m. when the bargaining contract is later overriden by the council as a whole . . . . From now on, let the union bargaining agent go directly to the council and not waste time with a bargaining committee in lengthy sessions negotiating a contract for wages, hours, and working conditions. [*419*]

This jibes with the experience reported from Philadelphia where on occasion councilmen have been on the bargaining team but not proved very useful because the other council members have not necessarily agreed with them.

George W. Noble reports the same problem in the Canadian municipalities where "the bargaining is generally conducted either by a committee of the council or by council as a whole." He reports, "municipal councils do not delegate to their nominee the same measure of authority as is exercised by the official in charge of bargaining for an industry, despite the fact that councils are clearly not suitable bodies to deal with skilled union negotiators in working out satisfactory collective agreements."

In any case, in his opinion the councils should not do the negotiating: they lack the "skill or knowledge necessary to deal effectively with the arguments put forward by experienced union representatives," cannot be expected to recognize the impact of union requests on management prerogatives, "find it difficult to maintain a united front" before the union, and "simply do not have the time to spend on the prolonged bargaining sessions sometimes necessary to achieve a satisfactory settlement." He believes they should limit themselves to establishing the labor relations policy, and appoint an experienced official or lawyer to conduct the bargaining meetings. [*296*, p. 259]

*Influence of the Bargaining Team.* Prominent among the points made by those quoted above is that the bargaining team should be such as to have real influence with the ultimate decision-makers. Plunkett states bluntly that "there is no use . . .

in a public management bargaining team attempting to carry out negotiations if for every minor point the team must wait for the results of a referral back to some administrative committee." [*309*, p. 190] At the same time, it must be recognized that the team cannot commit the public employer on the spot: it remains essentially an advisory group. After all, as noted in Chapter 2, industry negotiators also are advisers only to the company management. Probably much more decisive than the formal powers within the organization of the negotiators will be the personal regard in which they are held, based on the past experience with their recommendations.

*Qualities of the Negotiators.* This brings us to the question of the desirable characteristics of the members of the team. No one questions the need for familiarity with the legal structure, functions, and detailed operating problems of the jurisdiction, but, when it comes to personal characteristics, there is the usual tendency to set forth requirements in terms of superlatives. The negotiator obviously must be tactful, patient, flexible, and direct and firm enough to obtain the respect of the union representatives. More really cannot be said, because, as in everything else, much will be learned painfully from experience. Collective negotiations are very different from what most public officials are accustomed to in their daily routines.

Weiford quotes the Executive Director of the Wisconsin Council of County and Municipal Employees as follows: [*406*, p. 20]

> grossly apparent . . . is the complete lack of skill on the part of many public employers in bargaining with the union. There is an art to conducting negotiations. Over 90 per cent of the public employers have not mastered the basic fundamentals of the art. At the present time, city attorneys, district attorneys, city and county clerks, department heads and sundry other officials are all participating in bargaining. Continuity in the bargaining process is lacking and diversity of opinion is rampant.

Training programs are very desirable and they are functioning in some jurisdictions, but space makes it impossible for us to be concerned with the details of such programs in this book. New courses in educational institutions are also needed: in the spring of 1967, Professor Myron Lieberman of Rhode Island College taught a graduate-level course for future school administrators, entitled, "Collective Negotiations for Teachers," the first time such a course has been offered anywhere. [*62*]

*The Chief Negotiator.* It is generally considered desirable to have a chief negotiator or spokesman as sometimes he is called. His function is initially to present the management views and to summarize his team's reaction to the employees' proposals, and generally to exercise a leadership role within his group. When the team caucuses privately to go over its position, he directs its discussions and also is the main channel for checking back with the management on the employee organization's demands. He calls upon the other team members to contribute their particular skills and knowledge to the negotiations and assures their full participation. Obviously, he should be the most skilled negotiator in the group.

*Size of the Team.* There is general agreement that the team should be as small as possible, ideally from three to five members. This is one reason why full council participation, with the several councilmen added to the administrative branch representatives, makes for an unwieldy arrangement. Because of the scattering of responsibilities in many local governments, however, it may be necessary to include more administrative officials than would otherwise be desirable. The chief administrator should guard against the tendency to want to include every department head so as not to "leave anyone out." In jurisdiction-wide bargaining, there is no reason why all of them have to be represented. In any case, it is desirable to have alternate members also, because the regular ones may have to absent themselves from some of the negotiating sessions.

### Preparing for the Negotiations

The negotiation of each contract should be viewed as a special project, requiring a firm grasp by the management representatives of all the important facts bearing upon the particular issues involved. They should, first of all, have detailed knowledge of all the operating, personnel, and other problems of their own organizations which may come up during the negotiations. It would be embarrassing for the employee designates to know more about some of these matters than they do. The employee organization is constantly listening to its members' grievances and cannot survive unless it investigates the details and develops forceful arguments before the management to improve working conditions; its representatives usually come into the negotiations buttressed with what they consider the "facts" about given situations.

As Rollin B. Posey comments: [*312*, p. 64]

> The negotiating executives must be careful that they do not proceed upon the assumption that they already know everything there is to know about their own personnel policies and practices. This is an easy and common assumption, which is unfortunate, because the assumption is almost always an erroneous one. The written rules and regulations are usually incomplete; some practices and customs have never been reduced to writing. The personnel rules are not always followed, invariably and exactly, but are modified by tacit understanding or agreement.

Of course, the management negotiators cannot be expected to know in detail about every situation the employee leaders report, but they should demonstrate that they can get the facts quickly and that they are not far removed from operating realities.

### Need to Investigate Previous Contract Experience

Before the contract negotiations begin, the management team should talk in detail with department heads and supervisors to get their opinions about the problems which have arisen in the administration of the current and previous contracts; it should also obtain their suggestions as to proposals the management should make and the stand it should take on particular issues. It is also advisable to make a careful study of grievances filed by the employee organization under the present contract, to get some impression of the kinds of changes it may request in the new pact. While individual grievances will not be taken up during the negotiations, this review of past ones should pinpoint some of the areas of worker dissatisfactions.

Where the contracts provide for binding arbitration, as in the Canadian cities, recent arbitration awards should be studied. Donald G. Pyle, consultant to the Central Ontario Industrial Relations Institute of Toronto, states, "In this province, most of our arbitrators are judges, and for the most part they deal with disputes as to contract interpretation by the meaning to be taken from the written word, past practice notwithstanding. Private industry and public service have the same arbitrators, and their comments and observations on clauses or contract provisions as applied to a given situation can provide a fund of knowledge as to the rights and responsibilities or the freedom, discretion or restriction envisaged in any particular language or commitment." [*318*, p. 69] The management negotiators simply must keep up with developments, such as court decisions and the action of other public agencies in instituting court tests of the legality of certain recurring union requests, like that for the union shop.

## Value of Knowledge About the Employee Organizations

The management team should also familiarize itself with the program, past record, and personalities in the leadership of the particular employee organization. As we have seen, the orientation, position on specific issues, and even the membership composition (extent to which supervisors are represented) of these organizations vary. Every management negotiator should know enough about the employee organizations to know in advance the kinds of contract proposals their local representatives likely will make. There is no secret about their programs: they are clearly stated in their official organs, such as the AFSCME's *The Public Employee,* which ably summarizes their pending negotiations in the different parts of the country.

Employee organization leaders in both Canada and the United States generally need no lessons in government organization and procedures: even though collective negotiations with public agencies may be new, representations before administrative officials and lobbying with legislative bodies, in particular, have taken place for many years. By contrast, many government officials now drawn into contract negotiations have in the past had little reason to give much thought to the programs and functioning of public employee organizations. Knowledge of the political alliances of the organization, the relationships between the leaders and elective officials, and its past role in the community will also be valuable. After all, the employee organization makes similar assessments of the relationships within the government, but as Posey warns, "if information about the union does not come normally on a voluntary basis or through the union's house organ, then the information should not be secured. No under-handed method should be used to secure information about the union." [*312*, p. 65] On this point, Chester A. Newland observes: [*172*]

Posey's advice ... is consistent with best practices, but ... imported union leaders, or others who are not known in the jurisdiction, probably warrant background investigations similar to those which responsible management routinely conducts of unknown business contractors, applicants for sensitive positions, arbitrators, or community visitors. When routine, such investigations protect the public, employers, and responsible employee organizations from the rare but harmful few who are corrupt or worse. And, if handled as investigations are routinely practiced in scrutiny of business contractors, improper invasions of privacy and civil liberties should not even be approached, let alone threatened. Experienced unions likewise investigate management representatives, arbitrators, etc. When held to the usual limits, such practice is rather accepted, I find.

### The Necessary Wage and Related Data

All of this is essential background, but the management team must also obtain and carefully analyze essential wage and other data. Sometimes, the legal authorization for the collective bargaining will itself specify the items upon which the collective bargaining shall be based, as in the case of the Cincinnati ordinance: [*67*, p. 3]

1. Cost of Living Data
   a. Over-all consumers price indices as furnished by the Bureau of Labor Statistics for the latest complete twelve-month period.
   b. Bureau of Labor statistics food indices for the latest twelve-month period available at the time of negotiations.

2. Improvement Factors
   a. Improvements in the standard of living.
   b. Improvement in efficiency of city service.

3. National and Local Wage Surveys
   a. Bureau of Labor Statistics "family of four" budget estimates.
   b. Ohio Bureau of Unemployment Compensation average wage rates on covered workers.
   c. Other acceptable surveys by responsible fact-finding authorities.

4. Relationships among the salary rates of the various classes of city employment.

5. Comparative Salary Data
   a. Prevailing union wage rates for comparable jobs in local industry.
   b. List of local companies to be used for wage rate comparisons.
   c. Prevailing union wage scales in currently comparable cities where no local parallel exists for comparison of a job classification.

6. Such other items or issues as may be introduced during

meetings or conferences with city representatives, if, at the time they are offered, they are accepted as pertinent by both parties.

Data, as complete as possible, on compensation policies, rates, and fringe benefits of other employers, both public and private, for the same kinds of workers are essential. This information should be obtained as well from employers in other communities when the comparisons are still relevant despite the distance factor. The pattern, as well as the actual rates, of recent settlements, is important, for, as stressed by George W. Noble, the employee organizations try to obtain percentage wage increases and benefits equivalent to what they have obtained in other communities. [*296*, p. 255] It is here that the personnel department, with its responsibility for conducting periodic wage surveys, can be very useful, and, as noted earlier in this chapter, public agencies can cooperate to great advantage in their collection of wage and other data.

*Joint Management-Employee Fact-Finding Committees.* In the Tennessee Valley Authority, there is a Joint Committee on Wage Data, equally representing the TVA and the Tennessee Valley Trades and Labor Council. It reviews wage data and submits a written report to the co-chairmen (director of personnel and president of the council) of the annual wage conference, "including exhibits recording prevailing wage data as agreed upon by joint review together with written summaries of relevant argument made before the committee." [*102*, pp. 20-21]

The U.S. Civil Service Commission reports that, apart from the TVA, "some agencies have found it possible to make use of joint-employee-management committees as part of their fact-finding procedure. Where utilized, the size of such committees is best held to a minimum and complete arrangements should be agreed upon in advance both with the employee representatives and the employers to be consulted." [*378*, p. 6.03]

Mention might usefully be made of the Canadian Federal Pay Research Bureau which has been operating since 1958. Its functions have been to collect pay rate and benefit information on industrial, commercial and other governmental jurisdictions and make these data available to management and the appropriate employee organizations. The director of the Bureau was guided by an advisory committee on pay research comprised of representatives of the principal employee organizations and of the Civil

Service Commission and the Treasury Board. The cost of operating the Bureau was borne by the government and it was looked after administratively by the Civil Service Commission.

With the introduction of the new Canadian collective bargaining law, the Bureau was transferred to the administrative jurisdiction of the Public Service Staff Relations Board, and the director was given a more independent status. It is likely that both its continuing role and the cost of its operations will be negotiated. Meanwhile, it continues to function on behalf of both employee organizations and management, attempting to meet the needs of each through the extensive and effective data collecting systems the Bureau has developed over the past nine years.

*Use of Computers.* The Industrial Union Department of the AFL-CIO now uses computers to analyze the detailed provisions of existing contracts so that union negotiators will have this information before they go into the bargaining sessions. Jack Conway, executive director of the department, has said, "If we want to know how the pensions or vacations at G. E. compare with those at other companies, we can pull the information out of the computer in minutes." [250] As the volume of contracts in government increases, public employers should consider doing the same thing.

### Analysis of Employee Organization Proposals

When the employee organization proposals are received in an exchange of correspondence before the negotiations, they should, of course, be carefully studied. If these proposals are not obtained until the initial bargaining session, then the management team will have to make this analysis before the next meeting. A useful device is to mark in the margins of the existing contract, paragraph by paragraph, the changes, if any, sought by the organization. Another is to prepare a tabular comparison of the provisions of the civil service law and rules, on the one hand, and any conflicting clauses in the proposed contract.

Estimates should also be quickly made of the costs of each request if granted. Legal questions should be checked out with the legal officers, so that management can ready any position it wants to take in this respect. Before the negotiations start, the chief negotiator should ascertain, at least in a general way, what the thinking of management is on the possible terms of a

settlement. Exactly when and how this will be done is for him
to decide, since the circumstances vary so much.

### Negotiation Preliminaries in United States Post Office Agreement

Essential preliminaries for future negotiations are sometimes
written into the initial contract. Following are relevant parts
of Article VII, "Procedures Covering Local Negotiations," of the
United States Post Office agreement: [*12*, pp. 16-18]

Negotiations will commence October 10, 1966 and be concluded no
later than November 5, 1966.

The installation head shall arrange a meeting with representatives
of organizations having local installation exclusive recognition no
later than 5 days prior to beginning date of negotiations. Full committees of all negotiators shall meet for negotiation of agenda items
of interest to all crafts. Craft committees shall negotiate agreements
of specific concern to craft or crafts concerned.

In order to minimize disruption in operations and to provide an opportunity for full and complete discussion of items on the agenda,
negotiations may, by mutual consent, be conducted in the evening and
/or Saturdays and Sundays.

The covening, reconvening, and adjournment of negotiating meetings shall be by mutual consent. Recessing of negotiating meetings
shall be on a unilateral basis.

Formal correspondence shall be used prior to negotiations to designate each organization's chief spokesman-negotiator and his alternate
and the postal installation's chief spokesman-negotiator and his alternate.

Each party to the agreement shall unilaterally determine the makeup
of its principal, sub and working committees.

Subcommittees and working committees shall be established by
mutual consent of the parties. Ordinarily, the membership of such committees will not exceed six (6) in number, equally divided between the
two (2) parties.

The chief spokesman-negotiator or alternate of the parties by
mutual agreement will decide scope, authority, and operation of all
sub and working committees.... Specialists and technicians may be
added to the sub and working committees and will be in addition to the
six (6) members ... and will be selected in the same manner as those
members.

Generally meetings will be held at the postal installation and space
will be provided for caucus purposes. If meetings are held elsewhere
and a charge is made for the facilities the parties shall share the cost.

All parties agree that proposals on agenda items will be exchanged
at least one full working day before scheduled meetings. Proposals
on agenda items not listed on such agendas may be discussed and/or
negotiated if mutually agreeable by all parties.

It is most desirable that sufficient information be given in the agenda
items to give an opportunity for the other side to familiarize itself
with the subject matter so that it may be fully developed when it is
reached on the agenda.

If these procedural matters are not covered in the existing

agreement, they will have to be decided through prior exchange of correspondence, or at the first negotiation session. The Post Office Department is huge, and it has consequently developed a highly-structured pattern for the negotiations. Jurisdictions and departments with much smaller numbers of employees may prefer more informal arrangements, but in any case there should be an efficient procedure for conducting the negotiations, acceptable to both parties.

About the meeting place, some say that it is better to meet on "neutral ground," meaning neither on the premises of the public employer nor those of the employee organization. Others think the negotiators for both sides are sufficiently sophisticated to want to meet in the most conveniently located, suitable quarers, and that the availability of records and other information at the public employer's headquarters may convince both parties that this is the best place.

Minutes of each bargaining session should be kept; taping the proceedings is not necessary and could very well impede the negotiations by discouraging the negotiators from expressing themselves frankly. Although there is general agreement that the bargaining sessions should not be too long, some would limit them to two hours, others to three, but, of course, the pressures to reach a settlement may make it necessary to have some extended sessions. By its very nature, bargaining makes it impossible and also undesirable to keep within a very rigid framework on such matters. Obviously, it would be desirable to reach an agreement after only a couple of weeks of negotiations, but the reality is frequently otherwise.

### Secrecy and the Public's Right to Know

Another question is whether or not to open the negotiations to the public and the press. There has been much concern recently about the public's "right to know," and legitimately so, but most persons experienced in collective negotiations are convinced that, if a settlement is to be reached, the bargaining must take place in closed session. The "horse trading" and the eventual retreat from original positions, characteristic of the bargaining, simply would not take place with the public and the press present.

Essentially, nothing is being denied the public: it will be kept informed, in general terms, by statements, mutually released by the two parties, on the progress of the negotiations, and it will later be apprised of the proposed contract terms. Rollin B. Posey reminds us that the Constitution of the United States itself was written in closed session. Arvid Anderson comments: [*36*, pp. 38-39]

> Aside from the tactics and techniques of bargaining, the temptation of the public official, as well as the public employee representative, to make statements for the benefit of his constituents rather than to concentrate on how the positions at the bargaining table might be modified in order that an agreement might be reached is almost irresistible when he is faced with a television camera, a microphone, or a reporter's notebook. There is a difference between making the news and reporting the news. The public has a right to know about the recommendations made by its public officials to the legislative body, and certainly no formal and final actions can be taken on the tentative recommendations made at the bargaining table until they are made public at a formal hearing and fully debated before final action is taken thereon.

## Conduct of the Negotiations

Inevitably, discussions of preparations for the negotiations and their actual conduct will overlap, but now we turn to the distinct question of bargaining strategy. It becomes obvious from reviewing the statements made by persons competent in this area, that, as in international diplomacy, few sure leads can be given those anxious to learn. The approaches which succeed in one bargaining situation may fail miserably in another. Nonetheless, there are at least a few protections against certain failure.

### *Protections Against Failure*

One is to remain convinced of the desirability of collective negotiations, no matter how unreasonable the employee organization demands may seem and how unpleasant their negotiators may appear. There is no agreement on what good faith bargaining really is, but to refuse to consider any proposals to negotiate new personnel and other administrative policies and regulations definitely falls in that category. To justify being listened to, the employee representatives do not have to qualify by always being "reasonable"; their very emotionalism may be instructive as to the true situation with respect to the workers' feelings, justified or not. Any illusions that the employees really do not want a bargaining representative should be discarded. By joining the organization they have indicated they do want it, no matter what statements they may make to the contrary to supervisors and others. Unless employees vote to decertify the organization, which is unusual, the assumption must be that it is there to stay, and good faith bargaining must continue.

The management should avoid taking rigid early stands in the negotiations, if for no other reason than that it may find it necessary later on to back down. Bargaining means flexible manoeuvre, not battle from fixed positions. Of course, the governmental employer, out of its sense of responsibility to the public, may have no intention of granting certain requests, but it is significant that in industry many company negotiators see no point in greeting the employee representatives with edicts about the inviolability of management prerogatives. At the proper time, a clear, strong statement can be made as to exactly why a particular proposal is unacceptable.

Above all, employee representatives should be allowed to talk, because, apart from its value in making clear the reasons for their requests, it allows them to vent their feelings, one of the essential purposes of negotiations. Few individual workers will speak as frankly to management representatives.

Apart from this, little can be said by way of general prescription, except, of course, that deceit is unthinkable. Once the employee organization loses faith in the integrity of the management negotiator, he becomes a liability and should be replaced, but this, of course, assumes that the organization has good reasons for its suspicions. The organization generally respects firmness, even toughness, provided it is convinced that the management representative in question is fair, open-minded, and trustworthy. Although to some extent the bargaining may take place in an atmosphere of unreality, with both sides initially taking positions which make eventual agreement look unlikely to outsiders, this does not mean that insincerity is at a premium. It means nothing more than that the bargaining has commenced.

### The Bargaining Sessions Themselves

The first session or two will usually be devoted to reading and clarifying the employee proposals. For management, this is primarily a "listening" stage: it seeks to feel out the other side's position and nothing more. Some labor experts argue that management should at this time also present proposals of its own: this prevents collective negotiations from becoming a one-way street, with the employee organizations asking for a great deal and management simply trying to whittle down the requests.

Besides, this gives management the opportunity to press immediately for changes in the existing practices.

Others see no particular advantage, since management will have plenty of opportunity later on to express its views as to deficiencies in the current contract and essential provisions in the new one. Besides, it can make counter proposals at any time.

Some people recommend taking up the "non-economic items" first, presumably because they usually require clarification whereas the employee organization's desires as to wages and fringe benefits can be easily foreseen in terms of the one word—"more." On the other hand, particularly if the employee organization has already won certain status in the previous contracts, in response to the normal worker concern for early resolution of wage and fringe benefit terms, its representatives may ask that these be negotiated first. Common procedure is for all agreements on individual clauses to be considered tentative, and final only when concurrence is reached on *all* parts of the contract.

*Team Caucuses.* From time to time during the sessions, the negotiators for both sides will decide to request a break in order to caucus privately. During these caucuses, the management negotiators will exchange reactions about the employee requests and generally re-fashion their strategy. The leadership qualities of the chief negotiator may be tested as much during these internal team deliberations as during the actual negotiating sessions. He will also be in touch with the management decision-makers and receive new guidelines and/or specific instructions from them. If subcommittees have been named, as in the United States Post Office Department, they can explore knotty issues, propose settlements, and prepare drafts of contract language.

*Adroitness in Approaching a Settlement.* As the negotiations continue and become increasingly tiring, the endurance, perseverance, and the patience of the negotiators will be tested. If agreement cannot be reached on an agenda item, it can be put aside for the time being and attention given to other hopefully less "sticky" ones. Seasoned negotiators agree that sooner or later, the employee leaders will give "signals" as to concessions they might be willing to make. They want a settlement and, given flexibility on the other side, will modify their positions. Recognition of these signals is the sign of a good negotiator, just as is his timing and adroitness in sending up signals of his own. No doubt, after public jurisdictions have had more experience in negotiations, a good deal more will be known about the art of negotiating, but it will always remain exactly that, an art, rather than something which can be reduced to formulae and set procedures.

### The Final Steps

Although in some jurisdictions the parties see no need to put the final agreement into writing, where formal procedures prevail, a contract or other agreement is prepared. This document may be signed by the chief negotiators or all members of the two negotiating teams; in any event, it is signed for the public employer by its authorized agent or agents. If the agreement is not final until the legislative body approves it, the signatures will be those of its members. The procedure may also be followed of adopting the agreement by ordinance or resolution. Some employee leaders feel strongly that, whether or not the city council or other local governing body approves the contracts, adoption by ordinance is unnecessary; to them, this smacks of unilateralism.

Contract administration will be dealt with in detail in Chapter 8, but it should be said here that, immediately upon the approval of the agreement, the public employer should embark upon a thorough program of explaining its provisions to all supervisors and through them to the employees. The employee organization representatives will, of course, do the same for their members. In some situations, management and employee representatives find it helpful to explain jointly the new provisions to the employees, and this helps to insure more uniform understandings and interpretations. Whether or not satisfactory results are obtained with the contract, and just how satisfactory the relations with the employee organization are, will largely depend on the success of these efforts.

# 7

# Settlement of Impasses

THE ESSENCE of collective bargaining is the voluntary action of the parties; as noted in Chapter 4, the definition of the term in the Taft-Hartley Act makes clear that the parties are not compelled to come to an agreement. The hope, of course, is that they will, and, in fact, they do in the great majority of cases. Sometimes, they do not, so, realistically, provision must be made for effective machinery for resolving such deadlocks and avoiding costly strikes.

In both Canada and the United States, the inevitability of some strikes in the private sector is taken for granted, but, when it comes to public employees, the general expectation is that they should recognize a special obligation and not use the strike weapon in the same way as private industry workers—if at all. As noted in Chapter 2, this in turn places an obligation on the public employer, not only to bargain in good faith, but also to have available mutually acceptable procedures for settling any bargaining impasses. In a sense, passing a law prohibiting public employees from striking is like disarming them and rendering them defenseless before public employers who do not always give them the treatment they deserve. Apart from the question of fairness, even when prohibited by law, public service strikes do take place, as documented in Chapter 4, so on purely practical grounds dispute settlement procedures which work are essential. As will be elaborated below, devising and obtaining agreement on such procedures is far from easy, but it is unfortunate that so many citizens, legislators, and administrative officials still do not appreciate that this is a high priority problem, neglect of which may produce very undesirable consequences for all concerned.

In this chapter, we will first briefly describe industry dispute settlement techniques because they are being recommended for

231

government and already are being used to some extent. This will be followed by a detailed discussion of how this problem is currently being dealt with in labor relations in government, both in Canada and the United States, together with an analysis of the proposals which have been made for improvements.

### Dispute Settlement Techniques

The techniques are: *mediation*, or, as it is sometimes called, *conciliation; fact-finding; and arbitration.*

### Mediation

Mediation—the most frequently used method in industry— is the effort of a third party to persuade the disputants to come to an agreement. The mediator is usually a government official whose services are made available, but in some cases he is a private individual, often a labor expert, selected by both the employer and the union, sometimes in accordance with a specified procedure in the existing agreement. Mediators normally do not actually propose terms of settlement, because this is not considered to be their proper role, but, as we saw in Chapter 3 in the chronicle of the New York subway strike, there are unusual situations when they do.

In the United States, the mediator is often supplied by the Federal Mediation and Conciliation Service, an independent agency established by the Taft-Hartley Act. The mediator is assigned, either upon the request of one of the parties or on the initiative of the Service itself. Practically all the state governments also have "some kind of facilities, established by law or practice, for mediating labor disputes in industry generally," [*297*, p. 279] a development encouraged by Section 8 (d) of Taft-Hartley which defines the duty to bargain collectively also to mean that neither party may terminate or modify the contract without serving written notice upon the other party 60 days prior to the termination date, and to notify the Service or the appropriate state agency 30 days after filing of the notice if no agreement has been reached. [*132*, pp. 8-9]

The Federal Mediation and Conciliation Service concentrates on disputes with potentially substantial impact on interstate commerce; the state agencies deal with those of intrastate character or with only a minor impact on interstate commerce. In some states, the mediation agency must intervene when it learns of a strike or the threat of one; in some, it must when directed to do so by the governor and in others, upon petition of one or both of the parties. In still others, at the request of one of the parties or that of a state official, it can offer to mediate. In two states, it can mediate only upon request of both parties. [*297*, pp. 278-280] Several cities have also provided this kind of service, but "only in New York City is there a mediation service maintained which actively competes with state and federal agencies." [*297*, pp. 282-283]

In Canada, the term conciliation is preferred, but the service rendered is often essentially the same. In its review of practices in the private sector, the Preparatory Committee on Collective Bargaining in the Public Service wrote: "Although law and practice vary from one jurisdiction to another, a number of characteristics are common to most . . . . The parties are obliged by law to negotiate in good faith . . . . In the event of failure to reach agreement, they must comply with certain statutory requirements for conciliation before resorting to strike or lockout." [*324*, p. 19]

The provincial labor laws provide for the provincial minister of labor to name conciliators and, if necessary, conciliation boards. As we shall see later, the conciliation boards greatly resemble fact-finding panels. In the United States, it is hoped that there will be no strike or lockout before mediation is started or while it is going on, but unfortunately there are more than a few occasions when this happens. In Canada, in both government and industry, the statutory conciliation procedure must be exhausted before the workers may legally strike.

*Limitations and Possibilities of Mediation.* A study group of the Committee for Economic Development has cogently stated, "Extensive experience with mediation has disclosed two facts of primary importance about it. The first is that mediation works best when the parties themselves decide that it would be helpful. The second is that the individual mediator must command the respect and confidence of the parties. When an unqualified or unwanted man is thrust upon the parties, not only is he less likely to be successful, but confidence in mediation as a whole may be shaken." [*297*, pp. 92-93]

Laws providing for mandatory mediation, or requiring the mediation agency to offer its services when a potential strike situation develops, have their advantages, but in the final analysis a settlement cannot, and should not, be forced on the parties. The collective bargaining process should continue on the same voluntary basis, with the negotiations facilitated by the mediator, happily towards a prompt settlement, fair to both parties. Like all third party intervention, mediation prematurely offered or known to be readily available suffers from the limitation that it may induce the parties to hold back on concessions, hoping to come out better after the mediator enters the picture. On the other hand, as ably stated in an International Labour Office publication: [*119*, pp. 37-38]

> A skilled conciliator can often greatly assist the parties to reach agreement. During the unsuccessful negotiations they may have committed themselves to irreconcilable demands; neither side can give way directly without seeming to show weakness. Or the parties may have failed to reach agreement because neither side has been able to judge whether the other side has made its final offer or whether there is still a possibility of winning further concessions. A conciliator can bring a new approach to the problems. He has the advantage of being able to meet the two parties separately, and each can tell him privately what they would not say to the other and indicate to him how far they would be willing to go in making concessions. He can see the attitudes of both sides more clearly than is possible for the parties themselves at the conference table because, as part of the technique of bargaining, each side may conceal something from the other. He may learn from one side that it would make a concession on one matter if the other side would make an equivalent concession on some other point. They may each accept suggestions from him which, if made by either side, would involve "loss of face." Such suggestions often open the way to agreement.

### Fact-Finding

Fact-finding refers to the investigation of a bargaining impasse or other dispute between the parties, by an individual, panel, or board which issues a report of the key facts, usually also containing recommendations for a settlement. Fact-finding is generally thought of as following unsuccessful mediation, but in some cases it is used instead of mediation or precedes it. Again, the fact-finding procedures may be required by law or voluntarily written into collective agreements. Laws requiring fact-finding usually prohibit strikes and lockouts until a stipulated period after issuance of the fact-finder's report.

In the Canadian private sector and in the municipalities, fact-finding is a function of the conciliation boards referred to above. For example, in Ontario, as described by Jacob Finkelman, until recently chairman of that province's Labor Relations Board, "after a conciliation officer has been appointed and if he fails in his endeavors, the Minister of Labor has authority in his discretion to appoint a tripartite board of conciliation, consisting of one nominee of each of the parties and a neutral chairman .... The recommendations of a conciliation board, where a board is appointed, are not binding upon the parties. Seven days after the release of the report of the conciliation board, the union is entitled to call a strike. Usually, the report of the conciliation board constitutes a new point of departure for further bargaining." [*97*, p. 130]

Obviously, the exact sequence of mediation (conciliation) and fact-finding varies from place to place and from situation to situation; furthermore, the titles of the boards and panels and their true functions—conciliation or fact-finding—may not coincide. The same mediators or conciliators may also become fact-finders, as with Lindsay's mediation panel in the subway strike.

*Experience with Fact-Finding.* The hope behind fact-finding is that publication of a neutral body's dispassionate report of the issues and the facts will stir the press, opinion leaders in the community, and the public in general to demand a proper settlement. If the fact-finders also make recommendations, presumably these are the correct ones to follow and the public will so insist. But fact-finding suffers from the same limitation as mediation: the parties may only go through the motions of bargaining, expecting fact-finding to be invoked and for it to turn out more favorably for them.

Particularly when special fact-finding boards are frequently established, as in the United States under the Railway Labor Act of 1926, there are too many reports and crisis situations for the public to pay attention to in the critical way envisaged. Furthermore, even if the public reacts strongly in the right way, there is no guarantee that the parties will bow to its wishes. It is also true that the "facts" may call for substantial increases for the employees, and the "public" is made up of taxpayers who may prefer to ignore these facts. Yet, as we shall see later, fact-finding has proved its value in solving public employee disputes, and it is being strongly recommended as an important part of the disputes settlement procedures in jurisdictions still lacking such effective procedures.

### Arbitration

Arbitration has been defined as a "method of settling disputes through recourse to an impartial third party whose decision is usually final and binding. Arbitration is often used in the interpretation of *existing* contract language, but it is seldom used in settling disputes arising from negotiations of provisions of a *new* contract. Arbitration is *voluntary* when both parties, of their own volition, agree to submit a disputed issue to arbitration, and *compulsory* if required by law to prevent a work stoppage." [*399*, p. 14]

There is an element of compulsion in voluntary arbitration in those cases where the parties are bound by the award. On the other hand, all they may agree to is *advisory arbitration,* under which they are free to accept or reject the decision. This, in effect, is virtually the same as fact-finding with recommendations.

Arbitration is compulsory: [*119*, p. 104]

> . . . when the State requires the parties to a dispute to appear before an arbitration tribunal, which, after examining the facts and arguments submitted to it and considering any other relevant information, makes an award. Usually the laws concerning compulsory arbitration provide that the terms of the award shall be binding on the parties and that strikes and lockouts are illegal. However, . . . compulsory arbitration can exist without prohibition of strikes and lockouts. Also compulsory recourse to arbitration does not necessarily imply that the awards are binding on the parties; the latter may be required to submit the dispute to arbitration and to refrain from strikes or lockouts during the arbitration proceedings but be free to reject the award. Yet there is little point in having compulsory arbitration unless the awards are binding.

*In the United States.* In both the United States and Canada, binding arbitration of grievances arising out of the interpretation of the existing contracts is standard procedure. In a report published in November of 1964, the United States Bureau of Labor Statistics reports that in 94 per cent of 1,717 major industrial agreements studied, binding arbitration was the terminal point of the grievance procedure. [*390*, p. 1] In return for the employer's willingness to submit such grievances to binding arbitration, the union usually agrees not to strike over such issues during the life of the contract.

In Canada, the provincial labor acts typically require every collective agreement to contain a provision for settlement, by arbitration or otherwise, of such disputes, including any question as to whether the differences are arbitrable, without any work stoppage or refusal to perform the work. We are deferring consideration of "grievance administration," as it is frequently called, to the next chapter; here we are concerned with arbitration, in all its different forms, as part of the machinery for settling deadlocked negotiations over the terms of *new* contracts.

The first definition of arbitration above states that arbitration is seldom used to resolve bargaining impasses. This is particularly true in countries like the United States and Canada, which emphasize "voluntarism" in labor relations. This word has been used by Nathan D. Feinsinger, the chairman of the Lindsay panel of mediators in the subway strike; in an interview afterwards, he said, "in the modern world, compulsion of any sort is no longer of paramount consideration in disputes, not only in labor but in civil rights and in international affairs .... The problem then ... is how are you going to get disputes settled? By some kind of voluntarism." [*175*, p. 23]

Compulsory arbitration of new contract terms is so unusual in the United States that, when in 1963 Congress passed such a law to settle a railroad dispute, it was the first time it had done so in the peacetime labor history of the country. Even so, because it was "reluctant about ordering this, it set a time limit on the arbitration order," which lapsed on March 31, 1966. [*365*] A similar law was passed by Congress in July of 1967 to force settlement of another railway labor dispute, and it appears that this may be required in the future for most such disputes.

A few state governments "experimented with compulsory arbitration for short periods after both world wars," but "a majority of these laws became inoperative as a result of a 1951 Supreme Court decision involving the New York law." [*297*, pp. 396-397] Presently such laws exist in Nebraska for publicly owned utilities, and in Minnesota and New York for charitable hospitals. [*297*, p. 471]

In Rhode Island, a recent statute provides that, in case of an impasse between a school committee and the teachers' bargaining agent, and if mediation and conciliation have failed or not been sought, *one* of the parties may request arbitration, the awards being binding "on all matters not involving the expenditure of money." [*105*, E-4, E-5] The same state provides for "final and binding arbitration of the terms of employment for firemen and policemen." [*34*, p. 145]

Maine has a law requiring that, if a municipal employer and a fire fighters' bargaining agent cannot agree on a contract, "within 30 days from and including the date of their first meeting," the dispute must be submitted to arbitration. It is provided, however, that a "majority decision of the arbitrators shall not be final and binding" upon either party. [*343*, 672-2, 3]

*In Canada.* In Canada, some use has been made of compulsory arbitration, either through *ad hoc* legislation to deal with particular disputes or laws applying to certain classes of employees in essential services where strikes are considered intolerable. When, in the summer of 1966, efforts to settle a national railway strike had failed, the federal Parliament passed a law requiring the 120,000 railwaymen involved to return to work. The emergency legislation granted them an interim pay increase, ordered negotiations to resume, and provided for a federal mediator to make a settlement binding on both sides if they could not reach an agreement by a specified date. [*244*] As an example of such *ad hoc* legislation at the provincial level, in 1962 the Ontario Legislative Assembly compelled arbitration of a dispute in the provincial hydroelectric system. [*97*, p. 121]

As to legislation not limited to particular disputes, "Most provinces recognize a distinction between general municipal employees . . . and policemen and firemen for whom special provision is usually made. Generally speaking, municipal policemen and firemen are permitted to organize and bargain collectively but are required to submit disputes to binding arbitration. Strike action by such employees is prohibited in some provinces but not in all." [*324*, p. 20]

Yet, as Frankel stresses, in Canada "arbitration is not a normal part of  private industrial relations because the strike is." [*98*, p. 51]

*Compulsory Arbitration in Australia.* Whenever compulsory arbitration is discussed, the case of Australia is likely to be cited. In Australia, all labor disputes, including those in the public service, must be submitted to arbitration, and the awards are legally binding. The procedure followed is that the Australian Commonwealth Court of Arbitration fixes decent living wages for unskilled workers, as well as supplements to be paid to typical semi-skilled and skilled workers. It also awards bigger supplements than usual for particular occupations, if after hearing the arguments of both the employers and the unions, it is convinced that higher skill requirements or special conditions relating to such jobs justify such action. [*119*, p. 106]

Although the Court's wage declarations and awards apply only to interstate industries, every state has "either an arbitration court or wage board which regulates wages and conditions within its jurisdiction, taking into account in doing so the standards set by the Commonwealth Court." The employers' organizations and the unions "conduct their collective bargaining on the basis of the standards laid down by the Court, but often fix higher wages and conditions by agreement." [*119*, p. 107] Extra-legal and wildcat strikes commonly do occur, largely to register a union's dissatisfaction with a given award or to press employers to agree to a settlement without going to arbitration.

As to compulsory arbitration in the Australian government, there is a Public Service Board, attached to the Prime Minister's department, which has "an overall responsibility for the coordination of policy and administration affecting all other departments." [*324*, p. 23] Employee organizations seeking better pay or improved working conditions prepare claims which are either first discussed with the Public Service Board or immediately brought before the public service arbitrator. For a claim to be submitted, it is not necessary that a dispute with the public employer first exist.

The arbitrator sends copies of the claim to the Public Service Board and all departments with employees affected. Any minister or board may object to the claim within 14 days; if none does, the arbitrator must approve it. If objections are filed, he must send copies to the organization which initiated the claim and to all other parties originally apprised of it. The next step is for him, in accordance with his schedule for the disposition of important matters, to call in the parties for a private conference to try to reach an agreement. If these efforts fail, he then arranges for a public hearing. The employee organization presents its case, the Public Service Board gives its refutation, and then the employee representatives make final arguments and answer the Board's points.

After weighing all the evidence, the arbitrator issues his award in the form of a formal document specifying the pay rates and working conditions he has approved. Copies are sent to all interested parties, including the Prime Minister, who arranges for one to be tabled in both houses of the Commonwealth Parliament. If after 30 days, neither house has passed a resolution rejecting the award, it automatically goes into effect. [*81*, pp. 90-91]

In general, the Australians consider compulsory arbitration, both in the private and public sectors, a success. The system was adopted early in the present century, with the support of most of the employers and workers, to end the previous bitter industrial strife. If both sides "did not normally find the awards generally acceptable and were willing to give up various advantages they gain from the system, they could easily make it unworkable"; instead, they "actively support the system, even though it greatly restricts the right to strike and lock out." [*119*, p. 106]

According to Edward E. Crichton, many problems have developed with the system in the government, largely because of the inability of the public service arbitrator to "comprehend the whole of the effects of his decisions." His responsibility is to decide the specific case before him, that of the Public Service Board being to implement the decision and decide whether or not to extend it to other workers. Crichton writes: "Frequently either the arbitrator's original decision or the consequential action taken by the Public Service Board gives rise to further claims by the same or other unions. The end result is that, although the arbitration process is designed for settling claims, it is very rare indeed that the settlement of any one claim ends disputes on matters which are incidental to, or as a consequence of, that claim."

Still, he concludes: [*81*, p. 92]

> The Australian employee is committed to the principle of arbitration and so are the main political parties. The fact that he is a public servant, engaged in manual, trade, clerical, administrative, or professional work, or even executive work, makes no difference . . . . He believes in arbitration and although he may grizzle about its cost, delays, even its results, he will resist change and become vocal if there is any attack on his belief. Arbitration is one of Australia's settled policies and, as such, its existence in a highly specialized form in the commonwealth public service is now taken for granted.

*Attitude of Employers and Workers in the United States.* In the United States, employee organizations in both industry and government have generally strongly opposed compulsory arbitration of wages and other economic benefits, and most private and public employers are also against it. Despite the growing concern over strikes affecting the national interest, and the use of compulsory arbitration in two recent railroad disputes, this solution is rejected by most labor-management experts, and it is not being seriously considered in Congress. The objection has long been that it would stultify collective bargaining, and might even lead to government price fixing to protect the profit margins of businesses whose wage bills are set by the compulsory awards. It is even feared that ultimately the government would, through subsidies and otherwise, replace the traditional role of private enterprise, and that the "free" market system would disappear completely.

The immediate concern is over the inhibiting effect on· the collective bargaining process, as ably expressed in a recent policy statement by the AFSCME Executive Board: "If both parties know that, ultimately, an outside party will be brought in to make a binding decision on such matters as wages and hours there is not only no pressure on the parties to reach an agreement but even a fear of making any change in their original bargaining positions, lest the final arbitrator use this attempted compromise as a starting point for further compromise." [*400*, p. 404]

Walter P. Reuther, president of the United Automobile Workers' Union, recently said: "The idea that you can legislate a little bit of compulsion is like the idea that someone can be a little bit pregnant . . . and can only lead to greater strictures of free bargaining." [*277*]

Still, before the New York state legislature in 1963 passed a law permitting either party in labor disputes in nonprofit hospitals to invoke compulsory arbitration, its joint Legislative Committee on Industrial and Labor Conditions, after studying the Minnesota experience with similar legislation, concluded that "mature collective bargaining can be carried out even when employees lack the right to strike." The Committee reported:

> One of our informants suggested that parties often seem as anxious to avoid the intervention of a third party as a strike. Another suggested that the desirability of avoiding the costs of arbitration might well provide an incentive to settlement. Whatever the reasons, the fact is that most hospital negotiations in Minnesota have ended in agreement and there is no evidence that those agreements would have been significantly different if the consequences of disagreement had been a strike rather than arbitration. [*177*, p. 69]

*Changed Viewpoints in Canada.* In Canada, as in the United States, most employers and workers in both the private and public sectors have historically been opposed to compulsory arbitration, but there has long been some sentiment for it. At the turn of the century, John J. Carson calls to our attention, the *Labour Gazette* noted ". . . that there had been on the part of many organized labour organizations a pretty general demand that legislation having in view compulsory arbitration should be enacted. . . ." [*53*, p. 51] In 1957, the Canadian Labour Congress proposed collective bargaining and arbitration for public servants, without the right to strike. [*53*, p. 51]

In 1962, Frankel could comment that "it is precisely because the civil service associations feel that they must deny themselves the strike weapon that they regard arbitration as the only safeguard against unilateral action by the government." [*98*, p. 51] And, of course, the federal government's new Public Service Staff Relations Act, supported in the main by the public employee organizations, provides for compulsory arbitration as one of two options for dispute settlement. [*350*, pp. 29-41] Likewise, in sponsoring the new legislation, the federal government completed the process of discarding the old arguments about not yielding sovereignty.

### Review of Existing and Proposed Machinery for Impasse Resolution

We now turn to a detailed review of existing programs, at all levels of government in the United States and Canada, for settling bargaining impasses.

#### In the United States Federal Government

The Kennedy Task Force opposed arbitration of such impasses, arguing that, "in the developing stages of employee-management relations [it was] quite likely that the availability of arbitration would have an escalation effect whereby the parties, instead of working out their differences by hard, serious negotiation, would continually take their problems to a third party for settlement." [*315*, p. 19] The provision on advisory arbitration in the Kennedy Order accordingly makes clear that it "shall extend only to the interpretation or application of agreements or agency policy and not to changes in or proposed changes in agreements or agency policy." [*400*, p. 354]

To support its position, the Task Force pointed out that the Tennessee Valley Authority, which has provisions for arbitration of impasses in its agreements with the Tennessee Valley Trades and Labor Council and the Salary Policy Employee Panel, had been consulted and had recommended against it. Under both TVA agreements, if the parties cannot agree on contract terms, either one may invoke the services of a mediator whom they jointly select from a previously agreed-upon panel of five persons.

In the agreement with the Trades and Labor Council, if the mediator fails to obtain a settlement, he must immediately try to persuade both sides to submit the dispute to arbitration. If they concur, each appoints one arbitrator, with the third named by the mediator. A majority decision of the arbitrators is final and binding on both parties. [*102*, pp. 9-10]

In the TVA agreement with the Salary Policy Employee Panel, if the mediator fails, either party, with his assistance, may ask the other voluntarily to invoke arbitration. If arbitration is agreed to, the dispute then goes to an impartial referee, jointly selected by the parties from a previously mutually-designated panel of five persons. The arbitrator's decision is also final and binding. If the TVA rejects arbitration, the mediator, at the request of the Salary Panel, must go before the TVA Board of Directors to "present his recommendation and the basis therefor," and, if the dispute still remains unresolved, he must then "submit a statement of his final recommendation to both parties." [*39*, p. 3] In all the history of the TVA, however, not a single case had gone either to mediation or arbitration until 1967, when one went to mediation.

As we shall see shortly, some federal employee organizations are now convinced that mediation and arbitration are essential and that the TVA's record in avoiding impasses is unique and hardly likely to be duplicated. At the time of consideration of the Kennedy Order, the AFL-CIO proposed mediation using the services of the Federal Mediation and Conciliation Service, with disputes still unresolved to be referred to a "special labor relations panel empowered to hold hearings and issue a binding decision." The 1963 AFL-CIO convention "urged amendment of the executive order to allow arbitration of negotiation deadlocks and of unfair labor practices charges." [*303*] The Brewster bill, mentioned in Chapter 2 and again in Chapter 5, provides for a final step, binding resolution of bargaining impasses by a government labor-management panel appointed by the President; details will be given below. [*91*, pp. 14-15]

Early in the history of the federal program, the employee organizations began to complain that some agencies were simply terminating the negotiations when disagreements developed, on the assumption that they had met their responsibilities under the Order and done all they could. The reader will recall a charge to that effect by John F. Griner, head of the American Federation of Federal Employees, quoted in Chapter 5. Whatever the truth of these allegations, in December of 1965 U.S. Civil Service Commission Chairman John W. Macy, Jr., noting that the agencies were making little use of mediation, called upon them to employ more frequently this "effective instrument" for impasse resolution. He also asked them to review their delegation of authority to assure that "meaningful negotiations can be accomplished at the establishment level." [*161*] Another complaint of the employee leaders was that all too often heads of local installations did not have the power to negotiate over very many items.

*U.S. Civil Service Commission Letter to Agencies on Impasses.* On February 7, 1966, the Commission sent a letter to the agencies in which it pointed out that Section 6 (b) of the Order provides, not only for meetings between the parties to negotiate agreements, but also to determine "appropriate techniques, consistent with the terms and purposes of this order, to assist in such negotiation." [*382*, p. 711-3(1)] Although specifically mentioning arbitration only, the Kennedy Task Force had pointed out that there were many other devices for producing settlements, and it had recommended that "such techniques should themselves be the subject of negotiations, with each department and agency devising means most appropriate to its own needs and circumstances." [*315*, p. 19]

The Commission now requested the agencies to decide what techniques suited them best and to try to get agreement on this with the employee organizations concerned before negotiations began, assuming that they had not already written such a procedure into an existing contract. Furthermore, the agencies were advised to "delegate to management at the negotiating level sufficient authority to negotiate with employee organizations on dispute-solving procedures and authority to use appropriate procedures when mutually agreeable to both parties."

Pointing out that fact-finding, mediation, and referral to higher authority were the techniques generally used, the Commission stated that more than a quarter of the existing agreements in the federal service called for fact-finding and more than 10 per cent for mediation. Some agencies were referring unresolved disputes to "higher management levels" for possible settlement.

The Commission thought that mediation probably offered the most promise, but to avoid premature mediation, it recommended that the consent of both parties be required and that they have to share the costs. The mediator's function was to help the parties come to an agreement, without his taking sides, and he was to make no public recommendations on "negotiation issues" or "public statements of findings of fact," nor any "public statement or report" evaluating the merits of the positions of the parties. The same considerations were in general to apply in the case of fact-finding. If the mediator prepares a report, it should be limited to a statement of: the meetings held and the participants; the unresolved issues when mediation began; the issues resolved through the mediation; and the unresolved issues, if any. [*382*, pp. 711-3, (1), (2)]

*American Bar Association Recommendations.* Despite the issuance of the Commission's letter, in its 1966 report the American Bar Association Committee still reported that it had "found that very few collective bargaining agreements make provisions for deadlocks in negotiations," and that "the problem of impasses in the process of negotiations has apparently created a great deal of frustration for all parties concerned." Examining the various possibilities, it believed that the referral of deadlocks to "higher authority" had produced good results in the Post Office where at the national level they are taken to the Postmaster General and, on the local level, to regional officers.

The Committee recognized that the Federal Mediation and Conciliation Service had no authority under the Kennedy Order to mediate, but still it could supply a list of mediators from which the parties could choose one or more, sharing the mediation costs. The Committee also raised the possibility that the Order be amended to permit advisory arbitration of impasses, pointing out that the experience with this procedure in bargaining unit determinations had been excellent. [*16*, pp. 134-135]

*Mediation in the Post Office.* In August of 1966, the Post Office Department did adopt "mediation without mutual consent," meaning that if requested by one of the parties, mediation would be compulsory for any bargaining impasse. The new mediation procedures were to begin with the negotiations in the summer of 1967 for a new contract, with the mediators drawn, if needed, from among university professors, lawyers, and other labor relations specialists, not from the Federal Mediation and Conciliation Service which is already overworked. Interestingly, the new procedures were offered to the employee organizations by

Postmaster General Lawrence F. O'Brien, and it was contemplated that the mediator, if necessary, would also make private and confidential recommendations to him for settling disputes. [*403*]

The present Post Office Agreement contains the following definition of impasse: "it is mutually agreed that an impasse occurs after both parties have presented proposals and counter-proposals in good faith and both parties have considered the proposals and counter-proposals of the other party in good faith and despite such honest and diligent efforts no agreement can be reached on the subject being negotiated." [*12*, p. 52]

The full procedure is as follows: [*12*, pp. 52-53]

1. When it is agreed that an impasse has been reached, the item is laid aside. After all items on which the parties can agree have been negotiated, the parties must attempt "once more" to resolve all existing impasse items.

2. If either concludes that an impasse still exists, it may request mediation, notifying the other party in writing.

3. Within 5 days after such notification, the parties must jointly request the Federal Mediation and Conciliation Service to provide either its own mediation services or a list of 5 qualified mediators.

4. Within 5 days after receiving this list, the parties must meet to select the mediator by alternately striking names until one remains; he becomes the "duly selected mediator."

5. The mediator tries to resolve the dispute. He makes no public statements "on the impasses involved, the merits of the parties' positions nor agreement or lack of agreement of the parties." If he is unsuccessful, he "will be empowered to make a report, with any recommendation on unresolved impasses that he deems necessary, privately and confidentially only to the Postmaster General." Mutual consent of the parties is not necessary for the mediator to take such action.

6. Mediation expenses are shared equally by the parties.

7. Impasses not resolved by mediation must be submitted to the Postmaster General, and the unions may meet with him and submit briefs and other evidence. His decision is final.

*Dispute Settlement Provisions of Brewster Bill.* During a Federal Mediation and Conciliation Service seminar in early January, 1967, employee organization leaders renewed their requests for third party mediation to settle bargaining disputes. [*278*] In this, they were supported by Assistant Secretary of Labor for Labor-Management Relations, James J. Reynolds, who predicted that such procedures would soon be adopted because of the employees' frustrations over not being "treated with the honesty and dignity which they deserve." Macy, also present, said that the matter deserved careful study, but that creation of such machinery was not imminent. [*278*]

What the American Federation of Government Employees and other federal unions want is mediation through a little NLRB arrangement, such as proposed in the Brewster bill. Under the latter, it will be remembered from the discussion in Chapter 5, the Labor Department would administer the "federal employee labor-management" program, one aspect of which would be the following procedure for settling impasses: [*91,* pp. 14-15]

1. Either party may invoke the services of the Federal Mediation and Conciliation Service which would be required immediately to "assign one or more of its mediators . . . using every effort to bring the parties to an agreement."

2. Should these efforts fail, either party may submit the dispute to a government labor-management relations panel, to be established by the President and to consist of a chairman, an executive secretary, and not fewer than four nor more than six additional members. The President would appoint all members except for the executive secretary, to be selected by the panel itself.

3. The panel would try to get the parties to settle the dispute "through whatever voluntary methods and procedures it may consider to be appropriate."

4. If these first efforts by the panel fail, it must promptly hold hearings at which both parties are given a full opportunity to present their cases.

5. Upon completion of the hearings, the panel must, "with due dispatch," give its decision in writing, which "shall be final and binding upon all parties."

The full procedure contemplated, then, is mediation, followed, if necessary, by binding arbitration, with the consent of only one of the parties necessary for invoking either the mediation or the arbitration. Because of the very broad scope of negotiations proposed in the Brewster bill, many conditions of employment could ultimately be decided through binding arbitration. It is interesting that the AFL-CIO is supporting these proposals, because, as we have seen, labor in the United States has generally opposed binding arbitration of disagreements over contract terms. However, the Brewster bill provisions summarized above do not require the unions to use the arbitration; they can do as they please on this, and presumably the agency managements would not be so enamored of these procedures that they would want to take the initiative and force the unions to arbitration. The controversy in the federal service over impasse resolution is now approaching the "boiling" stage, with the outcome still uncertain.

### In the Canadian Federal Government

In the Canadian federal government, various methods have been employed in attempting to resolve negotiation deadlocks. Government conciliation boards tried unsuccessfully to prevent the nation-wide rail walkout in the summer of 1966; their recommendations were rejected by the unions. The labor minister's mediation efforts also failed, and, as stated earlier in this chapter, the Parliament passed special legislation to stop the strike.

The government-owned Air Canada closed down for ten days in November of 1966 after the International Association of Machinists rejected the proposals of the chairman of a three-member mediation board appointed by the two parties to try to resolve the dispute. [262] In May of 1966, a threatened strike of the Canadian Broadcasting Corporation was called off, but only after the government moved to name Stuart Keate, publisher of the *Vancouver Sun*, as mediator.

Employees of crown corporations, such as Air Canada and the CBC, have long had the right to strike, since these entities come under the 1948 Industrial Relations and Disputes Investigation Act, the Canadian parallel for Taft-Hartley. When, after unsuccessful negotiations, the postal strike broke out in the summer of 1965, the government was able to persuade most of the strikers to return to work, pending the report of a special commission, but postal workers in some of the nation's largest cities rejected the settlement terms and continued on strike. The government hurriedly appointed a special commissioner to investigate, but his initial proposals were voted down by some 3,000 Montreal postal workers. [115] When this strike was finally settled, much sentiment had solidified for passage of collective bargaining legislation for federal employees in general, with effective dispute settlement procedures.

*Recommendations of Preparatory Committee.* The Preparatory Committee on Collective Bargaining in the Public Service had released its report just before the postal strike, and it had concluded that, "if a strike should ever occur, the Government would not be without means to cope with it." It reasoned also that the great bulk of Canadian federal employees did not have the right to strike anyway and were already subject to disciplinary action should they participate in a walkout. [*324*, pp. 36-37] The Committee proposed arbitration of the "principal economic elements in the relationship between employers and employees," [*324*, p. 34] following the model of the system in effect in the United Kingdom since 1925. (The reader will recall the reference to arbitration in Britain during the discussion of "sovereignty" in Chapter 2.)

The British system, embodied in an agreement between the employee organizations and the government, provides for referral to a Civil Service Arbitration Tribunal of disagreements over emoluments, weekly hours of work, and leave; emoluments are defined to include pay, bonuses, overtime and subsistence rates, and travelling and lodging allowances. The Tribunal consists of a chairman appointed by the Minister of Labour after consultation with the parties, and of two members named by the chairman from panels of individuals representative of the interests of the government and the employee organizations. The Committee recommended creation of a similar tribunal for Canada, the chairman to be appointed by the Governor in Council for a fixed term, and the two other members to be selected by the chairman of the Public Service Staff Relations Board from panels composed in the same way as in Britain. [*324*, pp. 34-36]

Specifically, bargaining impasses were to be dealt with as follows: (1) they could first be made subject to conciliation, upon the joint request of both parties or whenever, in the opinion of the chairman of the Public Service Staff Relations Board, this would help resolve the dispute; (2) either without attempted conciliation, or after unsuccessful such efforts, they would have to be submitted to the proposed arbitration tribunal for settlement.

The Committee's reasoning was that, since arbitration would be required in any case, whereas it is not in the Canadian private sector, conciliation could be skipped. Conscious of the "difficult role" the arbitration tribunal would have, the Committee recommended that the legislation direct it, "in determining the terms and conditions of employment to be established by an award, to have regard, among other things, to the personnel requirements of the service, to conditions prevailing outside the service, to the need for appropriate internal relationships, and to what is fair and reasonable in relation to the nature of the jobs concerned and the qualifications required for their performance." [*324*, p. 36]

*Provisions of Public Service Staff Relations Act.* As already mentioned in Chapter 4, the new Canadian Public Service Staff Relations Act does contemplate the possibility of strikes and, indeed, it gives them legal sanction in certain cases. The full disputes settlement procedure is as follows:

1. When it applies for certification as bargaining agent, the employee organization must specify which of two procedures it elects to come under: arbitration or conciliation. [*350*, p. 20]

2. In bargaining units coming under arbitration, as determined under (1) above, if the parties, after bargaining in good faith, cannot come to an agreement, either one may request the secretary of the Public Service Staff Relations Board (PSSRB) to invoke arbitration. [*350*, pp. 30-31]

3. Where one or both parties have requested arbitration, the chairman of the PSSRB shall refer the dispute to a Public Service Arbitration Tribunal, created in the legislation. [*350*, p. 32] This Tribunal consists of a chairman, appointed by the Governor in Council upon recommendation of the PSSRB, and of two other members selected by the chairman of the PSSRB from panels established by the Board to represent the interests of the employers and employees respectively. [*350*, p. 30]

4. After considering the case, the Tribunal issues a binding award, "subject to the appropriation by or under the authority of Parliament of any moneys that may be required by the employer thereof." [*350*, p. 36] Decisions are made by a majority vote or by the chairman if the majority of the members cannot agree. Arbitral awards may deal with "rates of pay, hours of work, leave entitlements, standards of discipline, and terms and conditions of employment directly related thereto," but not with the "standards, procedures, or processes governing the appointment, appraisal, promotion, demotion, transfer, lay-off or release of employees." [*350*, p. 34] In making the awards the Tribunal is required to take into account the same factors as those enumerated by the Preparatory Committee. [*350*, pp. 33-34]

5. In bargaining units coming under conciliation, as determined under (1) above, either party to deadlocked negotiations may request the chairman of the PSSRB to provide a conciliator to help settle the disagreement. [*350*, pp. 27-28] In any case, with or without a previous request for the appointment of a conciliator, either party may request the chairman to establish a conciliation board to investigate and conciliate the dispute. The chairman complies, unless, after consultation with both parties, he concludes it is unlikely that this will produce a settlement. On his own initiative, without a request from either of the parties, he can, however, institute a conciliation board if he thinks one is needed, but he must notify the parties of his intention to do so.

As stated in Chapter 4, no conciliation board may be formed until the parties have agreed on, or the Board has determined, the employees in the bargaining unit whose services are "necessary in the interest of the safety or security of the public."

Conciliation boards are to consist of three persons, one designated by each of the parties and the third member, to be the chairman, selected by the first two members, all appointments to be made officially by the chairman. The conciliation board determines its own procedures, but must give "full opportunity to both parties to present evidence and make representations." It must make a report of its

252 Management-Employee Relations

findings and recommendations to the chairman of the PSSRB within 14 days of his delivery to them of a statement setting forth the matters which they are to investigate. By mutual agreement of the parties or determination of the chairman, however, this period may be extended. Conciliation board decisions are by majority vote; they are not binding on the parties unless by previous mutual agreement in writing they have so elected. No conciliation board report may contain "any recommendation concerning the standards, procedures or processes governing the appointment, appraisal, promotion, demotion, transfer, lay-off or release of employees." [*350*, pp. 38-41]

6. In no case, may an employee designated as providing "essential services" strike, and the same applies for those in bargaining units under arbitration. For all others, strikes are prohibited unless the following circumstances exist: (a) a conciliation board has been established but seven days have passed since the receipt of its report by the chairman of the PSSRB; (b) a board was requested but he has notified the parties that he will not name one. [*350*, p. 48]

*Debate Over the New Legislation.* Those who believe there should be a flat statutory prohibition of all public employee strikes obviously will not approve of this law. Its proponents, however, argue that, in view of the strong feeling of the unions against such a prohibition, its inclusion might invite strikes and that, in any event, there is no way of eliminating strikes completely. Arbitration is made available, but not forced on employee organizations which do not believe in it. As already mentioned in Chapter 4, employee organizations after three years can change their minds and opt for the other procedure, so there is flexibility. It is also maintained that collective bargaining will not be stifled, because, as noted earlier in this chapter, arbitration need not have that effect.

Jacob Finkelman reports that in Ontario the experience with that province's Hospital Labor Dispute Arbitration Act, passed in April of 1965, has been that arbitration is rarely invoked, with most agreements negotiated freely through the collective bargaining process. [*97*, p. 126] The Civil Service Federation of Canada wants the employee organizations also to have the right to elect conciliation or arbitration during the initial stages of the actual negotiations. It argues that it may not be clear until then which procedure is better from the employee standpoint, but the government's position is that this would enable the bargaining agent to threaten one sanction or the other as a tactical manoeuvre during the negotiations. [*400*, pp. 49-50] Those concerned with public employee relations in the United States and many other countries will be watching with great interest Canada's experience with this new legislation.

### In State and Local Governments in the United States

Wisconsin has now had extensive experience with dispute settlement procedures under its 1962 statute covering the cities and all other political subdivisions of the state. [*347*] The law, which prohibits strikes, authorizes the Wisconsin Employment Relations Board to mediate disputes at the request of both parties, and it also provides for fact-finding; the WERB "has chosen fact-finding with recommendations as its preferred procedure for settling collective bargaining deadlocks in the public area." [*347*, p. 3 ]

Fact-finding may be initiated in two ways: (1) upon the request of either or both parties "if after a reasonable period of negotiation the parties are deadlocked"; or (2) by the Board itself when it decides that the employer or employee organization has refused to "meet and negotiate in good faith at reasonable times in a bona fide effort to arrive at a settlement." Upon receipt of a petition to initiate fact-finding, the Board must investigate and determine whether or not the above conditions exist. If it so decides, the next step is for it to appoint a "qualified disinterested person" as the fact-finder from a list it has previously established. If both parties so request, the Board names a three-man panel from the same list instead of one person. The fact-finder may hold hearings, "where feasible in the jurisdiction of the municipality involved," conducting them "pursuant to rules established by the Board." When they are completed, he submits his "written findings of fact and recommendations for solution of the dispute" to the municipal employer and the union. Costs of the fact-finding are equally divided between the two parties. [*347*, p. 4]

*Evaluation of Fact-Finding in Wisconsin.* This is the formal procedure, as stated in the law; in practice, a "WERB staff member holds informal hearings to determine whether an impasse exists. One or all of the three WERB commissioners will occasionally conduct more formal hearings for the same purpose." Actually, the WERB at this point looks for a chance to mediate the dispute informally; [*347*, p. 4] its success is attested to by the fact that, of the 73 fact-finding petitions filed during the first three years of the law, 35 were settled by mediation in this way.[*347*, p. 5]

If these efforts at mediation fail, the fact-finder schedules hearings in the local jurisdiction where the dispute arose. He tries to complete the hearings in one day and frequently is able to do so. Although there is no requirement that his report must be published, the WERB reproduces it and sends it to the local newspaper and to other interested parties. Professor James L. Stern of the University of Wisconsin, upon whose research we are relying, reports that "in most cases the award is accepted and the impasse resolved." [*347*, p. 5] Disposition of the 35 petitions by mediation left 38 petitions, of which two were withdrawn, and two dismissed by the WERB on technical grounds. Six of the remaining ones were consolidated, leaving 28 cases which went to fact-finding. Of these 28, in only seven were the awards rejected.

In his detailed study of the first 73 petitions referred to above, Professor Stern [*347*, pp. 5-8] found that:

1. They originated in a wide variety of local governmental units;

2. The bargaining units concerned ranged greatly in size, "from a 3,000-person Milwaukee public works group to a six-person custodial group in the Wood County Courthouse";

3. The employee organization involved in most of the petitions was the American Federation of State, County, and Municipal Employees, with "local independent unions and affiliates of the Teamsters, Operating Engineers, Fire Fighters, Professional Policemen's Association, Wisconsin Federation of Teachers, and Wisconsin Education Association" also using the procedures;

4. Both white and blue collar employees initiated fact-finding when they thought it necessary;

5. The fact-finders were either economists or attorneys and in practice appointed by the WERB, although the formal

selection procedure calls for each party to strike out names alternately from the list of five persons until one remains;

6. The fact-finder's fee, fixed by the WERB, is $150 per day for hearing and $100 per day for preparing his report; in a typical case, he spends one day on the hearing and two and one-half days on the report, the fee for his services thus averaging $400, to which travel and subsistence costs must be added;

7. Considering the "out-of-pocket costs incurred by the parties for such items as legal fees where outside attorneys are used, pay for lost time, fees paid for the preparation of the case, and charges for miscellaneous expenses," the total cost to each party was about $500, but could be as low as $300 or as high as $15,000;

8. There was no evidence to prove that these costs were so low as to induce the parties to make undue use of fact-finding, but neither was there evidence they were so high as to discourage them from requesting it;

9. "The time schedule for a typical case was two to three months from the date of petition until the first day of hearing, one to two months from the last day of hearing to the date of the fact-finder's report, and another three months until the parties reached an agreement."

Apart from the statistical evidence of so high a proportion of acceptance of the awards, "all of the winners praised the procedure and only a few of the losers criticized it." In every one of the seven cases where the fact-finding failed, the employer was a county or small city in a rural or suburban area where the "managements did not look with favor upon any part of the process of collective bargaining." In the rural communities the employee organizations' lack of political strength was a possible explanation. Once the award is announced, the party anxious to see it adopted will try to mobilize public opinion in favor of it. In fact, Stern suggests that "the high degree of acceptance of awards suggest that political pressures may offer an effective substitute for the conventional economic pressures in securing acceptance of positions arrived at by collective bargaining procedures." [*347*, p. 12]

*Belasco's Thesis.* James A. Belasco, in his study of dispute settlement procedures in a number of states, including Wisconsin, comes to the same conclusion. He quotes the statement by Professor Edgar L. Warren that "fact-finding is not so much a case of finding facts of which the parties are ignorant, but rather of sharpening the consequences of the facts already known." [*44*, p. 542]

In the case of Minnesota which, like Wisconsin, relies a good deal upon fact-finding with recommendations, Belasco analyzed 35 cases and found that they were all accepted entirely or in part by the two disputants. In four of them, the public employer at first rejected the recommendations but then accepted them in part "after the union conducted an advertising campaign in the local papers, bannering and the distribution of leaflets to the general public." [*44*, p. 543] Belasco's thesis is that public employees make up for their weakness in economic power by exploiting their political and social power: [*44*, p. 542]

> It is logical to expect that the pressure of public opinion will weigh heavily on a government employer. This is a reasonable expectation since many of the individuals who represent the unit of government involved are either politically appointed or elected. In either case, such people usually possess themselves or report to people who possess political ambitions. A reputation for improper handling of labor relations, which results in unfavorable publicity, can be disastrous to such ambitions. Therefore, it is reasonable to expect that the employer representatives would be sensitive to the pressures of public opinion....
>
> In the private sector of the economy collective bargaining serves as an opportunity to ascertain the other party's settlement position. Once the other party's settlement position has been established, this enables the two parties to evaluate the consequences of non-agreement. In the private sector many of the consequences would be economic in nature. In the public sector, however, one of the major consequences is the adverse and intense pressure of public opinion. Since settlement occurs when the costs of management exceed the costs of the other party's proposal, public opinion pressure may replace economic power as the principal lever for securing agreement between public employers and their unions.

*Evaluation of Criteria to Guide Fact-Finding.* The question logically arises as to the criteria to be used by the fact-finders in reaching their decisions. Professor David B. Johnson of the University of Wisconsin lists four considerations: (1) wage and fringe benefit data, including recent salary increases, for comparable public and private establishments in the area and possibly also outside it; (2) changes in the cost of living since negotiation of the last contract or passage of the salary ordinance; (3) ability to pay, based on tax rates, economic conditions in the area, unemployment figures, population changes and trends, and the amount of state financial aid; and (4) productivity rates, comparing that for the work force concerned with the national figures which have shown annual increases in output per worker of 2½ to 3½ per cent. [*120*, pp. 42-43] He disputes the commonly-held belief that fact-finders "split the difference between the offer and the demand" and urges the parties to make "genuine offers and demands." [*120*, p. 44]

The new Wisconsin State Employment Relations Act requires the fact-finder to "take into consideration among other pertinent factors the logical and traditional concept of public personnel and merit system administration concepts and principles vital to the public interest in efficient and economical governmental administration." This statute specifically provides for fact-finding to settle either bargaining impasses or disagreements over "the application or interpretation of any provision of a collective bargaining agreement." [*345*, p. 7]

In Minnesota, the law requires fact-finding panels to consider:

> The tax limitations imposed by law or charter, if any, upon the governmental agency together with wages, hours and other conditions of employment of public employees performing comparable duties for other governmental agencies of a comparable nature and of employees performing comparable duties in private employment, internal consistency of treatment of employees in the several classes of positions in the governmental agency, as well as such other factors not confined to the foregoing as are normally or appropriately taken into consideration in the determination of wages, hours and other conditions of employment by the governmental agency. [*165*, 179. 57]

*Provisions of Other State Laws.* As stated in Chapter 5, the Connecticut and Massachusetts statutes authorize the state labor relations board (Connecticut) or commission (Massachusets) to order fact-finding with recommendations if it finds that either party has refused to bargain in good faith. Both laws also state that, if "after a reasonable period of negotiation over the terms of an agreement, a dispute exists between a municipal employer and an employee organization, or if no agreement has been reached sixty days prior to the final date for setting the municipal budget, either party or the parties jointly may petition the state board of mediation and arbitration [conciliation and arbitration in Massachusetts] to initiate fact-finding." Similarly, both laws require the "person selected or appointed as fact-finder" to hold hearings, if feasible in the municipality involved. [*30*, p. 329; *31*, p. 557]

In Connecticut, the fact-finder must make a written report of findings of fact and recommendations within 30 days of his appointment [*30*, p. 329] ; in Massachusetts, he is allowed 60 days [*31*, p. 557], but in both states the above identified board may for good cause extend this period. Costs of the fact-finding are shared equally by both parties, with the fact-finders' fees paid in accordance with a schedule established by the board. Both laws also make clear that nothing is to prevent the fact-finder from trying to mediate the dispute. This illustrates again the doubling up of roles, the same persons flexibly serving both as fact-finders and mediators. Since fact-finding with recommendations is sometimes referred to as advisory arbitration, the individual chosen to try to resolve the dispute may also be considered an arbitrator. The Connecticut and Massachusetts statutes (1965) are too recent for any extensive experience in disputes settlement to have accumulated; actually, while there has been more experience with the Wisconsin municipal law (1962), it is also still too new to "make a definite evaluation." [*347*, p. 19]

*Recommendations of the Rockefeller and Lindsay Panels.* When in 1966 the Rockefeller and Lindsay panels gave their attention to this problem after the subway strike, both groups could critically review the solutions attempted in different parts of the country and the proposals made from time to time by labor relations experts, union and business groups, academic researchers, and others.

*Proposals of Rockefeller Group.* Taking up the Rockefeller committee's report for New York State first, it begins by warning that, if impasse procedures are made too accessible, "the problem-solving virtues of constructive negotiations are lost." Pointing out that a "standardized dispute settlement procedure is not ideally suited to all parties and to all disputes," it also suggests that an impasse be considered to exist if the parties have not reached agreement "sixty days, or some longer period, prior to the budget submission date established by law for the agency or unit of government." Rather than wait until an impasse crisis develops, the parties should agree beforehand on procedures for resolving deadlocks. The procedures themselves should be made a subject for negotiations, and they should be incorporated in "every collective relationship between a governmental agency and an employee organization, which is reduced to writing." Even where the parties do not conclude their negotiations with a signed agreement, they should adopt a method for resolving impasses which "they may elect to reduce to writing." [*107*]

The committee[*107*] suggests as different possibilities that the parties agree in advance:

1. To submit the case to arbitration;

2. To settle it according to a "formula specifying that the wages, benefits or other conditions of employment in the locality and type of work in question shall be governed by those prevailing in private or public employment in other designated localities and types of work";

3. To refer it to fact-finding with recommendations, with or without a previous commitment on the part of one or both of the parties to be bound by the recommendations;

4. To establish joint study committees to review "complex or difficult problems" and make "mutually agreeable recommendations to their principals prior to the next budget submission or legislative deadline"; and

5. To use mediation.

These methods could be used singly or in combination, with the parties altering them from time to time as their experience dictates.[*107*]

If an impasse could not be resolved through the parties' own procedures, then a proposed public employment relations board would enter the picture, either on its own initiative or upon the request of either or both parties. If this board, to consist of three members appointed by the governor and confirmed by the senate, found that an impasse did exist, it would "seek to resolve the dispute by further mediation, including the search for mutually agreeable procedures to resolve any remaining differences between the parties." Should this not produce a settlement, it would appoint a fact-finding board, to consist usually of three members, drawn from a list of recognized experts established by the board after consulting with the employee organizations, state and local government administrators, and industrial relations and personnel agencies. The fact-finding panel would hear the contending parties, obtain the data it needed, and "make a recommendation to resolve the issues in dispute no later than fifteen days prior to the submission of the budget or legislative deadline." Unless the parties so agreed, these recommendations would not be binding. If a fact-finding report with recommendations had already been made under the parties' own procedures, instead of invoking more fact-finding, the board would take whatever steps it judged advisable, "including the making of recommendations after giving due consideration to the recommendations and facts found by the first body." [*107*]

Expressing its confidence in fact-finding, the Rockefeller committee argues that it "requires the parties to gather objective information and to present arguments with reference to these data," and that "the ... report and recommendations provide a basis to inform and to crystallize thoughtful public opinion and news media comment." It also recommends that the public employment relations board collect and make available to both parties, as well as to the mediators and fact-finders, "statistical data relating to wages, benefits and employment practices in public and private employment applicable to various localities and occupations."

Since, as stated in Chapter 4, the Committee was against repealing the statutory prohibition on strikes, the final question was what should be done if the parties rejected the fact-finders' recommendations. Its proposal was that the dispute be taken to the "legislative and political arena rather than to the streets"; specifically, a legislative committee, or the entire legislative body, would hold a kind of "show cause" hearing at which the parties would explain their positions on the fact-finding report. The lawmakers would then enact the "appropriate budgetary allotment or other regulations." [*107*]

The New York Public Employees' Fair Employment Act, already referred to in Chapter 4, follows these recommendations closely. Public employees are granted the right of organization and representation, and the state, local governments and other political subdivisions are required to negotiate with, and enter into written agreements with employee organizations representing public employees which have been certified or recognized. [*317*, p. 1] The recommended Public Employment Relations Board is created [*317*, pp. 1-2], and it is charged with establishing procedures for the resolution of "disputes concerning the representation status of employee organizations" in the *state* service. Local government entities, through their legislative bodies, are empowered to institute similar procedures in the case of employee organizations with which they deal; if they fail to do so, the disputes over representation status of the local employees concerned must be submitted to the Board. [*317*, pp. 3-4]

Public employers, both in state and local government, are authorized to enter into agreements with employee organizations "setting forth procedures to be invoked in the event of disputes which reach an impasse in the course of collective negotiations." "In the absence or upon the failure of such procedures," either party may request the Board to render assistance, or else the Board can do so on its own motion. When providing such help, the Board must proceed as follows:

1. Appoint a mediator or mediators from a list of qualified persons maintained by the Board, in order to "assist the parties to effect a voluntary resolution of the dispute."

2. If the impasse continues, name a "fact-finding board of not more than three members" which "shall have, in addition to the powers delegated to it by the Board, the power to make public recommendations" for settling the dispute.

3. If the deadlock is not resolved at least fifteen days before the budget submission date, the fact-finding board, acting by majority vote, must transmit its findings and recommendations to the "chief executive officer of the government ... and the employee organization involved," simultaneously making the findings and recommendations public.

4. If a fact-finding board, established in accordance with procedures agreed to by the parties, has already made public its findings and recommendations, the Public Employment Relations Board shall take whatever steps it deems necessary for resolving the conflict, "including the making of recommendations after giving due consideration to the findings and recommendations of such fact-finding board, but no further fact-finding board shall be appointed."

5. If either the public employer or the employee organization rejects in whole or in part the recommendations of the fact-finding board, the chief executive officer of the government involved must, within five days of his receiving the fact-finders' report, submit a copy of it to the legislative

body, together with his own recommendations for settling the dispute. The employee organization may also submit its recommendations to the legislature. [*317*, p. 5]

*Proposals by Lindsay Panel.* For New York City, the Lindsay group recommended that, by a specified time before the expiration of a collective bargaining agreement, the city or the bargaining agent be required to file a "bargaining notice" with the other party, with a copy to the Office of Collective Bargaining. Within 10 days after receipt of this notice, unless an extension were agreed to by the parties or granted by the OCB, the negotiations would begin. It then was to be the responsibility of the OCB director to follow the negotiations closely and to help the parties by furnishing them such data and information as they requested. On his own motion, or at the request of either party not less than 30 days after the beginning of the bargaining, if he believed it would help the negotiations, he was to make available a mediator or mediators from an OCB register of mediators. The mediator was to carry out his duties under the direction of the director, and the parties were to cooperate with them in every way to resolve the dispute if possible without resort to a dispute panel.

Upon the request of both parties or upon the recommendation of the director, and if a majority of the Board found that "collective bargaining, with or without mediation" had been "exhausted," the director was to establish a dispute panel. He was to submit to the parties a list of seven persons drawn from another OCB register, and each party was to state its preferences with respect to these seven persons; if "these preferences fail to disclose agreement," the director was to go ahead and set up the dispute panel. The latter was to "mediate, hold hearings, ... and take whatever action it considered necessary to settle the dispute." If it was unable to resolve the dispute, it would make recommendations for a settlement and file them in writing with the OCB chairman who, with the advice of his board, would determine when the recommendations would be "released to the parties and the public."

In any case, the recommendations were to be released not later than seven days after the dispute panel filed its recommendations. During the negotiations after the filing of a bargaining notice and, whenever a dispute panel was established, during the 30 day period after it filed its report, the city would refrain from making "unilateral changes in wages, hours, or working conditions," and the employee organizations would not engage in "any strikes, slowdowns, work stoppages, or mass absenteeism." [*131*] Both parties were to share equally the fees and expenses of mediators, arbitrators, members of dispute panels, and other costs incurred in the efforts to resolve the impasses.

The New York City ordinance establishing the OCB differs very little from these recommendations. The provision dealing with mediation provides for the appointment of panels, not a "mediator" or "mediators," and in no case may such a panel be named "less than 30 days after the commencement of negotiations, unless requested by both parties." [*144*, p. 5] The terminology "impasse panel" is used instead of "dispute panel." [*144*, pp. 5-6] The detailed provisions dealing with the approval of names to be placed on the registers of mediators and impasse panel members have already been given in Chapter 5.

Mediation, fact-finding, and other dispute settlement techniques have in the past been employed in New York City, but not in accordance with a uniform plan such as that provided in the OCB ordinance. Individual collective agreements have, for example, sometimes contained provisions requiring the parties to submit impasses to fact-finding, and on occasion the city has even agreed in advance to accept the fact-finder's recommendations, as it did in the case of the threatened mass resignation of hospital nurses in the spring of 1966.

Whatever one thinks about particular features of each, the Rockefeller and Lindsay plans both do provide machinery guaranteeing systematic attention to bargaining deadlocks, with steps automatically taken to assure that efforts to reach a settlement are continued. As stressed at the beginning of this chapter, settlements cannot be imposed on the parties if the free, collective bargaining system is to endure, but this does not mean that they should not be prodded to do everything possible to come to an agreement. With procedures of this type, it is likely that many more disputes will be resolved than in the past.

### "The Myth of the Magic Formula"

As former Secretary of Labor Arthur J. Goldberg and others have warned, it is an illusion to think in terms of that one method which surely will prevent strikes, either in the private or public sector. Goldberg calls this the "Myth of the Magic Formula—

the notion that there is some as yet undiscovered ideal method of settling labor disputes affecting the national interest." He believes that, actually, we have an "imperfect system which, historically, has worked reasonably well." [*104*]

Fact-finding offers real promise, but, in summarizing sentiment at the 1966 annual meeting of the National Academy of Arbitrators, A. H. Raskin wrote: "The largest question of all is whether the taxpayers, already writhing under the high cost of schools, slum clearance and other starved municipal services, are willing to let impartial fact-finders allocate enough money from the civic treasury to convince public employees that they are getting justice without strikes." [*320*] A recent apparently increasing tendency of the union members to reject proposed settlements makes the problem even more difficult. Secretary of Labor Wirtz has expressed concern that the rank and file in some unions were refusing to accept settlements recommended by their leaders as a device "to get more," a development he considers, "very, very dangerous for collective bargaining." [*274*] As Raskin portrays the real situation: [*320*]

> If Mayor Lindsay's mediation panel had acted before the transit strike to recommend an increase anywhere close to the one the Transport Workers Union extorted as the price for ending its 12-day shutdown, the panel probably would have been stoned out of town. Yet, any recommendation much short of that final figure might well have been rejected by fractious elements in the union rank and file, no matter what its leaders thought about the package. It is precisely the fear of membership rebellion that makes men who have spent their lives trying to encourage responsibility and reason in industrial relations so skeptical about any all-purpose device for prohibiting public strikes.

# 8

# The Grievance Procedure

I T IS sometimes said that the "negotiated grievance procedure is the heartbeat of collective bargaining."[*314*, p. 44]
From the standpoint of the employee organization, it is here that
the sincerity of management with respect to bilateral decision-
making is tested, for the purpose of the grievance procedure is to
make it possible to call management to account for any failure to
respect the agreement. But this, of course, works both ways: the
bargaining agent also has responsibilities under the contract,
and some agreements even provide that management may file
grievances against the employee organization.

### Importance of Contract Administration

The important point is that the contract unites management
and the bargaining agent in a very close relationship as each
day they confer on countless questions which arise under it.
All one has to do is to thumb through an agreement such as
that of the United States Post Office Department (138 pages),
or even the less lengthy ones such as that of the City of Winnipeg
with the Canadian Union of Public Employees, and one is
impressed with the many detailed points covered. The ability
of management and the employee leaders to negotiate the grievance procedure, rather than there simply being one unilaterally
decreed by the management, is itself strong evidence of the
vitality of the collective negotiations process.

Contract administration, however, poses a new challenge:
the agreement, which may even have been purposely left vague
in some respects, must be interpreted and applied to numerous
situations where its meaning may be far from clear. In the
United States, it is sometimes overlooked that failure to settle
disputes arising out of the interpretation of the contract can
lead to prolonged work stoppages; actually, the Bureau of Labor

Statistics reports that, in 1964, 1,319 or 36 per cent of all stoppages were caused by such disagreements. [*389*, p. 2] In its study of the 1,717 major agreements, the Bureau found that in only 45 per cent was there an absolute ban on strikes and lockouts during the contract term, and that work stoppages can and do occur when:

1. No grievance procedure is provided;
2. No final and binding arbitration is provided;
3. Certain issues are nonarbitrable;
4. Certain issues are excluded from the grievance and arbitration procedure;
5. The contract is deemed to be cancelled on particular types of contract violation;
6. Noncompliance with decisions and awards is charged; or
7. The grievance machinery breaks down. [*390*, pp. 2-3]

Since the strike threat is a real one in some public agencies, the possibility of walkouts over alleged contract violations is far from remote. When in October of 1966 some 600 New York City Welfare Department investigators went out on strike for two days, they accused the city of numerous violations of its contract with their union, including failure to pay back pay to which they considered themselves entitled. [*255*] Similarly, in January of 1967, a threatened strike of doctors employed by the city was averted with the reinstatement to active duty at Harlem Hospital of the president of the Doctors' Association of the Department of Hospitals, who had been relieved of his duties for refusing to retract his publicly-made charges of hospital abuses. [*276*] In Canada, however, "arbitrators or adjudicators rule on the final settlement of grievances *instead* of permitting the parties to strike or lockout during the term of their collective agreement."[*53*, p. 51]

But leaving aside the possibility of work stoppages, the kinds of relationships developed between management and the employee organization during the administration of a contract will have a great bearing on the success they have when the time comes to negotiate the terms of the next one. If they have been able to resolve their conflicts over contract administration without the creation of deep antagonisms which make it exceedingly difficult for them to agree on anything, then they should be in a good position to reach agreement on the new contract.

In Chapter 1 it was stated that "public personnel administration is now characterized by an increasing emphasis on understanding and trying to meet the needs of the individual employee." Perhaps the finest contribution of "bilateralism," now
spreading from industry to government, is that by focusing so
much on the worker's grievances—what he really has on his
mind—it makes it essential for the management to emphasize
human relations. If personnel officers really have meant it when
they have said they wanted to "understand" the worker, the
negotiated grievance procedure should give them every opportunity to gain this insight. There is no question that the union-
negotiated and union-protected grievance procedure makes possible what so often seems virtually unattainable: true upward
communication.

## The Grievance Procedure in Industry

As an introduction to the discussion of the grievance procedure in government, it is useful to refer further to the Bureau
of Labor Statistics findings on industrial grievance procedures.
Of the 1,717 agreements, 99 per cent included a grievance procedure and, in 94 per cent, there was provision for binding arbitration of some or all grievance disputes. [*390*, p. 1] While in
common usage grievance refers to any complaint a worker has relating to his job, in contract language, it means "any complaint or
dispute that a regular employee, group of employees, or the
union may submit to a management representative, to seek
an adjustment through part or all of the contract grievance
procedure." [*390*, p. 5] Thus, some of the workers' complaints
may not qualify as grievances under the contract; it all depends
upon how the latter defines a grievance.

In approximately 47 per cent of the agreements, the grievance
definition was unrestricted, meaning that it was stated or implied
that "any dispute or complaint could be processed as a grievance"
[*390*, p. 6] ; in about 53 per cent, "only disputes arising under or
relating to the specific provisions of the agreement were defined
as grievances." [*390*, p. 7] Although some agreements in each
category excluded one or more issues from the grievance process,
these exclusions "were not set forth as essential limitations
of the general grievance definition." [*390*, p. 6] As only one example, in some contracts disputes over merit increases could not
be invoked under the grievance procedure, no matter whether the

grievance definition was restricted or unrestricted. [*390*, p. 9]
The Bureau comments, "in the long run, as the history of labor-
management relations demonstrates, any substantial accumu-
lation of grievances not covered by the contract and not admissible into the grievance procedure will very likely work itself
out, either in open conflict or in a revision of the contract to
accommodate the issue or the type of grievance." [*390*, p. 7] As
we shall see later, the definition of grievance in the contracts
being negotiated in government also varies.

In most of the contracts analyzed by the Bureau, complaints
over what provisions the agreement ought to include were not
subject to the grievance procedure. [*390*, p. 5] Whether or not
they are union members, under the law employees "have equal
rights to have their grievances (as defined in the contract) processed through the grievance machinery specified in the contract."
[*390*, p. 17] Under Taft-Hartley, to which most of the agreements
studied were subject, the individual may, if he so desires, be
present and have his grievance adjusted without the intervention
of the bargaining representative, provided that the adjustment
is not inconsistent with the terms of the existing agreement and
that the "bargaining representative has been given the opportunity to be present at such adjustment." [*390*, p. 10]

Under some agreements, the "company, as well as the union
and the employee, could initiate a grievance"; [*390*, p. 20] in a
few, neither was allowed to do so. [*390*, p. 21] The agreements
frequently specified the number of grievance representatives to
be allowed, going into such details as their qualifications, how
they would be selected, their duties and privileges, and the rules
they had to observe. [*390*, pp. 23-28] At higher steps in the grievance procedure, many agreements provided for company and
union grievance committees. [*390*, pp. 29-30] The successive steps
in the grievance procedure were usually outlined, with three or
four steps provided in most cases. [*390*, pp. 33-37] For certain
kinds of grievances, usually those requiring quick resolution or
concerning matters "outside the limited authority of stewards,
foremen, or other lower echelon personnel," special handling was
provided, such as permitting initiation at some intermediate step,
or omitting or adding certain steps. [*390*, p. 36]

Time limits on some or all of the steps in the grievance procedure were also often specified. [*390*, pp. 37-41] Most of the
agreements required written presentation of the grievance at

some stage in the procedure, usually at the second step, although a few made it necessary at the first step and some at "another intermediate or the final step." [*390*, p. 41] Settlement of grievance disputes through non-binding mediation was stipulated in 45, or 2.6 percent, of the 1,717 agreements. [*390*, p. 52] Settlements mutually reached by labor and management at any step in the grievance procedure were generally final and binding on all parties concerned, and all but 88 of the 1,697 agreements with grievance procedures provided for arbitration of unsettled disputes. [*390*, pp. 54-56]

## The Grievance Procedure in Government

Appendix B reproduces, along with other materials, the grievance procedures of several collective agreements in government, and these procedures, along with others, will be cited at appropriate points in the discussion below of practices in the United States and Canadian public jurisdictions. There is no such thing as a "model grievance procedure," because the organizational structure and circumstances of government agencies vary so much. Furthermore, as we have seen, the procedure naturally takes its shape in accordance with the basic policy decisions made about the kinds of grievances to allow and whether or not to make arbitration available, on an advisory or binding basis.

### In the United States Federal Government

Although the Kennedy Task Force found that in general federal agencies took seriously their responsibility to establish and administer grievance systems in conformance with Civil Service Commission standards, it noted serious "shortcomings and deficiencies in many of the existing systems." Its principal criticism was that "for many Government agencies, complaints and dissatisfactions are considered to be purely personal problems which have no bearing on group or collective relationships," as contrasted with industry where ordinarily a company "will look upon its grievance system as part of an overall industrial relations structure."

It reported having found a disinclination in some agencies to deal with union spokesmen for employees with grievances, and it warned that "when the issues involved concern the implementation of an agreement by an agency and the exclusive representative of its employees, such an attitude could easily destroy the confidence and good will which are essential to such a relationship." Accordingly, it strongly recommended that the employee organizations be given a "recognized role in grievance systems" and, further, that the agencies consider including a provision for advisory arbitration of grievances in their agreements with exclusive bargaining agents. [*315*, p. 22]

Binding arbitration was ruled out because it would "undermine the final authority and responsibility of an agency head for his own operations." The issues to be subject to advisory arbitration would be clearly defined and be "confined to grievances, complaints and misunderstandings which are personal to an individual employee, and to the specific implementation of existing policies." [*315*, p. 23]

The Task Force also noted that, whereas in industry, "grievance" generally refers to any kind of employee complaint or dissatisfaction, in the federal service it was restricted to questions of working conditions and relationships, with many serious matters handled instead through the appeals procedure, available for those protesting adverse actions, such as separations and demotions. Particularly since it had found numerous "disparities" in the agency appeals systems, it recommended "that, to the extent feasible, appeals procedures in the agencies should be integrated into the agencies' grievance systems, that such systems should be developed in consultation or negotiation with employee organizations, that there should be a minimum number of levels of review, and that duplicate channels of appeal should not be permitted." [*315*, pp. 24-25]

*Relevant Provisions of the Two Kennedy Orders.* Executive Order 10988, previously referred to as the "Kennedy Order," authorizes the inclusion of grievance procedures in agreements with exclusive employee representatives, but such procedures must conform to U.S. Civil Service Commission standards and "may not in any manner diminish or impair any rights which would otherwise be available to any employee in the absence of an agreement providing for such procedures." They may provide for advisory arbitration, with "any decisions or recommendations subject to the approval of the agency head"; the arbitration is to apply only to the interpretation or application of the agreement or of agency policy, and to be invoked only "with the approval of the individual employee or employees concerned." [*400*, p. 354]

In a companion Executive Order, No. 10987 issued on the same day, the heads of each department and agency were required, in accordance with Civil Service Commission regulations, to establish systems "for the reconsideration of administrative decisions to take adverse action against employees." The Order specifies several principles to be embodied in the Commission's regulations; in general, these guidelines provide for a simple, orderly procedure, with the employee organizations given the right to be consulted in the formulation and operation of the system, and the individual employee to be "accompanied, represented, and advised by a representative of his own choosing in presenting his appeal." Department and agency heads are also "authorized to include provision for advisory arbitration, where appropriate, in the agency appeals system." [*112*, pp. 31-33]

*Analysis of Negotiated Grievance Procedures.* A Bureau of Labor Statistics' analysis of 209 federal agreements as of late summer 1964 showed that ninety-six included grievance procedures, and that of this ninety-six, two-thirds "permitted advisory arbitration of unsettled disputes as the next to the last step," the arbitrator's recommendations "to be considered by the designated agency official authorized to make a final and binding decision." [*388*, p. 62]

Other findings were:

1. The most common provision was for the employee organization to be notified or to be allowed to be present at formal grievance proceedings where the employee had not asked it to represent him;

2. The employee's right to initiate and process a grievance without the union's help was emphasized in about one-half of the contracts [*388*, p. 57];

3. "Generally, grievances relating to the interpretation and application of the agreement were admissible, as were complaints about working conditions";

4. Appeals against adverse actions were frequently excluded, being handled through separate procedures already provided for by law and/or regulations, this also being true for complaints over security clearances, reductions-in-force, and equal employment opportunities [*388*, p. 58];

5. The employee was sometimes allowed to choose between the negotiated procedures and those of the agency [*388*, p. 61];

6. The step-by-step process for handling grievances was specified in ninety-six of the nonpostal agreements [*388*, p. 59];

7. A joint hearing or fact-finding committee was brought into the process, usually at a later stage, in about half the agreements [*388*, pp. 59-60];

8. If advisory arbitration was permitted, the selection of the arbitrator was initially left to the parties, with the Federal Mediation and Conciliation Service or other organization called upon to furnish lists of qualified candidates if the parties could not agree; and

9. Arbitration costs were to be shared equally, although in some cases agency expenditures could not exceed an amount set by regulations. [*388*, pp. 62-63]

About 40 per cent of the agreements presently provide for grievance arbitration [*158*, p. 7]

*Union Criticisms.* Complaining about "the downgrading" of the negotiated grievance procedure, Otto Pragan of the AFL-CIO said in May, 1966, that the unions had three basic complaints: (1) the existence of dual procedures, one negotiated and the other the agency's; (2) the many exclusions from the negotiated procedure; and (3) the ineffectual nature in practice of advisory arbitration where provided. On the first point, Pragan found it significant that the negotiated procedure was sometimes referred to in the agreements as the "union procedure," and, in his opinion, the agencies' perpetuating this dualism betrayed "their still strong belief that settling of a complaint is a matter between the individual employee and management." As to the second point, he had even found agreements with fifteen exclusions from the negotiated procedure, such exclusions generally falling into five categories: (1) national security and discrimination (equal opportunity); (2) complaints over alleged violations of laws and of Civil Service Commission and agency regulations and directives; (3) position classification cases; (4) adverse actions; and (5) disputes between the union and the management over the interpretation and application of the agreement, not based on an individual grievance.

He had no objection to the exclusion of the first category, but he did to that of the four others, stressing that advisory arbitration is available only under the negotiated procedure. He said that, because of the numerous exceptions, "a considerable number, if not the majority of all complaints occurring in labor-management relations, are deprived of being reviewed by an outside arbitrator."

Acknowledging that the Civil Service Commission had, on February 7, 1966, sent the agencies a letter reminding them of the provisions for advisory arbitration in Executive Order 10987, Pragan charged that by using the words, "where appropriate," it would still permit unsympathetic agency officials to evade advisory arbitration. ("Where appropriate" comes directly from Executive Order 10987, dealing with adverse actions; what Pragan apparently wanted was for the Commission to come out strongly in favor of advisory arbitration.)

On the third point, he charged that, contrary to the plain intention in Executive Order 10988, in some agencies the same installation head who had rejected a grievance also made the decision on the advisory recommendations of the arbitrator to whom the case was taken on appeal. Only "great pressure from the unions" had persuaded the Civil Service Commission to state in its letter that "agency programs should provide, where rejection or modification of an advisory award is contemplated, for careful consideration and final decision at a higher administrative level than the agency official who made the original decision." [*314*, pp. 43-45]

The unions have also protested that the agencies can not only refuse to submit disputes to advisory arbitration but that they also can and do reject the arbitrators' decisions if unfavorable to them. These criticisms were made, for example, in December of 1965 when the Navy Department refused to accept an arbitrator's decision on an appeal processed under a negotiated grievance procedure. The Navy had filled a promotional position with someone who had previously occupied the job in question but had left it to work at another naval installation. The International Association of Machinists thereupon charged the Navy with violating the promotion provisions of its contract with the union, because it had filled the promotion from "without" rather than "within." The union's contention was that the promotion should have been awarded to one of the three employees at the top of the promotion register resulting from a competitive examination; the Navy insisted that it had the right to transfer or reassign employees and that it was entirely consistent with merit principles to reappoint the former occupant of the position. [*421*]

The arbitrator in this case was someone with a private industry background, and his ruling confirmed the widespread fear in federal personnel circles that outside arbitrators simply would not have the necessary knowledge of governmental merit system procedures. This, of course, is only one case, and no sure predictions about future decisions by the arbitrators can be made based upon it alone, but it does explain the worries of so many personnel officers. They do not have the confidence that the arbitrators would make rulings which consistently protect management rights and the merit principle.

The unions, on the other hand, have no faith in grievance and appeals systems which do not provide for *binding* arbitration by an impartial third party. In Chapter 2, reference was made to the Brewster Bill (see Appendix B, 1) which defines grievance very broadly and provides for binding arbitration. It should be noted that binding arbitration can be invoked on the initiative of the unions alone (Sec. 501, (f) (1) ) ; thus the government would be required by law to accept such a procedure even if it opposed it—as it very likely would.

In his strong criticism of the Rhodes-Johnston bills, which contained a similar provision on grievances, Wilson R. Hart wrote:

> Arbitration in industry is completely voluntary.... There is just as much difference between voluntary arbitration and compulsory arbitration as there is between voluntary matrimony and compulsory matrimony. To insist that anyone who is against the arbitration provisions of the Rhodes bill must be against arbitration generally is as fallacious as saying that a person who objects to letting someone else decide whom he will marry and when he will marry is against the institution of marriage.

In his opinion, the Rhodes-Johnston bills were so worded that the unions could embark on a policy of "come to us, we'll arbitrate anything," taking into account also that it was apparently intended that the government pay all the expenses of the arbitration. [*110*, pp. 163-165] The Brewster bill does require each party to meet the costs of its members of the proposed boards of arbitration, but this is the only significant difference with the Rhodes-Johnston provisions on grievances. Senator Brewster apparently believes that the attitude of the agency managements is such that arbitration must be forced on them by law, whereas in the private sector this has not been necessary because the great majority of companies have willingly accepted such procedures.

Although some of the union criticisms of the grievance and appeals procedures appear extreme to personnel and management officers, certain comments of Jack T. Conway, executive director of the AFL-CIO's Industrial Union Department, as reported by Mike Causey, make sense: [*56*]

> The most important feature in government-union contracts, Conway says, is the grievance procedures they set up. Many Federal officials frankly view them as a pain-in-the-neck. They see it as a way for union "crybabies" to bring up every minor item in the sun, items that aren't worth talking about and that actually impede work on more important matters.
>
> But Conway sees those so-called petty grievances as a 'measles chart' which will benefit Uncle Sam as much, if not more, than the unions.
>
> 'It's a constant pulse-taking action,' Conway explained. 'If a whole flock of grievances keep popping up in one area—as they probably will—it may mean some managers are acting in a club-footed manner.'
>
> He also feels that the "flock" of grievances will eventually subside, as both unions and management mature and learn to live with each other.

The Kennedy Order is also criticized because it does not limit representation of employees in grievances and appeals to exclusive bargaining agents; the same right is given employee organizations granted formal and informal recognition. Although no other organization can be granted formal recognition if there is an exclusive agent, still, in the opinion of Professor Cyrus F. Smythe, this has created undesirable competition in some agencies which "detracts from the reasonable and durable union-management relationships which might assist rather than hinder the operations of the federal service." If, on the other hand, says Smythe, the argument is made that this creates a "competitive environment for union organizations" which "strengthens federal management," then the Order could be viewed as seeming to give federal employees the same organization rights as in industry, "while at the same time creating real and frustrating obstacles to such organization and the organization's effectiveness." [*339*, p. 201]

This criticism is denied by those who see no evidence that the right of the individual employee to choose his own representative in a grievance action weakens the position of the exclusive bargaining agent. Organizations with informal and formal recognition do not have the same representation rights as those with exclusive recognition; furthermore, only the exclusive representative can negotiate separate grievances procedures, including advisory arbitration.

*Procedure in the Post Office.* The unions regard the grievance and appeals provisions in the Post Office Department Agreement, reproduced in part in Appendix B, 2, as more satisfactory than those in most other federal contracts. In analyzing the Appendix materials, and our comments which follow below, it should be remembered that the Post Office Department is very large, and that smaller agencies may not require as elaborate a procedure.

1. Grievances are not limited to disagreements arising over the interpretation or implementation of the contract, but neither are they defined so broadly that any and all management decisions could be made the subject of a grievance, as under the Brewster bill.

2. Separate procedures are provided for appeals against adverse actions and certain other kinds of cases. Thus, there is some of the "dualism" criticized by Pragan, who is quoted above.

3. The procedure evidences the willingness of the management to work out with the employee organizations the details of personnel procedures, consistent with provisions of law and Civil Service Commission regulations. An example is the section dealing with "Grievance Appeal from Salary Step-Increase Withholding." Unfortunately some personnel officers have assumed that, if there is a law or regulation dealing with some phase of personnel administration like salary increases, nothing related thereto can be negotiated with the employee organizations.

4. The entire "Adverse Action and Appeal Procedure" was negotiated by the department and the employee organizations, an excellent example of how, despite the numerous provisions of law relating to adverse actions, there is much room for management-labor cooperation in developing mutually-acceptable procedures, at the same time respecting these legal provisions and the regulations of the Civil Service Commission.

5. Some training material for the supervisors is included, for they are admonished to do everything possible to settle grievances informally.

6. Grievances must be filed within 30 days of the "action or condition giving rise to the grievance,"

7. An employee organization may file a grievance on behalf of one or more employees, provided the employee(s) concerned have so authorized it in writing.

8. At each step in both the grievance and the adverse action appeals procedures, action must be completed within a specified time period by the official to whom the case has been referred.

9. The employee is not required to put his grievance in writing when he initially takes it up with his immediate supervisor, or when it is not resolved at this stage and he elects to appeal to the installation head (usually the local postmaster). It is only if he does not wish to discuss it with the installation head, or does so and is still unsatisfied, that he must file it in writing.

10. The employee can be represented at any step in the grievance procedure by whomever he wants. If he does not select a representative of the exclusive organization, it still has a right to be present.

11. The exclusive organization has the right to be notified of the time and place of the proceedings, at each step of the grievance procedure beginning with the discussion with the installation head, and to be present and present its point of view at all steps, except the initial conversations with the immediate supervisor when the employee has not selected someone to represent him. It must also be furnished with a copy of any written decisions and summaries prepared at any step.

12. If the employee's grievance is rejected by the installation head, the employee can appeal, either with or without a hearing, depending on his wishes. If he requests one, the installation head must arrange for the establishment of a three-man hearing committee, one member to be named by the employee, one by the installation head, and the third (to serve as chairman) by the first two. All three members must be postal service employees. The committee's decision is binding unless appealed by the employee or the installation head to the regional director.

If the employee does not request a hearing, he files his appeal in writing with the regional director, sending a copy to the installation head who forwards the entire grievance file to the regional director, together with his answer to the grievance. The employee may request an "informal discussion," which is arranged for by the director of the personnel division in the regional office. The same request may be made by an employee whose appeal was rejected by the hearing committee referred to above. If the personnel director cannot resolve the case informally, it goes to the regional director for decision.

13. The regional director's decision may be appealed to the Board of Appeals and Review, in the Bureau of Personnel at headquarters, which, although the employee has no right to a hearing at this stage, may in its discretion hold one. The Board's decision is final and considered that of the Postmaster General.

*The TVA System.* In the Tennessee Valley Authority, the grievance procedures negotiated with the Tennessee Valley Trades and Labor Council and the Salary Policy Employee Panel both state that any "employee who believes he has been treated unfairly" or "disagrees with his supervisors as to the application of a policy to him as an employee, may file a grievance." [*102*, p. 49; *39*, p. 52] "Employee" is construed to include the union acting in behalf of a single employee, or a group of employees. In the agreement with the Council, it is made clear that grievances, the purpose of which is to obtain changes in existing policies and procedures, may not be filed, and that such changes can be made only through the contract negotiation process. An employee may be represented by a union spokesman at any stage in the grievance procedure, but, if he decides to represent himself, the personnel officer must inform the local union representative of the bargaining unit when a grievance is appealed beyond the immediate supervisor. The union representative is requested to attend all hearings and is given a copy of the grievance record.

*The Detailed TVA Procedure.* In the agreement with the Trades and Labor Council, the first step is for the employee to take up his grievance, orally or in writing, with "the supervisor immediately responsible for the action or notice of the proposed action which resulted in the grievance." He has 10 days to do this from the date he is notified of such action or proposed action, and the supervisor must give him an answer within 10 days. If the employee is not satisfied with the supervisor's decision, he may appeal under the grievance procedure to the division director, except that, depending on the nature of the proposed action, he may be entitled by federal law or regulation to take the case directly to the United States Civil Service Commission.

If he decides to appeal to the Commission, he must do so at this point, in which case his appeal will no longer be considered under the TVA grievance procedure. The employee must, within 10 days of the supervisor's decision, make known his desire to appeal, preferably by filing a notice in writing with the division head. In the next stage, he either presents his case in writing to the division head or he requests a hearing, although the division head may himself decide to hold one whether or not the employee requests it.

The hearing must be held within 30 days of the receipt of the employee's notice of appeal. Before a decision is made in the case, the verbatim transcript of the hearing must be submitted to the employee and the supervisor to check for accuracy, with each party given a reasonable amount of time to review the transcript and make comments. The division director must make his decision within three weeks of his receiving the appeal, or if a hearing is held, within three weeks from the date of obtaining the completed record of the hearing. If the employee does not appeal within 10 days of receiving the division director's written decision, the grievance is considered closed.

If he does appeal, it must be in writing to the director of personnel, and he does so personally or through the international representative of the bargaining agent. If personally, the director of personnel must inform the international union representative of the appeal; he makes his decision, which is final, within three weeks of receiving the appeal. If the international union representative appeals on behalf of an employee, the director of personnel confers with such representative on whether a conference should be held before a decision in the case is reached. If such a conference is held, those present are the supervisors involved in the appeal, the international union representative, such other representatives of the Trades and Labor Council as its officers may designate, and the director of personnel. He tries to get the parties to agree on a solution, but, if he is unable to do so, he gives his written decision within two weeks of holding the conference.

If the Council is not satisfied with the decision, it has the right to request the director of personnel to submit the case to an impartial referee. The director of personnel secures the services of such a referee and furnishes him with the complete record of the case in dispute; within 10 days of the referee's receiving this material, both TVA and the Council send him "such written comments on the factual and argumentative information considered in earlier steps of the grievance as they may wish." If requested by either the TVA or the Council, or if he independently judges it necessary, the referee holds a hearing.

Within two weeks from the date of his receiving the complete record, the referee makes his decision, "which must not be inconsistent with the General Agreement and its Supplementary Schedules," an important proviso because the General Agreement recognizes that "TVA must operate within the limits of its legally delegated authority and responsibility." The referee's decision must be accepted as final by both parties, and the expenses for his services are shared equally by the TVA and the Council. [*102*, pp. 49-53]

*Comment on TVA Procedure.* Attention should be called to two features in the TVA procedure, one not really unusual but the other very much so. The first is that appeal to the director of personnel is one of the important steps in the procedure. The second is that neither the employee nor his union can have a case arbitrated by the referee; this can be achieved only by the Trades and Labor Council, or by the Salary Policy Employee Panel in the case of the white collar employees under an agreement which is very similar to the one for the blue collar workers. [*39*, pp. 52-54] The reasoning is that at this stage the dispute is no longer an individual matter but rather one between the TVA and the Council. In requesting the services of a referee, however, the Council acts upon the recommendation of a constituent union which is dissatisfied with the director of personnel's decision. General Manager Van Mol states that "at the third level there is an innovation in that either the union or the director of personnel can request a conference before he makes a decision." [*395*, p. 92]

*The Bonneville Procedure.* In the agreement of the Bonneville Power Administration with the Columbia Power Trades Council, it is stated that "the adjudication of grievances extends only to the interpretation and application of this agreement and other management policy." The first step is for the aggrieved employee to discuss his problem informally with the immediate supervisor, except that if he believes that his relationship with him is such "that he cannot reasonably discuss the matter with him," he may take it up with the "next level of supervision."

If the grievance is not settled within five days, or if the employee is not satisfied with the decision of the immediate supervisor, he or his representative may, within the next ten days, submit the grievance in writing to the area manager or branch chief. When either of the latter receives a written grievance from an employee or group of employees, directly or through a representative, he must immediately inform the Council through the labor relations officer of the date and time when the grievance will be heard. If the matter in question is not excluded from the grievance procedure by departmental regulations, the area manager or branch chief attempts to adjudicate it, and gives his decision to the employee and, through the labor relations officer, to the Council within 14 days after receiving the case.

If the area manager or branch chief cannot settle the grievance to the employee's satisfaction within 14 days, the employee may, within the next 10 days, take it up directly with the administrator or submit it to the Joint Grievance Board. The latter is made up of four members, two appointed by the Council and two by the administrator. The employee and his representative, as well as "appropriate representative" of the management must be allowed to appear before the Board. The Board must "apply its best efforts to determine pertinent facts" and attempt by majority vote to recommend a settlement.

If the Board makes a recommendation or cannot agree on one, the employee and the Council are informed, and the employee has ten days in which to request the Joint Grievance Board to appoint an arbitrator. After studying all the records in the case and making such investigations as he finds necessary, the arbitrator recommends a settlement to the administrator. The latter's decision, whether based upon the direct appeal of the employee or upon the recommendations of the arbitrator, is final and binding upon both parties. [*73*, pp. 15-19]

### In the Canadian Federal Government

The Public Service Staff Relations Act of 1967 defines grievance as a complaint in writing made "in accordance with this Act" by an employee on his behalf or that of himself and one or more other employees; in the case of grievances, persons serving in a managerial or confidential capacity are not considered employees. [*350*, p. 3] The employee may file a grievance if it arises from: the "interpretation or application in respect of him" of the "provision of a statute, regulation, by-law, direction or other instrument made or issued by the employer, dealing with terms and conditions of employment; or the provision of a collective agreement or arbitral award"; or any other "occurrence or matter affecting his terms and conditions of employment," provided that in these cases there is no other "administrative procedure for redress" in any other law, e.g. the Public Service Employment Act which provides for appeals on promotion.

An employee may not present a grievance relating to the effect on him of any provision in a collective agreement or arbitral award unless "he has the approval of and is represented by the bargaining agent for the bargaining unit to which the collective agreement or arbitral award applies." Furthermore, the employee may not be represented by any "employee organization, other than the employee organization certified as such bargaining agent." [*350*, pp. 41-42]

The reader will recall the discussion in Chapter 4 of the rights of minorities, as well as the criticism, mentioned earlier in this chapter, of the Kennedy Order for not limiting employee representation rights to the exclusive agent. This is another reason why it will be instructive to follow the Canadian experience under this new legislation, for it will reveal how individual employees and minorities react to this stronger role for the employee organizations.

The Public Service Staff Relations Board (PSSRB) is authorized to make regulations covering:

1. The procedure for filing a grievance;

2. The maximum number of levels of officers to whom grievances may be presented;

3. The time limits for each step in the procedure;

4. The "circumstances in which any level below the final level in the grievance process may be eliminated"; and, in case of doubt, whether a particular matter shall be considered a grievance.

These regulations shall not apply "in respect of employees included in a bargaining unit for which a bargaining agent has been certified by the Board, to the extent that such regulations are inconsistent with any provisions contained" in the collective agreement in question. [*350*, pp. 46-47]

If an employee has exhausted all steps in the internal agency grievance procedure, and his complaint has to do with the interpretation or application of a collective agreement or arbitral award or a disciplinary action resulting in discharge, suspension, or a financial penalty, he may take the case to adjudication (arbitration). [*350*, p. 42] This means that some grievances may not be adjudicated, e.g., those arising out of the application to the employee of agency rules dealing with working conditions. In the case of grievances arising from the interpretation or application of a collective agreement or arbitral award, the bargaining agent must agree that the grievance should be adjudicated and be willing to represent the employee in the adjudication proceedings. To carry out adjudication under the Act, the Governor in Council, upon the recommendation of the PSSRB, appoints a panel of adjudicators and, also upon the recommendation of the Board, designates one of them to serve as chief adjudicator.

The aggrieved employee states whether an adjudicator is already named in any applicable collective agreement; if none is, he specifies whether he wants the case heard by an adjudicator selected by the chief adjudicator or by a board of adjudication. If the grievance arises out of a collective agreement and an adjudicator is named therein, the chief adjudicator refers the case to such person. If the employee requests a board of adjudication, and the employer does not object, the chief adjudicator establishes such a board, but, if no board is requested, he himself selects an adjudicator from the above-mentioned panel. When a board of adjudication is named, it consists of three members, an adjudicator selected by the chairman and one member nominated by each party. No one may serve on such a board who has "any direct interest in or in connection with the grievance, its handling or its disposition."

The board of adjudicators, or the single adjudicator, as the case may be, gives both parties the opportunity to be heard; in the case of a board, decisions are reached by majority vote. No decision may be made the effect of which would be to require amendment of the collective agreement or an arbitral award. If the decision "requires any action by or on part of an employee or a bargaining agent or both of them, the employee or bargaining agent, or both, as the case may be, shall take such action." If an adjudicator is named in a collective agreement, his salary and expenses shall be paid in accordance with the provisions therein, but, if the contract is silent on this matter, these costs are shared equally by both parties. If the grievance is referred for adjudication but is not heard by an adjudicator named in a collective agreement, and the employee has been represented by the bargaining agent, the latter is "liable to pay and shall remit to the Board such part of the costs of the adjudication as may be determined by the Secretary of the Board with the approval of the Board, except that where the grievance is referred to a board of adjudication, the remuneration and expenses of the nominee of each party shall be borne by each respectively."

If either the employer or the bargaining agent complains that the other party has failed to meet an obligation arising out of a collective agreement or arbitral award, and it is an obligation which cannot be made the subject of an individual employee grievance, either may refer it to the chief adjudicator who personally hears and determines the case. This enables either party to file grievances against the other, totally apart from individual employee complaints. [*350*, pp. 43-46]

Finally, the PSSRB also is authorized to issue regulations covering the detailed steps in the adjudication process, including time limits, procedures to be followed by the adjudicators, and the form of their decisions. [*350*, p. 47] Although the Preparatory Committee on Collective Bargaining had recommended that, in cases where "the national interest is at stake," the Governor in Council have "the power to amend or set aside an arbitral award," [*324*, p. 37] no such provision appears in the final legislation. Since Parliament can always legislate, presumably it could set aside an award, although it should be remembered that in Great Britain this has never happened.

### In United States State and Local Governments

There is little reference to the grievance procedure in the new state laws. As noted in Chapter 5, the Connecticut statute makes the services of the state board of mediation and arbitration available to municipal employers and employee organizations "for purposes of mediation of grievances or contract disputes and . . .arbitration of disputes over the interpretation or application of the terms of a written agreement." It also encourages the parties to set up their own arbitration machinery for such purposes, and the Massachusetts law has similar provisions.[*30*, p. 329; *31* p. 558] As mentioned in Chapter 7, the new Wisconsin State Labor Relations Act provides for the Wisconsin Employment Relations Board to initiate fact-finding, not only in disputes arising out of deadlocked negotiations but also those over the application or interpretation of contract provisions. [*345*, p. 7] In these and other states, the parties negotiate the grievance procedure, so it is to the agreements themselves we must turn in analyzing the practices in state and local governments.

The problem arises at once of which contracts to use as examples from the very large number already operative. No detailed, comprehensive analysis has been made of the agreements in government, similar to that of the Bureau of Labor Statistics for industry. There is the valuable analysis by Joseph Krislov and Jacob Schmulowitz of "Grievance Arbitration in State and Local Government Units," based on 44 usable responses to a questionnaire sent out to 101 state and local government units in late 1962, but the data is limited to the question of arbitration and many other contracts have been signed since then. [*130*] We will use as examples the grievance procedures in five contracts (see Appendix B) which, although in no sense "typical," illustrate the various approaches followed. We will not comment on every detail in these procedures, because in some respects they are not different from those of the United States Post Office and other agencies discussed above.

*Department of Mental Health, State of Delaware and Laborers' International Union of North America, Local 1029, AFL-CIO.* The bargaining unit here is the State Hospital for the Mentally Retarded. Note first that the definition of the grievance is broad, but not so broad as to encompass complaints about any management decisions, as in the case of the Brewster bill. Only grievances dealing with the "application, meaning, or interpretation" of the agreement can be carried through the fifth or last step, which is binding arbitration; all others can be processed through the first four steps.

In the first step, the employee must present his grievance in writing to his immediate supervisor. A hearing must be held at the third step, which is appeal to the facility (hospital) head. The employee may be accompanied by not more than three representatives, and someone from the office of personnel must be present. All testimony must be recorded, and a transcript be made available to the union upon request. The final decision in all grievances not subject to arbitration is made by the head of the Department of Mental Health, the commissioner. For arbitrable disputes, it is agreed that the Voluntary Arbitration Rules of the American Arbitration Association will govern the proceedings. If the Department of Mental Health has a disagreement with the union over the interpretation of the contract, it presents it to the union's grievance committee, but, if this does not settle the difficulty, it may be appealed at the fourth step in the grievance procedure (level of the commissioner), and, if still unresolved, be submitted to arbitration.

*Levy Court of New Castle County, Delaware, and the American Federation of State, County, and Municipal Employees, AFL-CIO, Local 459.* This agreement, now superceded, was referred to in Chapter 2 during the discussion of possible conflicts between union contracts and the merit principle. Note first that "grievance" includes *any* dispute between the parties. Whereas in the first step, the only union representative is the steward, in steps two and three he is joined by the chairman of the union grievance committee and the president of the local union. In the third step, the grievance is taken up with the Levy Court, a combined legislative-administrative body which has since been replaced by a county council limited to legislative functions. Since, as explained in Chapter 2, the contract covered important aspects of the personnel function, the scope of the binding arbitration is very broad. If the parties fail to nominate their arbitrators, either or both must request the State Mediation and Conciliation Service to provide a panel from which presumably a selection must be made.

*City of Milwaukee and Milwaukee District Council 48, AFSCME, AFL-CIO and Its Appropriate Affiliated Locals.* Here grievances are limited to disagreements over the interpretation, application, and enforcement of the contract. By the third step, it is either the employee or the union which has the right to appeal, and, if the grievance is still unsettled, it is the union which invokes the fourth step which is referral to the department head. If the dispute remains unresolved, either party can take it to binding arbitration; the latter is also available for any grievance initiated by the city which cannot be resolved through conferences with the union.

The circumstances under which binding or advisory arbitration may be invoked are carefully defined so as not to conflict with the legal obligations of the city. The case may be heard either by a single arbitrator or a board of arbitrators, with one party able to require establishment of such a board. What the arbitrator can and cannot do is carefully specified; he is instructed not only to confine himself to the issues in the case but also to make no statements which are not "directly essential" in deciding the case. He has, however, the initial authority to determine whether or not the case is arbitrable under the agreement.

The unusual provision is for advisory arbitration of disciplinary actions instituted by department heads under the civil service regulations. A special step is provided in the procedure, permitting the union to request the City Service Commission to appoint a panel of advisory arbitrators who investigate the facts and then present their findings and recommendations to the Commission. If unable to reach a decision on the basis of the arbitrators' report, the Commission may reopen the case to obtain more evidence, but, in any case, it makes the final decision.

Some people think that advisory arbitration of grievances, not arising out of a contract provision but rather under the civil service system, is a promising middle ground between the hard-line management rights' advocates, on the one hand, and the unions, on the other, with their demands for binding arbitration of grievances. It is much too early, however, to draw any conclusions from the Milwaukee experience, because the advisory arbitration provision has been invoked only twice since the contract went into effect on January 1, 1966. In both cases, the arbitrator upheld dismissal action taken by the city. [*1,137*]

*District Council 33, AFSCME, AFL-CIO and Personnel Director, City of Philadelphia.* A typical complaint is that management makes changes in policies without first consulting the union and giving it the opportunity to present its views. The first paragraph in the Philadelphia agreement takes care of this objection. As to disagreements over the interpretation or application of the contract, note the function of the advisory board of six members, three appointed by the personnel director and three by the union, and that it mediates, rather than arbitrates. The personnel director has an important role, because he speaks for the city in these contract disputes.

*City of Winnipeg and Local 500, Canadian Union of Public Employees*. Although the employee may file a grievance if he believes "he has been unjustly dealt with," only "controversies concerning the meaning, interpretation or violation" of the agreement can be submitted to binding arbitration. The arrangements for the selection of the arbitrators are not unusual, in the light of the examples already given in this chapter, but note that the arbitrators decide who is to pay the costs "or any part thereof" and they also may "tax or settle the amount thereof." The grievance procedure itself also permits appeal to the city council as one step in the procedure.

### The Common Law of the Collective Relationship

In concluding this chapter, these words of Professor Cyrus F. Smythe are particularly appropriate:

> The grievance process gives union leadership the opportunity to probe, on a daily basis, the scope of allowable bargaining. To those familiar with private industry collective bargaining, grievance processing has long been recognized as the more important of the two basic union functions of contract negotiation and contract administration. For it is in the administration of a collective agreement that the common law of the collective relationship is established. [*339*, p. 201]

# 9

# Collective Negotiations in Public Education

$A$S WE shall see later in this chapter, there are significant differences in the philosophies and tactics of the two leading organizations of school teachers, the National Education Association (NEA) and the American Federation of Teachers (AFT), but they are in solid agreement on the new image of the teacher: he regards himself as a true professional, demands corresponding recognition, and is increasingly getting it as his services rise in the public esteem. Three high-ranking staff members of the NEA, in explaining teacher "militancy," stress "the impact of a rapid emergence of a new status for public employees in general," based on the "greatly increased levels of preparation . . . demanded," levels which "apply with peculiar emphasis to teachers." [*348*, p. 5] A recent AFT publication quotes the statement made a few years ago by the president of one of its locals: "The day of the prim, meek, frustrated teacher submissive to the caprices of the school board, administration, politicians, the parents and the students is past." [*142*, p. 80] In this same publication, the comment appears: [*142*, pp. 1-2]

> In the popular image of the 18th and 19th century the school teacher was most often a young woman earning a meagre living while waiting for marriage, and somewhat less frequently, a spinster who was too old to change jobs or too dedicated to want to change. The teacher in the 20th century and those interns who will undoubtedly be teaching well into the 21st century are far removed from this popular image. *They see themselves as professionals who are dedicated to the instruction of youth.* They want their rights and obligations clearly defined, both by the organizations to which they belong, and by the school administrators for whom they work. They insist that these clear guidelines be the work of *mutual* action among the board of education, the administrators, and the teachers themselves. (Italics ours.)

Stinnett, Kleinmann, and Ware report that, whereas only ten years ago one-fourth of the school teachers in the United States did not have a college degree, "in 1965, fewer than 10 per

cent of public school staffs (about 1,800,000) had not completed
the bachelor's or higher degrees," and "about one fourth had
completed the master's degree." Noting that as late as 1946
about two-thirds of the states did not even require a degree
for beginning elementary teachers and that "the requirements
ranged downward to less than high school graduation and the
passing of an examination based on elementary school content
in some states," they comment that the public's "low opinion" of
teachers presumably "reflected these low requirements." Furthermore, the "great gap" between the preparation of elementary
and high school teachers which existed 10 years ago has been
largely closed. In all, to the public the teacher is now viewed
as an "employee of undoubted quality, and worthy of respect
and the dignity accorded all professional people." [*348*, p. 177]

### Reasons for Teacher Militancy

The sense of power teachers derive from their vastly-
increased numbers was noted in Chapter 1. In recent years, of all
government employees, the teachers have increased the most
in numbers; whereas in 1947 public school instructional personnel numbered 887,130, by 1964 this had climbed to 1,788,805.
[*348*, p. 175] Of the total of 10½ million state and local government employees, the school districts employ the highest percentage, a little less than a third, as contrasted with nearly
one-fourth each by the municipalities and the state governments.
From 1957 to 1964, full-time public employees in education rose
by 60 per cent, surpassed only by the 62 per cent increase in
those in public welfare. [*76*, p. 3] The one and three-quarter
million teachers are also very highly organized, with more
than 90 per cent of them members of the NEA or of its state
and local affiliates [*409*, p. 113], and about another 163,000 in the
AFT.

Of 4,308 school districts responding to a questionnaire sent
them by Professors Charles A. Perry and Wesley A. Wildman
of the University of Chicago's Industrial Relations Center, only
323 indicated that they had no local active teacher organization.
[*305*, p. 135] Since the questionnaire was sent only to school
systems which in the 1963-64 school year had a pupil enrollment
of 1,200 or more (of which there were 6,023), the survey
excluded the very small districts, but the researchers did not
consider this significant "in light of the distribution of classroom

teacher employment by size of school district and the trend toward fewer but larger school districts through consolidation." [*305*, p. 134]

The number of written agreements between the teacher organizations and the school boards is increasing at a rapid rate. As of September 20, 1965, the NEA reported that 388 "professional negotiation agreements," as it terms them, had been filed with it, and that perhaps another 1,000, of which it had not yet received copies, had been consummated. [*348*, p. 18] In 1955, the AFT membership was only about 46,500. [*286*] In October, 1967, the AFT estimated that it represented 146,477 teachers under "collective bargaining contracts"; [*29*, p. 8] previously it had predicted that by 1970 this figure would exceed one million. [*63*] The exact nature of the NEA "professional negotiation agreements" and the AFT's "contracts" will be discussed later in this chapter. Clearly, the teachers represent a solidly organized phalanx in society which is providing much of the momentum to the collective negotiations movement in the public service.

### Resentment over Economic Injustice

Since the labor-oriented views of the AFT are well-known, the reasons for teacher militancy are probably better conveyed by again referring to the opinions of NEA staff members, Stinnett, Kleinmann, and Ware, and also adding substantial information from other sources. Besides teacher "professionalism" and force of numbers, they cite "the mounting impatience of teachers with what they consider to be economic injustice," namely, low pay which has often even lagged behind that of unskilled workers; "teachers dislike the resistance of the public to reasonable adjustments in their pay in an affluent society which they have had a significant part in creating." [*348*, p. 4]

The teachers propose to correct this situation, and, according to a recent report of the United States Department of Labor, they have already done so to some extent, because the rate of salary increases for school teachers began to go up in 1966, particularly in the big cities. Significantly, this improvement was attributed in large part to the "new militancy" of the teachers, as reflected in the AFT's doubling of its membership since 1959 and the "increasingly forceful policies" of the NEA. Nevertheless, their percentage salary increases and fringe benefits in the big cities in the last five years have fallen behind factory workers and most other occupational groups. The Labor Department reported that the average teacher salary was $6,862, with some teachers in cities of 100,000 or more earning as little as $2,950. [*270*]

Former NEA President Richard D. Batchelder said, "it is nothing short of sinful that in this affluent society two out of three teachers must moonlight in other jobs in order to make ends meet . . . . The average teacher is growing younger. Young teachers along with their experienced colleagues are becoming impatient. They are not content to wait for their share of the fruits of the country's affluence." [*222*]

Based on its own study of teacher salaries in fifty cities, the AFT in February of 1967 put the average salary at $6,820, which it said was less than that for freight rate clerks and construction workers. [*281*] Dr. Bernard E. Donovan, the New York City Superintendent of Schools, frankly states that one of the major reasons for "militant teacher organization is a natural envy on the part of the profession toward those outside the profession who have improved their working conditions by the traditional tactics of private unionism." [*87*]

### Bitterness over Neglect of Schools

Stinnett, Kleinmann, and Ware also stress that "as an integral part of their own search for economic justice, teachers have grown increasingly bitter at the neglect of schools by our affluent society," evidenced by the "obsolete school buildings, inadequate facilities and supplies, overloaded classrooms, and the general deterioration in the quality of education offered children." [*348*, pp. 4-5] It has been pointed out that the working conditions of the teachers encompass practically all phases of the educational program; for example, if budgets are unrealistically low, classes are too large, equipment and supplies are rationed, building maintenance is neglected, and teachers are forced to perform many clerical and housekeeping chores.

The handicaps under which many teachers struggle are revealed in the responses of 9,526 of them in California to the following query in a questionnaire sent them several years ago by a state senate fact-finding committee: "Is there any specific thing which you think calls for state action to help teachers do a better job of teaching?" Most frequently mentioned were: smaller classes; less pupil supervision; a duty-free lunch period; more clerical help; more supplies and equipment; more preparation time; and more state aid. Better salaries were also stressed, but in California, as in all other parts of the country, it is clear that the pay check is only one element in widespread teacher dissatisfaction over their working conditions.

One teacher responded, "Few teachers have an opportunity to relax during 'lunch period.' I have often eaten my lunch while standing yard duty." Another reported that funds were so short that some teachers were buying badly-needed instructional materials and paying for them out of their own pockets.

One said: "If the average teacher has 5 classes a day with an average of 35 pupils per class, that is 175 pupils. If the teacher spends 5 minutes per pupil correcting papers, that is a total of 14½ hours. How often does a teacher have 14½ hours outside of school to go over a pupil's work . . . ?"

Disciplinary problems were another major source of concern: one recommendation was for non-academic schools for the "student who actively rebels against school, isn't wanted by the parents, isn't wanted by the juvenile authority or principals, and thus is forced to stay in the class where he is surrounded by more than 30 highly impressionable teenagers, and finally finds he can get some sort of recognition from the class by doing disruptive things."

Being required to attend numerous meetings after school hours also rankled, as did the frequent interruptions during the school day for assemblies, social activities, and other functions unilaterally arranged by the school administration. Better textbooks, and a voice in their selection, were also requested, and there were complaints about inadequate lighting, ventilation, and other poor physical working conditions making the teaching difficult. [*355*, pp. 21-46] These California findings are not at all unusual, but they are still unappreciated by many members of the public.

### The Teacher's Loss of Identity

The element of impersonality, mentioned in Chapter 2 as an important psychological reason for employees joining unions, also assails the school teacher who increasingly works in large-size school districts. Noting that the number of school districts in the United States has declined from about 130,000 in 1930 to some 27,000 at present, Stinnett, Kleinmann, and Ware quote the saying that " 'in the small community, the teacher is everything; in the great city he is nothing.' " In this environment of bigness, "there is unwittingly the pitfall of complex administrative machinery and unintentionally a kind of paternalism .... This has a devastating effect upon the spirit of any human being, especially upon the articulate, perceptive teacher. He resents the loss of identity." [*348*, p. 5] The NEA strongly dissents from the AFT view that the "administration" of the public school systems now resembles the "command" structure of corporate enterprise, but clearly both organizations are gaining new members and increased strength from the lonely teacher's feeling that he is only a hired hand in a bureaucratic machine.

### Influence of Civil Rights Movement

Although Stinnett, Kleinmann, and Ware speak for themselves only and not officially for the NEA, it is evidence of the growing social "activism" of educators in general that they should state their belief that the "dramatic push of American Negroes for human and civil rights" has also had "a psychological effect on teachers." Just like the Negroes, the teachers have viewed themselves as "oppressed"; "they have viewed their treatment by society as being far less that commensurate with the importance of their contribution to the general welfare." [*348*, pp. 5-6] The AFT has been very active in the civil rights movement and in fighting segregation and has frequently criticized the NEA for alleged failure to take strong action in this area, but rank and file members of both organizations have reacted to what they consider injustice in much the same way as many of the civil rights groups.

The agony of the teacher is seen in the following statement by Pete Schnaufer of the AFT:

> The commitment to integration of faculties, which many association and union leaders hold, conflicts with a concern to protect hard-fought-for seniority rights, and, even more importantly, with the pragmatic prediction that the overwhelming majority of experienced teachers who are forced to teach in slum schools won't; they'll quit, they'll go to the suburbs, they'll worm their way into administrative positions, but they won't teach where they believe it is impossible to teach, or dangerous to teach. [*332*]

Just recently the United Federation of Teachers in New York City, alarmed by cases of student assaults on teachers, requested the state legislature to provide for teacher disability insurance.

## Growing Acceptance of Collective Action in Educational Administration

Finally, the above-mentioned NEA staff members see the teachers' "demand for recognition and participation in policy formation" as "a product of the times." Like many other individuals, they are caught up in the "commitment of peoples throughout the world to a new status and dignity," in the "twilight of colonialism as a political philosophy—and of paternalism as its companion piece." [*348*, p. 5] Many teachers say they are tired of being treated autocratically: "for a long time superintendents and boards of education have publicly proclaimed their devotion to democracy in school organization. Unfortunately, what has been meant is a type of 'engineered democracy' under which teachers were allowed to discuss, but then were expected to accept the judgment of the supervisor or the board of education without question." [*87*]

These winds of change are not lost upon the administrators themselves; in a recent report of the American Association of School Administrators, the membership of which consists largely of school superintendents, frontier "individualism" is rejected as a relic of history, and collective action, including that by teachers, is lauded as a "characteristic" of American society. [*14*, pp. 11-13]

## The Stronger Bargaining Power of Teachers

Not specifically mentioned above, but implied, are two other factors: the greater importance given to education in American society, and the critical shortage of teachers. These contribute greatly to teacher bargaining power: the schools are viewed as an integral, rather than an incidental, element in the nation's plans for meeting pressing problems, and the teachers must be found to man them. As unfilled positions have increased, so has teacher militancy, not out of any malicious desire to exploit the situation but inevitably as a response to the radically altered supply and demand equation.

This is particularly noticeable in the universities and colleges where jobs were relatively scarce not too many years ago because the enrollments were then much lower. The AFT now claims a membership in higher education of more than 25,000, with AFT locals in 14 of California's 18 state colleges where the great increase in enrollments has placed new strains on the already overworked faculties. An AFT organizer said, "When colleges had fewer professors each could bargain for himself, but now they hire them by the gross." [*398*] The state college teachers find their salaries, benefits, and working conditions "intolerable," not only by comparison with private employers, but also with the University of California which under the state's master plan for education receives preferred treatment as far as salaries, teaching loads, research time, library, and other expenditures are concerned. [*40*]

## The Legal and Other Background

The points made in Chapter 4 about the legal status of public employees' rights to organize and negotiate collectively also apply to the school teachers; it is well, however, to review the background of their struggles because this constitutes an important part of labor relations developments in the public service.

### *Teachers' Right to Organize*

Just as in the case of some other government workers, early teacher efforts to organize were strongly resisted in some jurisdictions and denied by the courts. In an Illinois decision rendered in 1917, the court rejected the petition of a union of high school teachers for an injunction to prohibit the school board from enforcing a resolution making employment conditional on non-union status. The court said: "Union membership is inimical to proper discipline, prejudicial to the efficiency of the teaching force, and detrimental to the welfare of the public school system . . . . The board has the absolute right to decline to employ or reemploy any applicant for any reason whatever or for no reason at all . . . . The board is not bound to give any reason for its action." [*394*, p. 6]

This decision was cited by the Washington Supreme Court when in 1930 it upheld a lower court ruling sustaining the right of the Seattle school board to require all teachers, under penalty of dismissal, to sign an oath to the effect that they were not members of a newly-formed local of the AFT. In an article entitled "Teachers and the Yellow Dog Rule: The Seattle Story," published recently in the AFT journal, *Changing Education*, Frank Morris relates that the school board attorney, in defending the board's action in court, said that it had the right to bar union members from the classroom, just as it did to "refuse to hire women teachers or those over 40 years of age." [*166*, p. 24]

The school board charged that, if the union gained its ends, board policies would be determined by "a class organization, instead of the duly elected and appointed representatives of the schools." [*166*, p. 23] But, although as Morris puts it, the union, in existence only a few months, was "temporarily 'dead,'" in 1931 a new school board rescinded the "infamous anti-union contract clause." [*166*, p. 25]

Although, as pointed out in Chapter 4, legislatures can bar public employees from forming or joining organizations, in recent years the teachers, with few exceptions, have been free to organize and affiliate with the outside labor movement if they so desire. The NEA warns "nevertheless, since there have been some limitations on this right in the past, legislation on the subject of teacher negotiation should contain a provision that teachers may organize. Also, the provision should not limit the type of organization to which teachers may belong (provided it is organized for legitimate purposes)." [*399*, pp. 8-9]

### The Compulsory Membership Issue

As we saw in Chapter 4, in the absence of legislation barring or permitting the union shop, its legality depends upon rulings of legal officers and, ultimately, of the courts. In 1959, in the first case of this kind involving school teachers, the Montana Supreme Court declared invalid a clause in a contract with a local board of education which disqualified teachers who were not members of the union from receiving salary increases negotiated by the union. The court said:

> It is not competent for the school trustees to require union membership as a condition to receiving the increased salary. So far as this case is concerned it is sufficient to say that the Legislature has not given the school board authority to make the discrimination sought to be imposed there. . . . As well might it be argued that the Board of School Trustees might provide that the increased salary shall not be allowed to those who do not affiiliate with a certain lodge, service club, church or political party. [*348*, pp. 29-30]

In a 1961 case in Missouri, the court ruled that a local school board, under its broad statutory powers to manage school affairs, had the right to provide in the salary schedules that anyone refusing to join certain named professional organizations would not receive the "benefits" of the schedule. It reasoned that the teacher was not compelled to join the organizations and that he was free to negotiate his salary on an individual basis. Furthermore, drawing a distinction with the Montana case, it argued that membership in professional organizations, unlike that in unions, promoted "professional competence," and that it was the board's "duty to adopt rules and regulations to elevate the standards of teachers and the educational standards within their district." [*348*, pp. 31-32] Since this case, there have been no other court decisions on this issue, but, interestingly enough, teachers usually do not push for the union shop.

In Schnaufer's review of 88 contracts negotiated by both the NEA and the AFT, he found only one or two union shop clauses; these were in AFT agreements in Montana. As he explains it, the AFT's position here is really a defensive one, for, if it can be sure that teachers will not be coerced into joining NEA affiliates, then it will not press the union shop issue. An AFT agreement in Hurley, Wisconsin, has the following clause: "Teacher application forms and oral interview procedure shall omit therefrom any reference to the teacher applicant's membership in teacher-employee organizations in compliance with (Wisconsin) law."

Schnaufer writes: "What makes this so attractive is that the practical reason for favoring a union shop, or any other form of controlled membership, is that, if a bargaining agent does not negotiate it, the superintendent can deliberately hire 'antiunion' or 'nonunion' types in an effort to break the organization. This reportedly happened in one school district in Southern Illinois. If the union insists that hiring be free of antiunion bias, and then enforces such an agreement, the need for the union shop will be lessened." [*332*] The AFT's Ad Hoc College Committee, in a draft program it presented early in 1966, made clear that the AFT was not seeking the union or closed shop. [*23*, p. 9]

The California senate fact-finding committee referred to earlier in this chapter concluded that there was "little doubt that ratings, employment, promotions, and recommendations for tenure are, on a widespread basis, dependent on membership, not just in 'any professional' organization, but explicitly on membership in the California Teachers Association and its affiliates." [*334*, pp. 16-17] The CTA, an NEA affiliate, is the largest state-wide professional organization in the United States.

The Wisconsin Employment Relations Board, finding a joint city school district in the Milwaukee area guilty of favoring a Wisconsin Education Association affiliate over an AFT local, ordered it to cease and desist from coercing employees in the exercise of their right to be represented by labor organizations of their choice. [*418*] The NEA has denied many of the AFT's charges of such coercion, and it is not our purpose here to make a full appraisal of this controversy but rather to discuss the union shop briefly in relation to each organization.

There are different opinions as to the future lines of development: one observer believes that ultimately the AFT and the NEA will both insist on compulsory membership in the exclusive bargaining agent. He writes:

> A step in this direction has already been taken in New York City, where the UFT has negotiated a provision that prevents an officer of any other teacher organization from representing a teacher who has a grievance. In the near future, pressure from locals will force a change in the position of the AFT on this issue. The NEA will find itself in the same situation .... The Milwaukee Teacher Association, which won a representational election last spring, has petitioned the Wisconsin Employment Relations Board to deny the Milwaukee Teachers Union the right to a dues checkoff and to prohibit the MTU from representing teachers when they have grievances. This type of local pressure will produce a change in the NEA's national policy, and eventually the NEA will have to find some euphemism for the "union shop" and begin to advocate it for "professional" reasons. [*168*, p. 458]

### The Right to Bargain

The former doctrine that collective agreements in government are illegal unless specifically authorized by statute is also giving way in cases affecting teachers. Until very recently, "the leading decision representing this departure" was *"Norwalk Teachers' Association v. Board of Education of Norwalk,* where the court held that, absent statutory prohibition, there is no reason why public school teachers may not organize and engage in collective bargaining." [*394*, p. 15]

In the November 9, 1966, case already cited in Chapter 4, *Chicago Division of the Illinois Education Association v. Board of Education of the City of Chicago,* what was at issue was the authority of the Chicago Board of Education to sign a collective bargaining agreement with an exclusive bargaining agent.[*142*, pp. 188-198] The background here is that the Association, an NEA affiliate, and the Chicago Teachers Union, an AFT local, were competing hard for the support of the city's school teachers, and finally the Board of Education passed a resolution calling for an election to select an exclusive representative. The Association, joined by intervenor-plaintiff, James D. Broman, a private citizen, failed in circuit court to get the election stopped, and, when the case was heard on appeal by the Appellate Court of Illinois,

First District, it rejected the contention that specific legislation, lacking in Illinois, was necessary for such an election to be held. (It was held in June, 1966 and won by the Chicago Teachers Union.)

The Appellate Court sustained the Board's argument that, while such collective negotiations could not legally take place if barred by state law, in the absence of such prohibition it had ample authority under the school code to hold the election. The Chicago Teachers Union, intervenor-defendant in the case, had maintained all along that the sweeping powers given the Board in the code to prescribe the duties, compensation, and terms of employment of its employees, as well as to manage the public school system and issue by-laws, rules, and regulations with the force of ordinances, clearly permitted it in its discretion to authorize collective negotiations. This case is also very significant, because the Appellate Court agreed with the Board of Education and the union that the Board's decision to enter into collective negotiations and recognize an exclusive bargaining agent in no way represented an unlawful delegation of authority conferred on it by the legislature.

John Ligtenberg, AFT general counsel, had argued in a preliminary memorandum to the Board of Education: [*141*]

> The fact that the board cannot delegate its functions or its authority does not necessarily lead to a conclusion that it cannot bargain collectively on subjects where the law does not foreclose its discretion. In the event an agreement is negotiated it is within the scope of its discretion to adopt such rules and regulations as are necessary to carry out the agreement and it does not thereby delegate anything. It does so no more than a private corporation under the same circumstances. The board of education can and should guard its statutory duties and its managerial prerogatives with equal vigor.

While governing boards can voluntarily enter into collective negotiations and recognize exclusive bargaining agents, they cannot be forced to do so unless, on the other hand, they come under a mandatory bargaining law. [*348*, p. 41] Since very few states prohibit collective negotiations, the way is open for the teacher organizations to bring pressure on the school boards to agree to bargain the terms of employment, and both the AFT and the NEA have recently been very successful in these efforts.

### Definition of "Professional Negotiations"

At first, the NEA was lukewarm about sponsoring the principle of majority recognition since it is part of labor's credo, but by 1965 the following definition appeared in one of its publications: [*170,* p. 51]

Professional negotiation is a set of procedures, written and officially adopted by the local association and the school board, which provides an orderly method for the school board and the local association to negotiate, through professional channels, on matters of mutual concern, to reach agreement on these matters, and to establish educational channels for mediation and appeal in the event of impasse.

This definition is to be found in the second edition of the NEA's *Guidelines for Professional Negotiation,* which "clearly reflects a more realistic approach" than the first edition, "an admittedly somewhat naive document, at least by comparison with collective bargaining guidelines in private industry, developed over years of experience." [*348,* p. 17] The second edition comes closer to bargaining as practiced in industry, but it really is impossible to compare the AFT and NEA versions of majority recognition because the NEA thinks in terms of the local education association, rather than any union, being the exclusive bargaining agent.

Furthermore, whereas the AFT is opposed to proportional representation of the different teachers' organizations on joint bargaining councils, as in California under the Winton Act passed in 1965, the NEA does not preclude such arrangements, and its local affiliates sometimes fight for them as a way of holding back the AFT. The California Teachers Association was very influential in obtaining the passage of the Winton Act which provides for teacher negotiation councils in the school districts of from five to nine members, with proportional representation of the various teacher organizations and unions, each selecting its own members. In the elections held so far, the CTA has dominated these councils, and former AFT President Charles Cogen has charged that this and similar legislation introduced in other states is an attempt to "foil union gains among teachers." [*58*]

### Bargaining Strategies of the NEA and AFT

It should be stressed that the NEA affiliates naturally adjust their strategy to the exigencies of the local situation, the principal consideration being how to win out over the AFT. This sometimes means swinging somewhat to the right of the national NEA position, or somewhat to the left, meaning closer to the AFT labor-oriented stance. The NEA affiliates in Oregon and Washington supported the passage of recent teacher representation statutes in both states which "at least by implication, disavow 'collective bargaining' ... and leave the final decision in the hands of each school board." According to one newspaper writer, "both laws ... were inspired by concern that teacher organizations in the Pacific Northwest would take the union tack."[43] Conversely, when the NEA-affiliated District of Columbia Education Association, claiming 4,085 of a total of about 6,000 teachers, petitioned the District of Columbia School Board for exclusive bargaining rights, the rival AFT Teachers Union, with fewer than 1,500 members, urged the board to adopt a policy along the lines of the Kennedy Order, permitting the recognition of both organizations.[108]

In February of 1967, at a public hearing to consider proposed revisions of the Wisconsin municipal employee bargaining law, the AFT's Wisconsin Federation of Teachers strongly opposed the agency shop whereas the Wisconsin Education Association supported it. The reason was that the WFT is "outnumbered in most schools" by the WEA "and its members could be forced to pay fees to the rival WEA if agency shops were allowed."[419]

Illustrative of these local variations, it is reported that in one Detroit suburb where the Michigan Federation of Teachers is well-established, the rival Michigan Education Association chapter was attacking it as "conservative." [21, p. 8] When the NEA affiliates are for such labor-approved arrangements as the agency shop, and when, as mentioned in Chapter 4, they also do go out on strike, it is apparent that the differences between "professional negotiations" and "collective bargaining" may in practice be very slight. The competition between the AFT and the NEA has definitely caused the latter organization to become more labor-oriented than it is willing to admit, and their rivalry, interacting with other factors, adds fuel to the collective negotiations movement in education.

### Impact of New York City Agreement

Stinnett, Kleinmann, and Ware themselves concede that, although teacher demands "for participation in policy-making ... antedate the New York City turmoil by some years," they were "given great impetus by the collective bargaining election in New York City in 1961, and the resulting contract between the board of education and the United Federation of Teachers." [348, p. 6, p. 2] Writing in late 1964, Professor Wesley A. Wildman, whose research was previously referred to in this chapter, gave three reasons for the importance of this contract:

1. It was the first time a large, metropolitan school district practiced collective bargaining;

2. The UFT, an affiliate of the AFT, gave a convincing demonstration of the effectiveness of "tough" bargaining and probably secured "a larger total money package both in 1962 and 1963 than would have been offered in the absence of overt and dramatic action"; and

3. Compared with existing AFT local and NEA affiliate teacher agreements, it was "unique in its complexity and in the comprehensiveness of its coverage." [*408*, p. 9]

Evidence of the swift pace of events is that the New York City contract is no longer "unique," because similarly comprehensive pacts have since been negotiated in quite a few other school districts, both large and small. (A review of the wide scope of these contracts will be presented later in this chapter.) Although the NEA Educational Policies Commission had affirmed as early as 1938 that it was "sound procedure to provide for the active participation of teachers in the development of administrative policy," it was not until 1960 that what Stinnett, Kleinmann, and Ware term a "mild resolution . . . proposing the formalization of the negotiation process" was introduced in its Representative Assembly. This resolution was referred to the NEA board of directors for further study, but the issue came to a head fast, because in July of 1962 the Representative Assembly adopted a resolution sufficiently strong to mark "the official entry of the NEA into the area of professional negotiation." [*348*, pp. 6-12] Thus, in just a few years, the NEA had swung its position around to correspond closely with that of the AFT. The NEA is now just as vocal as the AFT in demanding bargaining rights for teachers and status for them as "full partners in the school enterprise," these being the quoted words of former NEA President, Richard D. Batchelder. [*222*]

### Present Teacher Organization-School Board Relationships

In their research Professors Perry and Wildman made a thorough analysis of the results achieved by the teachers in their drive for collective negotiations, and of the nature of the "teacher organization-school board relationships" which have emerged. [*305*, p. 133]

### The Perry-Wildman Research

This survey questionnaire elicited information not only about the existence of active local teacher organizations, but also about the procedures for "collective interaction or negotiation" and the "instances of impasse or persistent disagreement not resolved through the normal negotiation process." [*305*, p. 134] Four structural models were used for classifying the collective relationships—two representing "informal or non-bargaining types of interaction," and the other two evidencing "more formal or 'true'" negotiating relationships. Within each classification, a separation was made between cases where the teacher organization interacted with the superintendent of schools and where they dealt instead with the school board. The accompanying diagram shows the research design employed: [*305*, pp. 137-38]

|  | **Structural Models** | |
| --- | --- | --- |
|  | *Informal* | *Formal* |
| Interaction with: | | |
| Superintendent ................. | Consultation | Superintendent Negotiations |
| Board ................................ | Testimony | Board Negotiations |

"Consultation" was defined in the questionnaire as sporadic meetings between leaders of the teacher organization and the administration for the purpose of discussing matters of mutual interest, but as lacking any active or sustained attempt by the organization to represent the teachers on questions of salaries and/or working conditions.

"Testimony" was defined as an effort by the teacher organization to present teacher views on salaries and working conditions largely through appearances and presentations (not negotiations) at regular board meetings. This choice offered the possibility of occasional meetings between the superintendent and teacher organization representatives, but not for the purpose of developing mutually acceptable recommendations to be taken before the board.

"Superintendent negotiations" was defined as meetings between the superintendent (or his representative) and the teacher organization for the express purpose of developing mutually acceptable proposals on salaries and/or working conditions for submission to the board.

"Board negotiations" was defined in the questionnaire as meetings between representatives of the teacher organization and the board (or a committee including at least some board members) from the outset of negotiations for the express purpose of developing mutually acceptable policies on salaries and/or working conditions.

*Findings on Teacher Organization-School Management Relationships.* Of the school districts with an active teacher organization, 3,910 checked one or more of these "predetermined relationship forms," with 45 per cent reporting a formal relationship, meaning negotiations with the superintendent or the board, 39 per cent indicating "purely informal relationships," and 16 per cent showing "mixed formal and informal" interaction. [*305*, p. 139] Almost 60 per cent indicated that teacher organization-school management relationships were considered an administrative function and that, therefore, at least at the outset, the management was represented by the superintendent in these relationships. In another 15 per cent of the responding districts, the administration shared the responsibility for the interaction with the board, and in almost one-fourth of the responding districts, it played "no significant role on the management side of the relationship." Although there was some evidence that "in formal relationships, affiliated education associations deal more frequently with the superintendent (as opposed to the board) than do locals of the AFT," there was little difference in the practices of both organizations as far as relationships with the school superintendent are concerned. [*305*, p. 138]

The NEA believes that the superintendent can "participate in negotiations as a third party, serving as a resource both to the teachers and the board" [*348*, p. 113]; the AFT flatly rejects this interpretation and views him strictly as an agent of the "boss," meaning the school board. This is one of the principal differences between the two organizations: the NEA, because it admits the superintendents and other supervisors to membership, is considered a company union by the AFT. The latter used to grant membership to a few supervisors but recently decided to deny it in the future to any school administrators of the rank of principal or above. [*25*, p. 4]

In the districts where both an NEA affiliate and AFT local were active, in only three cases did they employ a "single joint approach" in their dealings with either the superintendent or the board; there were, however, 190 districts in which they "used the same approach but independently." In 23 other districts, they "pursued different approaches . . . with some tendency for the union to deal with the board and for the association to deal with the superintendent." A very significant finding was that "the existence of more than one active teacher organization tends to encourage a more active role for the board in the relationship," for in districts with more than one active organization, the board "enjoyed partial or sole responsibility for the interaction in 56 per cent of the cases as opposed to 39 per cent of districts reporting a single active organization." [*305*, pp. 138-139]

Whereas the affiliated education associations had formal relationships in 1,661 districts, this was true of the AFT in only 127 cases. On the other hand, the data showed clearly that the NEA's strength is principally in the smaller districts, and that, when it comes to total number of teachers represented, the AFT is a very formidable rival. "Nearly seventy-five per cent of the formal relationships of affiliated education associations" were reported from the two "smallest size strata" of districts used in collecting the data, with the "AFT's proportionately greater strength in the largest districts" reducing "significantly the differential between the two organizations in numbers of teachers represented in formal relationships," and this did not take into account the AFT victories in representation elections conducted in Philadelphia, Cleveland, Detroit, Baltimore, Washington, D.C., and other large cities after completion of the research. [*305*, p. 139] When in October, 1967, the AFT claimed that it represented 146,477 classroom teachers in bargaining units, it said this compared to only 50,134 for the NEA, [*29*, p. 8] but this count is based on the results of contested, secret ballot representation elections, and in any event is challenged by the NEA which claims that the teachers are turning to it rather than its rival.

Perry and Wildman conclude that "teacher organizations have been active in representing teachers, in some sense, in a large percentage of the nation's 6,000 largest school districts," but that "the precise nature of such representational activities is difficult, if not impossible, to assess accurately from a distance." [*305*, p. 141] Their field work produced strong evidence that, particularly in the large districts, after initial experiences with a negotiating relationship in a school system, the "administration," meaning the superintendent and his staff, tend to take over the bargaining with the teachers, and they predict that inevitably it will be necessary in all "systems large enough to justify it" to employ "specialized staff . . . to administer the relationship with the teacher organization." [*305*, pp. 150-151]

*The Data on Impasses.* As to impasses, 141 or 3.3 per cent of a total 4,308 districts responding, "reported the occurrence of one or more cases of persistent disagreement in the teacher organization-school management relationship." These impasses "were somewhat concentrated in the larger systems" and in those parts of the country where teacher collective activity has "generally been high." Although the affiliated education associations, which, incidentally, were the only active organizations in more than 75 per cent of these districts, were involved in a majority of the deadlocks, these constituted only 60 per cent of the reported cases. The districts with AFT affiliates, although representing only 0.5 per cent of those in the sample, "accounted for almost 10 per cent of all impasses." In 88 of the 141 cases of reported impasses, outside parties were called upon, with a tendency for this to occur more often in the larger school districts, but "there was no significant difference as to the use of outsiders on the basis of teacher organization involved." [*305*, pp. 141-142]

The most frequently used machinery for attempting to resolve impasses was a review board consisting of "an equal number of representatives of the board and the teacher organization and an impartial third party" chosen by both sides to investigate and make recommendations for a settlement. The third party almost always was either selected on an *ad hoc* basis for the particular dispute or an educator named in the agreement. Perry and Wildman comment that the fact that these educators ". . . may have perceptions quite different from those of lay boards of education has not deterred boards from agreeing to their use, nor have teacher organizations been reluctant to rely upon state superintendents despite the potential bias such officials may have toward administration." [*305*, pp. 146-147]

If the reader refers back to the NEA's definition of "professional negotiations" quoted earlier in this chapter, he will note that "educational channels" are to be used for the resolution of impasses. This is another major difference with the AFT which opposes using school superintendents, state superintendents or boards of education, or any other part of the supervisory structure in public education for mediating impasses. Charles Cogen, former AFT president, has made clear that the third party must be a "true" neutral, as in industry, although he has said that "perhaps standing educational mediation panels could by approved by state teacher organizations and the state school boards association." [*71*, p. 9] Again illustrating the difference between statements of the national organization and the actions of its local affiliates, the NEA's Delaware State Education Association recently sponsored a bill providing for the kind of impasse settlement machinery usually sought by the AFT: an impartial committee of three persons, one each chosen by the exclusive bargaining agent and the school board, and the third member selected by both. [*113*]

### Issues Highlighted

The collective negotiations movement in public education highlights in a very interesting way some of the key policy issues in public employee relations referred to throughout this book.

### Education, Labor, and the Public Interest

Ideologically, the AFT identifies with and supports the goals of the labor movement; the NEA argues that teachers should serve all groups in society and ally themselves with no one special interest bloc. The NEA emphasizes that teachers are professionals and, as such, should not join unions, to which the AFT replies that actors, musicians, entertainers, and many other "professionals" have seen nothing undignified in becoming union members. The reader will recall the discussion in Chapter 2 of the "public interest"; the NEA and the AFT both believe they speak for it and that the other does not.

The AFT tells proudly of how America's first public school was established in Philadelphia because of the efforts of a group of labor people, and of how at the first convention of the Federation of Organized Trades and Labor Unions (later renamed the American Federation of Labor), it was resolved that "if the state has the right to enact certain compliances with its demands, then it is also the right of the state to educate its people." It points to its consistent, subsequent support of public education, and maintains that organized labor is the largest single segment in society. Using the Census Bureau's estimate of 3.5 persons per family, it states that the families of organized workers represent more than 60 million people, better than one-third of the country's population. [*18,* pp. 5-6]

It is also happy to quote the following statement by John Dewey:

If our programs of study in our schools are still too academic and too pedantic, too remote from contact of life, it is largely because the educators, administrators and the teachers are themselves so far remote from the actual problems of life as they are met by the great mass of the population. If all teachers were within the teachers' unions and if they were not merely somewhat nominal members, who try to keep their dues paid, but active working members who came into contact with the labor unions, with the working men of the country and their problems, I am sure that more would be done to reform and improve our education, and to put into execution the ideas and ideals written about and talked about by progressive educators and reformers than by any other one cause whatsoever, if not more than by all other causes together. [85]

*Criticisms of AFT's Labor Ties.* The NEA believes that affiliation with the labor movement undermines the "professional independence" of the teacher, makes him think in terms of the "conflict of interests which has generally characterized relations between labor and management," and promotes "a cleavage between teachers and administrators" which "can be all but catastrophic to the quality of a school." It does not deny that teachers and school administrators will have differences of opinion, but it views these as family quarrels within a basic community of interest. It warns that parents and taxpayers will lose confidence in teachers who affiliate with a "single segment of society," and that in so doing teachers as a group will lose influence with "legislators and other officials representing other views or other constituencies." [*169,* pp. 3-4]

In an address at the NEA's 1962 annual convention, William G. Carr, its executive secretary, said: "Teachers and school administrators are colleagues, not opponents. They do not occupy a master-and-servant, or boss-and-hired-hand relationship. . . . The public school serves all the children of all the people—laborers, craftsmen, professional people, office workers, farmers, public officials, managers, and businessmen. Its personnel should not be affiliated to any one segment of the population." [*51,* p. 6]

Emphasizing that the NEA is consistent in this philosophy, Carr also said: "The principle that American education should be free from alliances with any single segment of American life is not applicable only to labor. When hundreds of local school boards find it appropriate to set up very close cooperation with the Chamber of Commerce but no similar cooperation with labor and other community groups, there is room to wonder, especially when we recall that the U. S. Chamber of Commerce is the arch foe of adequate national support for education." [*51*, p. 7]

The NEA is very critical of the financial and other support given the AFT by the AFL-CIO; the AFT is glad to get this help as evidence of organized labor's sincere interest in teacher welfare and the quality of public education. The AFT is now a member of the AFL-CIO Industrial Union Department, and the IUD has been very active in teacher organization drives, with Walter Reuther at the 1962 AFT convention calling for an eventual one million membership. [*408*, pp. 7-8] Some business groups regard this tie-in between the AFT and the IUD as "dangerous": witness these statements in a report of the Delaware State Chamber of Commerce: [*83*, pp. 4-6]

> *The American Federation of Teachers merely serves as a front for organized labor in general, and the Industrial Union Department in particular in their drive to unionize white collar workers and professionals in American society.* . . . The big push amongst the teachers will be the pattern for assistance in the rest of the non-blue collar and professional fields. The organization of the nation's one and three-quarters million school teachers will merely be a stepping stone to the organization of the millions of white collar workers in government, our new space industries and business.
>
> It is extremely important that you are aware of another motivation in this unionizing drive for teachers in particular. This second motivation represents to us one of the most dangerous threats that American education will ever face. An article appearing on the front page of the *Albuquerque Tribune* of October 16, 1965, began with the following statements:
>
> "A fiery plea to educate the nation on the labor movement by capturing the classroom was made today to the 10th annual convention of the New Mexico State AFL-CIO at Alvarado. Herrick Roth, president of the Colorado State Labor Council, told delegates the labor movement will not reach its ultimate in America until 'union shop signs are hanging in every classroom.' "

The authors of this report cite instances in which the AFT's affiliation with the labor movement has damaged the public school system and the teachers' image in the community. In Granite City, Illinois, the schools had to be shut down on April 6, 1964, when the teachers' union supported a strike by janitors and cafeteria workers; in New York, unionized teachers picketed Bloomingdale Department Stores. They also refer to the pressures exerted by the United Federation of Teachers and the AFL-CIO to get the New York City Board of Education to end purchases of textbooks and other teaching materials printed by the Kingsport Press Company of Kingsport, Tennessee.

The background here is that a council of several AFL-CIO printing trades unions had for several years been out on strike against this company which had continued to operate by hiring replacements. In giving the union its customary help, the AFL-CIO regarded it as proper to make such representations to the Board of Education which in March of 1966, by a 5-4 vote, did decide to curtail purchases of Kingsport Press textbooks when other books of "equal value" were available. The *New York Times*, which is not ultra-conservative in its views on public employee unions, did in this case strongly criticize the Board of Education for permitting "pressure backed by political power to outweigh the proper considerations of educational trusteeship." The *Times* thought the Board's action had the "earmarks of a secondary boycott," and it noted how its outvoted president, Lloyd K. Garrison, had warned that yielding to such demands would lead to similar pressures on principals to select textbooks "against their better judgment." [*227*] The Board of Education's decision was overturned in the courts, and the four-year strike ended in April of 1967. [*288*]

As to the union shop signs in the classroom, this has never been stated by the national AFT leaders as one of their objectives. Both the NEA and the AFT seize upon intemperate statements made by individuals connected with the other organization, which is to be expected in view of the intense competition between them. The AFT official position is that school teachers should present a full and unbiased picture of American history and society, and, accordingly, that the labor movement should not be neglected or falsely-represented. In answer to a statement by former NEA president Batchelder that the AFT sought to "indoctrinate high school students with the importance of the labor movement," former AFT president Cogen said: ". . . omit the question-begging word 'indoctrinate' and there is nothing whatsoever wrong with the intent indicated. The history of labor unionism has been a much-neglected area in our history courses . . . certainly in comparison with the treatment given to the development of business and the 'free enterprise' system." [*23*, p. 16]

Actually, this has been a relatively minor part of NEA objections to AFT labor affiliation; it has concentrated more on calling attention to what it considers concrete evidence of union actions detrimental to the school systems. It has charged, for example, that some state and local labor councils have on occasion opposed sales, cigarette, property, beer, and other taxes badly needed for school support; in this connection, it claims that in Philadelphia, in 1963, officials of the Hotel, Motel, and Club Employees' Union, the American Federation of Musicians, and the Brewery Workers' Union opposed a state legislative program for local school support, objecting to small taxes on hotel and motel rooms, cigars, state liquor stores, and beer distributors. [*52,* pp. 11-12] Cogen has said:

> The fact that organized labor, as well as teachers, frequently opposes sales taxes, is no evidence of labor control of teacher union policies. Such opposition flows from a principle, generally recognized by economists, that a sales tax is regressive and bears heaviest on those who can least afford it. In special cases, however, there have been instances where both labor generally and teacher unions have not opposed the sales tax because of the extreme exigencies of the situation. [*23,* p. 16]

*Mutual Accusations of Rigidity.* The NEA believes the AFT's labor orientation makes it conservative and rigid in its outlook; the AFT thinks that the NEA's "professionalism" is a cover for unreceptiveness to change. Scoring labor's preference for "standardization and preservation of the status quo" and its sponsorship of "tired old precepts" like "worker-boss conflict, seniority, union shop, and strike," George W. Denemark, Dean of Education at the University of Wisconsin, argues that "the rather rigid controls of a union hardly seem suited to the dynamic nature of the modern teaching-learning process." [*84,* p. 26]

The AFT points to the vested interests of school superintendents and boards in opposing desirable changes, such as consolidation of school districts in the interests of economy and efficiency. During the Oklahoma "school crisis" of several years back, to be discussed later in this chapter, critics of the Oklahoma Education Association charged that it gave consolidation lip service only, because it was dominated by school board members who feared losing their jobs. [*72*] As to the image of the school teacher, the AFT maintains that for the most part pupils and parents respect the militant teacher and appreciate his contributions to improved school systems.

### Conflict of Interest—But Favoring Which Side?

The NEA's policy, not only of granting membership to

supervisors, but also of seeing nothing wrong in their being in the same bargaining unit as the classroom teachers, runs counter to most conceptions of collective negotiations. The traditional view is that supervisors, meaning those who have "the authority to hire, transfer, suspend, promote, discharge, assign, reward, or discipline employees, adjust their grievances or to effectively recommend such action," should not be in the same bargaining unit as their subordinates. [*36*, p. 36]

The Wisconsin Employment Relations Board has ruled that, while membership of supervisors in an employee organization in and of itself does not prove "domination or interference with the organization by the municipal employer employing such supervisory personnel," it may "raise a suspicion." [*418*] The last-quoted words are from a WERB decision in which it concluded that a local affiliate of the Wisconsin Education Association which included the school superintendent and "various supervisors and principals" was not a "dominated labor organization."

*A Possible New Pattern.* The presence of supervisors in the bargaining unit, however, can terminate in their identifying with the rank and file, a very real possibility which many people have overlooked. Wesley A. Wildman has pointed out that "if teacher organizations are truly interested in changing significantly the pattern of lay control of education in this country or in diminishing the power of administrators and placing the relationship of administrators to teachers on a truly collegial basis, one might expect that a prime tactic would be the early absorption of the administrative hierarchy into the more numerous and potentially powerful teacher group."

Wildman observes that "traditional collective bargaining is, after all, in essence, an affirmation of and adaptation to the status quo" and that "generally it leaves the entire control (managerial) structure of the organization wholly intact, operating only to moderately modify its behavior." [*409*, pp. 121-122] He already sees indications that school boards, if they are going to have to accept the principle of collective negotiations, would prefer "to have it modeled on the traditional pattern with their policy-implementing administrative staff left wholly intact and out of the rank and file organization"; in this way they would continue to retain the superintendents as "effective spokesmen at the bargaining table." [*36*, p. 37]

Other "professional" organizations, such as the nurses' associations, have, in states like Delaware, pressed for inclusion of supervisors in the bargaining unit, which raises doubts about the long-held belief of the AFT and other labor affiliates that a bargaining unit with supervisors in it must be employer-dominated. It is precisely because public employee organizations, unlike the labor unions, have so many supervisors in their membership that the collective negotiations movement in government is evolving along untraditional lines. The labor historians may have to revise some of their interpretations which have been based primarily on the experience in industry.

### The Right to Manage

Where history is really being made is in the wide scope of the collective negotiations in public education. In no other area of labor relations in government has the management agreed to co-determination of so many basic policy questions; in quite a few school districts the teacher organizations are in effect sharing responsibility with the school management for formulating the educational program. The fact is that in this area of government the "right to manage" is becoming restricted to the school administrations carrying out jointly determined policies, with the teachers having an important role in policy execution. When class size is specified in the contracts and even made subject to binding arbitration under the grievance procedure, as in Stratford, Connecticut, it becomes clear that a quiet revolution is going on in education.

In Stratford, the superintendent of schools may, if he deems it necessary, allow the class size limits specified in the contract to be exceeded, but he must notify the education association which, if in disagreement, can invoke the grievance procedure. In his analysis of  49 NEA and 39 AFT contracts, Schnaufer determined that 11 of the NEA's and nine of the AFT's have "effective class-size limits," which he defines as: "either (1) limits *with* exceptions stated but with those exceptions subject to arbitration; or (2) limits *without* exceptions regardless of whether binding arbitration was a part of the contract."

While a good example, particularly when combined with the binding arbitration, class size limits constitute only one area where administrative discretion is being curtailed. Schnaufer [*332*] reports that the East St. Louis teachers (AFT affiliate)

. . . have torn out of the hide of their board such meaty hunks as: election of department heads; classroom interruptions prohibited; faculty meetings held to one a month and allowed to extend only 20 minutes beyond school time; teacher parking lots closed to parents transporting children; the principal barred from making a change in teaching conditions without the approval of the majority of the faculty; tuition reimbursal; room choice by school seniority; teachers permitted to leave their schools during their lunch periods or unassigned preparation period for any reason; and summer positions filled by seniority.

Significantly, although he himself is connected with the AFT, he finds both organizations "usually equal when it comes to negotiating most of the important clauses."

In Ecorse, Michigan, teachers, in Schnaufer's opinion, have more time to prepare to teach than in "almost all other school districts in the country": the AFT-negotiated contract defines the school day as "six hours and 25 minutes," excluding the lunch period, and allocates 300 minutes for instruction, 60 consecutive minutes for preparation in the secondary schools and 60 minutes cumulative in the elementary schools, and 25 minutes administrative time, as assigned by the principal. Fourteen of the 49 NEA contracts, and 17 of the 39 of those of the AFT, had clauses granting teachers in secondary schools at least five preparation periods a week, and those in elementary schools at least one such period a week. Fourteen of 38 AFT contracts and 17 of 48 NEA ones provide for teacher participation in textbook selection or curriculum planning. In North Dearborn Heights, Michigan, the AFT local conducts an election for teacher-members of all educational study committees; the contract also has a "mumps" clause, meaning that teachers who catch measles, chicken pox, or mumps from the students are charged with only a half day's, rather than a full day's, sick leave for each day out. In Philadelphia, teachers working after school on such activities as the yearbook and serving as senior class sponsors, receive $7.50 an hour; in Taylor, Michigan, the agreement calls for soundproofing of the band, chorus, and shop rooms. Eleven of 48 NEA, and 14 of 38 AFT, agreements also provide for a duty free lunch period of at least 45 minutes. [*332*]

Bilateralism also extends to civil rights and social action programs in the community. In May, 1966, the Inkster Federation of Teachers and the local school board in this suburban Detroit community wrote a "civil rights plank into their new collective bargaining agreement." Besides a statement of principle in which they "mutually recognize that the most significant social movement occurring in America today is the civil rights revolution," the school board agreed to the following teacher demands: purchase of "integrated elementary textbooks to be used as the basic reading text"; a promise to supply pupils in American history classes with teaching materials which describe in detail the contributions to the nation's development of Negroes and other minority groups; full integration of all faculties as quickly as possible; establishment of a community action committee of union, board, civil rights, and church leaders to eliminate de facto school segregation; elimination of the "class orientation" in achievement and intelligence tests; and creation of a joint committee to work for open occupancy in the community and generally to implement the civil rights provisions of the contract. [*24*, p. 9]

Although the NEA has not emphasized civil rights to the same extent as the AFT, it has by no means lagged behind the AFT in obtaining victories for the principle of bilateralism in educational policy making. In fact, whereas under the first agreement between the United Federation of Teachers and the New York City Board of Education such matters as class size and teacher assignments were "discussable but non-negotiable," in December of 1962 the NEA's Denver Classroom Teachers' Association signed a "recognitional agreement" with the Denver School Board providing for negotiations on any matter affecting the "professional or economic improvement" of teachers, the "advancement of public education," or "attainment of the objectives of the educational program." [*15*, p. 150]

An American Bar Association committee, noting that under this and similar NEA agreements, "anything within the dimensions of the teachers' interests as teachers" was subject to negotiation, pointed out that "concepts of what is bargainable and what is non-bargainable, drawn from the decisions of the National Labor Relations Board, are irrelevant." It defined the "central question" as " ... whether this concept of the scope of bilateralism in the relationship between school teachers and boards of education or an 'industrial relations' concept delineating between 'working conditions' and 'management prerogatives' will prevail." [*15*, p. 151]

From the evidence already presented, it is obvious that the teachers' concept is the one which has prevailed. Nor is this true of secondary and elementary school teachers only, for AFT college locals are seeking contracts with clauses on teaching loads, student teacher ratio, "reasonable" class sizes, and "efficient scheduling of class hours." [*19*, pp. 5-6] Indeed, the AFT's first collective bargaining contract with an institution of higher education, that with the Board of Education of the City of Dearborn, Michigan and the Henry Ford Community College, not only contains teaching load limitations but also the college calendar showing when classes begin and end each semester, the college week, and the length of the summer session. [*8*]

## Bargaining Without Full Financial Powers

Because school boards typically obtain their funds from several different sources, and because the great increase in enrollments places critical strains on these sources, the problem of the management's having to bargain without knowing where the money will come from is all too apparent in public education. Commenting on the teachers' strike in New York City in April of 1962, Fred Hechinger, education editor of the *New York Times*, said, "In industrial disputes labor confronts a management that knows what its assets are. Teachers bargain with a board of education, which lacks fiscal independence in the form of taxing powers. It is a kind of shadow boxing. At best, they can expect a promise that the board will recommend a certain amount to the city authorities."

He believed the bargaining between the UFT and the school board was pure ritual, because the real stumbling block was the disagreement between Mayor Wagner and Governor Rockefeller over the amount to be given the city in state aid for education: "Realistically, it might make more sense for teachers and school board to bargain on the same side of the table against those who control the budget." [*74*, p. 22]

Max Lerner assigned some of the blame to Mayor Wagner for "giving the school board $16 million less than it asked for in its budget" and some to Governor Rockefeller for making a change in the timing of state aid payments which caused $48 million the city would have received to disappear "into the cloudy nowhere." He made this telling observation:

The nub of the difficulty for Charles Cogen, the hard-pressed union leader, is that he can't decide whom the strike is supposed to be against. In other labor disputes it is clear that the strike is against the employer. Cogen has said that this strike would be aimed at both the city and the state—but more against the state. The trouble is that many people, already overready to blame any kind of worker, will say the strike is against the children and the public. [*74*, p. 21]

Although many school boards do have taxing power, the New York City Board of Education does not, and it usually does not know until mid-spring what its operating budget will be because the state and city authorities do not act until then. Furthermore, the Board is not in the picture alone as far as pensions, group insurance, and other benefits included in the bargaining are concerned; the state legislature or various city legislative or administrative bodies also have an important role in these matters.

After the collective bargaining election in December of 1961, won by the United Federation of Teachers, the decision was to start the negotiations immediately and " . . . reach agreement on working conditions and monetary items and then to include in the Board's budget request to the City those items of agreement which would necessitate increases in the Board's expenditures." This stage was completed in February, 1962, and then, when early in April the Board "was advised of its operating budget for the 1962-63 school year, it resumed discussions with respect to salaries and other items as yet unresolved." (Certain changes had to be made in the agreements reached in February because the "actual budgetary appropriation was somewhat less" than that requested.)

In early May, general agreement was reached on "salaries and working conditions requiring budgetary allotment." This did not conclude the contract negotiations, because agreement still had to be reached on the grievance procedure, a no-strike clause, and other matters not requiring expenditure of funds. Since the Board is required to adopt its operating budget before the end of the fiscal year, it passed a resolution to that effect, including in the budget the amounts agreed to for salaries and "other monetary items." The negotiations on the remaining issues continued throughout the summer, with the final contract being signed in October of 1962, but made effective as of July 1, 1962, so as to cover the entire 1962-63 school year. [*15*, pp. 145-146]

In the negotiation of successor contracts, the same problem has arisen, with the Board of Education uncertain as to how much money it will receive from city hall and Albany, the state legislature distrustful of the city, and the mayor and the governor not united in their views. Needless to say, this has also been true in other places because of the complications of school financing. When Quebec teachers struck in February of 1967, it was commented that "one difficulty . . . is that teachers bargain with local school boards that have jurisdiction but lack funds to cover salary increases. The money would have to come from additional grants from Mr. Johnson's Government [the Quebec Provincial Government], which at the moment is economy-minded." [*280*]

## *"Finding the Management" in Higher Education*

From what has been said above, it is obvious that "finding the management," a problem discussed in Chapter 2 of this book, is particularly difficult in public education. This is also true in higher education, as a brief review of the developments in the California State Colleges will show.

Several different teacher organizations are competing in California, namely, the AFT, the Association of California State College Professors (ACSCP), the American Association of University Professors (AAUP), and the University Faculty Association (an affiliate of the California Teachers Association), with many college teachers members also of the California State Employees Association (CSEA). The background is that in 1965 the AFT College Council embarked on an intensive campaign to add members and obtain support for the principle of collective bargaining. The ACSCP State Council was at first opposed to collective bargaining and still does not favor it in the form practiced in industry, but, by its own admission surprised by the strong faculty sentiment in favor of some kind of "bargaining," shortly came out in favor of "an elected faculty bargaining agency." [*41*, p. 3] In fact, on December 9, 1966, the San Francisco State College faculty, in the first representation election on the state college campuses, elected the ACSCP over the AFT as its bargaining agent, by a vote of 351 to 289. [*42*, p. 2]

*The Difficulty in Determining the Bargaining Framework.* The AFT had circulated petitions requesting the California State College Board of Trustees to hold an election to select an exclusive bargaining agent for all the college faculties. Its plan was to negotiate a contract with the trustees and then ask the legislature to vote the necessary funds. If the trustees refused to bargain collectively, then it was prepared to take whatever steps it found necessary to achieve its objective. [*41*, p. 1] Not only does the problem exist of deciding whether to establish the bargaining on a state-wide or individual campus basis, or to utilize some combination of both plans, but also there are complications owing to the division of responsibilities for determining the colleges' budgets. To the AFT, this is not an insuperable problem because it believes that experience elsewhere has proved that the basic problem is the willingness of the employer to bargain; once he decides to do so, then he cooperates in developing an appropriate framework for the negotiations.

Within the ACSCP and the other teacher organizations, the problem has not seemed so simple. Writing in the *ACSCP Newsletter*, Marc R. Tool said:

> At the state level now, the Chancellor's office, the Board of Trustees, the Coordinating Council [an advisory group representing the State University, the State Colleges, and private institutions of higher learning in the State], the State Department of Finance and the Legislature all have varying degrees of influence and discretion on policy questions of vital interest to the faculties. With which one of these would a body representing the faculty bargain? [*41*, p. 6]

Trying to answer this question himself, Tool noted that the legislature had the basic responsibility for "financial support, mission of segments, student access and general responsibility for higher education," but he did not see how anyone could envision "placing the legislature, in the role of employer, in a collective bargaining setting." As to the coordinating council, although it was influential in the decisions made on opening new campuses and although its recommendations on faculty salaries and budgets had weight, still it remained an advisory body, which he thought disqualified it as a bargaining agent. The department of finance, in view of its key position in making budgetary recommendations to the governor and the legislature and in exercising "line item budget control," was also very much in the picture, but it, too, was advisory and thus inappropriate as a negotiating agent. As to the Board of Trustees, although the legislature had delegated it power in certain areas, it could not expend state funds without legislative authorization, so "collective bargaining with trustees would be basically a synthetic and 'game playing' affair."

Tool concluded:

> Consequently any effort to employ the industrial model of collective bargaining in the State Colleges seems destined to founder, if for no other reason, because the identification of appropriate bargaining units

and their specific realms of power is most difficult. Hard, meaningful, good-faith bargaining would appear inaccessible because of the vague and obscure power relationships which exist on both sides. Determining a representative bargaining unit with authority to negotiate for enforceable contracts on the 'employer' side seems virtually impossible. Defining a bargaining unit on the 'employee' side seems destined to mount an interminable internecine hassle diverting faculty energies and attention from the more productive facets of their profession. [*41*, p. 6]

His solution was to give real policy-making powers to the academic senates on each campus and to the state-wide senate (established several years ago and representing the faculty on all the campuses). [*41*, pp. 6-7]

These senates have naturally been much concerned with the collective bargaining issue, because faculty members have traditionally looked to them as their vehicles for effective participation in the formulation of the academic program. Significantly, the AFT has made clear that collective bargaining would be limited to "economic welfare issues," such as salaries, fringe benefits, teaching load, sabbatical leaves, reimbursement for professional travel, and secretarial assistance.

Educational issues, such as hiring and firing, tenure rules, and promotion policy, would be the sphere of the academic senates on each campus, negotiating with the college authorities, and of the state-wide senate, dealing with the trustees and the chancellor. The distinction is a difficult one to maintain, however; for example, the change from a semester to a quarter system, opposed by many teachers for "professional" as well as "economic" reasons, fits into both categories. [*374*]

*The ACSCP Conception of Collective Bargaining.* In defining its position after the bargaining agent election at San Francisco State, the ACSCP Executive Committee both eschewed a "further reinforcement of the bureaucratic hierarchy, in the name of 'professional' disdain for 'industrial' collective bargaining," [and the] . . . "additional superimposition of a consolidated power alliance [arising out] of any permanently binding agreement in which a few selected representatives of the community of professionals and a few selected representatives of the employing agency are authorized jointly to establish fiscal and operational policies." [*42*, p. 2] It freely uses the term "collective bargaining," but obviously it seeks to fashion a higher education version which preserves the important role of the academic senates. As it sees it, ACSCP bargaining agents would construe their role as:

1. Accepting as their goals those adopted by the faculty which are "contingent upon fiscal support";

2. Organizing "whatever educational and professionally responsible sanctions are deemed necessary and appropriate to elicit the requisite fiscal support to achieve these goals";

3. Taking its "instructions from the faculties regarding whether or not to draft written contracts of employment and what kind of draft"; and

4. Leaving the establishment of "any and all State College policies and procedures" to the faculties, "acting as a whole or through their elected academic senates."

This conception of collective bargaining would put the ACSCP bargaining agent under the firm control of the academic senate, for in addition the views of the faculty as a whole would be controlling as to choice of sanctions and the timing of their application. As to the question of "bargaining with whom," all channels would be kept open, for "the heart of the ACSCP approach to collective bargaining will be the designating and organizing of sanctions, rather than making a choice among channels and methods of negotiations." [*42*, p. 2, p. 5]

The ACSCP's conception of collective bargaining has little resemblance to that in industry, but, of course, the structure of colleges and universities is different from that of a corporation. What we are witnessing is a continued searching in government for those patterns of collective interaction which will produce the results many teachers and other professionals associate with the accomplishments of "collective bargaining." The ACSCP apparently is going on the assumption that most teachers do not care exactly what form of bargaining emerges, so long as it puts the faculty in the strongest possible position before those who control the purse strings. In a statement it presented to the Board of Trustees in the summer of 1966, the ACSCP said:

... the term "collective bargaining" has become a symbol. To some it is but the newest expression of an old protest against intolerable conditions about which too little has been done too slowly. To others it is only an epithet to be used against those who are pressing for change and who are challenging the right of those who have prevented change to continue managing the establishment. What is most important today, however, is the rapidly increasing number of CSC faculty who see it as a symbol of effective protest and who will vote for it and support its implementation, not because they are enamoured with collective bargaining, but because they despair of improving the conditions of their professional lives by traditional means. [*40*, p. 7]

In a poll conducted in May of 1967 on all 18 state campuses, 2,741 professors voted for, and 3,015 against, collective bargaining, but two years previously, "even the proposal to vote on the issue ... would have been laughed away." [*45*] In September of 1967, a task force of the American Association for Higher Education, after making a study of faculty-administration relations at twenty-eight public and six private institutions, said, "Strikes by faculty members and even the need for collective bargaining on college and university campuses usually can be avoided at institutions where there is an effective local faculty organization which can share authority with administrative officers." [*66*]

### The Ultimate Weapon—Strikes or Sanctions?

As mentioned in Chapter 4, until very recently the NEA favored the use when necessary of "professional sanctions" instead of strikes, but now it approves of both weapons. In the fall of 1967, at the same time that it gave support to teacher strikes in Michigan and elsewhere, it was applying sanctions to the state of Florida. [*326*] Sanctions are by no means a light weapon, for, if fully invoked against a school district, they could succeed, not only in deterring teachers from the outside from accepting positions in it, but also in inducing those already in the district to refuse to sign contracts for the following school year.

The purpose behind the sanctions is to force the school authorities and/or the legislative bodies to correct certain unsatisfactory conditions, not limited to teacher salaries and benefits, but extending to the whole question of the level of financial support for the school system. The NEA has viewed the sanctions as a professional device for calling attention to educational deficiencies which make it impossible for teachers to function effectively and for school children to receive the kind of education they deserve. The sanction weapon was adapted from the "censure of administration" policy of the American Association of University Professors. [*348*, p. 134] The AAUP investigates college and university administrations which are charged with unfair treatment of faculty, and, when convinced that the accusations are true, places the institution's name on a "censured list" so that teachers all over the country will heed the message and avoid the place.

*The Utah and Oklahoma Cases.* Sanctions may be employed by NEA local affiliates acting alone or in cooperation with the state association, and in some cases the national organization will, upon request, join with the local and/or state organizations and also apply sanctions. The usual procedure is for the national organization to send a team to investigate the situation before it takes action, which may cause some delay, as in the case of Utah where there was a time lag of about a year (spring, 1963) between the request of the Utah Education Association and the voting of the sanctions by the NEA Executive Committee (spring, 1964). The sanctions were voted against the state's entire school system, just as was done in early 1965 in the case of Oklahoma and in June of 1967 in that of Florida. In all three states, teachers complained not only about their salaries and working conditions, but also the failure of the state legislatures to vote the funds needed to correct a growing deterioration in the school systems.

In Utah, the sanctions lasted 300 days until finally the legislature authorized an additional $26.4 million for school support. Utah teachers were not requested to refuse to sign contracts for the following school year, but those in other states were "enjoined from accepting positions in Utah." While the sanctions played an important part in "forcing remedial action," a successful political campaign by the Utah Education Association "to elect a governor and members of the legislature known to be friendly to the teachers' cause" proved decisive, with the legislature voting the increased funds in the spring of 1965. "Apparently the NEA sanctions were most effective in forcing a shift in the adamant opposition of the state's economic forces. The report is that many industries invited to build plants in the state refused to do so while the schools were under the ban of NEA." [*348*, p. 142]

The Oklahoma Education Association requested sanctions in late 1964, the NEA investigated, and the sanctions were voted in April of 1965, this time on a more inclusive basis than in Utah. Not only were teachers outside the state warned not to accept jobs in it under penalty of being found guilty of unprofessional conduct and being expelled from the NEA if they did, but also the NEA told the teachers in the state that they would help them get jobs elsewhere and set up five teacher relocation centers in Oklahoma for that purpose. At the same time, graduates of schools of education were warned against working in the state. [*348*, p. 144] The NEA mounted an intensive campaign to persuade business and other groups in Oklahoma to support legislative and other action to improve the schools, and within four months' time the sanctions achieved their objective. [*348*, pp. 143-145]

In essence, the rationale behind NEA sanctions is to "shock" the people into action to correct school deficiencies. The NEA naturally cannot count upon certain success when sanctions are employed, but it is hopeful about favorable reaction from the public. Some of the newspaper accounts of the public reactions in Utah and Oklahoma indicate that the citizens, far from being persuaded by the NEA campaign, were displeased with the adverse publicity being given the state. Former AFT President Charles Cogen calls sanctions a "strangulation" approach, [*71*, p. 10] because they can stretch over a long period of time and perhaps do permanent harm to the school systems they are invoked against; he reminds that teacher strikes have rarely lasted more than one day. [*71*,p.9]

Although it has not renounced sanctions for strikes, the NEA's decision in the summer of 1967 to support strikes was far from unexpected, because it was obvious that many rank and file members favored methods that would produce quicker results. After the strike by the Newark Teachers' Association and the one-day walkout of the Kentucky Education Association in 1966, Leonard Buder wrote in the *New York Times*, "Ironically, although the NEA eschews labor union tactics and regards strikes as unprofessional, the organization appears to be moving away from its reliance on 'sanctions' . . . to more sterner, union-type tactics." [*50* ]

In 1965, the NEA's Commission on Professional Rights and Responsibilities suggested no fewer than 19 "quick action procedures," to be "considered as supplements to sanctions, or as forerunners of sanctions." Evidencing the continued trend towards greater militancy, they included such techniques as: massive motorcades (a "drive-in to call attention of public to teachers' grievances") ; mass attendance at board meetings to force the board to find a larger meeting room; presentation of teacher grievances at mass meetings of citizens; and "immediate limited withdrawal of services," particularly of extracurricular activities. [*348*,p.147]

To many members of the public, these methods are just as "unprofessional" as the picketing and other activities of the AFT. These "quick action procedures," and the strike if necessary, are now emerging as principal weapons of the NEA, rather than as mere "supplements to sanctions." Perhaps the best explanation of this can be found in remarks attributed to Francis Keppel when he was United States Commissioner of Education: "I am opposed to any action that shuts down a school or disrupts the educational system. And I am just as opposed to the public neglect and apathy that drives dedicated, high-minded, normally unaggressive people to that kind of action." [*180*]

# 10

# Responsibilities and Results

---

T HROUGHOUT this book, there has been some discussion of the determination of responsibilities for formulating and carrying out the labor relations program within the government. It has also been stressed that the developments have come so fast that too often arrangements have had to be made hastily, which makes it all the more desirable that the public employer now pause to consider very carefully the basic question of who should do what. In the first part of this chapter, a summation of this entire question of responsibility will be attempted, but necessarily in general terms because of the varying circumstances which make solutions that are desirable in one jurisdiction unwise in another. In the second part, the problem of evalution of the effectiveness of the program, i.e., whether or not it is producing the desired results, will be discussed briefly.

## Responsibilities of the Various Participants

It is probably best to start with some observations about the interest of the general public in the way the government manages its relationships with its employees, for ultimately the extent and character of the collective negotiations movement will be related to the degree of public support.

### Interest of the Public

As the evidences of public employee militancy increase, many thinking citizens are figuratively scratching their heads, wondering what it is all about; others angrily denounce the "unions." Some silently or vocally applaud what is happening; as mentioned previously, leading newspapers like the *New York Times* and the *Los Angeles Times*, while sharply critical of some employee demands and actions, have called attention to the abysmal working conditions in the schools, public welfare, and other govern-

327

ment offices. The situation is complicated enough for students of government to analyze and form opinions about; for the typical citizen, absorbed with many other matters, the tendency may be to conclude quickly that it is all "another mess."

Throughout this book, the author has tried to present a balanced view, and he has expressed reservations about the direction of some public employee organization policies. In this final chapter, he must stress that the era of collective negotiations in government is definitely upon us. A change is taking place in the role of public employees both in the United States and Canada, and, while the resistance to such change will no doubt continue for some time in some quarters, it can no longer be dismissed as a spasm of activity doomed to subside. When organizations like the NEA, with its tremendous membership of more than a million, are on the same side as a union like the AFT in the demand for bilateralism, an objective to be attained quickly rather than at some indefinite time in the future, then clearly we are witnessing a real mass movement. And the same holds true for many other kinds of public employees; they would not be joining employee organizations in such increasing numbers, and nurses' associations and others viewed as far from militant in the past, would not be dropping "no-strike" pledges, unless they had strong convictions about what they are doing.

None of this means that the public should support any and all public employee demands; it should realize, however, that the world of government, previously relatively untouched by the collective negotiations concept, is now proving a very receptive environment for it as far as large numbers of public employees are concerned. Looking back on the development of collective bargaining in industry, the efforts of some to hold off the unions are now largely viewed as unrealistic; the evidences of a social movement in full evolution are now so clear that the same statement can be made about fighting "bilateralism" in government.

*Public Should Support "Comparability" Principle.* The public should support the principle of paying public employees salaries and fringe benefits which compare favorably with those offered by private employers for comparable positions. Since government salaries have lagged so far behind those in industry, the full application of this principle will take some time, but most employee leaders recognize this and do not expect the change to be accomplished overnight. Since the Federal Salary Reform

Act of 1962, the United States government has been committed to "comparability," and, while the employees have chafed over what has seemed too slow progress in implementing the principle, they would be much more dissatisfied if the government continued to assume that it should not be expected to match industry salaries.

As to state and local governments, those familiar with the procedures traditionally used in fixing pay rates have long recognized the built-in injustices. Salaries of teachers, policemen, firemen, welfare workers, and others in occupations peculiar to government have been set by making comparisons with the rates in other public jurisdictions for such positions. That the general practice has been to pay too little, in terms of the skills required and the responsibilities exercised, has generally been disregarded as irrelevant; the prevailing rate had to be paid because no one jurisdiction should start a revolution, so to speak, by deviating widely from it. This explains why so many public employees have been underpaid for so long: the original under-evaluation of the importance of their positions has been perpetuated.

Clearly, the "union" movement in government is largely responsible for the substantial improvements now being made in the pay of teachers, nurses, law enforcement officers, and many others. Traditional pay practices, which presumably would have continued indefinitely, have given way to the employee pressures, a very good example of the innovating effect of bilateralism.

Even very good newspapers like the *New York Times* fail to appreciate fully the great discontent of public employees over "perpetuated" pay injustices. While *Times* editorials were blasting Michael Quill for the subway strike, its reporters were writing articles to the effect that the subway workers had legitimate grievances and were indeed underpaid. The position of the Lindsay administration was that it could not be expected to correct these inequities all at once. The responsibility for the strike may have been largely Quill's, but, so long as pay policies are unfair, the danger of such strikes will exist. Lindsay obviously had not been in office long enough to overhaul the city's pay structure, and there is always the question of where the money is to be found. On the other hand, some jurisdictions allow these conditions to continue when they should at least be making a beginning towards correcting them.

Very recently, the *Christian Science Monitor* published the following editorial, under the heading, "Ditchdiggers and Policemen":[65]

> In thousands of communities throughout the country, Americans look to the police to spearhead the war on crime. If that war is to be successfully prosecuted, these communities are going to have to attract to the force men of exceptional ability and dedication. And to get such men, they are going to have to pay them a decent salary.
>
> That they are not doing so is underscored by the experience of a police chief in a northern city. In looking for able men, he found a ditchdigger who had previously served for 13 years with different police departments. When the chief made him an offer to return to the force, the worker declined. Why? Because it would have meant a $1,500 cut in salary.
>
> The President's Commission on Law Enforcement and Administration of Justice reported the median annual pay for a patrolman to be $4,600 in small cities, $5,300 in large. And "typically, the maximum salary for nearly all positions is less than $1,000 over the starting salary."
>
> Need we say that the report stated flatly that "police salaries must be raised"? When communities right across the nation are unwilling to pay for fighting crime what a firm is willing to pay a man for digging ditches, what are we to conclude? If the American people are concerned about the crime menace, let them begin now by working in their own community to obtain a decent salary for those men charged with enforcement of the law.

*Public Should be Alert to Undesirable Union Requests.* The employee organizations may be asking for too much, which brings us back to the fear expressed by Frank Zeidler (see Chapter 2) that the employee groups, because of their political power, will be much more influential with legislatures than the responsible administrators in the executive branch. Not only may the employees' economic demands (salaries and fringe benefits) be excessive, but they also may be making proposals which would weaken the merit system. In such cases, the responsibility of the general public and of civic groups such as the League of Women Voters is to support the administrators before the legislature in protesting such employee demands. There is no reason to suppose that the employees, anymore than the administrators, will always be right.

Naturally, no person or group wants to be labelled "anti-union," but to oppose particular proposals of the employee organizations is not to be against their very existence. It is possible that some public officials make too quick an assumption that union political power will prevail. Perhaps these officials should actively seek the support of various community leaders and groups and counter union pressures with pressures of their own. Obviously, exactly what should or can be done along these line will depend on the situation. Of course, there are independent power centers like the press that will activate themselves, and the officials should make every effort to pursue policies which result in favorable press reaction and generally create a good image for the public employer in the community.

### Role of the Legislature

In many public jurisdictions, administrative officials are uncertain as to what policies to follow in relation to employee organizations because there is no law dealing with the subject in a comprehensive way. In Chapter 1, a *Los Angeles Times* editorial published in the summer of 1966 criticizing the Board of Supervisors for failure to establish "orderly and effective negotiating procedures" was quoted. [151] At that time, there was no state statute in California requiring collective dealings between public agencies and employee organizations. (Such legislation was passed in June of 1968, and became effective on January 1, 1969.) The *Times* believes there should be an ordinance which would specify the bargaining rights and responsibilities of both sides, and, as the result of its editorials and other community pressures, the draft of such an ordinance was prepared by the chief administrative officer and the director of personnel; it was finally passed in September of 1968, and became effective the following month. [90]

Whether or not there is state legislation, the time has passed when local governing bodies can get by without a formal policy, because the employee pressures now usually make it necessary to act and to do so according to some plan, rather than haphazardly or capriciously. In Los Angeles, "in unhappy succession the Supervisors approved a 5.5 per cent increase, then an 11 per cent hike, then rescinded it (after the wildcat hospital worker strike) and finally restored the 11 per cent increase following the social workers' return to their jobs." [148]

Of course, the employee groups may not like the particular plan, as was clear, for example, from following the different employee organization views on Mayor Lindsay's proposal for an Office of Collective Bargaining in New York City. But ever since issuance of Mayor Wagner's Executive Order in 1958, New York had been relatively sophisticated in its labor relations procedures: it had a formal plan for collective negotiations, whereas places like Los Angeles County did not. In this area of public policy, it is better to do something, rather than nothing; furthermore, the chances are excellent that to do something will be to improve the relationships with the employees and protect the efficient functioning of the public services.

*Changing the Citizen's Sense of Values.* Legislative bodies should vote the funds required to put the comparability principle into effect and to maintain adequate levels of service in the different government programs. Much of the initiative in this respect may have to come from individual legislators, because of the strong opposition of some taxpayer groups to increased spending. Obviously, the political reality is that the people do not like to pay higher taxes, but there is another reality: the need to awaken the citizens to see their own best interest in improving, let alone preventing further deterioration of vital public services. This point is made effectively in a recent newspaper editorial:

> Education is hardly the place to start pinching pennies. If there is any public service which pays off in the long run, it is surely the schools. Given the money which Americans spend for cigarettes, liquor, cosmetics, and other luxury items, it is hard to believe that, if their sense of values were right, they could not afford what it takes to provide quality education for the nation's children.[64]

Americans are justifiably much concerned about crime on the streets but hardly so much about policemen's salaries; the same contradiction exists when it comes to other public services in which the citizen professes a great interest. Certainly, the political leaders should bear some of this responsibility for inducing this change in the citizens' sense of values.

*Evaluating Costs and Effectiveness of Labor Relations Program.* Legislatures should also provide the funds needed for proper administration of the labor relations program. Not only will personnel office staffs have to be enlarged, but training programs will also be needed to prepare supervisors to carry out properly their responsibilities under the agreements. If anything is clear, it is that collective negotiations in government, just as in industry, will consume a great deal of time and involve many employees. This is mostly time they would have spent on other matters, which means that the personnel services budget should be increased accordingly.

In the long run, the improved employee morale should compensate many times over for this initial extra expense; future research, conducted inside or outside the government, should attempt to evaluate the long-run impact of bilateralism on the organization's health, i.e., the condition of its human assets. It is only natural that the legislators, along with administrative officials, should be afraid that the time and money devoted to collective negotiations may fail to produce good results. The area is new and the complexities of dealing effectively with the employee organizations so great that it is understandable why these reservations exist. Once the element of newness disappears and the bargaining relationship becomes customary, as in industry, these fears should disappear. If collective bargaining has strengthened management in industry, as many persons claim it has because of the stimulus to improve policies and procedures and avoid union complaints, it should have the same effect in government.

In the spring of 1966, the House Appropriations Committee rejected a budget request of the Post Office Department for two million dollars to train postal managers in how to deal with the unions. [93,] Representative Steed of Oklahoma, already quoted in Chapter 6, was so concerned about the expense of administering the Post Office's labor relations program that he asked the General Accounting Office to make a detailed study of both its costs and effectiveness. The GAO's report, released in March of 1967, "although it gave no hearty endorsement to the program, . . . accorded it the stiff and guarded comments that pass for approbation." Steed's verdict was that the report gave the impression that "this is a very adequate program, that management is meeting the employee groups halfway."

An important objective of the GAO report was to determine the accuracy of Post Office Department estimates of the costs of the program per se as distinguished from the other operations of the Department. It is difficult to separate out the costs, but the GAO's verdict was that the Post Office's estimates for fiscal 1967 of $376,000 for national expenses, and of $738,000 for regional office costs were reasonable. It thought the $629,000 estimate for local costs was too low, but Assistant Postmaster General Richard J. Murphy pointed out that the "underestimate" was very small in a total budget of more than six and a half billion. [93] Congress usually gives weight to GAO reports, because it regards this agency as a congressional arm which will give it the straight story and not cover up any inadequacies in the executive branch. The Civil Service Commission conducts its own inspection program pursuant to its responsibilities under the Kennedy Order, but what Steed wanted was an investigation by the Congress' own agency for making business-type audits of costs and efficiency.

At this point, we are touching upon the question of evaluation, which we said would be taken up in the second part of this chapter, but this is necessary because one of the most important functions of legislatures is to review the activities of the administrative agencies. Certainly, legislatures should give the same critical scrutiny to budget requests for labor relations activities that they give to all other programs. While the Post Office Department is a very large one, the total estimated expense of $1,743,000 for the labor relations program in fiscal 1967 was a considerable one, the need for which had to be carefully investigated. [*93*]

This author will express no opinion as to how much money the Congress should give the Post Office and other departments for training supervisors and others in their labor relations responsibilities, but he will emphasize that there are numerous reports of inadequacies attributable to the lack of such training. The same reports come from state and local governments, as well as from Canada. The truth is that the budgets for so complex an activity as labor relations can be expected to escalate, as the detailed activities of determining bargaining units and certifying exclusive agents, conducting negotiation sessions, and hearing grievances get under way. Many of the programs are still so new that their full dimensions and costs have not been understood.

*Need for "Lead Time."* In the United States, there is some opinion to the effect that relationships with the employees are worse, rather than better, as the result of passage of state collective bargaining statutes. Based on the experience in Michigan, Roger Rapoport of the *Wall Street Journal*, asserts that "the record shows that the laws lead to more, not less, militancy and strife." He states that "during the first year of legalized collective bargaining in Michigan, there were a dozen strikes by municipal employees—compared with only 13 during the previous 17 years"; this he attributes to "bargaining bungles, stemming from the apparent unwillingness of some public employers to bargain, insufficient help from mediation services and basically inept negotiating on both sides." He quotes Robert Howlett, chairman of the State Labor Mediation Board, as saying, "We inherited a monster"; the Board, operating with a small staff and modest budget, was deluged with 560 bargaining right petitions and 88 unfair labor practices charges. [*319*]

Robert D. Krause, former staff member of the Milwaukee City Service Commission, maintains that the city was making slow but sure progress in developing effective relationships with the employee organizations when the Wisconsin legislature passed legislation in 1962 providing for immediate adoption of collective negotiation procedures in the municipalities. He says that "Milwaukee inherited a whirlwind," with "all of the unsolved problems of labor relations ... placed immediately on the table," and that clearly "the major problems in Milwaukee arose almost entirely from the abrupt adoption of the 1962 legislation." [*129*, pp. 306-307]

Neither the Milwaukee nor the Wisconsin experience, nor that in any other state with this kind of legislation, conclusively demonstrates that it is better not to have such laws or even that the Michigan and Wisconsin legislatures acted prematurely. Clearly, however, ample lead time should be allowed in putting the legislation into effect, and this may be the real error which was made. The new Canadian Public Staff Relations Act gives every evidence of having been planned for gradual implementation, with its staggered time schedule for action upon bargaining unit petitions. Even with lead time, the novel nature of the legislation and the inexperience of many management and union officials will in most jurisdictions inevitably create some confusion. There is nothing strange or unprecedented about difficulties in putting new programs into effect; these administrative pains can be compared to those of birth—and certainly many a lusty child has been born.

*Desirability of Some "Bi-Partisanship."* While it would be preposterous to argue that political parties should not develop points of view, sympathetic or otherwise, about labor groups, there are circumstances when some form of "bi-partisanship" in the legislature is highly desirable. Despite the obvious ineffectiveness of the twenty-year-old Condon-Wadlin law, it was not until April 2, 1967, that the New York legislature repealed the "old monster." [*331*]

As we saw in Chapter 2, some of the employee organizations do not like the new legislation, and we will not take sides on the issue. We do believe that the *New York Times* was entirely right in criticizing the legislature for failing to remove from the statutes a law which had become a farce as different groups of public employees violated it and then were forgiven by passage of special legislation. If it can be argued that the deadlocked negotiators in labor disputes should recognize the public interest and work out an agreement, the same can be said about legislatures which are split over issues like Condon-Wadlin. Surely the lesson of the transit strike was that the law was unworkable and that the legislators should not tarry in working out a formula which would "couple justice for public employees with dependable protection for all the citizens of New York State." [*282*]

*"Good Faith Bargaining" and the Legislature.* In Chapter 6, various viewpoints were presented as to whether legislative bodies should participate directly in negotiations with employee organizations. Before making this decision, the legislators should ask themselves how they can best serve the interests of the community in this area of public policy. In the smaller jurisdictions, they may elect to participate directly, in which case they should define clearly the responsibilities of any negotiating committees they create and their relationship to the full governing body. If the negotiations are entrusted to a team within the administrative branch, the governing body should follow the negotiations closely and make its point of view on the various issues clear to the chief administrative officer. Arvid Anderson states:

> Whether . . . bargaining teams are made up solely of members of the legislative department, the executive department, or a combination thereof is secondary to the establishment of a negotiating team with authority to make effective recommendations. Such authority being absent, the bargaining process will break down because employee representatives will bypass the formal bargaining table and go to the legislator or to the executive, whoever has the authority to make decisions.[*36*, p. 38]

To Anderson, good faith bargaining in the public service means that the employee organizations will "not attempt to improve on the terms of the bargain before the legislative body when the bargaining is to be ratified, if it agreed to forego such improvement during negotiations in consideration of other benefits granted." By the same token, the public bargaining representatives who have agreed to contract terms with the unions "should not renege on their promise to recommend acceptance of the proposal to the full legislative body (city council or county board) nor should they ask their fellow members of the legislative body to take them off the hook." [*36*, pp. 37-38] Anderson recognizes that employee lobbying before the legislature will and should continue; what he is against is failure by either party to respect its promises. Eventually, a code of ethical practices to guide collective negotiations in government may be developed, at least on an informal basis.

### Leadership by the Chief Executive

By "chief executive" is meant not only elective officials like the President, Prime Minister, state governor or mayor, but also appointive ones like the city and county managers and school board chairmen or superintendents. Some jurisdictions, of course, have both an elective head, like a mayor or county executive, and a professional manager (e.g., chief administrative officer).

Whether elective or appointive, these are leadership posts, and the incumbents should take the initiative in proposing effective systems for dealing with employee organizations. If they do not, the danger is that action will be delayed too long in the legislature. When President Kennedy issued his Executive Order in January, 1962, he was taking action which he felt was overdue: creation of collective negotiations machinery to parallel, at least to some extent, that in industry. Kennedy committed himself to recognition of the employee organizations in his presidential campaign and quickly made good on his promise. Some have said that he also wanted to head off Congressional passage of the Rhodes-Johnston proposals; if so, he accomplished this as well.

Similarly, Mayor Wagner's Executive Order in 1958 was an important act of political leadership, by no means a routine personnel decree. The author's purpose is not to single out certain political personalities for praise, but rather to emphasize that organized relationships with public employees are now one of the important concerns of chief executives. Whatever one thinks of the respective merits of the Rockefeller and Lindsay plans already previously referred to, they are clear evidence that these chief executives regarded the problem as important.

*Improving the Organization Arrangements Under the Chief Executive.* Since, as stated by the Rockefeller panel, "the organization for effective employee relations is usually underdeveloped in the government service," chief executives can make a major contribution by recommending new administra-

tive arrangements. [*107*, p. 76] Just what those arrangements
should be depends upon the circumstances in each jurisdiction,
and there will be the usual disagreements. Perhaps Mayor
Lindsay does not need a labor relations adviser on his staff
in addition to the city's director of labor relations, but he thinks
he does and the important thing is that as the chief executive
he has sought to develop the labor relations function.

As the Rockefeller group pointed out, it is not just a question
of making changes in the administrative structure, but, more
important, of bringing in "skilled and knowledgeable people"
to carry out the labor relations function in all its numerous
ramifications. It stressed that "employee relations problems in
the public service are usually complicated" . . . (and that) . . .
"there is . . . a unique requirement that such persons have knowledge of and experience with the legislative process, and how to
adapt collective negotiations to that process." [*107*, pp. 76-77]

All the best-intentioned of legislative bodies can do is approve
the basic labor relations program, provide the necessary funds,
and follow up on the results; it is the chief executive's job to
keep the system functioning efficiently and see to it that personnel officers, department heads, and others are properly carrying out their roles. As in other areas, if the department heads
know that he is keenly interested and wants good results, they
will be guided accordingly. The story is told of one department
head who in effect told his personnel officer not to respect the
terms of the union contract. Unfortunately, there will be un-
intelligent and dishonest people in management ranks, just as
in the employee organizations, but they are not apt to be around
very long when the chief executive is closely scrutinizing the
labor relations program.

*The New Organization in Los Angeles County.* Sometimes,
what is needed is a complete overhaul of the personnel machinery
to enable the chief executive to provide this leadership and
oversight. This has taken place in Los Angeles County as the
result of a charter amendment approved by the voters in
November of 1966.

The charter proposal was the result of a study by the Los
Angeles County Citizens Economy and Efficiency Committee
which criticized the then existing arrangements under which
the civil service commission was responsible for position classification, but the county administrative officer for fixing the

pay scales. The commission was bogged down in numerous details of the personnel program which should have been handled by the secretary and chief examiner, and there was no one in the county government with overall responsibility for the employee relations function.

The committee recommended that all personnel functions be consolidated in a new department of personnel, to be headed by a director of personnel, appointed by the board of supervisors, with the civil service commission to continue, but with appellate and advisory powers only. It further proposed that the new director of personnel be given the responsibility for the employee relations function. [*145*] These changes have since been accomplished on the basis of the charter amendment; the internal organization of the new department of personnel is shown in Appendix C. The county administrative officer is now in a much better position to oversee the development and administration of the employee relations function throughout the county government.

### The Civil Service Commission, the Director of Personnel, and the Departmental Personnel Offices

The organizational arrangements for personnel administration vary so much and this, coupled with the fact that the scope and character of the recently instituted collective negotiations programs also vary, makes it impossible to make statements of general application about the responsibilities of civil service commissions, directors of personnel, and the departmental personnel offices.

In the Canadian federal government, the new Public Service Commission will have a role in the employee relations program, because it is responsible for recruiting and retaining all employees and, accordingly, will have a continuing contribution to make in decisions on wages and working conditions. It will, however, have no direct role in the bargaining process. In the United States federal government, the Kennedy Order places the Civil Service Commission in an advisory role, with these responsibilities proving so great that in November of 1966 the Commission established a new Office of Labor-Management Relations. Commission Chairman John W. Macy, Jr. explained that the head of this new office, W. V. Gill, would report directly to him and that it was "being established in order to strengthen the Commission's central leadership and guidance services in response to increased needs that have developed in the employee-management cooperation program." [*377*]

In Oregon and Washington, as we saw in Chapter 5, the civil service commission and personnel board, respectively, function in some respects like labor relations agencies, with the personnel director their agent for administering the system. In Chapter 6, we recommended that the civil service commission or board not participate directly in the negotiations, but that they follow the negotiations carefully and make recommendations to the personnel director and the chief executive. Whatever the role assigned to them, the commission or board members should endeavor to make themselves as competent in it as possible. The advent of collective negotiations in the public service makes it just as incumbent upon them as upon the personnel officers and line officials to equip themselves to function effectively in this new and frequently baffling area.

In Chapter 6, the reasons for including the personnel director on the management bargaining team were discussed. In Los Angeles County, under the new arrangements, there is a staff of negotiators serving under a deputy director of personnel for employee relations. This places the labor relations function together with the personnel activities, all under the director of personnel. The Rockefeller panel wrote:

> There is as yet no counterpart in state and local government to the Vice-President of Industrial Relations in private industry. In modern corporations, the chief industrial relations executive plays two essential roles—that of employee relations *advisor* to the president and the chief operating officials and that of *assistant* to the line executives in implementing policy.[*107*, p. 75]

In a general way, the new position of director of personnel in Los Angeles County follows this industry model. Others prefer the structure in New York City where there is a director of labor relations reporting directly to the mayor, with labor relations not coming under the city's director of personnel. Cities like Philadelphia and Cincinnati have obtained good results with the personnel director serving as the principal labor relations officer under the chief executive, and on the balance this merger with the general personnel function appears preferable.

As for the departmental personnel offices, these exist only in the larger jurisdictions and departments, and it would have to be a very large department to justify an office of labor relations separate from the personnel activity. Since the personnel office will be dealing with so many questions arising in the administration of the contracts, it is desirable that it also provide the department head with specialized help in labor relations matters. If he wants the advice of outside labor relations consultants from time to time, he can always obtain it. Besides, the sooner personnel staffs are brought face to face with the employee organizations, the sooner they will be able to make the transition to personnel administration on the new model of "bilateralism."

### Department Heads and Supervisors

The department heads may join the management negotiating team when agreements with their departments are being negotiated, or they will be in close touch with the head of the team. Whether or not they do any actual negotiating, they should become thoroughly familiar with the problems of relationships with organized employees. This also applies to installation and branch heads, to many of whom in the United States federal agencies the responsibility for negotiating the agreements has been delegated. They will also be very much involved in contract administration, because the agreements obligate them to follow certain policies and respect various employee rights. The department head should not be expected to carry the entire load in labor relations, but he should know in detail what is in the contract and see to it that all levels of supervision are discharging their responsibilities properly.

As to the supervisors, they are the closest to the employees and they make many decisions which influence the subordinates' image of the management. They should be thoroughly versed in the contract provisions and be given the necessary training so that they do a good job in their relationships with the stewards and other employee organization officials. Some provision should be made for ascertaining their ideas on desirable changes in the existing contracts and, if possible, also on employee organization proposals for modifications. In large organizations, the effective way of accomplishing this is by having the supervisors submit their views to their department heads. Too often, the supervisor is simply told, after the agreement has been signed, of the new provisions with which he will be confronted. More need not be said in view of the references made earlier in this book to the important role of the supervisor.

### The Employee Organizations

Everyone has his point of view about the "unions," and much could be said about the responsibilities of the employee organizations if one were asked to expound his own opinions on public policy. Many people are shocked by public employee strikes, picketing, and other demonstrations, but what they think the unions should do and what the employee leaders have made clear they will do if necessary are two different things.

We will limit ourselves to saying simply that the employee organizations should behave responsibly. They should agree to, and respect the provisions for standards of conduct, such as those in effect in the United States federal service. In December of 1966, the Uniformed Sanitationmen's Association in New York City ordered a slowdown of refuse collections and other activities of the municipal sanitation department, because the sanitation commissioner had suspended 18 employees accused of accepting bribes from private refuse collectors using city dumping facilities. It was also charged that he had slurred employees of Italian descent by appointing as departmental inspector general a former state policeman who had led a raid on "reputed Mafia leaders at Apalachin, N.Y."[*269*]

Whatever the truth of the bribe allegations and the embarrassment created by the appointment of the former policeman, to threaten a slowdown in such a situation suggests that traditional labor weapons may be used indiscriminately, no matter what the nature of the controversy and with no consideration for the public at all. Earlier some 100 employees of Metropolitan Hospital, mostly kitchen workers, had walked off their jobs and joined a Teamsters' picket line which was trying to block the delivery of food and drugs to this city institution. This dispute was discussed in Chapter 3, "Political Factors," but it also illustrates union irresponsibility. Cases like these have been exceptional, but they do show that labor abuses in government are possible just as in industry.

Historically, the public employee organizations made a great contribution by joining the fight for merit practices. Their disillusionment with the paternalistic attitudes and unimaginative approaches of many merit system administrators is understandable, but they will jeopardize their own cause if they try to strip the civil service agency of most of its functions, relegating it to recruitment and examining functions only. The collective contract can justifiably appear more advantageous right now than the merit system, but bilateralism functioning within basic merit concepts is sound, whereas complete rejection of civil service is not. The political power of public employee organizations should be used to strengthen the merit system, and any suspicion that alliances are being made with the old-style patronage politicians can only hurt them in the long run. The political situation is a constantly changing one, and anti-labor administrations can succeed pro-labor ones, which makes it dangerous to be entirely dependent on the contracts which usually expire within relatively short periods of time.

Since public employee organizations are also plagued by inexperience in collective negotiations, they should organize suitable training programs, and they should cooperate with the management in explaining to the employees the provisions of the agreement. As noted in previous chapters, they should also help in the collection of pay and other data, and the development and successful functioning of labor-management joint programs, as in the TVA. Although the element of conflict will always remain, they should seek to expand the areas of cooperation with management as widely as possible.

### The Employees

A long catalog could also be presented of what the employees should and should not do. Clearly, the employee leaders, both in industry and government, are now often a more restraining force than the rank and file membership which has refused to accept passively the contract terms recommended by the leaders. This has occurred with enough frequency to raise doubts about the social science findings that small elites or other groups tend to rule large organizations: in some of the unions at least, the membership mass right now appears neither apathetic nor sluggish. Whether the memberships should not have rejected a particular contract is not the point; the outsider is usually unable to make an informed judgment on this anyway. It is the frequency of such rejections which is alarming; the reader will remember the concern expressed about this by Secretary of Labor Wirtz, who was quoted in Chapter 7. If the rank and file invariably know better than the leaders what a good contract is or what is feasible to achieve, then the whole concept of collective bargaining through designated teams representing both parties is in for trouble.

*Responding to a New Role.* If it is not correct for the employee leaders to go to the legislature to improve the deal after they have exchanged concessions with the management bargaining team, the same also holds for individual employees who may be tempted to put pressure on their elected representatives. The employees should make responsible use of the grievance procedures and respect all the contract provisions, just as the management should. Above all, "co-determination" means that the employee should do all he can to make constructive suggestions and otherwise contribute to improved work operations. He should recognize that he is being cast in a new role, that of active participant in the enterprise, and he should do what he can to make bilateralism a success. If it is true that his grievances are far more than economic, then he should respond to the challenge by showing appropriate enthusiasm and energy.

### Governmental Organizations and Institutions of Learning

There is a great opportunity for various kinds of organizations and groups to help both the employee organizations and the management in making a success of collective negotiations. The leagues of municipalities and similar governmental organizations have already entered this field, but much more remains to be done. Specifically, they can organize training institutes, provide materials, and take an active role in proposing and criticizing legislation on collective negotiations. Because of the reluctance of many local officials to change old ways of thinking, these organizations can carry on a badly-needed program of enlightenment with respect to the contributions collective negotiations can make to efficiency in government. Professional associations like the Public Personnel Association and the Society for Personnel Administration can, through their round tables, study groups, newsletters, and other publications, keep their memberships informed of the recent developments and of the problems and challenges. Such organizations have already made a significant contribution to the understanding of the collective negotiations movement in government, and our knowledge would be much less without their efforts.

*Contributions of Academic Institutions.* Academic and other researchers will find few areas in which research is as badly needed, and even fewer in which the scholarly exploration is as absorbing. While the bilateral relationships are frequently very new ones, some of the major issues have already become clear and invite careful analysis. What has the effect been on the educational program in school systems with class size and other limitations on management discretion? How often has binding arbitration been invoked, and with what consequences, in jurisdictions in which the contracts provide for it? Again, we are getting into the question of evaluation, but someone must have the responsibility for evaluating the results, and the detached analyses of the academicians can prove very valuable. Suffice it to say that an extensive agenda for research in public employee relations can be prepared right now, and that doctoral dissertations and masters theses on various aspects should be encouraged.

University bureaus of governmental research should be compiling information in this area and making analyses of existing legislation and current contracts. Very much in point also is the recommendation of the Rockefeller panel that "educational institutions preparing persons for careers in public administration intensify their programs in public employee relations and collective negotiations"; the trouble is that so few have programs addressed to the current needs. [*107*, p. 77] For example, every institution preparing students for careers in education and teaching should have at least one course on collective negotiations in government, but most do not. This is also a whole area for development in the programs of schools of public administration.

### The Problem of Evaluation

When laws and executive orders establish formal programs of collective negotiations, there are specific provisions as to bargaining units, representation elections, unfair labor practices and the like. The authorizing document may specifically designate an agency within the executive branch to be responsible for seeing to it that the program is implemented effectively; the Kennedy Order states that the Civil Service Commission shall "provide for continuous study and review of the Federal employee-management relations program and, from time to time, make recommendations to the President for its improvement." [*400*, p. 356]

The recent state laws referred to throughout this book make no mention of evaluation, but it should be remembered that they provide different patterns of relationships from those under the Kennedy Order. Either the existing state labor relations agency is also given jurisdiction over collective negotiations in government, or, as in Oregon, the central personnel agency is given certain responsibilities in this area. In these circumstances, in the absence of decentralized arrangements as in the federal service, it has not been feasible to make the state civil service commission the advisory and evaluating agency.

It can be expected that the Wisconsin Employment Relations Board, as one example, will evaluate the conformance of municipal employers with the law, and, indeed, it has made legal rulings relating thereto, but arrangements should also be made to analyze its effectiveness in carrying out its own duties under the law. The budget officers in state and local governments can fill this gap by making in-depth studies of the functioning of the labor relations agencies and of the employee relations programs in the individual agencies. Where there is an administrative management staff in the budget office, such surveys can be entrusted to them. Since the manpower is not available to make such studies in many state and local governments, much of the evaluation will have to come from the legislature, the leagues of municipalities, academic researchers, and others outside the administrative branch.

A study committee appointed by Illinois Governor Kerner, in presenting its detailed recommendations for passage of a mandatory collective negotiations statute, also proposed that the governor name "a seven-member Advisory Committee to review the effectiveness of the Statute and to recommend any changes in substance or procedures desirable." It said:

> Any new legislation must be regarded as experimental and subject to modification and improvement on the basis of experience. This is particularly true in an area as complex as public employee relations, involving so many different types of public authorities and occupations. Accordingly, it seems desirable to establish an Advisory Committee of employee relations experts to make periodic studies of experience under the Statute and to make reports to the Governor and the Legislature assessing the experiment and making appropriate recommendations.

It also proposed that the legislature establish a joint standing committee to "review all matters pertaining to the Statute and its administration, the reports and recommendations of the Advisory Committee, and such requests or recommendations arising out of employer-employee negotiations that may require legislative action." This joint committee would not only continuously review the effectiveness of the labor relations program, but also advise the legislature on the action it should take on "requests and recommendations from the parties," such as for changes in salaries and employee benefits and revisions of the personnel code. Later, the legislature might decide to "have legislators and outside experts serve together in a single committee, a procedure which has been effective in other technical areas." [*106*, p. 35]

Similarly, Michigan Governor Romney's Advisory Committee on Public Employee Relations stated that "in many respects our most important recommendation is for the establishment of a continuing Commission on Public Employee Relations." It said:

> Collective bargaining, like all human institutions, is imperfect, and both the policies and procedures of the Public Employment Relations Act should be subject to continuing analysis and examination with the objective of finding even better methods of providing for employee participation in the determination of their terms and conditions of employment within the framework of the American system of representative government.

The commission would be created by statute and the members be appointed by the governor; they would "include persons who are experts in industrial relations, preferably with knowledge also of labor relations in the public sector." [*2*, pp. 26-27] Continuing machinery of this kind, as recommended in the Illinois and Michigan reports, is highly desirable, because the passage of legislation really represents only the initial step.

### Inspection Program of United States Civil Service Commission

Appendix D reproduces in part the instructions issued by the United States Civil Service Commission to guide its Bureau of Inspections in evaluating the individual agency programs. The procedures are carefully worked out, and, while they are based on specific provisions of the Kennedy Order, the same approach can be used effectively in other jurisdictions. There is, of course, nothing new in these personnel inspection procedures; the Commission, because of the substantial experience acquired under its extensive program of decentralization to the agencies, has been able to develop them on a refined basis. It will be noted from the instructions that the inspectors speak not only with management officials but also with individual employees and the representatives of employee organizations.

At some future date, the Commission may want to enlist the help of the employee organizations in planning and improving the inspection program. Within the agencies, the labor-management cooperation committees established in the agreements should make evaluation of the employee relations program one of their responsibilities. A section of one of the Air Force contracts reads: "A regular meeting will be held monthly between management and the union. Purpose of these regular meetings will be to review management-employee relationships, to identify possible problem areas at any early stage, to provide management an informal report or 'feel' for employee morale and to discuss any current problems or impending actions. Time and place of this meeting will be arranged and announced by management." [*388*, p. 50]

### Role of the Employee Organizations

The employee organizations may want to make their own independent evaluations. This could be accomplished in part by getting the views of the stewards and other union officials with roles in the employee relations program, and by directly consulting the members. Representatives of the organizations' headquarters offices may suggest evaluation techniques; obviously, the employee leaders will want to be sure that the local bodies are making effective use of the collective negotiations procedures.

### Some Suggestions on Scope of the Evaluations

While the first priority must be to check compliance with the law and other authority for the program, the evaluation should probe into larger questions of relationships between productivity and the various indices of morale, inadequate as they are. As one example, intensive studies of grievances *before* and *after* inauguration of the collective negotiations could prove revealing. Employee attitude surveys should contain items on worker reactions to the detailed phases of the program. As a beginning, studies might be made in selected organization units to determine what specific benefits, if any, have resulted from bilateralism. Public reactions should also be analyzed to identify mistaken citizen attitudes which could be corrected, as well as to obtain valid criticisms which should be acted upon.

### Rising Expectations and Progress

As to employee reactions, it can be expected that there

will be numerous expressions of frustration, owing to the inevitable gaps between their rising expectations and their perception of gains actually obtained from the new arrangements. The gruff citizen reaction may be that "the more they get, the more they want," but the public also expects a good deal more from government these days. With everybody's expectations up, there are bound to be disappointments, but the long-term result of all this is progress, and that is the important consideration.

# A

## Appendix A—

## Subjects for Consultation and Negotiation

B ELOW IS A partial list of subjects that may be appropriate for consultation or negotiation. The list is representative, but is not exhaustive or complete. Moreover, not all the subjects listed are necessarily appropriate under all circumstances. Those items preceded by an asterisk (*) were contained in *Collective Bargaining Agreements in the Federal Service, Late Summer, 1964,* U. S. Department of Labor.

### 1. Working Conditions

*Rest rooms and rest periods.
*Safety equipment.
 Parking spaces.
 Cost of meals.
 Free inoculations—flu, polio, tetanus, etc.
 Uniforms—laundry of uniforms, type, weight.
 Physical examinations.
 Ventilation, light, heat.
 Required use of government quarters.
*Length of lunch periods (scheduling).
 Cleanliness and sanitation.
 Locker facilities.
 Space and arrangement.
 Noise.
 Building maintenance.
*Enforcement of safety rules.
*Responsibility for determining that working conditions are safe.
*Special procedures for hazardous work.
*Special qualifications for participation in hazardous work.

Provision of required physical examinations.
Provision of health services.
Benefits and services provided.

## 2. Leave and Hours of Duty and Pay

*Scheduling for holidays and overtime.
*Scheduling for rotation of shifts (notification of changes).
*On-call; standby.
*Posting of schedules in advance.
*Vacation schedules.
*Hours of work—beginning and ending of shifts (notification of changes).
*Leave for union activities.
*Procedures for leave requests.
*Premium pay; hazard pay.
  Special work rules for inclement weather.
*Rules pertaining to leaving the work site.
*Schedules changes.
*Time and method of reporting sick leave absence.
*Provisions to assure that employees will be able to use the leave they earn.
*Policies concerning granting of leave without pay.
*Policies concerning "administrative" leave.
  Travel and transportation.
*Activities which can be conducted on official time.
*Advance of sick leave.
*Doctor's certificate following sick leave.

## 3. Grievances and Other Appeals

  Standards of conduct.
  Code of penalties.
*Conduct of hearings.
*Use of arbitrators in lieu of hearing (advisory).
*Methods of settlement of grievances.
*Severity and appropriateness of penalty.
*Time of hearing—overtime for witnesses.
  Levels of review.
*Provisions to forbid discrimination, restraint, or reprisal.
*Union representation at hearings.
  Composition of hearing committees.
*Selection of members of hearing committees.
  Time allowed employee and representative to prepare appeal.
  Record of the hearing.

### 4. Disciplinary Action and Adverse Actions

Development of standard penalties.
Reckoning periods.

### 5. Promotion Policy

Areas of consideration.
*Means used for developing merit roll.
Seniority.
*Posting of vacancies.
Concurrent consideration of outside candidates.
Use of promotion examinations.
*Composition of promotion (evaluation) boards.
Information available to employees.

### 6. Wage Board Employees

Planning for survey.
*Selecting appropriate industries (or private hospitals).
Analyzing findings in industries.
Reconciling inequities between government services in a
  community.
Step increases.
*Uniform allowances (special clothing).
Method of payment, cash, check, mailing.
*Clean-up time.
Tools and equipment.
*Frequency of surveys.
*Union participation in surveys.
Use of surveys conducted by other agencies or organizations.

### 7. Training

*Development of programs.
Systematic planning for career development.
*Selection for training—selection criteria.
*Apprenticeship programs.
*Retraining because of change of work character.

### 8. Conditions of Employment

Out-placement under reduction-in-force.
Driving tests for vehicle operators—type of tests.
Reassignments within geographical area.

### 9. Institutional Needs of Unions

*Space for meeting and meeting time.
*Bulletin boards; messenger service.
*Space in house organs.

354 Management-Employee Relations

Membership drive cooperation.
*Reassignment practices (union officials).
Relationship between mobility and the promotion program.
Use of internal messenger service and inter-office mails.
*Coverage of union activities in official newspapers and employee publications.
*Right of management to review, approve, or change union material placed on bulletin boards, distributed through office mail, or published in official newspapers.
*Right of employee organizations to solicit membership, collect dues, and other business on government property.
Inclusion of information about employee organizations in employee orientation.
Listing of employee organizations and organization officials in the building directory and the telephone directory.

## 10. Relationships with Employee Organizations

*Negotiation procedures.
*Duration of the agreement.
Determination of management and employee organization representatives in negotiation.
Determination of the management level with which the organization deals.
*Negotiation on official time.
Procedures to insure enforcement of the agreement.
*Membership and participation in union activities.
*Determination of the type of positions which disqualify members from holding office in the organization.
*Identification of supervisory employees.
*Identification of management personnel.
*Identification of professional employees.
*Stewards and representatives.
*Leave without pay for union activities.
*Dues withholding.
*Cooperation committees.
*Fact-finding committees.

# B

## Appendix B—

## Materials on the Grievance Procedure

I N THIS APPENDIX the author has drawn on several sources to assemble information on the grievance process. These procedures will serve as guidelines in the shaping and operation of the grievance process. The sources are the following:

1. Excerpts from the bill entitled "Federal Employee Labor-Management Act of 1967," as introduced in the 90th Congress, First Session [S. 341], and subsequently referred to committee.

2. Agreement between United States Post Office Department and National Association of Letter Carriers, AFL-CIO, National Association of Post Office and General Services Maintenance Employees, National Association of Post Office Mail Handlers, Watchmen, Messengers and Group Leaders, AFL-CIO, National Association of Special Delivery Messengers, AFL-CIO, National Federation of Post Office Motor Vehicle Employees, AFL-CIO, National Rural Letter Carriers' Association, United Federation of Postal Clerks, AFL-CIO, effective September 24, 1966 to October 31, 1967.

3. Agreement between Department of Mental Health of the State of Delaware and Laborers' International Union of North America, AFL-CIO, Local 1029, effective November 1, 1966.

4. Agreement between Levy Court of New Castle County, Delaware and the American Federation of State, County and Municipal Employees, AFL-CIO, Local No. 459, effective July 1, 1966.

5. Agreement between City of Milwaukee and District Council 48, AFSCME, AFL-CIO and Its Appropriate Affiliated Locals, effective January 1, 1966.

6. Agreement between District Council 33, AFSCME, AFL-CIO and Personnel Director, City of Philadelphia.

7. Agreement between the City of Winnipeg and Local 500, Canadian Union of Public Employees, effective April, 1965.

## 1. Excerpts from Proposed "Federal Employee Labor-Management Act of 1967" (9th Congress, 1st Session)

### Title V—Settlement of Grievances

Sec. 501. (a) Any union of government employees shall have the right to present and process grievances informally and to submit to arbitration unresolved grievances on behalf of a member or members employed in any department, agency, activity, organization, function, or facility of the executive branch of the United States government.

(b) Grievance as specifically used in this title includes any dispute between any department, agency, activity, organization, function, or facility of the executive branch of the United States government by any union of government employees on behalf of its individual members or group of members concerning the effect, interpretation, or application of any law, rule, regulation, or provision of a collective bargaining agreement, governing any condition of employment, including but not limited to working conditions, work procedures, automation, safety, transfers, job classification, details, promotional procedures, demotions, rates of pay, reductions in force, hours of work, and disciplinary actions.

(c) Grievances shall be presented or taken up at any level by the representative or representatives of the union of government employees representing the employee or employees involved through established supervisory channels preferably starting with the lowest level of management in such government organization having competent authority to make a decision on the subject of the grievance, up to the designated chief supervisory officer concerned, as defined from time to time by the appropriate administrative head of the government organization involved.

(d) Failing prompt and satisfactory adjustment, an appeal can be taken by the union representing the employee or employees involved directly to the principal administrative officer of the government organization involved for investigation and settlement.

(e) Details of grievance procedures shall be established by each government organization in negotiation or consultation with representatives of unions of government employees with members employed in such government organization. Such procedures shall assure employees (1) the right to be represented through their union of government employees; (2) of fixed reasonable time limits for a decision at each grievance step; (3) of the right to call witnesses at each step of the procedure; (4) of no loss of pay to the aggrieved employee or employees, employee witnesses or employee representatives in the processing of such grievance.

(f) (1) Any grievance not satisfactorily settled in the grievance process shall be subject to arbitration upon the written request of the union of government employees representing the employee or employees involved. Such written request shall be directed to the principal administrative officer of the government organization involved and shall specify the name and address of person selected by the union to serve on a three-member Board of Arbitration to be constituted to hear and decide the case.

(2) Within five working days after receipt of such arbitration request, the principal administrative officer of the government organization involved shall advise the union of the name and address of the person selected by the government organization to serve on such Board of Arbitration.

(3) The two arbitrators so selected shall request the Secretary of Labor to furnish them with a panel of names of five arbitrators from which they will endeavor to select a third member who will serve as Chairman of the Board of Arbitration. If they cannot agree on the third member, they shall then request the Secretary of Labor to name the third member.

(4) The decision of the majority of the members of such Board of Arbitration shall be final and binding. Each party shall be responsible for the costs of its members of the Board of Arbitration. The fee and expenses of the Chairman and the general expenses incident to the arbitration shall be paid by the Secretary of Labor from an arbitration fund created for such purpose. No employee of the government organization involved in the arbitration shall suffer any loss in pay because of his participation in the proceedings, either as a witness, aggrieved employee, or employee representative.

## 2. United States Post Office Department Agreement

### A. Definition

1. A grievance is any cause for dissatisfaction outside an employee's control if the matter grows out of employment in the Postal Service and the remedy sought is within the authority of the Postmaster General or other postal official to whom such authority has been delegated. Grievances shall not be accepted for processing which are based upon matters such as the mission of the Department, its budget, the technology of performing its work, its organization, and assignment of personnel unless such assignment violates laws, regulations or policy.

2. Grievances on alleged violations of local agreements must be processed under the section of this procedure on violations of local agreements.

3. Grievances on promotions must be processed under the section of this procedure on promotion appeals.

4. Appeals on the denial of a salary step-increase when the denial is based on unsatisfactory service during the required period of satisfactory service must be processed through the procedures established in Paragraph S of this Article.

5. Appeals from adverse actions, determination of grade level, cases of alleged discrimination because of race, creed, color or national origin, and interpretations or alleged violations of this Agreement will be made through separate procedures. Dissatisfactions arising out of a decision appealed through compensation, adverse action or equal employment opportunity procedure are not subject to further appeal under the grievance procedure.

## B. Guides for Supervisors

1. Most grievances arise from instances of misunderstandings or problems that should be settled promptly and satisfactorily on an informal basis at the supervisory levels before they become formal grievances. The prompt settlement of these problems is desirable in the interest of sound employee-management relations. To this end, the practice of friendly discussions of problems between employees and their supervisors is not only encouraged but directed.

Every reasonable effort shall be made to avoid referral to the grievance procedure.

## C. Eligibility to Appeal

Any employee, except Christmas or seasonal assistants, may file a grievance appeal, provided action on such appeal is initiated within thirty (30) working days from the date of the action or condition giving rise to the grievance. An employee organization may file an appeal on behalf of an employee(s) provided the employee(s) has (have) so authorized the organization in writing.

## D. Grievance Steps at Installation Level

1. Whenever an employee considers himself aggrieved, he shall discuss the matter with his immediate supervisor. If he desires, he may be accompanied by a representative of his own choice. Both the aggrieved and his representative shall be allowed a reasonable amount of official time to present the grievance. There shall be no delay and normally the efforts of the supervisor to resolve the grievance shall not exceed three (3) working days.

2. If the immediate supervisor cannot resolve the grievance the employee has the right to discuss the grievance with the head of the installation or his designee, and to be accompanied by his representative. Both the aggrieved and/or his representative shall be allowed a reasonable amount of official time to present the grievance. The designee must have authority to resolve the grievance.

3. If as a result of such discussion at Step (2) the grievance is not resolved or if the employee does not wish to discuss the grievance at Step (2) it shall be reduced to writing and filed with the head of the installation.

4. The grievance shall be signed by the employee or, if he so authorizes in writing, it may be signed by his employee organization representative or by his own chosen representative. . . .

## E. An Individual's Right to be Represented

1. An employee has the right to select whomever he desires to represent him at each level of the grievance procedure. In the event that the person selected at the various levels is someone other than a representative of the exclusive organization, the exclusive organization at that level has a right to be present. . . .

## F. Right of Organization with Exclusive Recognition

The exclusive organization at each level has the following rights in grievance matters processed at that level:

1. To be notified of the time and place of the proceedings at each step of the grievance beginning with discussion with the head of the installation or designee.
2. To be present at all steps of the grievance procedure. (No right to be present at initial contact with supervisor if the aggrieved has not selected a representative.)
3. The organization, if any, with exclusive recognition at the level where the grievance is being processed shall be furnished with a copy of the written decision and summary, at any step at which a written decision and/or summary is involved.
4. If not the designated representative of the grievant, shall have an opportunity to state the exclusive organization's position on the grievance. This right shall be exercised only one time, at each step, and shall follow the presentation made by the employee and/or his representative.

## G. Installation Head's Decision

Within five (5) working days from the receipt of the written appeal, the installation head shall render a written dated decision to the grievant and submit a copy to the employee's representative, if any. The letter of decision shall indicate as clearly as is practicable, without a detailed analysis, the basis for the action taken and must advise the employee of his right to appeal including the right to a hearing. The installation head shall establish an official grievance file for use in the event of a further appeal.

## H. Appeal from Installation Head's Decision

1. If the grieved employee desires to appeal the decision of the head of the installation but does not desire a hearing, he shall appeal within five (5) working days after receipt of the decision in writing to the second level of appeal. A copy of the appeal to the second level shall be furnished to the installation head who shall forward the entire grievance file to the second level of appeal along with his answer to the grievance, within five (5) working days. The installation head's answer should indicate as clearly as is practicable the basis for the action taken, a copy of which shall be sent to the grievant. The grievant may within five (5) working days after receipt of the installation head's answer file exceptions to the Regional Director. The grievant's exception will become a part of the grievance file and must be considered by the Regional Director in arriving at a decision. . . .

## I. Hearing

1. If the employee desires a hearing either he or his representative must notify the installation head in writing, within five (5) working days of the installation head's decision. The installation head shall within three (3) working days arrange for formation of a three-man hearing committee and he shall arrange a place for the hearing. The hearing committee will consist of the following members: the grievant will name the person of his choice to be a member, the installation head will name the second member, and these two members will agree, within three (3) working days, on a third member who will act as chairman. All three members must be employees of the postal service. At those installations where there are ten or less employees, the grievant and/or the installation head is permitted to name members from nearby postal installations employing more than ten people.

2. The hearing committee shall act as an unbiased group to hear and evaluate such information pertinent to the grievance as may be presented by the grievant and management of the installation. While the hearing committee will listen to and ask questions of both sides, there shall be no confrontation of witnesses nor shall either side be permitted to cross-examine the

other. Persons appointed to the hearing committee must approach their duties with an open mind and their recommendations must be based on a fair evaluation of the facts without distortion or personal bias.

3. Conduct of the hearing shall be as informal as is consistent with an orderly presentation of the case. While the hearings will not be limited by legal rules of evidence and procedures, testimony should be within reasonable bounds of relevancy. Only one witness should be permitted at a time. The grievant and his representative shall be present throughout the hearing.

4. The installation head shall make available to the hearing committee all records and facts pertinent to the case, other than security or other classified material.

5. An abstract of the proceedings covering all pertinent facts shall be kept. The abstract shall be signed by and copies furnished to all members of the hearing committee. Within five (5) working days after the completion of the hearing, the hearing committee shall furnish the installation head, the grievant and his representative with a summary of the hearing together with its decision.

6. The decision of the hearing committee shall be binding at the expiration of ten (10) working days unless appealed at the next higher level by the grievant or his representative or the installation head within that period.

7. Because the decision of the hearing committee may have a substantial impact on the operations of the postal installation, it shall not be placed into effect until the installation head has had an opportunity to appeal at the second level. If no appeal is filed, the decision shall be carried out upon expiration of the appeal period. If an appeal is made by the installation head, the decision of the hearing committee shall be held in abeyance unless changed by the second level. The decision rendered at the second level of appeal is binding and shall be promptly implemented by the installation head.

### J. Official Time, Installation Level

1. The employee and his chosen representative shall have a reasonable amount of official time to present his grievance. A reasonable amount of time is determined by local management, except that the chairman of the hearing committee rather than local management determines the length and the conduct of the hearing.

2. In those cases where an organization with exclusive recognition represents the unit in which the grievant is employed, but is not the grievant's chosen representative, the exclusive

organization representative may attend all proceedings, as provided herein, with his attendance at the proceedings charged to annual leave or leave without pay at his discretion. (In no instance may such attendance be charged to official time).

3. Members of the hearing committee and representatives for management shall be granted official time for necessary absences from their assigned tours.

### K. Appeal from Hearing Committee Decision

1. If the decision of the hearing committee is not acceptable to the grievant or to the installation head, either party may appeal in writing within ten (10) working days from the hearing committee decision to the second level of appeal. The grievant shall request informal discussion at the regional level at the same time if he desires such discussion. As most postal installations are post offices the second appeal would be to the Regional Director and the procedures will be set forth accordingly. . . .

2. If the grievant appeals, a copy of the letter of the appeal shall be submitted to the installation head who shall promptly forward the grievance file to the Regional Director. Either party may file with the Regional Director exceptions to the summary of the hearing committee within the ten-day time limitation. The exceptions to the summary must be confined to the material appearing in the summary. In the event that either party to the grievance, or his representative, does not appear to make any presentation or give testimony, that party shall be denied the right to provide exceptions to the summary. If the installation head appeals he should submit the grievance file with the letter of appeal to the Regional Director and copy of the letter of appeal to the grievant.

### L. Decision of the Regional Director

1. If the grievant or his representative requests informal discussion prior to the decision, the Director of the Personnel Division shall then arrange for the employee and/or his representative to meet with him for informal discussion designed to arrive at a settlement. All travel and other costs on the part of the organization, the grievant or his representative shall be at his own expense. However, the Regional Director shall arrange to have annual leave or leave without pay granted at the option of each employee involved.

2. If the Director, Personnel Division, at the region is not able to arrive at an informal settlement of the grievance, he shall within three (3) days following the informal discussion submit the case to the Regional Director who shall render a decision

based on the merits as contained in the record of the official grievance file within ten (10) days. If no informal discussions are held the decision will be rendered within ten (10) days after receipt of the file by the Regional Director.

3. No additional information shall be solicited by the Regional Director. However, the Regional Director may accept new relevant and material evidence which was not available at the hearing upon a showing by the party presenting the new evidence that it was not previously disclosed through no fault of the party making request for its consideration. Copies of the decision shall be forwarded to the grievant, his representative and the installation head. The basis for the decision shall be stated as clearly as practical and the grievant shall be notified of any further appeal rights.

## M. Appeals from the Regional Director's Decision

The decision of the Regional Director may be appealed to the Department by the grievant or his representative within ten (10) working days from the date of the Regional Director's decision. The appeal should be addressed to the Board of Appeals and Review, Bureau of Personnel, Post Office Department, Washington, D. C. 20260 . . . . The appellant or his representative shall send a signed copy of the letter of appeal to the Regional Director. Upon receipt of this copy of a letter of further appeal, the Regional Director will promptly forward the entire grievance file to the Board of Appeals and Review, Bureau of Personnel.

## N. Review by Board of Appeals and Review, Bureau of Personnel

1. The Board of Appeals and Review, Bureau of Personnel, will docket the appeal, notify the employee and other interested parties of its receipt, and schedule it for review. There is no right to a hearing at this level, but an additional hearing may be granted if such is deemed warranted. If a hearing is not held the grievant and/or his representative may discuss the case with the Board of Appeals and Review. If a hearing or discussion is scheduled at this level, the national exclusive organization, if not the representative, will be so notified and will be given an opportunity to be present throughout the proceedings and to state its position on the grievance.

2. The Board will render a decision on the appeal which shall be considered as the decision of the Postmaster General. . . .

## P. Termination

A grievance will be terminated when so requested by the grievant at any stage of the proceedings. . . .

## 3. Delaware Department of Mental Health Agreement

### Grievance

Any employee having a problem regarding his employment shall first discuss the problem with his immediate supervisor. If the problem is not settled to the employee's satisfaction, the employee, if the problem is a grievance, shall follow the grievance procedure outlined below.

### Definition of a Grievance

A grievance is a complaint regarding working conditions or the unjust application of rules and regulations of the department or the terms of this agreement.

### Grievance Procedure

Any grievance which may arise between the parties including the application, meaning or interpretation of this agreement shall be settled in the following manner. However, grievances of other than the meaning or interpretation of the agreement shall be fully exhausted after the reply to the grievance at Step 4.

*Step 1.* The employee and his union representative, if he desires such representative, shall within ten (10) days of the date of the grievance or his knowledge of the grievance, present the grievance in writing to his immediate supervisor and discuss the grievance with his immediate supervisor. The supervisor shall have five working days in which to consider the grievance of the employee and make a decision, in writing to the employee.

*Step 2.* In the event the decision of the immediate supervisor is not satisfactory to the employee, the factual details of the complaint or grievance shall be submitted in writing within five (5) working days to the head of the department of the facility who shall meet within ten (10) working days, with and discuss the grievance with the employee and his union representative, if he desires such representative. The head of the department has five (5) working days to reach his decision and reply in writing to the employee.

*Step 3.* In the event the decision of the head of the department does not satisfy the grievance of the employee, the employee may within five (5) working days present in writing the grievance to the facility head. The facility head shall arrange to meet within ten (10) working days with the employee, the employee's representatives, not to exceed three in number, witnesses to both sides of the dispute and a representative of the office of personnel. The facility head shall have recorded all testimony at the hearing and shall issue his decision to the employee in writing within five (5) working days. A copy of the transcript shall be made available to the union upon request. In addition, the union upon request shall be furnished payroll or time records that are appropriate to the hearing.

*Step 4.* In the event the employee is still not satisfied regarding the grievance, he may within five (5) working days request in writing a review of his grievance by the Commissioner. The Commissioner or his designee shall within fifteen (15) days meet and discuss the grievance with the employee and his union representative, if he desires such representative, and reply to the employee in writing within thirty (30) days.

### Arbitration

1. Any unresolved dispute, claim or grievance arising out of or relating to the interpretation of this Agreement shall be submitted to arbitration under the Voluntary Labor Arbitration Rules of the American Arbitration Association.

The parties further agree to accept the arbitrator's award as final and binding upon them.

The cost of the arbitrator's fee and expenses shall be borne equally by the parties.

2. The arbitrator shall have no power to add to or subtract from or modify or extend or renew any of the terms of this Agreement; nor to establish or change any wage rate or the job content of any occupational classification.

3. In case of a grievance involving any continuing or other money claim against the department, no award shall be made by the arbitrator which shall allow any alleged accruals prior to the date when such grievance shall have been presented to the department in writing.

4. Any grievance which the department may have against the union involving the interpretation of this Agreement shall be presented to the Grievance Committee of the union.

In the event the matter is not satisfactorily adjusted within ten (10) days after such presentation, it may be appealed at the fourth step in the grievance procedure.

If the matter is not satisfactorily settled at this meeting, it may be appealed to arbitration as provided for in Section 1 above.

### 4. Levy Court of New Castle County Agreement

### Article III. Grievances and Arbitration Procedure

*Section 1.* Any grievance or dispute which may arise between the parties, including the application, meaning or interpretation of this Agreement, shall be settled in the following manner:

*Step 1.* The union steward, with the aggrieved employee, shall discuss the grievance or dispute with the immediate superintendent with 10 days of the date of the grievance or his knowledge of its occurrence. The immediate superintendent shall attempt to adjust the matter and shall respond to the union steward within 3 working days.

*Step 2.* If after a thorough discussion with the immediate superintendent, the grievance has not been satisfactorily resolved, the union steward, the chairman of the grievance committee and president of the local union, and the aggrieved employee shall, after written appeal, discuss the grievance with the department head, within 3 working days after the immediate supervisor response is due. The department head shall respond in writing within three (3) working days.

*Step 3.* If after a thorough discussion with the department head, the grievance has not been satisfactorily resolved, the union steward, the aggrieved employee, the president of the local union, and the union representative shall, after written appeal, discuss the grievance with the Levy Court within 5 working days after the department head's response is due. The Levy Court shall respond in writing within 5 working days.

*Step 4.* If the grievance is still unsettled, either party may, within 15 days after the reply of the Levy Court is due, by written notice to the other, request arbitration.

The arbitration proceedings shall be conducted by a board of arbitrators consisting of 3 persons, one selected by the employer, one selected by the union. The two arbitrators shall then select a third mutual arbitrator who shall act as chairman of the board.

If the parties fail to select an arbitrator, the state mediation and conciliation service shall be requested by either or both parties to provide a panel of 5 arbitrators.

Both the employer and the union shall have the right to strike two names from the panel. The party requesting arbitration shall strike the first name; the other party shall then strike one name. The process will be repeated and the remaining person shall be the arbitrator.

The decision of the arbitration board shall be final and binding on the parties, and the arbitration board shall be requested to issue their decision within 30 days after the conclusion of testimony and argument.

Expenses for the arbitrator's services and the proceedings

shall be borne equally by the employer and the union. However, each party shall be responsible for compensating its own representatives. The employer shall require all persons pertinent to the grievance, and including those requested by the employee to be given time off from duty, without loss of pay, to appear at the hearing.

*Section 2.* Time limits may be extended under this Article by mutual agreement of the parties.

## 5. City of Milwaukee Agreement

### Part III. Section I—Grievance and Arbitration Procedure

1. Only matters involving the interpretation, application or enforcement of the terms of this Agreement shall constitute a grievance under the provisions set forth below. If an employee has a grievance, he shall first present the grievance orally to his immediate supervisor, either alone or accompanied by a union representative.

2. If the grievance is not settled at the first step, it shall be reduced to writing and presented to his immediate supervisor. Within two working days, the supervisor shall furnish the employee and the union with a written answer to the grievance.

3. If the grievance is not settled at the second step, the union or employee shall have the right to make an appeal in writing within ten working days to the bureau or division head. The bureau or division head may confer with the aggrieved and the union before making his determination. Such decision shall be reduced to writing and submitted to the aggrieved employee and the union within ten working days from his receipt of the appeal.

4. If the grievance is not settled at the third step, the union may appeal in writing within ten working days to the department head, who may confer with the aggrieved and the union and notify the aggrieved and the union in writing within ten working days from receipt of the appeal.

5. If a union grievance is not settled at the fourth step, or if any grievance filed by the city cannot be satisfactorily resolved by conference with appropriate representatives of the union, either party may proceed to the next step as hereinafter provided.

### Section II—Final and Binding Arbitration

Arbitration may be resorted to only when issues arise between the parties hereto with reference to the interpretation, application or enforcement of provisions of this Agreement, except, however, that the following subjects shall not be submitted nor subject to either advisory or binding arbitration:

1. Provisions of the Agreement which relate to or in any manner affect the obligations of the city as expressed or intended by the provisions of Chapter 65, Wisconsin statutes.

2. The statutory or charter obligations which by law devolve upon the Common Council.

3. The legal principles except dicta, expressed either by Wisconsin Supreme Court determination or in the general body of legal principles which are applicable to municipalities and their municipal functions.

4. Any matter which is covered by Wisconsin Statutes and relates to the operation and jurisdiction of the City Service Commission, including rules which the Commission is authorized to promulgate, except as provided in Section III.

5. The elimination or discontinuance of any job, except as provided in the contracting and subcontracting provision.

6. Any pension matter.

The specific exceptions noted above are not intended to limit the right of the union to proceed to final and binding arbitration in disputes affecting the entitlement of employees to existing and established wages, hours, and conditions of employment as specifically set forth and referred to in Schedule "A" attached hereto unless otherwise noted in said schedule.

For purposes of brevity, the term "Arbitrator," as used hereinafter, shall refer either to a single arbitrator or a panel of arbitrators, as the case may be.

No issue whatsoever shall be arbitrated or subject to arbitration, either advisory or binding, unless such issue results from an action or occurrence which takes place following the execution of this Agreement, and no arbitration determination or award shall be made by any arbitrator, either advisory or binding, which grants any right or relief for any period of time whatsoever prior to the execution date of this Agreement.

In the event that this Agreement is terminated or breached for any reason, rights to arbitration, either advisory or binding, thereupon cease. This provision, however, shall not affect any arbitration proceedings which were properly commenced prior to the expiration or termination of this Agreement.

It is contemplated by the provisions of this Agreement that any arbitration award, either advisory or binding, shall be issued by the arbitrator within 60 working days after the notice of appointment unless the parties to this Agreement shall extend the period in writing by mutual consent.

In matters where the no-strike, no-lockout provision becomes subject to arbitration as herein provided for, the arbitrator shall issue the award within 15 days from the commencement of arbitration proceedings. No extension of this period shall be permitted unless the grieving party consents thereto in writing. No item or issue may be the subject of arbitration, either advisory or binding, unless such arbitration is formally requested within 60 working days following the action or occurrence which gives rise to the issue to be arbitrated. This provision is one of limitation, and no award of any arbitrator, whether advisory or binding, may be retroactive for a period greater than 60 working days prior to the formal request for arbitration as herein provided, but in no event shall it be retroactive for any period prior to the execution of this Agreement.

Final and binding arbitration may be initiated by either party serving upon the other party a notice in writing of an intent to proceed to arbitration. Said notice shall identify the Agreement provision, the grievance or grievances, the department, and the employees involved. Unless the parties can, within five working days following the receipt of such written notice, agree upon the selection of an arbitrator, either party may in writing request the Wisconsin Employment Relations Board to submit a list of five arbitrators to both parties. The parties shall within five working days of the receipt of said list meet for the purpose of selecting the arbitrator by striking names from said list until one name remains. Such person shall become the arbitrator.

Whenever one of the parties deems the issue to be arbitrated to be of such significance as to warrant a panel of three arbitrators, each party shall, within five working days of the notification of the request to proceed to arbitration, appoint one arbitrator, and the two arbitrators so appointed shall attempt to agree on a neutral person to serve as the third arbitrator and chairman of the arbitration panel. If no mutual agreement is reached within five working days on the selection of the third arbitrator, said third arbitrator and chairman shall be selected in the manner and in the time specified for the selection of a single arbitrator.

The arbitrator shall neither add to, detract from, nor modify the language of this Agreement in arriving at a determination of any issue presented that is proper for arbitration within the limitations expressed herein. The arbitrator shall have no authority to grant wage increases or wage decreases.

The arbitrator shall expressly confine himself to the precise issues submitted for arbitration and shall have no authority to determine any other issue not so submitted to him or to submit observations or declarations of opinion which are not directly essential in reaching the determination.

All expenses which may be involved in the arbitration proceedings shall be borne by the parties equally. However, expenses relating to the calling of witnesses or the obtaining of depositions or any other similar expense associated with such proceedings shall be borne by the party at whose request such witnesses or depositions are required.

The arbitrator so selected shall hold a hearing at a time and place convenient to the parties within ten working days of the notification of his selection, unless otherwise mutually agreed upon by the parties. The arbitrator shall take such evidence as in his judgment is appropriate for the disposition of the dispute. Statements of position may be made by the parties, and witnesses may be called. The arbitrator shall have initial authority to determine whether or not the dispute is arbitrable under the express terms of this Agreement. Once it is determined that a dispute is arbitrable, the arbitrator shall proceed in accordance with this article to determine the merits of the dispute submitted to arbitration.

For the purposes of receiving testimony and evidence, the provisions of Section 298.06 and 298.07 of the Wisconsin Statutes shall apply. The arbitration award shall be reduced to writing, subject to Sections 298.08 through and including 298.15 of the Wisconsin Statutes. . . .

In addition to all other exceptions, disputes or differences regarding classifications of positions; promotions of employees; pensions; and eliminations of positions, except as provided in the contracting and subcontracting provision; are expressly not subject to arbitration of any kind notwithstanding any other provision herein contained.

### Section III—Advisory Arbitration

It is recognized by the parties to this Agreement that the City Service Commission as organized under state law is a quasi-judicial body exercising quasi-judicial duties. In that respect it is a public agency operated for the benefit of the public and not specifically operated for either the city or the employee. Only the union may request advisory arbitration on behalf of an employee who has been disciplined, provided that the action is properly appealable under the provisions of Section 63.43 of the Wisconsin Statutes in accordance with the rules and regulations promulgated thereunder by the Commission; and, provided, further, that the union shall file with the Commission within three days following the determination by such department head, an appeal in writing requesting advisory arbitration. Upon receipt thereof, the Commission shall appoint from a panel of 15 arbitrators previously submitted by the Wisconsin Employment Relations Board, the person who shall act as advisory arbitrator. Pending the advisory arbitration proceedings, the discipline determination shall be in all respects operative and not be stayed. It is intended by the provisions of this paragraph providing for advisory arbitration that it shall operate consistent with the full exercise by the Commission of its duties, responsibilities and obligations under the provisions of the Wisconsin Statutes with respect to city service, and nothing herein is intended to override or supersede any rule promulgated by the Commission within its authority under the Wisconsin Statutes. It is further the intention of this provision that full faith and credit shall be afforded to the provisions of the City Service Act. All expenses incurred shall be paid in the same manner as in final and binding arbitration herein.

The advisory arbitrator shall submit in writing his findings of fact and his advisory recommendations.

The advisory arbitrator shall neither add to, detract from, nor modify the language of any civil service rule or regulation in arriving at his recommendation. The advisory arbitrator shall expressly confine himself to the precise issue submitted for advisory arbitration and shall have no authority to make a recommendation on any other issue not so submitted to him.

The City Service Commission alone has the power to render a final and binding determination of the matter. The award of the advisory arbitrator shall be advisory only, and if upon review the Commission determines that it is unable to render a final determination on the record, findings of fact and recommendation of the advisory arbitrator, it may reopen the record for the purpose of taking additional evidence. The provisions of Chapter 298 of the Wisconsin Statutes are hereby expressly negated and are of no force and effect in advisory arbitration under this provision.

### 6. City of Philadelphia Agreement

**Grievance Procedure**

1. There shall be prior notice to the union regarding changes in, or institution of rules and regulations pertaining to working conditions, and opportunity for discussion of same wherever possible.

2. The city agrees to receive and consider any specific complaints from the union regarding alleged abuses under civil service Regulation 5.11, entitled "Temporary Change in Assignment," and will sincerely attempt to correct such abuses where the complaint is found to be justified.

3. In the event that any difference concerning the interpretation or application of the Agreement shall arise, the procedure to be followed in an effort to reach a mutual understanding shall be in the order as herein indicated:

   a. The question shall be discussed between the business agent of the local union and the personnel officer, or authorized representative of the particular department, board or commission; and upon failure to agree

   b. Between the business agent of the local union and the head of the particular department, board or commission; and upon failure to agree

   c. Between the business agent of the local union and the personnel director of the City of Philadelphia.

In the event that the above steps fail to resolve the difference, it shall then be submitted to an advisory board consisting of three (3) members appointed or named by the personnel director and three (3) members appointed or named by the union. The advisory board, consisting of six (6) members, shall endeavor to settle the issue. The advisory board shall not sit as a board of arbitration but shall serve in a mediating capacity for the purpose of endeavoring to have the personnel director and the union mutually agree on the issue under discussion.

If a majority of this board fails to agree, then its members shall select a seventh member, who shall act in the capacity of chairman of the board. A quorum shall consist of the full board. A majority vote of this board shall be required to decide the difference or question, and such decision shall be considered as advisory only.

## 7. City of Winnipeg Agreement

### 52. Grievances

52-1. Should any employee subject to this Agreement believe he has been unjustly dealt with or that any of the provisions of this Agreement have been violated he shall, with the assistance of a representative of the union, if he so desires, take up the matter with his immediate superior and if he does not obtain satisfaction from his immediate superior, the case may be referred to the grievance committee of the union which will make its initial submission in writing to the head of the department concerned.

52-2. An individual employee, however, may make application to present his own grievance to the head of the department in which he is employed.

52-3. Should a settlement not be effected between the parties as provided in subsection 52-1, the matter may be taken up with the committee and if no agreement is reached, then to city council.

52-4. All conferences between the grievance committee and heads of the departments will be held by appointment during working hours, without loss of time to committee men.

52-5. It is further agreed that at the request of the grievance committee, the business agent of the union will be called in on any dispute that may be the subject of negotiations.

52-6. If it is found by either the department head, committee or council that an employee has been unjustly discharged or dealt with, such employee will be reinstated with full pay for all time lost.

52-7. The city agrees to recognize the grievance committee of this union and its representatives, as the sole representatives of the employees covered by this Agreement, but this will not prevent any employee from applying to be heard on his own behalf in any negotiations under this section.

52-8. An accredited steward will be recognized on behalf of the employees whom he represents by the immediate superior of such employees, and failing satisfaction by the more responsible officials in turn, to the head of the department.

## 53. Arbitration

In the event of any controversy concerning the meaning, interpretation or violation of this Agreement or any portion thereof, and in the event that a satisfactory adjustment cannot be reached between the parties as stated above, either party may submit such dispute to a board of arbitration; hereinafter referred to as the Board. Such Board shall consist of three members.

Each party to the agreement shall select one member of the Board of Arbitration within thirty days after failure to settle the controversy. The two members of the Board so selected shall within 14 days of their selection, select a third member. Upon the selection of such third member, the Board shall meet and appoint one of their members chairman.

If either party fails to appoint its arbitrator as herein provided, or if any arbitrator so appointed shall fail or be unable to serve, and another arbitrator is not appointed in his place, then the other party hereto may request the Minister of Labor of the Province of Manitoba to select such arbitrator.

If the two arbitrators appointed as herein provided shall fail within 14 days to agree upon the third arbitrator, the said two arbitrators shall forthwith request the said Minister of Labor to select such arbitrator.

Any question referred to said arbitrators shall be decided by a majority affirmative vote of the said arbitrators, and any such decision or award made pursuant thereto shall be final and binding on all parties to this agreement. The costs of any arbitration or award shall be in the discretion of the arbitrators who may direct to and by whom and in what manner such costs or any part thereof are to be paid, and may tax or settle the amount thereof.

# C

## Appendix C—

## Organization for
## Employee Relations

O<small>N</small> THE FACING PAGE is an organization chart of the Los Angeles County Personnel Department outlining the employee relations staff. Note that the Director of Personnel is shown at the top, with the areas of classification and compensation, of employee relations, and of employee development listed below. This chart is contained in a Memorandum from Gordon T. Nesvig, Director of Personnel, to all department and district heads, February 16, 1967.

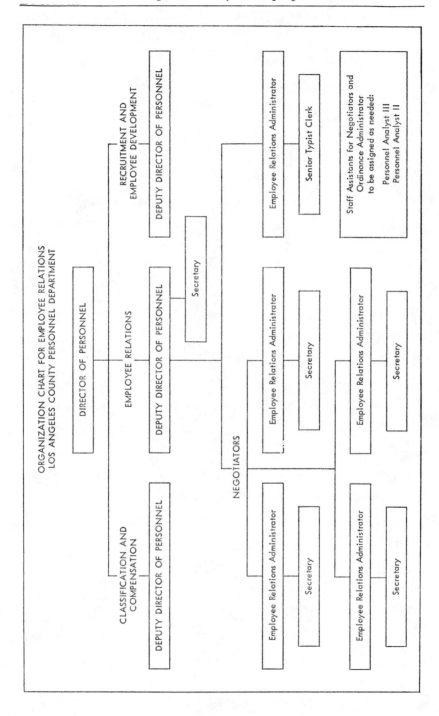

ORGANIZATION CHART FOR EMPLOYEE RELATIONS
LOS ANGELES COUNTY PERSONNEL DEPARTMENT

DIRECTOR OF PERSONNEL

CLASSIFICATION AND COMPENSATION

EMPLOYEE RELATIONS

RECRUITMENT AND EMPLOYEE DEVELOPMENT

DEPUTY DIRECTOR OF PERSONNEL

DEPUTY DIRECTOR OF PERSONNEL

DEPUTY DIRECTOR OF PERSONNEL

Secretary

NEGOTIATORS

Employee Relations Administrator

Employee Relations Administrator

Employee Relations Administrator

Employee Relations Administrator

Employee Relations Administrator

Secretary

Secretary

Secretary

Secretary

Senior Typist Clerk

Staff Assistants for Negotiators and Ordinance Administrator to be assigned as needed:
Personnel Analyst III
Personnel Analyst II

# D

## Appendix D—

## Evaluation Procedures

THE FOLLOWING evaluation procedures of the federal employee-management cooperation program are contained in the United States Civil Service Commission Federal Personnel Manual System, Supplement (Internal) No. 273-72, June, 1967.

### Employee-Management Cooperation

. . . Although Executive Order 10988 does not pertain to the relations between the Commission and employee organizations recognized by other agencies, inspectors will conduct their work in a manner which respects the Executive Order 10988 relationships existing at each establishment inspected. This policy closes no avenues of inquiry into the agency's personnel management program. It does place important responsibilities on the inspector, . . . . Here are three such responsibilities:

- Contacting each employee organization granted formal and exclusive recognition to seek its views on employee-management cooperation and agency personnel operations.

- Maintaining a clear distinction in soliciting the views of employees to assure that group views are solicited only from the designated representatives of employee organizations.

- Avoiding third-party involvement in situations of disagreement between management and employee organizations.

While the operation of the employee-management cooperation program is itself a discrete area of inspection coverage, the very nature of the program may cause its review to be interrelated with that of other aspects of personnel management. Wherever employee organizations are strong and active, inspectors may anticipate that the influence of activities under the program can be felt in virtually every area of personnel management. . .

Government employee organizations have demonstrated an admirable degree of concern for the public interest, but it is only fair to them to recognize that their primary concern must be for the economic and social welfare of their members. Even though they carry out their functions within a framework established by government, unions are not public organizations, but private membership organizations. What the employee organization does, and how it does it, is up to the organization so long as it maintains its representative strength and refrains from prohibited practices. Inspectors must bear in mind, therefore, that only the members of such an employee organization have any right or obligation to evaluate how well that organization performs its functions. Moreover, it is optional with the organization whether or not it exercises all of the rights which would be available to it under the Executive Order.

Certainly there are many tasks which the employee organization may undertake which would be very constructive from the agency's point of view. Whether an employee organization undertakes these or not in no way alters management's basic responsibilities with respect to agency mission. The task, for example, of facilitating understanding in communications between management and employees, if a union undertakes it, may make a very direct contribution to program effectiveness and agency mission accomplishment. The fact that a union is doing a particularly good job in this area, however, does not relieve management of the responsibility for assuring that communications are effective. The general application of this principle, however much the activities of employee organizations may assist management in getting the agency's job done, never relieves management of responsibility for seeing that the job is done. It follows, therefore, that the inspection activities must place primary emphasis on management effectiveness within the total program framework. The evaluation and report should be made in this context.

Under no circumstances should inspectors give the impression that they are evaluating the ability, attitude, or effectiveness of employee organization or their representatives. The Civil Service Commission does not inspect unions. Inspectors should be alert, however, for the views and attitudes which the parties to the labor-management scene express about one another. These should be reported if they all contribute to the reader's understanding of local relationships. . . .

The inspector should focus survey activities on the following:

*Character of Relationships and Dealings With Employee Organizations.* This item is concerned with the parties on the labor-management scene and the manner in which they deal with one another. Identify each employee organization along with pertinent information such as its approximate size; level of recognition, if any; occupational composition of the unit in which recognized; when recognized; whether an agreement has been negotiated; whether a higher level of recognition has been requested, etc. (Use revised form IC 74). [See page 387.] Consider the patterns of dealings and the type, frequency, and atmosphere of contacts with each organization. Identify significant changes which have developed because of the program in the number, size, and character of employee organizations. Do not ignore information on professionals, supervisors, and other personnel mentioned in section 6(a) of the order which may be useful in revealing trends in the patterns of dealing with these as well as other workers.

*Results of Consultations and Other Contacts.* Inspectors will concentrate on the substance of dealings and what they have meant to the parties involved. They should also identify problems and report suggestions and comments from persons interviewed (with attention to effective solutions successfully implemented), which would be helpful in revealing trends and assessing the overall effectiveness of the program. Consider major subjects discussed, decisions reached and other accomplishments, current needs and demands, unsolved problems, etc.

*Agency and Employee Organization Experience in Negotiating and Carrying Out Agreements.* Particular emphasis should be placed on the employee-management agreement and the influence its provisions have had on personnel management and agency mission accomplishment. Consider whether agreement provisions have led to significant changes in agency policies and operations. Review the results in terms of employees both in and out of the exclusive unit. Consider also the impact on the employee organization in terms of expanded activity, membership growth, inclusion in personnel program development, etc.

*Cases and Problems Involving the Application of the Standards of Conduct and the Code of Fair Labor Practices.* Situations, if any, involving the application of the Standards and Code issued to supplement Executive Order 10988 should be described in detail.

*Matters of General Interest and Concern to Employees and Employee Organization.* Normally, discussions with management and organization representatives covering items *2* and *3* above will elicit information on most matters of concern to employees. However, contacts with union representatives should provide ample opportunity to discuss items of general interest to union members (e.g. employee "unrest," impact of agency "contracting out" procedures, etc.)

## Factfinding Techniques and Sources of Information

Discussions with managers, supervisors, supporting staffs, employees and designated representatives of employee organizations.

During the course of each inspection the inspector will seek out and meet the designated representatives of each employee organization granted formal recognition or exclusive recognition by the activity being inspected. At the discretion of the inspector, such meetings may include other officials of these employee organizations. The essential purposes of these meetings will be to obtain comments from the representatives of these recognized employee organizations regarding the local program of employee-management cooperation and to provide such representatives with an opportunity to present their views . . . to our inspectors.

There is no requirement that inspectors seek out the representatives of employee organizations granted informal recognition. However, inspectors will continue to make themselves available to them and to employees upon request.

In some agencies it may be desirable to make additional contacts with employee organizations to assure adequate coverage and full exploration of matters of concern to employees. For example, added contacts might be desirable in agencies where there are very large or highly structured employee unions (e.g., extensive steward system), significant workforce dispersion, or a wide variety of occupational groups. The possibility of such contact (normally with chief stewards) should, of course, be discussed with both the employee organization and agency management to assure understanding and cooperation.

## On-site Inspection Action and Reporting

As a general rule, inspectors will refrain from discussing the substantive merits of individual cases with either management, employees, or employee organizations, avoid becoming third parties in disputes, and exercise care in all discussions of controversial matters and employee complaints.

Discussions by inspectors with representatives of employee organizations should cover the following areas:

- Obtaining comments and views about the local program of employee-management cooperation.

- Providing such representatives with an opportunity to present their views concerning personnel operations and any matters of general concern to employees.

- Responding to questions of fact which can be answered by reference to the Executive Order or to supplemental material the Commission has issued on the subject.

• Responding, where appropriate, to union representatives in response to leads furnished by them. The following illustrates the types of information an inspector may or may not properly supply in these circumstances:

If, as a result of a complaint by a union representative, an inspector investigates and finds that the matter is one over which the Commission has jurisdiction, he would inform the union representative either that management has complied with requirements or that it had not done so, and what corrective action (if pertinent) the Commission has initiated. (An example of such a lead would be information that particular selections for promotion had not been made in accordance with the published plan.)

A report to the union would need to be deferred if, in questionable cases, a decision was delayed pending discussions with the installation or its headquarters. Disclosure about case findings would be limited to cases called to the attention of the inspector by the union representative.

If a complaint is received regarding a matter over which the Commission does not have direct jurisdiction, the scope and depth of our inquiry would vary with circumstances. The inspector would inform the union representative of the Commission's role in the particular situation—one of interest in promoting effective personnel management practices, but not one in which the Commission may inject itself as a third party in individual cases. Our investigation could include an inquiry into what happened in the situation brought to our attention if it would be of assistance in appraising the personnel management program.

Our report to the installation head would include pertinent facts but would not express judgements about the merits of decisions within the agency's purview. Our response to the union would be limited to a clarification of jurisdictional areas, to an explanation about avenues of recourse, and to the fact that we were reporting to appropriate levels of management any matters pertaining to the agency program that we felt merited its consideration (details of these matters would not be divulged).

Our discussions with union representatives would seek to determine whether they have exhausted the procedures open to them locally. Should this be the case, it would be proper to tell them that their next recourse would be to their own headquarters if they feel they have a legitimate complaint which they seek to have pursued at higher levels of management.

In summary, our approach should be one which emphasizes

consultation with local management in matters relating to employee-management relations. We can look into situations brought to the Commission's attention and, when findings indicate, take action; but we must avoid specific promises of action, especially on matters outside the Commission's jurisdiction. On the other hand, it is very important that we convey to representatives our intent to develop complete facts, whatever they may be, so long as they have a bearing on the agency's stewardship of human resources.

In making program suggestions, inspectors should remember that the responsibility for implementing this program is vested specifically in the hands of agencies. They may, however, make such recommendations as:

- Management should inform employees promptly of their right to join or not to join an employee organization.

- Improvement is needed in management's efforts to inform employees of their responsibilities, rights and privileges.

- Improvement in training supervisors, management and staff to assist in more effective program participation and implementation.

As applicable and whenever possible, inspectors should provide assistance to management by giving technical advice and interpretation on program matters or questions for which there are established "ground rules" or precedent interpretation.

**Specialized Reporting Instructions**

Emphasis in reporting should be on program problems, actions and results. General statements of intent and descriptions of standard procedures or operations, recurring practices, agency-wide systems, etc., should be used only when essential to clear understanding of the local program. Inspectors should concentrate on providing complete and objective descriptions with pertinent details on such matters as:

- Significant problems encountered, how they were handled and effective solutions (successful methods of resolving impasses, etc.).

- What problems remain and what is being done to meet them.

- The impact or lack of impact as a result of program activity (policy changes which stemmed from consultation, etc.).

- Measurable impact on the program as a result of changes in other program areas (impact from new promotion program, agency reorganization, etc.).

- Critical or significant changes in the program due to increased union activity, new levels of recognition granted, newly organized locals, new or revised agency instructions, supervisory and management training, etc.

The above items should not be viewed as an all-inclusive list or a reporting format. They are intended to demonstrate the type of reporting needed to accurately measure program development, promote understanding in the agencies, and provide data for summary program reports.

The inspector should be careful not to characterize "a lack of unsolved problems" or "a lack of EMC program activity" as a "good EMC program." If a program is "good," then its accomplishments should be reviewed and reported in a way which clearly defines what the actual accomplishments are. It is just as important to know what problems have been solved, as it is to know that no unsolved problems remain. If, however, an establishment's EMC program is inactive, reporting need only deal briefly with the reasons for this inactivity (for example, lack of employee interest) if it is possible to identify them.

Where employee-management relationships are established and active, a narrative review following each of the coverage items should be included in the written report.

Where employee-management organization dealings are not an active part of the agency scene, a detailed response to any but the first coverage item may be unproductive. If, for example, the only pertinent observation in viewing the employee relations scene is something such as, "While Local X is recognized at the informal level in this establishment, it is relatively inactive and has not discussed anything with management in a year or more," then the report may say this and stop there.

A very limited level of activities in employee-management cooperation, in some instances, may be the result of attitudes or behavior contrary to Executive Order 10988 or the Standards and Code. If an inspector finds evidence of this he should cover the situation in detail in the inspection report.

Where the inspector determines that the local installation has problems from adherence to instructions issued by a higher headquarters, the problems will be brought to the attention of the Bureau of Inspection in a memorandum. Likewise, matters not covered by guidelines from the Commission's central office and matters which are controversial in nature should be brought to the attention of the Bureau.

Problems encountered in factfinding on employee-management cooperation; in securing information from activities; in discussions with management officials, employees, or representatives of employee groups; or in reporting the facts in the inspection report should also be included in the memorandum to BI. Any problems encountered which the regional director feels are of a priority nature or which require a prompt reply, may be made the subject of a separate memorandum, or if appropriate, a telephone call. The communication of such problems to the central office need not be delayed pending completion of the inspection or of the written report. Problems reported to the Bureau of Inspections will be negotiated between the Bureau and the appropriate agency headquarters as necessary.

To promote accuracy in reporting, inspectors are asked to familiarize themselves with the terms which have special meaning under this program.

Commission offices will not furnish inspection findings, opinions, or recommendations to employees or employee organizations, except under circumstances as outlined in (d) 2 above. Employees and employee organizations requesting inspection reports will be advised that the purpose of these reports is to inform installations, offices, and agencies in the executive branch concerning our appraisals of their personnel management . . . .

U. S. CIVIL SERVICE COMMISSION—
EMPLOYEE-MANAGEMENT COOPERATION

Date: _____

| A. Establishment and Location | B. Agency EMC Official | |
|---|---|---|
| C. Organizations Dealing with Management | D. Recognition | E. Unit Description |

(Where added space is needed for Items C, D, and E, a plain piece of paper may be used for an extension of the listing)

F. If no relationships have been established with employee organizations under Executive Order 10988, some of the following questions may be inapplicable. Please respond to those items checked.

Please Forward / Available Upon Arrival

☐ ☐   1. Has a statement of policy been issued concerning the employee-management cooperation program and/or the rights of employees to participate in employee organization activities? Please attach one copy of the most recent statement.

☐ ☐   2. Has training in employee-management cooperation been provided to top management, supervisors, or the personnel staff? Please describe briefly.

☐ ☐   3. Has a written agreement been negotiated with an employee organization? If so, please attach a copy of each current agreement.

☐ ☐   4. What impact has the Employee Management Cooperation Program had on personnel management and communications with employees? Be as specific as possible in identifying any achievements or changes in practices which have occurred.

☐ ☐   5. Have any problems arisen within the past two years in the operation of the EMC Program (granting recognition, definition of units, conflicts of interest, resolving negotiation impasses, carrying out the agreement, competition between employee organizations, cases under the standards of conduct or the code of fair labor practice, etc.)? Please explain each briefly.

☐ ☐   6. Is there an "employee council" or other group established and controlled by management? If so, please describe briefly.

IC Form 74 (Revised) June 1966

Form Used by United States Civil Service Commission Bureau of Inspections in Reporting on Employee-Management Cooperation in Federal Agencies.

# E

# Appendix E—

# Bibliography

American Association of School Administrators, *School Administrators View Professional Negotiations*. Washington, D.C.: 1201 Sixteenth St., N.W., 20036, 1966.

American Bar Association, Section of Labor Relations Law, *Annual Proceedings*. Chicago: American Bar Center.

American Civil Liberties Union, *Policy Statement on Civil Rights in Government Employment*. New York: 170 Fifth Avenue, April 13, 1959.

American Management Association, Inc., *Understanding Collective Bargaining: The Executive's Guide*. New York: 1515 Broadway, Times Square, 1958.

Beal, Edwin F. and Wickersham, Edward D., *The Practice of Collective Bargaining*. Homewood, Ill.: Richard D. Irwin, Inc., 1967.

Belasco, James A., "Resolving Dispute over Contract Terms in the State Public Service: An Analysis." *Labor Law Journal*, September, 1965.

Benson, E. P., "Recent Changes in the Approach to Personnel Management in the Canadian Public Service." *Public Personnel Review*, October, 1967.

Case, Harry L., *Personnel Policy in a Public Agency—The TVA Experience*. New York: Harper and Row, 1955.

Cevasco, Gerard, "Should We Arbitrate?" *Personnel Administrator*, January-February, 1967.

*Changing Education*. Quarterly Journal of the American Federation of Teachers, AFL-CIO. Washington, D.C.: Editorial and business offices, 1012 14th St., N. W.

Civil Service Commission of Canada, *Personnel Administration in the Public Service, A Review of Civil Service Legislation*. Ottawa: Queen's Printer, 1959.

*Collective Bargaining, A Worker's Education Manual*. Geneva: International Labour Office, 1960.

Cornell, Herbert W., "Collective Bargaining by Public Employee Groups." *University of Pennsylvania Law Review*, November, 1958.

Council For Administrative Leadership in New York State, *How Good Are Personnel Relationships in New York State?* Albany, N. Y. 12210: 1964.

389

Crichton, Edward E., "Arbitration Practices in the Australian Public Service." *Public Personnel Review*, April, 1965.

Cripso, John H. G. (ed.), *Collective Bargaining and the Professional Employee*. Toronto: Centre for Industrial Relations, University of Toronto, 1966.

Dartnell Corporation, *Handbook of Employee Relations*. Chicago: 1957.

Enright, Thomas C. and Adams, Harold W., *Collective Bargaining in State Employment, Oregon's Experience*. Oregon State Employees' Association, 1515 State Street, Salem, Ore. 97301, 1966.

*Examination of Grievances and Communications Within the Undertaking*. Geneva: International Labour Office, 1965.

Federal Mediation and Conciliation Service, *Annual Reports*. Washington, D. C.: U. S. Government Printing Office.

Foegen, J. H., "A Qualified Right to Strike—in the Public Interest." *Labor Law Journal*, February, 1967.

Frankel, Saul, *A Model For Negotiation and Arbitration Between The Canadian Government And Its Civil Servants*. Montreal: Industrial Relations Centre, McGill University, 1962.

——————— "Employer-Employee Relations in the Public Service." *Public Personnel Review*, October, 1964.

Frankel, S. J. and Pratt, R. C., *Municipal Labour Relations in Canada*. Montreal: Canadian Federation of Mayors and Municipalities, 1954.

Gallagher, Donald, *The Legal Aspects of Collective Bargaining for California Public Employees*. Sacramento, Cal.: California State Employees' Association, 1315 K Street, November, 1959.

Godine, Morton R., *The Labor Problem in the Public Service*. Cambridge, Mass.; Harvard University Press, 1951.

Governor's Advisory Commission on Labor-Management Policy for Public Employees, *Report and Recommendations*. Springfield, Ill.: March, 1967.

Governor's Committee on Public Employee Relations, State of New York, *Final Report*, March 31, 1966. Mimeographed. *See* Summary of Recommendations in Warner, Kenneth O. and Hennessy, Mary L., *Public Management at the Bargaining Table*. Chicago: Public Personnel Association, 1967.

Handsaker, Morrison, "Arbitration of Discipline Cases." *Personnel Journal*, March, 1967.

Hart, Wilson R., *Collective Bargaining in the Federal Civil Service*. New York: Harper and Row, 1961.

——————— "The Impasse in Labor Relations in the Federal Civil Service." *Industrial and Labor Relations Review*, January, 1966.

Heisel, W. D. and Hallihan, J. D., *Questions & Answers on Public Employee Negotiation*. Chicago: Public Personnel Association, 1968.

Heisel, W. D. and Santa-Emma, J. P., "Unions in City Government: The Cincinnati Story." *Public Personnel Review*, January, 1961.

Hodgetts, J. E. and Corbett, D. C., *Canadian Public Administration, A Book of Readings*. Toronto: The Macmillan Company of Canada Ltd., 1960. Note particularly Part III, pp. 249-433.

Holland, Ann, *Unions Are Here to Stay, A Guide for Employee-Management Relations in the Federal Service.* Washington, D. C.: Society for Personnel Administration, 1962.

Illinois Legislative Council, *Public Employee Labor Relations,* Publication 132. Springfield, Ill.: November, 1958.

Institute of Labor and Industrial Relations, Division of University Extension, University of Illinois, *Collective Bargaining for State and Local Public Employees. Three papers presented at the 18th Annual Central Labor Union Conference,* December, 1966.

International City Managers' Association, *Municipal Collective Bargaining Agreements.* Management Information Service Report No. 257. Washington, D. C.: 1140 Connecticut Ave., N. W., June, 1965.

Khanna, B. S., "Whitleyism—A Feature of Democratic Administration." *Indian Journal of Public Administration,* April-June, 1959.

Killingsworth, Charles C., "Grievance Adjudication in Public Employment." *American Arbitration Journal,* No. 1 (1958).

Klaus, Ida, *Report on a Program of Labor Relations for New York City Employees.* New York: Department of Labor of the City of New York, June, 1967.

Krinsky, Edward B., "Public Employment Fact-Finding in Fourteen States." *Labor Law Journal,* September, 1966.

Krislov, Joseph, "Prospects for the Use of Advisory Grievance Arbitration in Federal Service." *Industrial and Labor Relations Review,* April, 1965.

Labor Management Institute of the American Arbitration Association, *Report to Mayor Lindsay.* New York: 140 West 51st St., 10020, March 31, 1966.

League of Wisconsin Municipalities, *Municipal Employe-Management Relations, Proceedings of an Institute held August 10, 1964.* Madison, Wis.: 30 East Johnson St., September, 1964.

Lieberman, Myron and Moskow, Michael H., *Collective Negotiations for Teachers:An Approach to School Administration.* Chicago: Rand McNally & Company, 1966.

Ligtenberg, John and Andree, Robert G., *Collective Bargaining in the Public Schools, A Handbook of Information and Source Materials on Teacher Rights and Teacher Obligations.* Chicago: American Federation of Teachers Educational Foundation, Inc., 716 North Rush St., 60611, 1966.

McCart, John A., Murphy, Richard J., and Nigro, Felix A., "Labor-Management Relations—Where Do We Stand?" *Civil Service Journal,* July-September, 1967.

McKelvey, Jean T., "The Role of State Agencies in Public Employee Labor Relations." *Industrial and Labor Relations Review,* January, 1967.

Michigan Municipal League, *Requirements and Techniques for Municipal Employer-Employee Negotiations.* Ann Arbor, Mich.: Technical Topics No. 31, 1966.

Moberly, Robert B., "The Strike and Its Alternatives in Public Employment." *Wisconsin Law Review,* Spring, 1966.

Moskow, Michael, *Teachers and Unions.* Philadelphia: University of Pennsylvania, Wharton School of Finance and Commerce, Industrial Research Unit Study No. 42, 1966.

National Education Association, Office of Professional Development and Welfare, *Guidelines for Professional Negotiation.* Revised edition. Washington, D. C.: 1201 Sixteenth St., N.W. 20036, 1965.

_____ *Professional Negotiation: Selected Statements of School Board, Administrator, Teacher Relationships.* Revised edition, 1965.

National Foreman's Institute, *Strategy in Labor Relations.* Waterford, Conn.: 1963.

National Governors' Conference, *Report of Task Force on State and Local Government Labor Relations.* Chicago: 1967.

_____ *1968 Supplement to Report of Task Force on State and Local Government Labor Relations.* Chicago: 1968.

Newland, Chester A., "Trends in Public Employee Unionization." *The Journal of Politics,* August, 1964.

_____ "Variety: A Public Personnel Approach." *Public Personnel Review,* October, 1967.

New York State Joint Legislative Committee on Industrial and Labor Relations, *Report, 1960-1961,* Legislative Document No. 17. Albany, N. Y.: 1961.

_____ *Report, 1962-1963,* Legislative Document No. 38 (1963).

_____ *Report, 1963-1964,* Legislative Document No. 17 (1964).

Noble, George W., "Labour Relations in Canadian Municipalities." *Public Personnel Review,* October, 1961.

Northrup, Herbert R. and Bloom, Gordon F., *Government and Labor.* Homewood, Ill.: Richard D. Irwin, Inc., 1963.

Ocheltree, Keith (ed.), *Government Labor Relations in Transition.* Chicago: Public Personnel Association, 1966.

Perry, Charles A. and Wildman, Wesley A., "A Survey of Collective Activity among Public School Teachers." *Educational Administration Quarterly,* University Council for Education Administration, Spring, 1966.

*Personnel Administration,* January-February, 1963. Entire issue devoted to union-management relations.

"Personnel Opinions," *Public Personnel Review,* January, 1966.

Posey, Rollin B., "The Negotiating Session." *Public Personnel Review,* April, 1965.

Powell, Norman J., *Personnel Administration in Government.* Englewood Cliffs, N. J.: Prentice-Hall, Inc., 1956.

President's Task Force on Employee-Management Relations in the Federal Service, *Report of the President's Task Force on Employee-Management Relations in the Federal Service,* November 30, 1961. Washington, D. C.: Government Printing Office, December, 1961.

Prives, M. Z., *Unionism And The Merit System In Municipal Relations In Canada.* Montreal: Canadian Federation of Mayors and Municipalities, 1958. Mimeographed.

Public Personnel Association, *Public Employee Relations Library.* Chicago:

first issue published in 1968. Each issue deals with specific problems in employee relations.

*Report of the Preparatory Committee on Collective Bargaining in the Public Service.* Ottawa: Queen's Printer, July, 1965.

Research Division, National Education Association, *Negotiation Research Digest.* Published ten times a year, "to report objectively and comprehensively all significant data, trends, and developments concerning professional negotiations, collective bargaining, and similar types of group action procedures relating to members of the teaching profession." Washington, D. C.: 1201 Sixteenth St., N. W. 20036.

Salik, Richard L., *A Digest of Provincial Labor Laws Governing Municipal and Provincial Employees in Canada.* Personnel Report No. 664. Chicago: Public Personnel Association, 1966.

Saso, Carmen D., "Massachusetts Local Government Goes to the Bargaining Table." *Public Personnel Review,* July, 1967.

Somers, Gerald E. (ed.), *Collective Bargaining in the Public Service, Proceedings of the 1966 Annual Spring Meeting.* Industrial Relations Research Association. Madison, Wis.: 1966.

Spero, Sterling, *Government as Employer.* Remsen Press, 1948.

Steffensen, James P., *Teachers Negotiate with Their School Boards.* U. S. Department of Health, Education, and Welfare, Bulletin 1964, 40, OE-23036.

Stern, James, "The Wisconsin Public Employee Fact-Finding Procedure." *Industrial and Labor Relations Review,* October, 1966.

Stieber, Jack, "Collective Bargaining in the Public Sector," in Ulman, Lloyd (ed.), *Challenge to Collective Bargaining.* American Assembly, Columbia University. Englewood Cliffs, N. J.: Prentice-Hall, Inc., 1967.

Stinnett, T. M., Kleinmann, Jack H., Ware, Martha L., *Professional Negotiation in Public Education.* New York: Macmillan Company, 1966.

Subcommittee on Collective Bargaining, Industrial Relations Committee, National Association of Manufacturers, *When Management Negotiates, A Guidebook For Sound Collective Bargaining.* New York: 277 Park Avenue 10017, 1967.

Taylor, George W., "Public Employment: Strikes or Procedures?" *Industrial and Labor Relations Review,* July, 1967.

The Bureau of National Affairs, Inc., *Government Employee Relations Report.* Weekly publication privately circulated. Washington, D. C.: 1231 24th St., N. W. 20037.

The House of Commons of Canada, *Bill C-170, An Act respecting employer and employee relations in the Public Service of Canada.* As Passed By The House of Commons, 20th February, 1967. Ottawa: Queen's Printer, 1967.

——————— *Bill C-181, An Act respecting employment in the Public Service of Canada.* As Passed By The House of Commons, 20th February, 1967. Ottawa: Queen's Printer, 1967.

——————— *Bill C-182, An Act to amend the Financial Administration Act.* As Passed By The House of Commons, 20th February, 1967. Ottawa: Queen's Printer, 1967.

Thompson, Arthur A., "Employee Participation in Decision Making: The TVA Experience." *Public Personnel Review,* April, 1967.

Tompkins, Dorothy C., *Strikes by Public Employees, Professional Personnel and Social Workers: A Bibliography.* Berkeley, Cal.: Institute of Governmental Studies, 1966.

University of California at Los Angeles, Bureau of Governmental Research, *Organized Public Employee Relations; An Annotated Bibliography of Periodical Literature.* Los Angeles: August, 1961.

U. S. Civil Service Commission, Office of Labor-Management Relations, *Statistical Report of Exclusive Recognitions and Negotiated Agreements in the Federal Government under Executive Order 10988, As reported to the Civil Service Commission in August 1966.* Washington, D. C. 20415.

U. S. Department of Labor, Bureau of Labor Statistics, *Bargaining Agreements in the Federal Service, Late Summer 1964.* Washington, D. C.: Government Printing Office, August, 1965.

_____ *Major Collective Bargaining Agreements, Arbitration Procedures.* Bulletin No. 1425-6, June, 1966.

_____ *Major Collective Bargaining Agreements, Grievance Procedures.* Bulletin No. 1425-1, November, 1964.

_____ *Management Rights and Union-Management Cooperation.* Bulletin No. 1425-5, April, 1966.

U. S. Department of Labor, Office of Federal Employee-Management Relations, *Annual Reports.*

Van de Water, John R., "Union-Management Relations in Public and Private Education." *The Journal of the College and University Personnel Association,* November, 1965.

Vosloo, Willem B., *Collective Bargaining in the United States Federal Civil Service.* Chicago: Public Personnel Association, 1966.

Ware, Martha L., *Professional Negotiation With School Boards, A Legal Analysis and Review.* School Law Review Series, Research Report 1965-R3. Washington, D.C.: National Education Association, 1201 Sixteenth St., N. W., March, 1965.

Warner, Kenneth O. and Hennessy, Mary L., *Public Management at the Bargaining Table.* Chicago: Public Personnel Association, 1967.

Warner, Kenneth O. (ed.), *Developments in Public Employee Relations: Legislative, Judicial, Administrative.* Chicago: Public Personnel Association, 1965.

_____ *Management Relations With Organized Public Employees.* Chicago: Public Personnel Association, 1963.

_____ *Collective Bargaining in the Public Service: Theory and Practice.* Chicago: Public Personnel Association, 1967.

Wildman, Wesley A., "Collective Action by Public School Teachers." *Industrial and Labor Relations Review,* October, 1964.

Wisconsin Employment Relations Board, *Digest of Decisions Of The Wisconsin Employment Relations Board And The Courts Involving The Wisconsin Employment Peace Act And Section 111.07, Wisconsin Statutes (Municipal Employer-Employe Labor Relations Law).* Madison, Wis.: June 1, 1966.

Ziskind, David, *One Thousand Strikes of Government Employees.* New York: Columbia University Press, 1940.

# F

## Appendix F—

## References and Citations

THIS APPENDIX contains a numbered list of the sources that have been cited at various points in the main body of the book. To facilitate ready reference, the following coding method has been used:

a. In the body of the book, references appear enclosed in brackets at appropriate points; e.g., [*34*, p. 128].

b. Of the numbers enclosed in brackets, the one in italics is the code number of the particular reference source; e. g., Reference *34*.

c. Following the italicized reference number, the page number within the source is given; e. g., p. 128.

1. *Advisory Arbitration between The City of Milwaukee and Milwaukee District Council 48 AFSCME, AFL-CIO,* report of Thomas P. Whelan, Arbitrator, May 9, 1967; *Advisory Arbitration between The City of Milwaukee and Milwaukee District Council 48 AFSCME,* report of Philip G. Marshall, Arbitrator, August 3, 1967.

2. Advisory Committee on Public Employee Relations, *Report to Governor George Romney.* Lansing, Mich.: February 15, 1967. Mimeographed.

3. *Agreement between City of Milwaukee and Milwaukee District Council 48, AFSCME, AFL-CIO and Its Appropriate Affiliated Locals,* Effective January 1, 1966.

4. *Agreement between Department of Mental Health of the State of Delaware and Laborers' International Union of North America, Local 1029, AFL-CIO,* Effective November 1, 1966.

5. *Agreement between Levy Court of New Castle County and The American Federation of State, County and Municipal Employees, AFL-CIO, Local No. 459,* effective July 1, 1966.

6. *Agreement between New Castle County and The American Federation of State, County, and Municipal Employees, AFL-CIO, Locals 459 and 1607,* effective July 1, 1967.

7. *Agreement between State Tax Department of the State of Delaware*

*and Delaware State Office Employees Local 1385, AFSCME-AFL-CIO,* effective March 1, 1966.

8. *Agreement between The Board of Education of the City of Dearborn and the Henry Ford Community College Federation of Teachers, American Federation of Teachers, Local 1650, 1966-67.* Dearborn Public Schools, 4824 Lois Avenue, Dearborn, Mich.

9. *Agreement between the City Manager et al and District Council No. 51, American Federation of State, County, and Municipal Employees, AFL-CIO,* effective April 13, 1960.

10. *Agreement between The City of Winnipeg and Local 500, Canadian Union of Public Employees,* April, 1965.

11. *Agreement between the State Treasury Department and the Oregon State Employees' Association,* effective January 23, 1967.

12. *Agreement between United States Post Office Department and National Association of Letter Carriers, AFL-CIO, National Association of Post Office and General Services Maintenance Employees, National Association of Post Office Mail Handlers, Watchmen, Messengers and Group Leaders, AFL-CIO, National Association of Special Delivery Messengers, AFL-CIO, National Federation of Post Office Motor Vehicle Employees, AFL-CIO, National Rural Letter Carriers' Association, United Federation of Postal Clerks, AFL-CIO,* September 24, 1966 to October 31, 1967.

13. *Agreement between University of Delaware and the American Federation of State, County, and Municipal Employees, AFL-CIO, Local 439,* October 17, 1966.

14. American Association of School Administrators. *School Administrators View Professional Negotiation.* Washington, D. C., 1966.

15. American Bar Association. *Section of Labor Relations Law, 1963 Proceedings.* Part II. American Bar Center, Chicago: 1964.

16. American Bar Association. *Section of Labor Relations Law, Program of the 1966 Annual Meeting, Montreal, Canada. 1966 Committee Reports.* American Bar Center, Chicago: 1966.

17. American Civil Liberties Union. *Policy Statement on Civil Rights in Government Employment.* New York City, April 13, 1959.

18. American Federation of Teachers. *Questions and Answers about the American Federation of Teachers.* Chicago.

19. American Federation of Teachers. *Statement on the policies of the college locals.* Pamphlet. Distributed in California.

20. *American Teacher,* January, 1966.

21. *American Teacher,* Teachers' Mailbox, January, 1966.

22. *American Teacher,* March, 1966.

23. *American Teacher,* May, 1966.

24. *American Teacher,* June, 1966.

25. *American Teacher,* September, 1966

26. *American Teacher,* October, 1966.

27. *American Teacher,* December, 1966.

28. *American Teacher*, September, 1967.

29. *American Teacher*, October, 1967.

30. *An Act Establishing A Municipal Employee Relations Act*, Public Act. No. 159, General Statutes, State of Connecticut.

31. *An Act Providing for the Election of Representative Bargaining Agents with Political Subdivisions of the Commonwealth*, The Commonwealth of Massachusetts, Acts, 1965, Chap. 763.

32. *An Act Recognizing the Right of Public Employees to Organize*, Chapter 126, Volume 55, Laws of Delaware. Approved by the Governor, June 15, 1965.

33. *An Act To Establish A Merit System Of Personnel Administration for the Employees Of The State*, Chapter 443, Volume 55, Laws of Delaware. Approved by the Governor, July 1, 1966.

34. Anderson, Arvid, "Legal Aspects of Collective Bargaining," in Warner, Kenneth O. (ed.), *Developments in Public Employee Relations: Legislative, Judicial, Administrative. Chicago:* Public Personnel Association, 1965.

35. Anderson, Arvid, "The American City and Its Public Employee Unions," in Somers, Gerald G. (ed.), *Collective Bargaining in the Public Service, Proceedings of the 1966 Annual Spring Meeting, Industrial Relations Research Association*, Milwaukee, Wis. May 6-7, 1966.

36. Anderson, Arvid, "The U. S. Experience in Collective Bargaining in Public Employment," in Warner, Kenneth O. (ed.), *Collective Bargaining in the Public Service: Theory and Practice.* Chicago: Public Personnel Association, 1967.

37. Anderson, Arvid, "Wisconsin Employment Relations Board," in Ocheltree, Keith (ed.), *Government Labor Relations in Transition.* Chicago: Public Personnel Association, Personnel Report No. 662, 1966.

38. *An Ordinance to authorize the Mayor to enter into an Agreement with District Council 33, American Federation of State, County, and Municipal Employees, AFL-CIO, Philadelphia and Vicinity, regarding its representation of certain City employees*, approved April 4, 1961.

39. *Articles of Agreement Between the Tennessee Valley Authority and the Salary Policy Employee Panel*, negotiated December 5, 1950, Revised and Reaffirmed May 7, 1964, and *Supplementary Agreements* (As of May 7, 1964).

40. Association of California State College Professors. *A Report on Conditions in the California State Colleges.* Prepared for Presentation to the Board of Trustees, July 20, 1966.

41. Association of California State College Professors, *The Voice of the Faculties*, April, 1966.

42. Association of California State College Professors, *The Voice of the Faculties*, February, 1967.

43. Bauer, Malcolm, "Northwest teachers push for raises and benefits," *Christian Science Monitor*, March 17, 1966.

44. Belasco, James A., "Resolving Dispute over Contract Terms in the State Public Service: An Analysis." Reprint Series No. 180. New York State School of Industrial and Labor Relations, Cornell University, Ithaca, N. Y. Reprinted from *Labor Law Journal*, September, 1965.

45. Bernstein, Harry, "Teachers Try Militancy in Pleas for More Money," *Los Angeles Times*, June 15, 1967.

46. Berthoud, Paul M., "Techniques of Negotiation," in Warner, Kenneth O. (ed.), *Developments in Public Employee Relations: Legislative, Judicial, Administrative*. Chicago: Public Personnel Association, 1965.

47. Bolduc, Roch, "The Framework for Collective Bargaining in the Public Service," in Warner, Kenneth O. (ed.), *Collective Bargaining in the Public Service: Theory and Practice*. Chicago: Public Personnel Association, 1967.

48. Brooks, Thomas R., "Lindsay, Quill, & the Transit Strike," *Commentary*, March, 1966.

49. Brooks, Thomas R., "The Caseworker and the Client," *New York Times Sunday Magazine*, January 29, 1967.

50. Buder, Leonard, "A Warning to Strikers," education section, *New York Times*, April 3, 1966.

51. Carr, William G. *The Turning Point*. Reprint of address at annual convention of the NEA, July 2, 1962. National Education Association, Washington, D. C.

52. Carr, William G. *The Year of Decision*. Address by Executive Secretary of the National Education Association at its annual convention, Seattle, June, 1964. Mimeographed.

53. Carson, John J., "Collective Bargaining in Private Industry: The Lessons for Public Administration," in Warner, Kenneth O. (ed.), *Collective Bargaining in the Public Service: Theory and Practice*. Chicago: Public Personnel Association, 1967.

54. Causey, Mike, "The Federal Diary," *Washington Post*, May 2, 1966.

55. Causey, Mike, "The Federal Diary," *Washington Post*, August 15, 1966.

56. Causey, Mike, "The Federal Diary," *Washington Post*, September 5, 1966.

57. Causey, Mike, "The Federal Diary," *Washington Post*, November 8, 1966.

58. *Christian Science Monitor*, September 15, 1965.

59. *Christian Science Monitor*, January 26, 1966 and *New York Times*, February 4, 1966.

60. *Christian Science Monitor*, February 14, 1966, map on p. 10.

61. *Christian Science Monitor*, July 21, 1966.

62. *Christian Science Monitor*, January 28, 1967.

63. *Christian Science Monitor*, March 31, 1967.

64. *Christian Science Monitor*, editorial, April 18, 1967.

65. *Christian Science Monitor*, editorial, April 24, 1967.

66. *Christian Science Monitor*, September 28, 1967.

67. Cincinnati, *A Resolution Declaring a City Wage Policy, and repealing resolution, passed August 5, 1959, entitled "Declaring a City Wage Policy."* Passed April 6, 1960.

68. *Cincinnati, City Manager's Policy with Respect to Unions*. Mimeographed.

69. Civil Service Assembly, Committee on Employee Relations in the Public Service, Gordon R. Clapp, Chairman. *Employee Relations in the Public Service.* Chicago: Civil Service Assembly of the U. S. and Canada, 1942.

70. Civil Service Commission of Canada. *Personnel Administration In The Public Service, A Review Of Civil Service Legislation.* Ottawa: Queen's Printer, 1959.

71. Cogen, Charles, "Greater Status for Teachers, Collective Bargaining: The AFT Way," address at Rhode Island State College Conference on Collective Negotiations, July 8, 1965. Mimeographed.

72. Cohen, Jerry, "Angry Young Teachers Lead Battle for Reforms in Oklahoma Schools," *Los Angeles Times,* May 31, 1965.

73. *Collective Agreement between the Administrator, Bonneville Power Administration and Columbia Power Trades Council,* negotiated May 2, 1945, Revised June 19, 1964.

74. *Comment on the Strike of the New York City Teachers, April 11, 1962.* Pamphlet reproducing samples of "Editorial Opinion and Analysis by U. S. Newspapers and Broadcasting Stations." Washington, D. C.: National Education Association.

75. Committee for Economic Development. *The Public Interest in National Labor Policy.* New York: 1961.

76. *Congressional Record,* January 26, 1967. Statement by Senator Muskie of Maine in introducing The Intergovernmental Personnel Act of 1967.

77. Connecticut State Board of Labor Relations. *Twenty-First Annual Report.* Hartford, Connecticut, 1966.

78. Coppock, Robert W., "Union Agreements in Local Government in the United States," in Ocheltree, Keith (ed.), *Government Labor Relations in Transition.* Chicago: Public Personnel Association, Personnel Report No. 662, 1966.

79. Cornell, Herbert W., *Legal Aspects of Collective Bargaining by Public Employees.* Mimeographed.

80. Council of the City of Philadelphia, *Bill No. 656, An Ordinance, To authorize the Mayor to enter into an Agreement with District Council 33, American Federation of State, County, and Municipal Employees, AFL-CIO, Philadelphia and Vicinity, regarding its representation of certain City employees.*

81. Crichton, Edward E., "Arbitration Practices in the Australian Public Service," *Public Personnel Review,* April, 1965.

82. Cullen, Donald E., *Negotiating Labor-Management Contracts.* Pamphlet. Ithaca: New York State School of Industrial and Labor Relations, Cornell University, Bulletin 56, September, 1965.

83. Delaware State Chamber of Commerce, Research and Legislative Department. *Unionism vs. Professionalism in Public Education.* Research Report No. 2, May 11, 1966.

84. Denmark, George W., "Schools Are Not Factories," *NEA Journal,* March, 1964.

85. Dewey, John, "Why Teachers Need A Union." Brochure reprint of address which appeared in January, 1928 issue of the *American Teacher.* American Federation of Teachers, Chicago, Illinois.

86. Dominion Bureau of Statistics, Governments Division. *Federal Government Employment, December 1966.* Ottawa: Queen's Printer, August, 1967.

87. Donovan, Bernard E., "Management-Employee Relations in Transition: The Public School Experience." Talk at 1964 annual convention of Public Personnel Association, Los Angeles, California, October 5, 1964. Mimeographed.

88. Dymond, W. R., "The Role of the Union in the Public Service as Opposed to Its Role in Private Business," in Hodgetts, J. E. and Corbett, D. C. (eds.), *Canadian Public Administration, a Book of Readings.* Toronto: The Macmillan Company of Canada, Ltd., 1960.

89. "Employee Organizations in Government," *Good Government,* November, 1960.

90. *Employee Relations Ordinance of the County of Los Angeles.* Ordinance No. 9646, adopted September 3, 1968, effective October 4, 1968.

91. *Federal Employee Labor-Management Act of 1966,* 90th Congress, 1st Session, S. 341.

92. *Federal Employee-Management Cooperation Act of 1965,* 89th Congress, 1st Session, H. R. 6883.

93. *Federal Times,* March 29, 1967.

94. *Federal Times,* May 31, 1967.

95. *Federal Times,* October 4, 1967.

96. *Federal Times,* October 11, 1967.

97. Finkelman, Jacob, "When Bargaining Fails," in Warner, Kenneth O. (ed.), *Collective Bargaining in the Public Service: Theory and Practice.* Chicago: Public Personnel Association, 1967.

98. Frankel, Saul. *A Model for Negotiation and Arbitration Between the Canadian Government and Its Civil Servants.* Montreal: Industrial Relations Centre, McGill University, 1962.

99. Frankel, Saul, "Employer-Employee Relations in the Public Service," *Public Personnel Review.* October, 1964.

100. Gallagher, Donald, "The Legal Aspects of Collective Bargaining for California Public Employees." Sacramento, Cal.: California State Employees' Association, November, 1959. Mimeographed.

101. Garman, Phillips L., Comments on Nigro Manuscript, *Management-Employee Relations in the Public Service.*

102. *General Agreement between the Tennessee Valley Authority and the Tennessee Valley Trades and Labor Council,* negotiated August 6, 1940, Revised July 1, 1951, And Supplementary Schedules (Revised through February 26, 1967) Covering Annual Employment.

103. Goff, Tom, "Public Strike Answers Sought," *Los Angeles Times,* editorial section, October 10, 1966.

104. Goldberg, Arthur J., Address to the Seminar on Collective Bargaining of the Federal Mediation and Conciliation Service, Washington, D. C., January 9, 1967. Unpublished. Also see *New York Times,* January 10, 1967.

105. *Government Employee Relations Report,* The Bureau of National Affairs, Inc., Washington, D. C., May 23, 1966.

106. Governor's Advisory Commission on Labor-Management Policy for Public Employees, *Report and Recommendations.* Springfield, Ill.: March, 1967.

107. Governor's Committee on Public Employee Relations, State of New York. *Final Report.* March 31, 1966. Mimeographed.

108. Grant, Gerald, "Fight Likely Between Rival Teacher Groups Here," *Washington Post,* December 16, 1965.

109. Hamilton, Alexander, Madison, James, and Jay, John. *The Federalist.* New York: Modern Library edition, 1937.

110. Hart, Wilson R. *Collective Bargaining in the Federal Civil Service.* New York: Harper and Row, 1961.

111. Herman, Edward E., "Collective Bargaining by Civil Servants in Canada," in Somers, Gerald G. (ed.), *Collective Bargaining in the Public Service, Proceedings of the 1966 Annual Spring Meeting, Industrial Relations Research Association,* Milwaukee, Wis., May 6-7, 1966.

112. Holland, Ann. *Unions Are Here to Stay, A Guide for Employee-Management Relations in the Federal Service.* Washington, D. C.: Society for Personnel Administration, 1962.

113. House Bill No. 72, *An Act To Amend Title 14, Delaware Code, Relating to Education By Providing for Negotiations Between Boards of Education And Organizations of Public School Employees.* Introduced April 6, 1967.

114. Howlett, Robert G., "Problems of a State Public Employment Relations Law in Practice." Unpublished address at a conference on Public Employment and Collective Bargaining, University of Chicago, March, 1966.

115. Hutchison, Bruce, "New Deal for Canada's Civil Service," *Christian Science Monitor,* May 23, 1966.

116. Illinois Legislative Council. *Public Employee Labor Relations,* Publication 132. Springfield, Ill.: November, 1958.

117. Intergovernmental Personnel Act of 1967, 90th Congress, First Session. *Congressional Record,* January 26, 1967.

118. International City Managers' Association. *Management Information Service Report No. 257.* Washington, D. C.: June, 1965.

119. International Labour Office. *Collective Bargaining, A Workers' Education Manual.* Geneva: 1960.

120. Johnson, David B., "Fact-Finding," in *Municipal Employe-Management Relations, Proceedings of an Institute held August 10, 1964.* League of Wisconsin Municipalities, Madison, Wis., September, 1964.

121. Klaus, Ida, "Collective Bargaining in Public Employment: A Look Ahead." *Government Employee Relations Report,* March 28, 1966.

122. Klaus, Ida. *Report on a Program of Labor Relations for New York City Employees.* Department of Labor of the City of New York, June, 1957.

123. Klaus, Ida, "The Emerging Relationship," address before Conference on Public Employment and Collective Bargaining, at University of Chicago, February 5, 1965. Unpublished.

124. Kluttz, Jerry, "Federal Diary," *Washington Post,* August 9, 1966.

125. Kluttz, Jerry, "Federal Diary," *Washington Post*, August 13, 1966.

126. Kluttz, Jerry, "Federal Diary," *Washington Post*, August 17, 1966.

127. Kluttz, Jerry, "Federal Diary," *Washington Post*, August 22, 1966.

128. Kluttz, Jerry, "Federal Diary," *Washington Post*, October 11, 1966. and February 28, 1967.

129. Krause, Robert D., "The Short, Troubled History of Wisconsin's New Labor Law," *Public Administration Review*, December, 1965.

130. Krislov, Joseph and Schmulowitz, Jacob, "Grievance Arbitration in State and Local Government Units," *Arbitration Journal*, November 3, 1963.

131. Labor Management Institute of the American Arbitration Association. *Report to Mayor Lindsay*, March 31, 1966. Mimeographed.

132. *Labor Management Relations Act, 1947, as Amended by Public Law 86-257, 1959*. Public Law 101-80th Congress. Washington, D. C.: Government Printing Office.

133. League of Wisconsin Municipalities. *Statement at Hearing Held by Professor Nathan Feinsinger*, February 10, 1967, Madison, Wis.

134. Leich, Harold H., "Where We Stand On Union-Management Relations In The Federal Service," March 21, 1961. Unpublished talk.

135. Leonard, William, "The Rights and Powers of a Civil Service Association," in Hodgetts, J. E. and Corbett, D. C. (eds.), *Canadian Public Administration, a Book of Readings*. Toronto: The Macmillan Company of Canada Ltd., 1960.

136. Letter from Arvid Anderson to Felix A. Nigro, February 4, 1966.

137. Letter from Robert C. Garnier, Personnel Director, City of Milwaukee, to Felix A. Nigro, March 28, 1967.

138. Letter from Seymour S. Berlin, Director of Bureau of Inspections, U.S. Civil Service Commission, to Felix A. Nigro, October 10, 1966.

139. Letter from S. T. Ford, Assistant Director, Oregon State Civil Service Commission, to Felix A. Nigro, May 31, 1966.

140. Letter from Thomas C. Enright, Executive Secretary, Oregon State Employees' Association, to Felix A. Nigro, February 8, 1967.

141. Ligtenberg, John, "Legal Opinion on Collective Bargaining." Reprinted by the American Federation of Teachers from *Chicago Union Teacher*, September, 1963.

142. Ligtenberg, John and Andree, Robert G. *Collective Bargaining in the Public Schools, A Handbook of Information and Source Materials on Teacher Rights and Teacher Obligations*. Chicago: American Federation of Teachers Educational Foundation, Inc., 1966.

143. Little, S. A., "Union or Association Objectives: A Labor Viewpoint," in Warner, Kenneth O. (ed.), *Collective Bargaining in the Public Service: Theory and Practice*. Chicago: Public Personnel Association, 1967.

144. *Local Law No. 53-1967*, contained in the City Record, 2213 Municipal Building, New York, N. Y. 10007.

145. Los Angeles County Citizens Economy and Efficiency Committee, *Re-*

May 20, 1966.

editorial, May 25, 1966.

May 29, 1966.

May 30, 1966.

June 3, 1966.

June 10, 1966.

June 14, 1966.

June 19, 1966.

June 19, 24, 25, 1966.

August 13, 1966.

August 22, 24, 28, and September 3, 1966; *Washing-*
1, 1966 (also editorial of same date).

August 23, 1966.

August 23, 24, 28, and September 3, 1966.

August 31, October 29, and October 30, 1966.

September 3, 1966.

September 7 and 13; *Washington Post*, September 7,

itorial, September 9, 1966.

eptember 22, 1966.

eptember 25, 1966.

ctober 11, 1966.

litorial, October 15, 1966.

ctober 16, 1966.

ctober 23, 1966.

ctober 25 and 26, 1966.

ctober 29 and 30, 1966.

tober 31, 1966.

vember 4 and 5, 1966.

itorial, November 6, 1966.

vember 15, 1966.

vember 15 and 21, 1966.

vember 15 and 27, 1966.

torial, November 17, 1966.

vember 18, 1966.

vember 22 and 24, and *Christian Science Monitor*

vember 24, 1966.

torial, December 1, 1966.

ember 3 and 4, 1966.

port on *Civil Service Operations*, May 24, 1966, and on *County Personnel Organization and Administration*, July 26, 1966.

146. *Los Angeles Times*, June 17, 18, 20, 23, and July 5, 1966.

147. *Los Angeles Times*, June 20, 1966.

148. *Los Angeles Times*, editorial, June 23, 1966.

149. *Los Angeles Times*, June 25, 1966.

150. *Los Angeles Times*, editorial, June 29, 1966.

151. *Los Angeles Times*, editorial, July 5, 1966.

152. *Los Angeles Times*, July 10, 1966 and *New York Times*, September 3, 1966.

153. *Los Angeles Times*, July 12, 14, 15, and 28, 1966.

154. Love, J. Douglas, "Proposals for Collective Bargaining in the Public Service of Canada: A Further Commentary," in Somers, Gerald G. (ed.), *Collective Bargaining in the Public Service*, Proceedings of the 1966 Annual Spring Meeting, Industrial Relations Research Association, Milwaukee, Wis., May 6-7, 1966.

155. MacNeill, Robertson G., "Personnel Panorama—1963, Canadian Federal Developments in Employer-Employee Relationships," *Public Personnel Review*, January, 1964.

156. Macy, John W., Jr., "A Long-Standing Partnership in Progress," address before National Convention of National Federation of Federal Employees, Miami Beach, Fla., September 13, 1966.

157. Macy, John W., Jr., "Employee-Management Cooperation in the Federal Service," in Somers, Gerald G. (ed.), *Collective Bargaining in the Public Service*, Proceedings of the 1966 Annual Spring Meeting of the Industrial Relations Research Association, Milwaukee, Wis., May 6-7, 1966.

158. Macy, John W., Jr., "Employee-Management Relations in the Federal Service," address at the Federal Mediation and Conciliation Service Seminar, Washington, D. C., January 10, 1967.

159. Male, Raymond F., "Labor Crises and the Role of Management," in Warner, Kenneth O. (ed.), *Developments in Public Employee Relations: Legislative, Judicial, Administrative*. Chicago: Public Personnel Association, 1965.

160. Massey, John E., "Labor-Management Cooperation in TVA," *Public Personnel Review*, July, 1965.

161. Messaros, Henry W., "The Federal Notebook," *Philadelphia Sunday Bulletin*, December 19, 1965.

162. Messaros, Henry W., "The Federal Notebook," *Philadelphia Sunday Bulletin*, January 9, 1966.

163. Messaros, Henry W., "The Federal Notebook," *Philadelphia Sunday Bulletin*, January 30, 1966.

164. Messaros, Henry W., "The Federal Notebook," *Philadelphia Sunday Bulletin*, May 29, 1966.

165. Minnesota Statutes, Chapter 839-S.F. No. 1235(1965). An Act . . . amending Minnesota Statutes 1961, Sections 179.52 and 179.57; amending Minnesota Statutes 1961, Chapter 179, by adding sections thereto.

166. Morris, Frank, "Teachers and the Yellow-Dog Rule: The Seattle Story," *Changing Education*, Summer, 1966.

167. Morse, Muriel M., "Shall We Bargain Away the Merit System?", *Public Personnel Review*, October, 1963.

168. Moskow, Michael H., "Teacher Organizations: an analysis of the issues," *TC Record*, February, 1965.

169. National Education Association, Educational Policies Commission. *The Public Interest in How Teachers Organize*. Washington, D. C., 1964.

170. National Education Association, Office of Professional Development and Welfare. *Guidelines for Professional Negotiation*. Revised edition. Washington, D. C.: 1965.

171. New Castle County, Delaware, *Ordinance No. 67*, approved January 30, 1967.

172. Newland, Chester A., Comments on Nigro manuscript, *Management-Employee Relations in the Public Service*.

173. Newland, Chester A., "Trends in Public Employee Unionization," *Journal of Politics*, August, 1964.

174. *Newsweek*, September 29, 1966.

175. *New Yorker*, "Talk of the Town," January 22, 1966.

176. New York State Joint Legislative Committee on Industrial and Labor Relations. *Report, 1960-1961*, Legislative Document (1961) No. 17. Albany, N. Y.: 1961.

177. New York State Joint Legislative Committee on Industrial and Labor Relations. *Report, 1962-1963*, Legislative Document (1963) No. 38. Albany, N. Y.: 1963.

178. New York State Joint Legislative Committee on Industrial and Labor Conditions. *Report, 1963-1964*, Legislative Document (1964) No. 17. Albany, N. Y.: 1964.

179. *New York Times*, August 11, 1965.

180. *New York Times*, August 24, 1965.

181. *New York Times*, November 19, 1965.

182. *New York Times*, December 6, 1965.

183. *New York Times*, December 7, 1965.

184. *New York Times*, editorial, December 23, 1965.

185. *New York Times*, December 28, 1965.

186. *New York Times*, December 29, 1965.

187. *New York Times*, December 30, 1965.

188. *New York Times*, December 30, 1965; April 19, June 6, August 3, October 25, 1966; and September 13, 1967.

189. *New York Times*, December 31, 1965.

190. *New York Times*, January 1, 1966.

191. *New York Times*, January 2, 1966.

192. *New York Times*, January 3, 1966.

193. *New York Times*, January 4, 1966.

194. *New York*
195. *New York*
196. *New York*
197. *New York*
198. *New York*
199. *New York*
200. *New York*
201. *New York*
202. *New York*
203. *New York*
204. *New York*
205. *New York*
206. *New York*
207. *New York*
208. *New York*
209. *New York*
210. *New York*
211. *New York*
212. *New York*
213. *New York*
214. *New York*
215. *New York*
216. *New York*
217. *New York*
218. *New York*
219. *New York*
220. *New York*
221. *New York*
222. *New York*
223. *New York*
224. *New York*
225. *New York*
226. *New York*
227. *New York*
228. *New York*
229. *New York*
230. *New York*
231. *New York*

232. *New York Times,*
233. *New York Times,*
234. *New York Times,*
235. *New York Times,*
236. *New York Times,*
237. *New York Times,*
238. *New York Times,*
239. *New York Times,*
240. *New York Times,*
241. *New York Times,*
242. *New York Times,* ton Post, August 3
243. *New York Times,*
244. *New York Times,*
245. *New York Times,*
246. *New York Times,*
247. *New York Times,* 1966.
248. *New York Times,* e
249. *New York Times,*
250. *New York Times,*
251. *New York Times,* O
252. *New York Times,* e
253. *New York Times,* O
254. *New York Times,* O
255. *New York Times,* O
256. *New York Times,* O
257. *New York Times,* O
258. *New York Times,* N
259. *New York Times,* e
260. *New York Times,* N
261. *New York Times,* N
262. *New York Times,* N
263. *New York Times,* e
264. *New York Times,* N
265. *New York Times,* N November 29, 1966.
266. *New York Times,* N
267. *New York Times,* e
268. *New York Times,* D

269. *New York Times*, December 4, 1966.

270. *New York Times*, December 10, 1966.

271. *New York Times*, December 12, 1966.

272. *New York Times*, December 29, 1966.

273. *New York Times*, December 30 and 31, 1966.

274. *New York Times*, January 3, 1967.

275. *New York Times*, January 6, 1967.

276. *New York Times*, January 9, 11, and 12, 1967.

277. *New York Times*, January 10, 1967.

278. *New York Times*, January 11, 1967.

279. *New York Times*, January 17, 1967.

280. *New York Times*, February 12, 1967.

281. *New York Times*, February 28, 1967.

282. *New York Times*, editorial, March 3, 1967.

283. *New York Times*, March 16, 1967.

284. *New York Times*, March 17, 1967.

285. *New York Times*, editorial, March 20, 1967.

286. *New York Times*, April 2, 1967.

287. *New York Times*, April 3, 1967.

288. *New York Times*, April 28, 1967.

289. *New York Times*, May 3, 1967.

290. *New York Times*, May 10, 1967.

291. *New York Times*, May 24, 1967.

292. *New York Times*, July 8, 1967.

293. *New York Times*, September 10 through 21, 1967.

294. *New York Times*, September 25, 1967.

295. *New York Times*, October 5, 1967.

296. Noble, George W., "Labour Relations in Canadian Municipalities," *Public Personnel Review*, October, 1961.

297. Northrup, Herbert R. and Bloom, Gordon F. *Government and Labor.* Homewood, Ill.: Richard D. Irwin, Inc., 1963.

298. Office of the Mayor. *Executive Order No. 38, Duties, Responsibilities and Authority of the Director of Labor Relations.* February 7, 1967.

299. Oregon Laws 1963, Chapter 579.

300. Oregon Laws 1965, Chapter 543.

301. Oregon State Civil Service Commission. Rules, Division 9, Subdivision 8, Employee Representation, 98-200.

302. Oregon State Tax Commission. Memorandum to all Section Supervisors from C. H. Mack, Chairman, May 18, 1966.

303. Perlman, L. David, "The Government Worker Goes Union," AFL-CIO

Pamphlet Division. Reprinted from *AFL-CIO American Federationist*, March, 1964.

304. Perlmutter, Emanuel, "Pessimism on Transit, Economic and Political Factors Point to the Inability to Avert a Showdown," *New York Times*, December 31, 1965.

305. Perry, Charles A. and Wildman, Wesley A., "A Survey of Collective Activity among Public School Teachers," *Educational Administration Quarterly*, Spring, 1966.

306. "Personnel Opinions," *Public Personnel Review*, January, 1966.

307. "Personnel Panorama," *Personnel News*, Public Personnel Association, February, 1966.

308. Plunkett, T. J., "Rethinking Management Relations in the Public Service," in Warner, Kenneth O. (ed.), *Collective Bargaining in the Public Service: Theory and Practice*. Chicago: Public Personnel Association, 1967.

309. Plunkett, T. J., "The Seminar in Retrospect," in Warner, Kenneth O. (ed.), *Collective Bargaining in the Public Service: Theory and Practice*. Chicago: Public Personnel Association, 1967.

310. Porter, Robert G., "Collective Bargaining for Teachers." Brochure, American Federation of Teachers.

311. Posey, Rollin B., comments on Nigro manuscript, *Management-Employee Relations in the Public Service*.

312. Posey, Rollin B., "How to Negotiate with Labor Unions," in Warner, Kenneth O. (ed.), *Management Relations with Organized Public Employees*. Chicago: Public Personnel Association, 1963.

313. Powell, Norman J. *Personnel Administration in Government*. Englewood Cliffs, N. J.: Prentice-Hall, Inc., 1956.

314. Pragan Otto, "Panel Discussion: Is Private Sector Industrial Relations the Objective in the Federal Service?", in Somers, Gerald G. (ed.), *Collective Bargaining in the Public Service, Proceedings of the 1966 Annual Spring Meeting, Industrial Relations Research Association,* Milwaukee, Wis., May 6-7, 1966.

315. President's Task Force on Employee-Management Relations in the Federal Service. *A Policy for Employee-Management Cooperation in the Federal Service, November 30, 1961*. Washington, D. C.: Government Printing Office, 1961.

316. Prives, M. Z. *Unionism And The Merit System in Municipal Relations in Canada*. Montreal: Canadian Federation of Mayors and Municipalities, September, 1958.

317. *Public Employees' Fair Employment Act*, Chapter 392 of the Laws of 1967 of the State of New York.

318. Pyle, Donald G., "Negotiating The Collective Agreement," in Warner, Kenneth O. (ed.), *Collective Bargaining in the Public Service: Theory and Practice*. Chicago: Public Personnel Association, 1967.

319. Rapoport, Roger, "Militant Public Employees," *Wall Street Journal*, August 9, 1966.

320. Raskin, A. H., "Search for That Elusive No-Strike Law," *New York Times*, editorial page, Jan. 31, 1966.

321. Raskin, A. H., "Wanted: A Substitute for Condon-Wadlin," *New York Times*, April 17, 1966.

322. Rehmus, Charles M., "Panel Discussion: Is Private Sector Industrial Relations the Objective in the Federal Service?", in Somers, Gerald G. (ed.), *Collective Bargaining in the Public Service, Proceedings of the 1966 Annual Spring Meeting, Industrial Relations Research Association*, Milwaukee, Wis., May 6-7, 1966.

323. *Report of the Interim Commission to Study Collective Bargaining by Municipalities*, State of Connecticut, As Provided by Public Act No. 495 of the 1963 Session of the General Assembly. February, 1965.

324. *Report of the Preparatory Committee on Collective Bargaining in the Public Service.* Ottawa: Queen's Printer, July, 1965.

325. Reston, James, "Government Workers Affecting Union Goals," *Philadelphia Sunday Bulletin*, September 4, 1966.

326. Ripley, Josephine, "Teacher militancy backed," *Christian Science Monitor*, September 11, 1967.

327. Rodger, L. D., "The Role of the Departmental Personnel Officer," in Hodgetts, J. E. and Corbett, D. C. (eds.), *Canadian Public Administration, a Book of Readings*. Toronto: The Macmillan Company of Canada, Ltd., 1960.

328. Roser, Foster B., "Role of Staff Agencies in Employee Relations," in Warner, Kenneth O. (ed.), *Developments in Public Employee Relations: Legislative, Judicial, Administrative*. Chicago: Public Personnel Association, 1965.

329. Salik, Richard L. *A Digest of Provincial Labor Laws Governing Municipal and Provincial Employees in Canada*. Chicago: Public Personnel Association, Personnel Report No. 664, 1966.

330. Scarrow, Howard A., "Employer-Employee Relationships in the Civil Services of the Canadian Provinces," in Hodgetts, J. E. and Corbett, D. C. (eds.), *Canadian Public Administration, a Book of Readings*. Toronto: The Macmillan Company of Canada, Ltd., 1960.

331. Schanberg, Sidney H., "A Substitute for Condon-Wadlin—If It Works," *New York Times*, editorial section, April 9, 1967.

332. Schnaufer, Pete, "Collective Bargaining Contracts, From the Houses of AFT & NEA," *American Teacher*, March, 1967. Special section.

333. Schneider, B. V. H., "The British Post Office Strike of 1964," in Ocheltree, Keith (ed.), *Government Labor Relations in Transition*. Chicago: Public Personnel Association, Personnel Report No. 662, 1966.

334. Senate Factfinding Committee on Governmental Administration. *Compulsory Membership in Professional Organizations Among Credentialed California School Employees*. Sacramento, Cal.: Senate of the State of California, 1965.

335. Senate Factfinding Committee on Governmental Administration. *"Let Us Teach," Final Report on "An Analysis of the Helpfulness of Certain Aspects of the School Program to Classroom Teaching."* Sacramento, Cal.: Senate of the State of California, 1965.

336. Sharpe, Carleton F. and Freedman, Elisha C., "Collective Bargaining in Hartford, Connecticut," in Warner, Kenneth O. (ed.), *Management*

*Relations with Organized Public Employees.* Chicago: Public Personnel Association, 1963.

337. Simons, Jesse, "The American City and Its Public Employee Unions," in Somers, Gerald G. (ed.), *Collective Bargaining in the Public Service, Proceedings of the 1966 Annual Spring Meeting, Industrial Relations Research Association,* Milwaukee, Wis., May 6-7, 1966.

338. Sitomer, Curtis J., "State-employee lobby sways California," *Christian Science Monitor,* September 15, 1966.

339. Smythe, Cyrus F., "Collective Bargaining Under Executive Order #10988—Trends and Prospects," *Public Personnel Review,* October, 1965.

340. Society for Personnel Administration, *1965 Annual Conference Summary,* Washington, D. C., June 3-4, 1965.

341. Society for Personnel Administration. *1966 Annual Conference Proceedings,* Washington, D. C., May 26-27, 1966.

342. Spero, Sterling D., "Collective Bargaining in Public Employment: Form and Scope," *Public Administration Review,* Winter, 1962.

343. State of Maine, *Fire Fighters Arbitration Law,* Chapter 10, Title 26 of Revised Statutes.

344. State of Michigan, Labor Mediation Board, *Michigan Labor Mediation Act and Public Employment Relations Act.* Pamphlet. Lansing, Mich.

345. State of Wisconsin, *Assembly Bill 814,* Chapter 612, Laws of 1965, effective January 1, 1967.

346. State of Wisconsin, Office of Attorney General, Letter to the Assembly, dated July 12, 1965, Madison, Wis.

347. Stern, James L., "The Wisconsin Public Employee Fact-Finding Procedure," Reprint series No. 79, Industrial Relations Research Institute, University of Wisconsin. Reprinted from *Industrial and Labor Relations Review,* Vol. 20, No. 1 (October, 1966).

348. Stinnett, T. M., Kleinmann, Jack H., and Ware, Martha L. *Professional Negotiation in Public Education.* New York: Macmillan Company, 1966.

349. Tacoma, Washington, *Resolution No. 18848,* August 23, 1966.

350. The House of Commons of Canada. *Bill C-170, An Act respecting employer and employee relations in the Public Service of Canada.* As Passed By The House of Commons, 20th February 1967. Ottawa: Queen's Printer, 1967.

351. The House of Commons of Canada. *Bill C-181, An Act respecting employment in the Public Service of Canada.* As Passed By The House of Commons, 20th February 1967. Ottawa: Queen's Printer, 1967.

352. The House of Commons of Canada. *Bill C-182, An Act to amend the Financial Administration Act.* As Passed By The House of Commons, 20th February 1967. Ottawa: Queen's Printer, 1967.

353. *The Ontario Public Service Act and Regulations, Amended to February, 1965.* Section 9a through 9f.

354. *The Public Employee,* April, 1966.

355. *The Public Employee,* May, 1966.

356. *The Public Employee,* August, 1966.

357. *The Public Employee,* September, 1966.

358. *The Public Employee,* October, 1966.

359. *The Public Employee,* November, 1966.

360. *The Public Employee,* December, 1966.

361. *The Public Employee,* March, 1967.

362. *The Shield,* December 3, 1966.

363. Thompson, Peter M., "Negotiating with Unions: The Canadian Experience," *Public Personnel Review,* October, 1962.

364. Tolchin, Martin, "The Nurses' Gains," *New York Times,* May 28, 1966.

365. Townsend, Ed, "Mediators try to weld rail gap," *Christian Science Monitor,* April 15, 1966.

366. Townsend, Ed, "New York pushes negotiations," *Christian Science Monitor,* January 11, 1966.

367. Townsend, Ed, "N. Y. strike: guarded optimism," *Christian Science Monitor,* January 8, 1966.

368. Townsend, Ed, "N. Y. strike legislation asked," *Christian Science Monitor,* January 10, 1966.

369. Townsend, Ed, "Quill dangles on limb," *Christian Science Monitor,* January 5, 1966.

370. Townsend, Ed, "Strike aftermath forecast," *Christian Science Monitor,* January 15, 1966.

371. Townsend, Ed, "Unions tackle changing work force," *Christian Science Monitor,* September 2, 1966.

372. Townsend, Ed, "Unions top 19 million members," *Christian Science Monitor,* September 9, 1967.

373. Townsend, Ed, "Welfare strike assessed," *Christian Science Monitor,* February 4, 1965.

374. Trombley, William, "California Professors Divided Over Unionism," *Los Angeles Times,* June 6, 1966.

375. *Union Agreement between District Council 33, A.F.S.C.M.E., AFL-CIO and Personnel Director, City of Philadelphia.*

376. U. S. Civil Service Commission, Analysis and Development Division, Bureau of Inspections. *Employee-Management Cooperation in the Federal Service, A Review of Findings from Inquiries at 558 Federal Establishments,* October 16, 1963-October 31, 1964. November, 1964.

377. U. S. Civil Service Commission. *Civil Service News,* November 21, 1966.

378. U. S. Civil Service Commission, Bureau of Programs and Standards. *Employee-Management Cooperation in the Federal Service, Basic Training Materials.* Personnel Methods Series No. 15, August, 1962.

379. U. S. Civil Service Commission, Employee-Management Relations Section, Policy Development Division, Bureau of Policies and Standards. *Listing of Exclusive Recognitions and Negotiated Agreements in Federal Agencies under Executive Order 10988.* As reported to the Civil Service Commission, August, 1966.

380. U. S. Civil Service Commission. *Federal Personnel Manual.* Washington, D. C.: Government Printing Office.

381. U. S. Civil Service Commission. FPM Letter No. 711-2, *Explanation of the Provisions of the Standards of Conduct for Employee Organizations and Code of Fair Labor Practices in Employee-Management Cooperation in the Federal Service,* August 30, 1963.

382. U. S. Civil Service Commission. FPM Letter No. 711-3, *Guidance and Advice on Employee-Management Cooperation Programs and Problems,* February 7, 1966.

383. U. S. Civil Service Commission. FPM Letter No. 711-4, *Guidance and Advice on Employee-Management Cooperation Programs and Problems,* May 23, 1966.

384. U. S. Civil Service Commission. FPM Letter No. 711-5, *Guidance and Advice on Employee-Management Cooperation Programs and Problems,* August 1, 1966.

385. U. S. Civil Service Commission. FPM Letter No. 711-6, *Guidance for Agencies in Dealing with Employee Organizations Competing for Exclusive Recognition,* December 14, 1966.

386. U. S. Department of Health, Education, and Welfare. Personnel, *Instruction 711-1, Employee-Management Cooperation.*

387. U. S. Department of Labor, Bureau of Labor Statistics. BLS Report No. 247, *Work Stoppages, Government Employees 1942-61.* Washington, D. C.: 1963.

388. U. S. Department of Labor, Bureau of Labor Statistics. *Collective Bargaining Agreements in the Federal Service, Late Summer 1964.* Washington, D. C.: Government Printing Office, August, 1965.

389. U. S. Department of Labor, Bureau of Labor Statistics. *Major Collective Bargaining Agreements, Arbitration Procedures.* Bulletin No. 1425-6. Washington, D. C.: Government Printing Office, June, 1966.

390. U. S. Department of Labor, Bureau of Labor Statistics. *Major Collective Bargaining Agreements, Grievance Procedures.* Bulletin No. 1425-1. Washington, D. C.: Government Printing Office, November, 1964.

391. U. S. Department of Labor, Bureau of Labor Statistics. *Management Rights and Union-Management Cooperation.* Bulletin No. 1425-5. Washington, D. C.: Government Printing Office, April, 1966.

392. U. S. Department of Labor. *Summary of Activities of the Office of Federal Employee-Management Relations Under Executive Order 10988.* Washington, D. C.: Government Printing Office.

393. U. S. Senate Committee on Labor and Public Welfare. *Labor-Management Relations in the Bonneville Power Administration,* Report No. 192, 82nd Congress, 1st Session. Washington, D. C.: Government Printing Office, 1951.

394. Van de Water, John R., "Union-Management Relations in Public and Private Education," *The Journal of the College and University Personnel Association,* November, 1965.

395. Van Mol, Louis J., "The TVA Experience," in Warner, Kenneth O. (ed.), *Collective Bargaining in the Public Service: Theory and Practice.* Chicago: Public Personnel Association, 1967.

396. Van Riper, Paul P. *History of the United States Civil Service.* New York: Harper and Row, 1958.

397. Vosloo, Willem B. *Collective Bargaining in the United States Federal Civil Service.* Chicago: Public Personnel Association, 1966.

398. *Wall Street Journal,* November 29, 1966.

399. Ware, Martha L. *Professional Negotiation With School Boards, A Legal Analysis and Review.* School Law Series, Research Report 1965-R3. Washington, D. C.: National Education Association, March, 1965.

400. Warner, Kenneth O. and Hennessy, Mary L. *Public Management at the Bargaining Table.* Chicago: Public Personnel Association, 1967.

401. Warner, Kenneth O. and Hennessy, Mary L., "Public Management at the Bargaining Table," *Public Personnel Review,* October, 1966.

402. Warner, Kenneth O. (ed.). *Collective Bargaining in the Public Service: Theory and Practice.* Chicago: Public Personnel Association, 1967.

403. *Washington Post,* August 10, 1966.

404. *Washington Post,* editorial, September 27, 1966.

405. Washington State Personnel Board. *Merit System Rules,* Article XX.

406. Weiford, D. G., "Organizing Management for Negotiations," in *Municipal Employe-Management Relations, Proceedings of an Institute held August 10, 1964.* Madison, Wis.: League of Wisconsin Municipalities, September, 1964.

407. Weisenfeld, Allan, "Collective Bargaining by Public Employees in the U. S.," in Somers, Gerald G. (ed.), *Collective Bargaining in the Public Service, Proceedings of the 1966 Annual Spring Meeting, Industrial Relations Research Association,* Milwaukee, Wis., May 6-7, 1966.

408. Wildman, Wesley A., "Collective Action by Public School Teachers." Reprinted from *Industrial and Labor Relations Review,* October, 1964. Industrial Relations Center, the University of Chicago.

409. Wildman, Wesley A., "Representing the Teachers' Interests," in Somers, Gerald G. (ed.), *Collective Bargaining in the Public Service, Proceedings of the 1966 Annual Spring Meeting, Industrial Relations Research Association,* Madison, Wis., May 6-7, 1966.

410. *Wilmington Evening Journal,* May 27, 1966.

411. *Wilmington Evening Journal,* November 3, 1966.

412. *Wilmington Evening Journal,* November 16, 1966.

413. *Wilmington Evening Journal,* December 15, 1966.

414. *Wilmington Morning News,* editorial, September 21, 1967.

415. *Wisconsin Administrative Code,* Chap. 111.70, Sub-Chap. IV, "Right of Public Employees to Organize or Join Labor Organizations;" "Bargaining in Municipal Employment."

416. Wisconsin Employment Relations Board. *Decision No. 6200,* January 2, 1963.

417. Wisconsin Employment Relations Board. *Decision No. 6276,* March 15, 1963.

418. Wisconsin Employment Relations Board. *Decision No. 6544,* November 18, 1963.

419. *Wisconsin State Journal,* February 11, 1967.

420. Witkin, Richard, "Governor in the Wings, Key to Strike Believed to be in Albany Where Rockefeller Awaits Cue to Move," *New York Times*, January 8, 1966.

421. Young, Joseph, "Humphrey Calls on U. S. Workers to Back President's Program," *Washington Star*, December 9, 1965.

422. Zeidler, Frank P., "Rethinking the Philosophy of Employee Relations in the Public Service," in *Rethinking the Philosophy of Employee Relations in the Public Service*, Public Employee Relations Library, November 1, 1967. Chicago: Public Personnel Association, 1968.

# Index

on implementation of agreement, 34-35;

employee organization defined, 133;

bargaining unit determination, 151;

on managerial exclusions, 161-62;

on chief executive officer as negotiator, 214;

grievance procedure, 284-85

Connecticut State Board of Labor Relations, 127-28;

bargaining unit criteria, 152-53;

on professional employees in bargaining units, 155;

on supervisor participation in employee organizations, 163-64;

on showing of interest, 170

Connecticut State Board of Mediation and Arbitration, 128

Consultants, outside, as chief negotiators, 214-15

Consultation, in public education: defined, 304

Contract. *See* Agreement, collective

Conway, Jack T., on grievance procedure, 275

Councils of employee organizations, 84, 89:

in Tacoma, Washington, 203-04;

in TVA, 204, 278, 280;

in Bonneville Power Administration, 204, 280, 281;

in Dept. of Health, Education and Welfare, 204-05;

in Canadian federal government, 205-06

Court decisions, on collective negotiations by teachers, 299-300

Crichton, Edward E., on compulsory arbitration in Australia, 240

**D**

"De facto" bargaining rights, 20

Decertification, 116 *See also* Decertification elections

Decertification elections, 168-69, 170

Delaware, State of:

collective bargaining statute, 42, 152, 142-43;

State Dept. of Labor and Industrial Relations, 42-43, 57, 171;

State merit system, 42-43, 44-45;

State Tax Dept. agreement, 43-44;

State Dept. of Mental Health agreement, 174-75, 285-86, 364-65;

Levy Court of New Castle County, negotiated grievance procedure, 286, 365-67;

State Chamber of Commerce report on AFT, 310-11

Democracy, and employee relations, 13, 27

Denmark, George W., 312

Department heads, labor relations responsibilities of, 341

Department of Health, Education and Welfare (HEW):

and conflict of interest, 158-59;

and exclusive recognition, 165;

and decertification elections, 168-69;

and joint negotiations, 204-05

Department of Labor, 139-40:

report on teacher salaries, 291-92

Departmental personnel offices, and labor relations, 340-41

Dewey, John, on teacher unions, 309

Dewey, Thomas, and Condon-Wadlin Act, 113-14

Dispute settlement. *See* Impasse resolution

Donovan, Bernard E., 292

Dues checkoff, 83, 118

**E**

Election. *See* Decertification election, Exclusive recognition, Representation elections, Runoff elections

Employee organizations:

changed role concepts of, 12-15;

growth of, 14-18, 290-91;

in Bonneville Power Administration, 280-81;
state law provisions, 284-85;
in Delaware Dept. of Mental
Health, 285-86, 364-65;
of Levy Court, New Castle
County, Delaware, 286, 365-
67;
in Milwaukee, 286-87, 367-71;
in Philadelphia, 287, 371-72;
in Winnipeg, Canada, 288, 372-
74;
in education, 314
Negotiating sessions:
basic information for, 219-25;
length of, 226;
records of, 226;
physical arrangements for,
226;
confidentiality of, 226-27;
press and public interest in,
226-27;
good faith in, 227-28;
climate of, 228;
stages of, 228-29;
strategy in, 229-30;
final agreement in, 230
Negotiating team:
composition of, 206-17;
size of, 207, 219;
effectiveness of, 217-18;
personal qualities, of members,
218;
training of, 218;
preparations of, 219-25;
caucuses of, 229
Newark, Delaware, 36
New Castle County, Delaware:
merit system of, 42, 45-46;
union agreement of, 46;
personnel director of, as negotiator, 209
Newland, Chester A., 53-54, 221-22
New York City:
labor relations program, 20,
331;
Metropolitan Hospital strike,
58, 342;
Office of Collective Bargaining,
58-59, 130-32, 262-63;
subway strike, 60-75;
welfare worker strikes, 114,
196, 266;

teacher strikes, 117-18, 317-18;
management rights, 195-98;
Memorandum of Agreement,
197;
landmark first teacher agreement, 302-03, 316;
Board of Education and Kingsport Press Company, 310-11;
Board of Education, budgeting
and fiscal problems, 317-18;
*See also* Office of Collective
Bargaining, Subway strike
New York State Joint Legislative
Committee on Industrial and
Labor Conditions, report on compulsory arbitration, 241
New York State Public Employees'
Fair Employment Act, 107:
on strikes and strike penalties,
116-117;
experiences with, 117-18;
impasse resolution procedures,
260-62
New York State Public Employment Relations Board, 117, 118
New York State Civil Service Employees' Association, no-strike
pledge, 107
Noble, George W., 50, 223:
on joint bargaining, 202;
on city councils as negotiators,
217

## O

Occupational category, defined, in
Canada, 148-49
Office of Collective Bargaining
(OCB), New York City, 58-59,
75, 331:
union reaction to, 59;
functions of, 130-32;
impasse procedure of, 262-63
Office of Federal Employee-Management Relations, Labor Dept.,
147:
*Procedural Guide* for representation elections, 166
Oklahoma Education Association,
and sanctions, 312, 324-25
Ontario, Province of, and judges as
arbitrators, 220
Oregon State Civil Service Commission:

collective negotiations functions, 129;

rules on bargaining units, 151; and managerial exclusions, 162-63;

rules on representation elections, 171

Oregon State Employees' Association:

and representation elections, 151;

supervisor participation in, 164;

agreement with State Treasury Dept., 175

**P**

Patrolmen's Benevolent Association, New York City, work assignment demands of, 197

Pennsylvania Nurses' Association, no-strike pledge, 105

Perry, Charles A. and Wildman, Wesley A., school district questionnaire of, 290-91, 303-07

Personnel administration, background and current emphasis of, in government, 11-12

Personnel director:

responsibilities of, in Washington State, 129;

and TVA bargaining unit determination, 147-48;

on negotiating team, 207-12;

role of, in Philadelphia, 209-10;

and contract administration, 280;

and labor relations function, 340

Personnel policies, statutory, 182

Philadelphia:

encouragement of union membership, 82;

and modified union shop, 96-97;

composition of negotiating team, 209;

negotiated grievance procedure, 287, 371-72

Plunkett, T. J.:

on innovation in public service, 87;

on management rights, 180;

on composition of negotiating team, 206-07, 217-18

Policy questions, negotiation of, 196

Political activity, of employee organizations, 53-57

Political factors, in subway strike, 73-75

Posey, Rollin B., 220, 221, 227

Position classification:

TVA adoption of standards, 187;

union participation in, 190;

maintenance of integrity of, 190-91;

non-negotiability of, in Canadian federal government, 192

Post Office Department, U.S.:

and bulletin boards, 173-74;

and management rights, 188, 189;

agreement, provisions of, for consultation, 188-89;

procedures for negotiations, 225-26;

mediation procedures, 245-46;

negotiated grievance and appeals procedure, 276-78, 357-63;

labor relations program, 333-34

Powell, Adam Clayton, 69

Pragan, Otto, 183:

on bilateralism in wage surveys, 190;

on negotiated grievance procedure, 272-73

Preparatory Committee on Collective Bargaining in the Public Service (Canada), recommendations of, 21, 102, 284:

on administrative machinery, 125-26;

on managerial exclusions, 156, 160-61;

on negotiable items, 191;

on councils of employee organizations, 205;

on conciliation, 233;

on bargaining impasses, 249-250

Prevailing wage rates, union participation in setting, 186

Quill, Michael V., 61, 62, 64, 65, 66, 67, 71, 143

## R

Railway Labor Act, 235

Rapoport, Roger, 334-35

Raskin, A. H., 264

Recognition:
forms of, under Executive Order 10988, 91-92;
forms of, in Minnesota, 92.
*See also* Exclusive recognition, Representation election(s)

Rehman, Charles, on subjects for negotiation at the local level, 183-84

Representation election(s), 150:
and excluded positions, 163;
in U.S. federal government, 164-69;
sixty per cent rule, 167;
frequency of, 168, 169-70, 170, 171, 172;
in Canada, 169;
in state and local governments, 170-72;
in Chicago schools, 299-300;
in California State Colleges, 319

Residual rights, in collective negotiations, 179, 180. *See also* Management rights

Reston, James, on public employee organization, 17

Reuther, Walter P., 241

Rhodes-Johnston bills, 49, 274

Right to bargain, 18-19, 19-21, 21-23, 49:
need for, 37-38, 86-87;
in education, 299-300.
*See also* Executive Order 10988, New York State Public Employees' Fair Employment Act, Public Service Staff Relations Act

Right to organize:
restrictions on, 78-79;
background, 77-79;
in education, 296-97.
*See also* Executive Order 10988, Lloyd-LaFollette Act

Right to strike, 20:
in Canada, 21, 22, 101-02, 104, 111, 248, 252;
changed thinking on, 99-100;
employee organizations attitudes on, 104-106, 113

Right to work laws, 79, 93

Rochester, New York, 59-60, 97

Rockefeller Committee, 71, 338, 340:
on exclusive recognition, 89;
on strike prohibitions, 106;
on essential services, 110;
definition of strike, 115;
on injunctions, 116;
on bargaining units, 145-46;
on impasse resolution, 258-60;
on effective organization, 337-38;
on academic programs in public employee relations, 345

Roser, Foster:
on modified union shop, 96;
on role of personnel director in labor relations, 209-10

Rowlands, David D., 203

Runoff elections, 167-68, 170-72

## S

Salary Policy Employee Panel, TVA, 81, 187, 204, 242-43, 278

Sanctions, 322:
purpose of, 323-24;
examples of, 324-25;
public reactions to, 325

Saskatchewan, Province of, scope of negotiations in, 192-93

Saxon, James J., unfair labor practice charge against, 140-41

Schnaufer, Pete:
on teachers and civil rights, 294;
on union shop clauses, 298;
on co-determination in education, 314-15

School board negotiations, defined, 305

Scope of negotiations:
in New Castle County, Delaware, 46;
in Canadian federal government, 149, 192;
in industry, 177-78;